The Trade Union Movement of Canada

1827 - 1959

THE
TRADE UNION
MOVEMENT
OF
CANADA
1827
1959

Charles Lipton

NC PRESS
TORONTO
THIRD EDITION   1973

We would like to thank University of Toronto Press for permission to reprint "Canadian Unionism" by Charles Lipton from *Capitalism and the national question in Canada,* edited by Gary Teeple, 1972.

ISBN 0-919600-02-6, paper, $3.95.
ISBN 0-919600-20-4, cloth, $7.95.

Originally published by Canadian Social Publications Limited, Montreal, Quebec, 1967.

New Canada Publications, a division of
NC Press Ltd,
Box 6106 Terminal A,
Toronto 1, Ontario

Printed in Canada by Union Labour

TO JEAN

The Rosary parade in the Asbestos strike of 1949.

We are pleased to be reprinting Dr. Charles Lipton's **The Trade Union Movement of Canada 1827-1959**. *It is much needed at a time of swift change in the Canadian labour movement. The issues it raises are central to the further development of the labour movement and the survival of our country.*

We are also pleased to be reprinting, as a postscript, an article by Dr. Lipton, written in 1966, which was originally intended to be in the **Trade Union Movement** *but appeared earlier this year in* **Capitalism and the National Question in Canada**, *edited by G. Teeple, University of Toronto Press.*

Dr. Lipton concludes this article with a rousing call to Canadian workers: "The winning of a sovereign trade union movement—a sovereign Canadian union for each industry, a sovereign movement for the country as a whole—stands as a central class objective for Canada's organised workers."

Since **The Trade Union Movement of Canada 1827-1959** *was first published in 1967, there has been a new drive among Canadian workers to take up the fight for independent Canadian unions. There have been important struggles at Bristol Aerospace and Bell Foundry in Winnipeg, Texpack in Brantford, Puretex in Toronto, Alcan in Kitimat, Cominco in Trail, Cassiar Asbestos in Clinton Creek, Yukon, at Stanley Steel in Hamilton and in rail yards across the country.*

The new independent Canadian unions are growing: the Pulp and Paper Workers of Canada, the Canadian Union of Operating Engineers, the Canadian Textile and Chemical Union, the Bricklayers, Masons Independent Union of Canada, the Canadian Association of Industrial, Mechanical and Allied Workers, the United Oil Workers and the Transportation Employees Canadian Union. New unions, the Canadian Aluminum, Smelter and Allied Workers, the Canadian Workers' Union, the Canadian Miners' Union and others are being formed.

These new unions saw the need for a national centre for independent Canadian unions. In 1969, they called the founding convention of the Council (now Confederation) of Canadian unions in Sudbury, Ontario. Dr. Lipton attended as an observer. It was an historic occasion.

Canada's workers had taken the initiative in the struggle for the independence of Canada long before any other group by establishing their own class organisations at both the local and national level. Since then, the CCU has continued to grow in size and importance.

The **Trade Union Movement** *is* the *major work of its kind to date in an area of Canadian history little-known to the average Canadian reader, and it is the only one in print. It tells a story not taught in our schools—a story unknown in its entirety to most of the millions of Canadian workers who have sacrificed and fought to win a better life for all. They are the real heroes of this book.*

Many more histories remain to be written before we have the whole heroic tale; for instance, the true story of the role of Canada's political parties and especially those on the "left".

The two most powerful have been the Communist Party and the CCF-NDP. Although they have many differences, their attitude to Canadian unionism has been the same: they have almost invariably supported U.S. unions at the expense of Canadian unions. The root of this outlook is their failure to recognize U.S. imperialism as the key problem in Canada and the role of U.S. unions in promoting and supporting it.

The Communist Party of Canada led the initial organisation of hundreds of thousands of workers and many important class battles. However, Dr. Lipton points out, "The Communist Party of Canada which should be a leader in this field, (the building of sovereign Canadian unions—Ed.) has confined itself in practice to the 'Canadian autonomy' slogan. This has been one important factor holding up progress to building a Canadian trade union movement."

The Communist Party led the destruction of the One Big Union Movement. It organised the Workers Unity League in the depths of the depression as a centre for wholly independent Canadian industrial unions when the U.S. unions refused to organise industrially. But it dissolved the WUL in the name of 'unity' with U.S. unions in 1935.

It was under Communist Party direction that the CIO was invited into Canada when in fact Canadians were organising and continued to organise themselves. In each instance, the independent Canadian union movement was gaining strength and in each instance, the Communist Party used its influence to destroy it.

In recent years, the most powerful supporter of U.S. unions has been the NDP. It was formed in a coalition between the CCF and the Canadian Labour Congress, the latter being completely dominated by U.S. unions. The NDP is financially dependent on enforced dues checkoffs from members of the large U.S. unions, especially the United Autoworkers and the United Steelworkers of America.

Many party officials and organisers are paid representatives of these unions who have been appointed to their union and party posts by headquarters in the U.S. Their power can be seen in their successful explusion of the Waffle Group from the NDP in Ontario when they feared that the Waffle would support Canadian unions.

This has meant that many progressive-minded Canadians who should be supporting the struggle for independent Canadian unions are not doing so. The only organisation which wholeheartedly supports the struggle for independent Canadian unions is the Canadian Liberation Movement.

Great changes are coming. Canadian workers are on the move. Canadian unions will be won. It is up to Canadians in all walks of life to line up side by side with Canadian workers and join the fight. It would be a great tragedy if those who consider themselves progressive continue to count themselves enemies of the struggle.

This book answers the question "why do we need independent Canadian unions?" Every Canadian should read it. This is why its republication in a more economical edition is so important at this time.

We are pleased to report that Dr. Lipton is working on a sequel. We look forward to seeing it in print in the near future.

The Editors, NC Press

PREFACE

The writer hopes that the public will welcome this work, which spans some 130 years of Canadian trade union history. He thanks the staffs of the Department of Labour Library at Ottawa, the McGill University Library and the Purvis Institute, both of Montreal, for their patience and kind assistance. He also thanks all those who contributed to this work either by reading the manuscript or by making materials available. Miss Beatrice Ferneyhough, M.A. served as research secretary during most of the period of preparation of this volume. Mrs. Jean Lipton typed preparatory materials and the manuscript again and again. The writer emphasises that he is solely responsible for the material in this volume.

In a work of this scope, some errors of fact or judgment are almost inevitable. The writer will welcome communications from the readers correcting or questioning points of detail and evaluation. Beyond that he will welcome communications of all types concerning this book. All such communications should be sent care of the publishers.

CONTENTS

PART 1

BEGINNINGS TO 1900

PART 2

1900-1919

PART 3

1919-1939

CONTENTS

PART 4

1939-1959

PART 1
BEGINNINGS TO 1900

CHAPTER 1

ORIGINS TO CONFEDERATION
1827-1867

1. DEVELOPMENT OF INDUSTRY AND CAPITALISM

Emergence of the Working Class:

Records of efforts by Canadian working people to improve their conditions go back to the 18th century. In 1778, an official of the North West Fur Trading Company sent a memorandum to the Governor of Canada, Sir Guy Carleton, asking him to take action to keep the workers (voyageurs and canoemen) from quitting their employment and going elsewhere to work for higher wages. It appears there was a demand for these skilled workers, who were key men in the fur industry. Wages were rising and they were taking advantage of this to go from one job to another.[1] On August 3, 1794, voyageurs went on strike for higher wages at Rainy Lake (Lac la Pluie). They did not win, and their leaders lost their jobs, at least for the time being.[2]

As capitalist industry grew, the wage-earning class or working class emerged. The process was slow. In 1809, a sawmill was established at Hawkesbury, Ontario. It employed 80.[3] Shipbuilding developed at Montreal.[4] The textile industry can be traced at least as far back as 1816, when a small fulling and carding mill was established at Montreal.[5] In the 1820s, bar iron was being manufactured at Marmora, Ontario. It was said at the time that "if (the) superb works of Marmora .. were brought into full play" Canadian dependence on imports of iron would cease.[6] By 1831, not just ships but ships' engines were being produced in Montreal.[7] In Toronto, in 1833, 80 workers were employed at the "elaborate works of Messrs. Sheldon, Dutcher and Company".[8] That same year, the coal stove was introduced at Montreal and Toronto.[9] Two years later it was reported that "manufactures are rapidly advancing in Toronto".[10]

Industrialization brought with it a shortage of labour. At the same time, in Great Britain, a surplus of labour had developed. This was due to the ruin of artisans by advancing large-scale industry, and to displacement of small farmers by advancing large-scale capitalist farming. In order to reduce this surplus, the colonial authorities encouraged immigration to Canada.[11] Between 1828 and 1830, many British immigrants came to Canada. No great concern was shown for these immigrants. Sometimes, they were transported in unseaworthy ships, and wrecks were frequent.[12] Many of them were Irish. A chronicler of the times speaks of the "fever-stricken, naked and friendless Irish, a people truly scattered and peeled, who year after year are thrown in shoals upon the wharves of Quebec from ships which ought to be called itinerant pesthouses. These unwelcome outcasts are crowded . . . into vessels fitted up almost slave-ship fashion by the agents of . . . unprincipled landlords". He goes on to describe the dilapidated houses in Quebec into which the immigrants were put: "The filthy and crowded state of the houses, the disgusting scenes going on in them can only be guessed . . . I have trod the floor of one such house (littered with) churned and sodden garbage, animal and vegetable. It required dissecting-room nerves to bear it."[13]

Another important group of immigrants were the Scottish. Many were textile workers from the district around Glasgow and Paisley. They were hard-pressed by mechanization and other conditions in the industry. Their wages, 25 shillings per week in 1803, dropped to 5 shillings in 1819. Dissatisfaction and revolt spread among them. In 1819, a frightened British Government adopted the Seditious Meetings Prevention Bill. Some of these textile workers decided to come to Canada. In 1820, 1,200 set sail from Grenoch. In 1821, 1,883 more set sail. One of them, John MacDonald, kept a diary, in which he described conditions on the boat—the fierce storms, then the long and difficult trip by wagon and boat from Montreal to Lachine through the Rapids, and 120 miles onward to Prescott. "At Prescott we began to feel the effects of our rough journey. Some had fever and many died after two days' illness." In Brockville the wagons overturned with men, women and children in them. "One boy was killed on the spot." Finally, they arrived at their destination, in the district now known as Lanark County, by a stream called the "Little Mississippi".*[14]

As capitalism developed, it brought with it economic crises. One

---

* In later years, the textile experience of these immigrants, and also the favourable water resources, helped make this district a centre for the woollen industry in Canada.

took place in 1825, another in 1833-1837, yet another in 1847.[15] They were crises of overproduction due, among other things, to exploitation and anarchy of production; the dependence of capitalism in Canada on the cycle of world capitalism, in general; more particularly, its dependence on the stronger capitalism in the United States and Great Britain.

On May 13, 1834, the Quebec *Gazette* stated: "We trust that the improving state of things in the United States will be felt in Canada. We have borne a fair share of the weight of the evil."[16]

What was the impact of such crises? A writer of the times speaks of the "Bills drawn by houses of long standing and the highest respectability being returned dishonoured ... The unparalleled suddenness of so unexpected a commercial calamity prevented the most cautious and experienced from guarding against the ruin which awaited them".[17] A letter in *La Minerve*, March 13, 1837, describes conditions around Rimouski:

"If the correspondent were to travel at this moment through the least afflicted district of the province, he would still see scenes similar to that of which he has given us so passionate a picture. He would come upon a frightful number of families driven from their homes by hunger on to the streets, going from door to door beseeching rich and poor alike. If he were to enter the houses, he would see a far greater number than one would imagine of pale and shivering children seeking for bread, while the mother had nothing left but tears to offer them, for she has shared her last crust with them the day previous. The husband, weakened with hunger is seeking somewhere for work, but often in vain, for those who formerly employed the poorest here have run short themselves."

2. RISE OF THE UNIONS

Quebec, 1827-1834:

Wherever workers are massed to produce the wealth of society, they begin to organize, to unite and fight for decent wages and conditions. Combinations begin, unions, transitional first—then durable. In Canada, this process was under way between 1827 and 1836. Some say Canada's first union was the Quebec City printers' organization, founded, it is believed, in 1827.[18] More definite is this union's activities from 1836. Certain it is that in 1830, in Montreal, a shoe workers' union was functioning, also a tailors' lodge.[19] In 1832, St. Lawrence River pilots organized against speed-up. An indignant correspondent in *La Minerve* denounced their action as "a conspiracy against the public". He said: "(It is) foolish to combine against the new practice of towing 5 or 6 vessels up the river by steamboat ..."[20] In 1833, unions of printers, tailors and carpenters were established in Montreal.[21] A statement of the Journeymen Tailors Union for December 1833 provides an early instance of negotiations. It says the committee will be on hand at the "House of Call", there to wait on the master tailors.[22]

The carpenters were pioneers. In 1833, they organized the Montreal Mechanics Mutual Protective Society. It was born in the fight for the shorter working day. At the time, journeymen carpenters were becoming restless at the treatment handed out to them by the master carpenters. They said that one of their men had fallen sick because of the "long and heavy labour" imposed on him. His master had docked him "until you get strong enough to take a good day's work" and then had held back his wages.[23] Their main grievance was long hours. In 1833, a journeyman carpenter said:

"I don't know what Master Carpenter would call a fair and honest day's work, but this I know, after working 12 hours a day, sleeping 7 hours a night, I cannot do as much work the next day than if I had worked 10 hours."[24]

The carpenters decided to organize. On February 5, 1833, they gathered at Lavoie's Hotel, then a well-known centre for union men, located on St. Lawrence Boulevard. Their aim was to discover "the most efficient (means) for accomplishing a diminution of the hours of labour".[25] They decided by unanimous vote that "ten hours a day is as much as a man can work". They decided, also, that a fund be raised in addition to that already in the hands of the treasurer "to assist the members of this society who are endeavouring to obtain justice, and through the obstinacy of their employers (have) been thrown out of employ".[26] The master carpenters were to be asked "to appoint a deputation to meet one from this body". Finally, they decided that, if the negotiations did not succeed, they would conduct a "general strike" to begin March 18.[27] A clear warning was issued against strike breaking: "We hereby pledge ourselves not to work for any employer whose men are on a turnout for wages or time, and . . . any member so offending shall be expelled from this society."[28]

The journeymen's efforts proved successful. Their hours were reduced. But the following year, 1834, the master carpenters decided to turn the clock back, to restore the additional hour to the workday. The union men readied for action. On February 13, they held a meeting and adopted measures to tighten organization.[29] Members in arrears were told to pay up. The first Tuesday of every month was set aside for a "show of cards"—a check-up on dues standing. It was decided that a "book of prices" (wage schedule) be put out in English and French, and arrangements were made for strike pay.[30] A week later, the journeymen issued a circular addressed to brother mechanics in other centres, cautioning them not to come and work in Montreal: "Every person whether Society or not Society ... will not debase himself so low beneath the dignity of his nature, as to work for any of these employers until some arrangement be made for them and their journeymen."[31]

The master carpenters replied in a statement published in the Montreal *Gazette* on March 4, 1834. They said they were determined to increase the working day to 11 hours, between April 1 and November 1. They doubted the effectiveness of the Society's strike. Ninety of the Society members were back on the job, and of these all but 25 had "expressed themselves as dissatisfied with the conduct of the Society". They condemned the Society in these terms:

"This Society is calculated to produce the worst consequences ... such a body of men cannot be considered competent to what they have undertaken, neither are they likely to confine themselves to decent and becoming order. They are dangerous to the peace and safety of good citizens."[32]

The union men did not stand idly by. Their response is indicated by this comment of a member or sympathizer: "The present demand would cost the Master Employer 16 shillings a year per Journeyman ... What danger is there in that to the peace and safety of our good citizens?" He expresses the strikers' spirit in these words: "Your walking men are firm as mountains."[33] The strike's effectiveness is reflected in the master carpenters' complaint that the Society was using "combined threats to force peaceful men to leave their working employ".[34]

At Montreal, in the spring of 1834, not only journeymen carpenters were in action, but other workers. The operative masons and stonecutters joined the fight for the 10-hour day. At a meeting held March 12, 1834, they decided that after April 1 "no man would work ... longer than 10 hours a day".[35] The tailors' union went on strike—the master tailors denounced them as a "powerful combination".[36] Other unions included the Journeymen Bakers, Cordwainers and City Firemen.[37]

Out of this upsurge came an early city central council, or at least the project for one—the "Trades Union". Its rules and regulations, decided at a meeting held March 12, 1834, provided that the working classes of Montreal and surrounding villages (would) form themselves into a union for the purpose of securing their rights and advancing their interest in society. The new body was to be located in Montreal, with a council of "delegates from any particular trade".[38] It was to be a body of action "ready to act in case of an emergency". There is some indication that the Trades Union passed the project stage and became a factor in the shorter hours movement. A notice of the Merchant Tailors, published June 30, 1834, speaks of the Journeymen Tailors' strike as "under the combination with the Trades Union".[39] Beyond that, the organizers of the Trades Union likely had more far-reaching objectives. The rules provided "that the working classes in other towns and districts in Canada shall be invited to form unions of the same kind".[40] The movement seems to have spread to Quebec City. A letter dated April 29, 1834, says: "Last evening there was a meeting in the City (Quebec) of different trades to take into consideration the necessity of forming a trades union."[41] A year later, a meeting of all trades was held in Quebec City, and chaired by a tailor, John Teed.[42]

Ontario and the Maritimes, 1830-1836:

During the 1830s, unions of coopers, stonemasons, tailors, bricklayers, carpenters and printers developed in Upper Canada.[43] In 1830, journeymen shoemakers in Toronto went on a "turnout" (strike) against "scanty wages... beds of straw... tyrannical oppression".[44] In 1831, the "United Amicable Society of Bricklayers, Plasterers and Masons", joined the fight for the 10-hour day. From its headquarters on Dorchester Street, the Society issued the following statement:

"(We have) ... mutually resolved not to work for any employer who shall in future require (us) to work... from sunrise to sundown... In future we will work... from six in the morning until six in the evening, and deducting therefrom two hours for meals... ten working hours per day."[45]

In 1833, the Toronto Carpenters Union went on strike for "more punctual payment" of wages. The Union described its aims as "mutual protection" and "mutual aid in sickness and in poverty".[46]

An important event was formation of the York Typographical Society. In 1832, master printers at York (Toronto) decided on a wage cut whose effect was to bring journeymen's wages down to the level for unskilled labour. A journeyman, J. H. Lawrence, called a meeting for October 12 at the York Hotel. In the chair was another journeyman, W. C. H. Myers. The printers adopted a resolution constituting themselves the "York Typographical Society".[47] The preamble to the constitution said:

"Owing to the many innovations which have been made in the long-established usages of the professors of the art of printing, and those of a kind highly detrimental to their interests, it is deemed expedient by journeymen printers of York that they should form themselves into a body similar to societies in other parts of the world, in order to maintain that honourable station of respectability that belongs to the profession."[48]

A key clause in the constitution stated: "No member of this society shall engage in any printing establishment in this town at prices below those stipulated by the Society, viz: I pound 15 shillings per week." Another section provided for overtime: "When any member shall work over the usual number of hours, ten per day, he shall receive ten cents per hour for such extra service." Dues were fixed at 1 shilling and 3 pence a month.[49]

The new body seems to have prospered. In 1833, it celebrated its first anniversary at a banquet held at Ontario House, on October 15. Noteworthy was the arrival, at 11 p.m., of a journeyman printer from Hamilton, John F. Rodgers. He brought greetings from the "auxiliary society of Typographers of Hamilton", and told the brethren "it has taken me 4 days to make the trip".[50] In 1834, the Toronto Society petitioned the Legislature for better regulation of apprentices' conditions.[51] In 1836, it went on strike for $1 more per week (the rate then was $7 per week); the 10-hour day; overtime pay of 10 pence per hour. These demands the master printers resisted, and their lawyer said unions were illegal. For their part, the journeymen printers sent a message to Montreal asking the men there not to go down to Toronto for work.[52]

So much for development in Ontario. In the Maritimes, labour organization dates back to at least 1816. That year, an Act was adopted by the Nova Scotia legislature directed against workers in Halifax and other centres who "by unlawful meetings and combinations are endeavouring to regulate the rate of wages."[53] In 1837, a printers' organization was functioning in Nova Scotia.[54] In New Brunswick, in 1833, mechanics protested against legislation drafting them for roadwork. So it seems, at least, from this manifesto poem, printed in the New Brunswick *Courrier* that year, entitled "The Humble Petition of Mechanics and Others of the Province of New Brunswick to their Representatives now sitting in the House of Assembly".[55] The mechanics' proud spirit is shown in the opening lines:

"Pray harbour not that vain conceit,
That yon high Legislative seat
Makes you our Lords or Masters;
We've learnt our dignity of late,
Our servants now we designate—
M.P.'s as well as Masters."

The poem concludes with the warning that the workers' ranks will grow. More of "Auld Jack's Kin" will flock to the banners, not "Merchants, Doctors or Lawyers" but "the barefoot and hobnail, ragtag and bobtail". It is signed as follows:

    For Painters and Glaziers—Benjamin Brushman
    For Shoemakers—Ephraim Screwfeet
    For Brick and Stone builders—Gregory Groundwork
    For Carpenters—Oatmeal Okum
    For Ironworkers—Vulcan Bellows

Canadian Labour and World Labour:

Canadian Labour and World Labour—their union—this is a law of Canadian labour history. The rise of unions in Canada was connected with the rise of the world labour movement. "Producing classes everywhere have awakened from a long slumber", says a Montrealer in a letter printed in a Montreal newspaper, March 11, 1834. He defends the Montreal workers' struggle for the 10-hour day by pointing to the example of "other cities in Europe and America".[56] And indeed much was astir this year, 1834: In France, the general strike of textile workers at Lyons; in Britain, "the universal strike" of cotton workers for the 8-hour day;[57] the founding of the world's first national trade union centre, the Grand National Consolidated Trades Union of Great Britain and Ireland. The Grand National claimed 800,000 adherents. It sought higher wages and shorter hours, but, some of its leaders also believed the organized workers should take over society and run industry. The founder, Robert Owen, looked to a society "in which well-directed industry and virtue shall merit its just distinction and reward, and vicious idleness its merited contempt".[58]

Another event which shook Britain in 1834, and—as it turned out—linked itself to Canada's destiny, was the struggle of the Tolpuddle Martyrs. Five agricultural labourers were arrested at Tolpuddle on a charge of combination, and thrown into jail. There, one of them, George Loveless, wrote this poem:

    "God is our guide, from field and wave,
      From plough, from handle, and from loom
    We come our country's right to save,
      And speak the tyrant actions' doom.
    "We raise the watchword Liberty,
      We will, we will, we will be free.
    "God is our guide, no swords we draw,
      We kindle not God's battle fires,
    By reason, union, justice, law,
      We claim the birthright of our sires.
    We raise the watchword Liberty,
      We will, we will, we will be free!"[59]

The Five were tried and found guilty. Before pronouncing sentence, the judge asked Loveless, "Do you have anything to say?" Loveless passed a slip of paper to the judge on which he had written these words:

"My lord, if we have violated any law, it was not done intentionally ... We were uniting together to preserve ourselves, our wives and families from utter starvation and degradation ..."[60]

The labourers were sentenced to deportation to Australia. Loveless was put on a convict ship. His arms and legs were riveted in irons. Before departing from his homeland he wrote his wife:

"Thank you Betsie, for the kind attention you have always given me... Although we may part for a while, I shall consider myself under the same obligation as though living with you. Be satisfied, my dear Betsie ... it will work for good and we shall yet rejoice ... Don't send me any money to distress yourself. For He who is the Lord of the winds and the waves, will be my support in life as well as in death."[61]

The campaign to free the Five began. Petition after petition descended on the Government. On April 1, 1834, thousands of labour men, led by Robert Owen, paraded in London. Terrified, the Government mustered 5,000 special constables, 29 pieces of artillery, 8 battalions of infantry, the light guards and the household troops. Despite this, the fight for amnesty was won, and Loveless and his comrades came back to England. Looking back on the events of the past year, Loveless set down his conclusions in these words:

"I believe nothing will ever be done to relieve the distress of the working class, unless they take it into their own hands. With these beliefs I left England, and with these views I have returned. Notwithstanding all I have felt and seen, my sentiments on the subject are unchanged. Nothing but union can obtain the great and important object, namely the salvation of the world. Let the producers of wealth firmly and peacefully unite their energies, and what would withstand them? The power and influence of the non-producer would sink into insignificance. The conquest will be won. Our victory is certain."[62]

Some time later, Loveless and his family set sail for Canada. With him were three more of the Tolpuddle Five—James Loveless, John Stanfield, and James Byrne. Conditions were difficult, and Loveless' daughter died in transit. The boat landed in New York, and then began the arduous trip by sailboat and oxcart through Buffalo, on to Port Stanley, Ontario, and then to the point of settlement, near London, Ontario. Loveless settled on a farm. He remained true to his principles to the end of his days.[63]

3.　THE REVOLUTION OF 1837

Labour and the Patriots, 1833-1836:

"Strike, the conflict is begun,
　Freemen, soldiers, follow me

Shout—the victory is won—
Canada and liberty!"*[64]

The fight for Canada was opening up. Labour played its part. In 1834, Montreal union members supported the 92 Resolutions.**[65] In 1836, workers in Quebec City joined with other citizens in an Address of Approval presented to Papineau.[66]

Labour's patriot activities alarmed Montreal capitalists. Their supporter, the Montreal *Gazette,* spewed hatred of the working class and patriot cause. A letter published there in October 1834 exhorts merchants to ensure their employees vote against the patriots. The merchants' duty is to "exercise the control which you are entitled, nay bound, to exercise, over those to whom you afford the means of daily sustenance".[67] The opposing standpoint is expressed in a letter appearing in the Montreal *Vindicator* on April 22, 1834. It says the mechanic is "being singled out, marked and punished, because he presumes to entertain a different set of political opinions from the gentlemen . . . to whom he gives . . . his day's labour in exchange for a dollar". Another letter in this journal, on November 16, 1834, declares that workers have lost their jobs because of political activities. It is signed "One of the Proscribed".

In Upper Canada, too, Labour linked with the patriots. In 1833, William Lyon Mackenzie was guest of honour at the York Typographical anniversary banquet. The Printers' Minute Book says: "All . . . was sweetness and jollification . . . The glass and song went merrily around . . ." In his address, Mackenzie endorsed the union. He said he had been doubtful at first, but "since he has investigated the principles of the constitution, he could find nothing therein but a consistent and moderate policy . . ."[68]

Mackenzie was not consistent in his support for Labour. He opposed the printers' strike of 1836. Perhaps his business as master printer got the better of him then. But, basically, he was a working journalist, a fighter for Canada. The logic of Canada's progress demanded a positive attitude to the workers. Mackenzie put patriotism first, not business, and responded to that logic. In 1834, he was striving to set up mass organizations based on the workers. On May 18, he summoned the mechanics to a meeting aimed at forming "ward committees of vigilance". The meeting took place next day at 6.30 p.m. in the Old

---

* From William Lyon Mackenzie's *Colonial Advocate.*
** The 92 Resolutions were a program of demands for responsible government. Sponsored by Louis Joseph Papineau, they were adopted by the Lower Canada Assembly in 1834.

King's Bench Court House of York (Toronto). The hall was packed to overflowing, and hundreds stood outside. The meeting decided to organize select committees "to canvass the wards". Soon after, "a grand committee was convened".[69] Mackenzie's concern about workers' support is shown in his arrangements for these meetings. In organizing one in the mid-summer of 1834, he set the time at 6 p.m. "when the mechanics and labouring classes can most conveniently attend".[70]

This relation between Labour and the Patriots expressed itself elsewhere too. In 1834, mechanics at Kingston turned out to meetings sponsored by the Reform candidate. He promised to work for social legislation. There was mention of a bill "to prevent the provincial penitentiary from being an injury to mechanics"—presumably a reference to prison labour.[71] In 1836, Irish labourers at work on the canal near Cornwall also supported the Patriot candidate. Once they so terrified the opposing Family Compact candidate that he appealed to Lieutenant Governor Sir Francis Bond Head for troops.[72] That year, 2 union men in Toronto, James H. Lumsden and Patrick Burns, members of the Toronto Typographical Society, were arrested on a charge of "disloyalty to the Government". The union busied itself on a defence fund. Every member contributed, and six pounds, eight shillings and six pence was collected.[73]

1837 — Lower and Upper Canada:

When the fateful year 1837 came, Labour continued to be active. In Lower Canada the Coercion Bill was the big issue. Introduced in the British House of Commons by Prime Minister Lord John Russell, the bill trampled on the rights of the Assembly of Lower Canada, provided for appropriation of money without the Assembly's consent, and thus diminished the prospect for peaceful transition to responsible government and home rule.[74] Pursuing this policy of coercion, the British government clamped a ban on meetings in Canada. The Patriots did not back down. Their committee said: "We treated with contempt the silly proclamation of an ignorant government against these meetings."[75] And, indeed, many meetings did take place this June of 1837—at Montreal, Quebec, St. Hyacinthe, in Yamaska, Vaudreuil and Richelieu counties. One meeting in the county of Montreal was attended by 4,000.[76]

The workers must have been active at these meetings. A newspaper account of one meeting, held in Quebec City, May 1837, says that those present were largely from the "mechanics and operative classes", and that they adopted the resolution "with an intensity and demonstration of feeling far beyond any anticipated ... These were men who can be relied on in the hour of need".[77] At another meeting, held on the public square of St. Paul's Market in Quebec City, and attended by between 2,000 and 3,000, the chief speaker was the trade unionist, John Teed.[78]

Meanwhile important help was coming from British workers. An organization which led the way was the London Workingmen's Association, an early Chartist body founded in 1837. It took up the fight against the Coercion Bill by organizing a mass meeting for "Canadian rights". The meeting was held April 3, at the Crown and Anchor Tavern in the Strand, London. Two thousand were present, and there was much enthusiasm.[79] Concerning the meeting, a London journalist commented: "Workingmen (in respect to the democratic issue) are really in advance of the middle class in point of knowledge."[80]

Then the Chartists launched a petition against the Coercion Bill. They aimed at 500,000 signatures. They had some success, and the movement spread to other cities. Among those rallying to the Canadians' cause were British textile workers. They said: "The cause of liberty was the same the world over."[81] Following upon this petition campaign, the Chartists sent an Address to the Patriots. Signed by a dozen workers, including engravers, goldsmiths and carpenters,[82] it stated: "Do not, therefore, believe that the working millions of England have any feelings in common with your oppressors."[83]

These solidarity actions by British workers encouraged the Patriots. From the Lower Canada meeting of May-June 1837, came votes of thanks to "les industriels" (the workers) of Britain. The Chartists' Address was received with "lively acclamation" by the Central and Permanent Committee of Patriots of the County of Montreal.[84] It was decided that several thousand copies be printed and that county and parish committees arrange for its reading "at the doors ... of parish churches".[85] Also, a committee was struck off to draft a reply. This was read to a meeting held October 12, 1837. Those signing it included: Louis Joseph Papineau, C. N. G. Delormier, Georges Etienne Cartier, E. B. O'Callaghan and Robert Nelson.[86]

This Patriot Address to the Chartists is a great document. Its opening passage proclaims the primacy of Labour in Canadian democracy: "Nearly our whole population is dependent for subsistance on manual or mental labour ... We despise the idler ... a mere consumer of what other men produce." The Address refers to Canada's past—Indian tribal society—a kind of primitive communism. "The aboriginal masters of the American wilderness knew neither lords nor kings but freely chose the best deserving heads of council and chief in war." Turning to the present, it points to the lot of the British workers. The wealth they had created had become now "the instrument (of their) political subjection". But, despite this subjection, the British workers, in coming to the aid of the Canadian Patriots, had dissociated themselves from the crimes of their ruling class, and affirmed the principle that a people was "responsible for the deeds of their rulers". For this the Patriots thanked them and pledged: "Whatever course we shall be compelled to adopt, we have no contest with the people of England. We war only against the aggression of their and our tyrannical oppressors." Finally, the Address warns: "Our arms are now the argument of justice and reason. They can easily be changed for more decisive weapons, if the eyes of the invaders of our rights continue too dull to see, and their ears too obtuse to hear."[87]

Behind this solidarity between the Patriots and Chartists was not just principle but practicality. The point was to combine the Patriot fight in Canada and Labour's fight in Britain. Conversely, the British ruling class attack on Canadian rights was part of its attack on British Labour. This was seen at the time. The Patriots' Address warned that the British authorities were preparing "an unholy scheme for destruction" of British liberties and that Lower Canada was to be the theatre for the experiment.

Why make Canada a target? Because Canada had become a battlefield in the world struggle for freedom. Quebec was one of the few places in the world where radicals had a majority in the legislature, and Toronto one of the few cities in the world where a rebel was elected and re-elected as mayor. A London correspondent to a Montreal newspaper wrote in 1837 that Lord John Russell's Coercion Bill would not have been possible if the British "had as good a House of Commons as the Canadians enjoyed".[88] So, Canadians were scoring success in an arduous world fight. The French Revolution of 1830 and the British Reform Bill of 1832 had brought modest advance. But France had no social liberty, and its workers did not have the right to organize. In Britain, the workers did not have the vote. Germany was still backward, divided, semi-feudal. In Russia, the Decembrist uprising of 1825 had been crushed. So victory or defeat in Canada meant something to the world fight for labour and democracy.

The events in Lower Canada, including solidarity with the British Chartists, reflected the labour content in the Revolution of 1837. So did events in Upper Canada. Early in 1837, the Tories carried through an electoral swindle which helped bring about the defeat of reform candidates. Jubilant over the result, a spokesman of the Family Compact said it was good that "blacksmiths and carpenters, reeking from daily labour" had been replaced by "gentlemen of intelligence and information". Mackenzie replied: "Sir Francis Bond Head can pretend to despise such men as Messrs. Park, Lount, Moore, Duncombe, M'Kay, because they are carpenters, blacksmiths, farmers and millers (but) labour ought not to be held dishonourable in a country which is upheld by the farmer and mechanic."[89]

Later that year, Mackenzie hit on a bold plan for power. Assemble a task force. Take Government House in Toronto by direct assault. Arrest Sir Francis Bond Head. Seize artillery and small arms. Arm the people. Proclaim a provisional government. Who would compose the task force? Mackenzie looked to the workers—in his words, "Dutcher's Foundrymen and Armstrong's Axemakers; all of whom could be depended on".[90] This was a good plan. Perhaps it could have succeeded. Most people in Toronto supported the Reformers. But, when Mackenzie submitted the plan to the Reform Committee, he was rebuffed. He departed, a disappointed man.[91] As matters turned out, the reactionaries seized the initiative. The Patriots had to resort to arms in any case, and they were defeated. But the principles they fought for were bound to prevail. One such principle, if only in embryo, was the union of democracy and labour. A Patriot convention held in the York Hotel, Toronto, toward the end of 1837 consisted—so the *Colonial Advocate* reported—of farmers, mechanics, labourers and other inhabitants of Toronto.[92] The Patriots' constitution for a free Canada said: "There shall never be created within this state any incorporated trading companies or incorporated companies with banking powers ... Labour is the only means of creating wealth."[93] In later years Mackenzie used to say: "My creed has been social democracy or equality of each man before society, and political democracy, or the equality of each man before the law."[94]

This reflected the labour content in the Revolution of 1837. So did the class composition of those arrested in both Lower and Upper Canada. First, Lower Canada. Here, one list shows the following:[95]

Trade	Number Arrested	Trade	Number Arrested
blacksmiths	6	painters & decorators	1
clerks	10	woolcombers	1
masons	4	printers	8
bakers	3	tanners	2
shoemakers	3	merchants	3
tailors	2	seigneurs	1
porters	2	bourgeois	1
coopers	1	gentlemen	2

A breakdown by occupation of another group of prisoners tried by court martial, includes the following: Blacksmiths 5; carpenters-joiners 2; shoemakers 2; wheelwrights 2; clerks 1; millers 1.[96]

Rev. J. D. Borthwick gives this division by occupation of a group of prisoners on the H.M.S. Buffalo, bound for Australia in 1839: Labourers 6; bakers 1; carpenters 2; blacksmiths 2; joiners 1; wheelwrights 1; millers 1; clerks 1; machinists 1; gentlemen 2.[97]

Now, Upper Canada. Here Lindsey lists 885 people arrested and jailed on charges of insurrection and treason. They included 61 indicted for high treason, of whom 37 were yeomen (farmers) and 13 workers. A breakdown of most of this list, by occupation and number, follows:[98]

Trade	Number
labourers (workmen or artisans)	429
yeomen	396
intellectuals	28
merchants and gentlemen	18

One of the best known of the martyrs of 1837 was the blacksmith, Samuel Lount, a comrade of Mackenzie. While in jail he was told his life would be spared if he informed, but he refused, and went to the scaffold, says a contemporary report, "with entire composure and firmness of step".[99]

Thus ended the Revolution of 1837. Defeat meant a great opportunity lost, a halting zig-zag course to Canadian history; partial victory later, the winning of responsible government and independence, but victory in stages and inadequate, when it might have been swift and sweeping. And why? Because Canada's businessmen, such as they were then, did not want to win with the people, but on their backs. When the chips were down, they preferred collaboration with, and subordination to, foreign capitalists—in this case, the ruling class in Britain—to alliance with workers and farmers in Canada, the "mechanics" and "yeomen". The result was that economic power passed from the Family Compact of Upper Canada and their counterpart in Lower Canada, the Seigneurs, not to the people, but to the new Family Compact of Capital. Substantial elements of colonialism persisted and the productive forces grew haltingly.

The likelihood is that even had the Revolution succeeded, capitalism—then on the ascendent across the world—would have prevailed in Canada. New conflicts would have been generated among the victors in the Revolution. Tensions would have arisen between the people of Lower Canada, predominantly of French Canadian stock, and of Upper Canada, predominantly of British stock. Nevertheless it is fairly probable that Canada's independence and economic growth would have been speeded, and also her unity—the total union of the founding races, on the basis of the total conservation of their individuality—a free Quebec and French Canada in a free, integrally united Canada.

Defeat in the Revolution meant that these durable, positive drives of Canadian history—though not destroyed—could only prevail through defeat, vicissitudes and partial success. Unity was held back. Independence was held back. So was the progress of labour and industry. Problems were handed down to the present (1967). Almost certainly they would have existed in any case. But they were rendered much more acute.

4. FROM THE REVOLUTION OF 1837 TO CONFEDERATION 1837-1867

The Toronto Printers:

From 1837 to 1867 the unions grew slowly. Progress was difficult, due probably to political defeat in 1837, along with lagging economic development and frequent depression. In the 1840s a revival began. Again, the Toronto printers led the way. In 1843, they began moves to revive their union, dissolved earlier. The immediate cause was a move by Toronto master printers to cut wages to the Kingston level. What happened is described in the Minute Book of the Toronto Typographical Society:

"These gentlemen (the employers) thought it prudent to attempt to accomplish by coalition that which they despaired of achieving single-handed. While this and other matters were under the consideration of the employers, a move was made in another quarter. The men, too, determined that they would have their combination."[100]

The printers moved with care. First they held meetings in their homes. Then, in September 1844, they set up their organization, with a constitution based on the constitution of 1832, plus additions from the Printers Rules of Quebec City and Montreal.[101] Once organized, the printers gave the employers a copy of their constitution and "scale of prices".

One of the first tasks was the combat against unemployment. The master printers used to bring in journeyman from other cities to wait around Toronto for a job, while union men walked the streets.[102] The union opposed this. Another decision, in May 1845, was to collect statistics of the trade in order to get a clear view of the wage and job situation.[103]

In 1845, the employers began a counter attack. Their leader was George Brown, editor of the *Globe* and a famed Liberal. Among his employees were 2 union officers, Clindinning and Carter. One day late in April 1845 Clindinning was called to the head office. This interview took place:

Brown: "You are president of the Society?"

Clindinning: "I am."

Brown: "I am determined not to employ anyone belonging to your Society."

Clindinning: "For my part I could not make up my mind to work much longer in your office at the present rate of wages. It is too little. I object to working until 12, even 1 and 2 o'clock in the morning, on publication for $7.00 a week. It is very hard-earned money indeed. The hours taken in lieu of such work will not compensate for the injury to my constitution, and already I seem to feel much the worse for it."

Brown: "Oh, Mr. Clindinning, I have no objection to giving you $7.00 a week, if you will leave the Society. But I will not be dictated to by the Society as to what wage I must give the men belonging to it. I will not be compelled to pay every hand $7.00 a week. I intend to start discharging you as soon as I can secure a hand to fill your place, which I can soon do."

Clindinning: "I will defend the interest of my brethren, the journeymen printers of Toronto with whom I have long acted. There must be an established and fair rate of wages."

Brown: "There are only two offices in this city willing to support the Society ... the rest are against you."

Clindinning: "I will not desert the Society."

Soon after, Brown called the other union officer, Carter and had a similar conversation with him. Later he dismissed both.[104]

What made Brown so sure he could replace Clindinning? Clancy. Clancy was a "scab". That meant, in the words of the Printers' Minute Book:

"A monster of so hideous a mien,
  That to be hated needs but to be seen."

The Minute Book says Clancy broke ranks with the union and "underhandedly engaged" to work for Brown at $6 a week.[105] The union took strong action. An emergency meeting was called, at which the members pledged to uphold the constitution, and denounced George

Brown for "tampering with members". Clindinning and Carter were voted 15 shillings a week to keep up the fight. Stern treatment was meted to Clancy. He was condemned as "one who had sold himself to George Brown of the *Globe* and *Banner* for $6 a week". By vote of the membership, Clancy and another "scab" named Davies were expelled, and their names ordered struck from Society rolls.[106]

In July 1845, the fight with George Brown was still on. The union decided on a bold step. It issued a leaflet to the public, entitled "A Plain Statement of Facts". Here is the text:

"The Journeymen Printers of the City of Toronto, in consequence of recent proceedings in a certain quarter seriously affecting their interests, deem it their duty thus publicly to state the following facts and circumstances in order to refute several mis-statements industriously circulated which are calculated greatly to injure them . . .

"While they disclaim all intention of assuming a position dictatorial to any employer, they are resolved firmly but respectfully to maintain by all legitimate means in their power, their just rights and privileges, as one of the most important and useful but perhaps the most inadequately rewarded classes in the industrious community.

"For a number of years, a certain scale of prices has prevailed in this city, which are considered perfectly fair and reasonable by all the employers, as evident from the fact that not the slightest objection to it was offered by any of them, and which continued in operation without exception until about two years ago; when a person from the neighbouring Republic commenced living here who has ever since been unremitting to his "liberal" endeavours to reduce as low as possible the justly considered fair and equitable rate of remuneration due the humble operative.

"The first effort of this 'patriotic individual' shortly after his arrival in furtherance of his object was to call together by circular the master printers for the professed purpose of regulating the wages of the journeymen. None or very few attended. No steps were taken either by them to regulate or reduce the fair and long-established rates of wages.

"On the part of the journeymen it was thought prudent by them to form a Society, the object of which should be to promote by every lawful means the interests of the employees, as well as the employer, to uphold the respectability of the members of the printing profession in this City of Toronto, to preserve from encroachment the present established new rate of prices, and to afford the pecuniary assistance to those of the profession who might require it.

"To these objects, together with the scale of prices as set forth in their printers constitution, the journeymen are not aware that any objection was expressed by the master printers. On the contrary, by most they were cordially approved of.

"This individual, though foiled in his first attempt, did not relinquish his design, and has constantly endeavoured by various means to accomplish it. At present it may not be necessary to give in minute detail the scheme resorted to. Suffice it to say that after nearly filling his office with boys, some two or three who were apprentices or had absconded from offices at a distance, and four who have left different offices of this city—about two months ago, he discharged two of his journeymen, professedly because they were members of the Typographical Society, but really because they refused to work for less than a regular and established rate of wages.

"In connection with this proceeding, the printers of Toronto deem it just to mention that two individuals who at present may not be named, have Judas-like betrayed their fellow journeymen in a manner most despicable and mean. These two 'worthies' along with one of a nearly similar stamp, form a trio under the 'banner' of that 'liberal' and 'responsible' establishment.

"Having given these few plain and unvarnished facts, the journeymen printers leave a generous and discerning public to avow their decision on the motives and conduct of the parties in question, trusting they will bear in mind that the printers of Toronto are but acting on the defensive, and contending for no additional remuneration. (They seek) nothing exorbitant or unreasonable, but on the contrary are only endeavouring to maintain that which is considered by all respectable proprietors, as a fair and just reward for their labour and toil.

"The 'labourer is worthy of his hire'!

"Toronto, July 1845. The Journeymen Printers of Toronto."[107]*

This battle was not the last. In 1854, the Toronto Printers went on strike again when employers rejected their price scale. The employers tried to break the strike by arresting union members on a 'conspiracy' charge. The penalty imposed was not serious, but the arrests exposed the insecure condition of workmen's combination.[108]

Amidst difficulties, the printers persisted. They seem to have succeeded in unionizing every newspaper in Toronto, and stoutly defended the conditions they had won. Their rate was $7 per week, and working day 10 hours per day—conditions comparing favourably with those in the United States.[109] Also, they consolidated their union and established a pattern for collective bargaining. In those days more elaborate techniques of negotiations had not developed. The procedure was for union men to gather at a meeting and fix a date when they would get a given rate for their work. They would so advise the employer. If he agreed, good. If he did not agree, and the moment was opportune, they withdrew their services. If the moment was not opportune, they bided their time.[110]

As the years went by, they developed an organizational apparatus. The elements of a stewards body was set up,[111] and rules of order were laid down for union meetings. Frequently, committees were set up to

---

* In 1964, this same union, now Local 91 of the International Typographical Union, CLC, was on strike against the *Globe's* successor, the *Globe and Mail* of Toronto.

carry out decisions and report to the general meeting. Generally, the printers shunned hasty action. If a problem was taxing, they put it on the table for the next meeting. Another innovation, begun in the 1840s, was the annual report. Presented usually in January, it summed up the financial position, state of membership, relations with the employers, and drew conclusions for the future. These reports were models of working class presentation.[112]

The printers were always concerned about discipline. An entry in their minute book for April 5, 1848, states: "We must reject those who have never atoned their betrayal of our rights, who have never relented for espousing the form of that detested vermin which has for ages so cruelly symbolized the dishonourable of our craft." A disciplinary procedure was established. When the printers suspected that a member had broken ranks and was working below the agreed rate, they would lay charges and set up an investigating committee. If the member was found guilty, the penalty might be suspension. Sometimes the sword of discipline reached across the decades. The printers' Minute Book for 1894 reports that a member was fined for "scabbing" 20 years earlier. Also, the Society pressed for an active membership. A meeting of February 1849 reprimands "those who feel quite satisfied to reap and enjoy the benefit which has been brought about by the labour and expense of others, while on their part they seldom think proper to attend a Society meeting or to come forward and pay their subscription."[113]

Many printers must have been interested in politics. In January 1850, after debating the matter, the Society invited the Governor General, the Earl of Elgin, to its annual dinner. A year earlier, Elgin had been a target of a Montreal capitalist clique, who wanted to hand Canada to the United States—the same clique that was pro-British Empire in 1837. There was some controversy about this in the Society, the invitation to Elgin was rescinded and later the President submitted his resignation.[114]

All in all, the printers persevered amidst toil and trouble. When things were difficult, they said: "Though our members are few, and our finances low, yet if we will exert ourselves, in a very short time our members will increase to many, and our finances rise higher."[115] In 1850, the Society looked back to six years of life and set forth its prospects with poetic vigour:

"The future is big with hope and promise. The foundations of your Society are too broad and too secure to be easily shaken. The twig, planted some years ago, has become a fair and stately tree; and your committee with every confidence predicts that when the blasts of winter shall have gathered to Mother Earth, the leaves which at present adorn its branches, a future spring shall call forth its more than past-time vigour."[116]

Growth of Other Unions:

Other unions were being built in Ontario, the Maritimes, British Columbia and Quebec. One union, the Hamilton printers, was functioning in 1846. In 1848, organization developed among shipwrights and caulkers at Kingston.[117] In the 1850s, at Toronto, unions of bakers and tailors were organized, and there were strikes of bricklayers, carpenters, moulders and shoemakers.[118] In the 1860s, building trades unions were organized at Ottawa.[119] At London, Ontario, the London Bricklayers Protective Association was established in 1863.[120] In the Maritimes, organization centred on the shipping industry—a ship's labourers society at Saint John, New Brunswick,[121] a strong union of shipwrights and caulkers at Halifax, Nova Scotia.[122] In British Columbia, organization grew in the shipbuilding industry—a shipyard workers union was functioning there in 1862.[123] Organization was built also in the mining industry. In 1858, coal miners were on strike at Nanaimo, Vancouver Island.[124]

Unions were also built in Quebec. At Montreal, unions of cigar makers and wharf workers were founded around 1865,[125] and metal trades organization developed in 1866 (at the Robert Mitchell Plumbing and Brass Works). At Quebec City, the shipping industry was a centre of organization—a union of sail makers founded 1858; [126] a longshoremen's, 1859; a Ship Labourers Benevolent Society, 1862.[127] The Longshoremen's Union, called "L'Association du Bord", was a powerful body. Tribute to its effectiveness is a complaint by pro-employer elements in 1862 that normally it cost only 62 cents per thousand sheets to load lumber "but with men who are members of the Society, the cost was $1.10 per thousand".[128]

Outstanding among Quebec City's unions was the Canadian Typographical Union. Organized at least as far back as 1836, it grouped both English-speaking and French-Canadian printers. In 1839, it drafted a petition to the master printers, demanding a raise in wages because of rising living costs.[129] The text stated:

"You master printers are heads of families yourselves. You must be aware of the high price of food, of firewood, of lodging, of clothing, of all that is necessary to life. The high cost of living in Quebec City has long since forced our wives to scrimp and save and economize at every point. And, despite all this, there are very few among us who are or will not be in debt this winter."

Many signing this petition were later prominent in the labour, cultural and political life of Quebec City. In 1844, the Union went out of existence. Reorganized in 1852, it functioned only a few months.[130] In 1855 there was a further reorganization. The new body called itself the Quebec Typographical Society.[131] In the years that followed, it flourished, co-operated with its sister union in Toronto, and participated in Quebec patriotic endeavours—on June 24, 1862, its members marched proudly in the parade of the St. Jean Baptiste Society.[132] From the reorganization of 1855 to the present (1967), this union has functioned continuously—one of Canada's pioneer unions.[133]

Beginnings of International Unionism:

We turn to a major development—the beginnings of international unionism. Until now, the movement had been almost completely Canadian, with no outside connections. An exception was the Amalgamated Society of Engineers, a British organization with affiliates at Toronto, Hamilton, Kingston and Montreal.[134] In the 1860s, affiliation to U.S. unions began, to a significant degree. Among the first to do this were the moulders. In 1861, Montreal moulders joined the U.S. National Moulders Union; in 1863, Toronto moulders joined;[135] later, the Hamilton moulders.[136] Then came the printers. In the middle 1860s, there were Canadian unions of printers at London, Hamilton, Toronto, Montreal, Quebec, Saint John and Halifax. In 1865, the Saint John, N.B. printers' local affiliated to the National Typographical Union.[137] In 1866, the Toronto Typographical Society affiliated. In the next few years other typographical unions did likewise.

This process has sometimes been described as an "opening up of branches" by U.S. unions in Canada. The term was used by H. A. Logan in his *Trade Unions in Canada*.[138] To an important degree, the facts suggest otherwise. The process often entailed Canadian affiliation to U.S. unions. Consider the printers. When the Quebec City Printers joined the NTU in 1872, they had been in existence 17 years.[139] Their records refer to a motion "to request a charter of affiliation from the national union".[140] The same applies to the Toronto printers. When they joined the U.S. union, they had been a Canadian union for 34 years—as from their founding in 1832—and 22 years, as from their reorganization in 1844. So Toronto printers had their own union 27 years before there was a national union in the U.S.A.

How did their affiliation come about? At a meeting of the Toronto Typographical Society in February 1859, the committee reported that a letter had come from New York inviting the Society to join the National Typographical Union. The matter was referred to a standing committee.[141] At a later meeting the committee reported that "it had not sufficient information to decide whether it should join in subordination to the National Typographical Union of the United States".[142] Six years later (1865) the NTU renewed its invitation. The terms of its letter are revealing. They proposed a "union of Societies in the British provinces with the national body of the United States".[143] The Toronto printers discussed this with their usual care, and in 1866, decided to affiliate.[144] Their annual report for that year states: "This (affiliation) has not been effected without careful consideration and after many pressing solicitations from our United States brethren."

A year later, the Society was vigorously upholding its rights against centralizing tendencies in the national (international) union. The national union had proposed measures which, the Toronto members felt, diminished their right to alter their constitution and by-laws—a right, which they said, "must remain with the subordinate unions". A committee from the Society visited the shops and discussed the proposed constitutional changes with the members. Later, the Society adopted a motion disapproving the changes and opposing also an increase in per capita tax.[145]

Why affiliation to U.S. unions? Here are some reasons: The undeveloped condition of the Canadian economy; its interflow with the U.S. economy; Canadians' need for jobs in the United States; trade solidarity; the Canadian workers' desire for organization, and their readiness to use anything to get it—east, west, north, or south of the border.

A few details: Because of the low level of Canadian industry, many Canadians used to go to the U.S. for jobs. The union card could help. There was one motive for affiliation. It operated in the case of the Toronto Typographical Society—the members were informed that affiliation would help those "seeking employment in the United States".[146]

A further motive was solidarity. It was natural for the workers in a trade, for example carpentering or typesetting, to combine. And it was natural for them to extend this combination to south of the border. This was the more so because craft production was still strong as compared to large-scale industrial production; and most industrial units were small, employing a comparatively small group of workers. This meant that in the building trades for example, carpenters who wanted a strong union, would look first to carpenters in other centres rather than, say, to bricklayers, painters or masons or unskilled workers on their own job—at that, perhaps a small, short-term job. And if carpenters in Canada were few and isolated, why not become stronger by combining with a larger craft organization of carpenters in the U.S.?

It follows that the origin of international unionism in Canada was connected with the *lower* form of craft production and craft unionism, as distinct from the *higher* form of large-scale industrial production and industrial unionism. In turn, this reflected and fused with a situation where the Canadian economy as a whole was underdeveloped, lacked internal connection and self-sufficiency. This strengthened the *emerging* Canada-U.S. attraction and *continuing* Canada-British attraction, as compared to the *inter-Canada* and *Canada-world* attraction of our day.

So, U.S. affiliation was a *mode* of solidarity proper to the times. Moreover, it was a two-way street. In 1860, the Toronto Printers said: "We trust that we shall ever be among those in the front ranks in assisting any typographical brother who may need our assistance."[147] More than once, the Toronto printers sent contributions to U.S. printers' locals at Brooklyn, New York and Chicago.[148]

Still more sweeping in significance, is the origin of the term "international union". That term, and its substance, *was almost exclusively a product of Canadian membership*. Throughout their history down to the present (1967), international unions have had little or no membership in any foreign country save Canada. For example, the National Typographical Union changed its name to International Typographical Union *after* it acquired membership in Canada. Other unions such as the Brotherhood of Locomotive Engineers kept their original name but *took on* the status of international unions *solely because of membership in Canada*. In sum, throughout their history, the international unions have in practically every case been unions originating in, and based predominantly on, the United States, but with membership in Canada or claims to membership there; and gradually, through the years, they have come to consider various trades and industries in Canada as part of their jurisdiction.

A further factor. The United States unions were then in their pioneer, progressive phase. National unions were being formed, and trade union centres—first the National Labour Union, then the Knights of Labour, later the American Federation of Labour. U.S. organized workers were soon to be involved in major battles for the 8-hour day and the right to organize. The leaders of many U.S. unions such as the Moulders, Typographers, Cigar Makers, Carpenters—were inclined to socialism. McGuire, a leader in the carpenters union was a socialist in his early days. Samuel Gompers of the Cigar Makers—later to become an arch reactionary—says of his youthful years: "I studied German in order to read Karl Marx' *Capital* in the original!"[149] Sylvis, founder of the National Moulders Union, corresponded with Karl Marx.[150]

●

These then are some circumstances which help explain Canadian affiliation to U.S. unions. Plainly this was no thundering descent of U.S. super organizers on Canada, but rather the formation of a fraternal relationship which was subsequently to become — as will be shown in later chapters—one of domination. In sum, the evidence belies the idea that Canadians did not originate their trade union movement, were passive beneficiaries of U.S. unions, and were always dependent on U.S. Organized Labour.

CHAPTER 2

RISE OF A CENTRAL LABOUR MOVEMENT
1867-1880

1. CONFEDERATION
THE TORONTO TRADES ASSEMBLY

Reasons for Confederation:

At the time of Confederation, Canada was a backward country, its economy predominantly rural.[1] Its population was 3½ million, of which four-fifths was rural. Only 13% of the population was engaged in manufacturing and handicraft production. Construction took up another 18%.[2] Factories were small—usually in boot and shoe, woollens, and similar secondary industry. Average capital per industrial establishment was somewhat under $2,000.[3] Industry was slowly developing. In 1871, in Ontario, there were 58 people per thousand in the "industrial" class, as compared with 47 per thousand in 1851.[4] For Quebec, the figures for the same period are 55 persons per thousand in the "industrial" class, as compared with 29 persons per thousand in 1851. Growth of urban population is indicated in the following table:[5]

City	1851	1871
Toronto	30,775	56,092
Hamilton	14,121	26,716
Montreal	57,715	107,225

The condition of wages at Confederation is reflected in this data:[6]

Trade	Wage Rate
Compositor	$5 to $8 per week
Labour in Soap and Candle Factories	$1 per day
First Class Furrier	$8 to $9 per week

Second Class Furrier	$5 to $7 per week
Skilled Woman Worker	$3 to $5 per week
Farm Labourer	$1 to $1.50 per day plus board

Why Confederation? One reason was that Canada's political structure had become incompatible with the expanding economic forces. Growth of production demanded unification in a central state. The grouping of scattered provinces no longer sufficed. Railroads and canals were needed. Whence the money to build them? In the 1850s and 1860s, large-scale railway and canalization projects were mainly financed by loans from governments in the provinces—by 1866, $33,000,000 had been loaned to railroads.[7] Such disbursements were increasingly beyond the capacities of the separate governments in the provinces.[8] In short, capitalist private enterprise was too weak to develop the productive forces. The central action of the state was needed.

Another reason for Confederation was that economic and political tutelage to foreign capital was blocking Canada's progress. Unification could diminish dependence, increase independence from Great Britain and the United States. In the U.S., capital was expanding. Some ruling circles there wanted to take over all North America. Frontier incidents were developing, as American settlers pressed toward Canadian mid-western territories. The issue was being posed: Would Canada's scattered provinces be welded into one great country, or would they be absorbed, first economically, then politically, by the United States?[9]

Confederation decided the issue, at least for the time being; and it was followed by territorial unification, railroad building and protection—the National Policy.[10] Progress was swift. The territories of the Hudson's Bay Company were taken over. Manitoba was founded. In 1871, British Columbia joined the Dominion. Then came the decision to build a railroad entirely through Canadian territory; also the imposing of duties on goods from Britain and the United States, particularly the latter.[11]

So Confederation was a great step forward. There were serious shortcomings. Much of the immediate fruits went to large employers based on Montreal and Toronto. For labour, for the farmers, for the Maritimes, for Quebec, there were grave inequities. But historically most decisive was the growth of Production, Labour, Canada.

The Toronto Trades Assembly, 1871:

The birth of Canada as a central state was followed by the birth of a central labour movement. The Toronto Trades Assembly was a move in this direction. Its origins go back to the late 1860s, when Toronto unions used to meet at annual picnics. In February 1871, the Toronto Coopers Union struck off a committee to visit other unions, "for the purpose of agitating the question of forming a central body to be known as the Toronto Trades Assembly".[12] On March 27, 1871, a gathering was held with delegates from a number of unions, including the Knights of St. Crispin, a shoeworkers union, the Bakers Union, the Cigar Makers Union, and the Iron Moulders Union.[13] On April 12, a further meeting adopted this motion: "Be it resolved that the delegates now assembled will now proceed with formation of an Association to be known as the Toronto Trades Assembly. And the same is hereby formed."[14] John Hewitt of the Coopers Union was elected president, and J. S. Williams of the Toronto Typographical Society, secretary.

Organization of the unorganized was the first task undertaken by the Assembly. For this it set up a special committee. On June 9, this committee reported that "Hatters are moving in our direction" and that "the men at the rolling mills want a union".[15] The Assembly set up another committee to visit unions not yet affiliated.[16] Also, it issued a list of union and non-union shops, and helped in strikes.[17] The Assembly's success in bringing together unions is indicated by the following list of affiliates in the Minute Book for 1872:[18]

Building Trades
Builders Union
Bricklayers and Masons Unions
Carpenters Union
Painters Union
Stonecutters Union

Woodworking
Cabinet Makers Union
Chair Makers Union
Upholsterers Union
Varnishers and Polishers Union

Carriage Making
Carriage Makers Union
Coach Makers Union
Harness Makers Union
Hackmen's Association

Metal Trades
Amalgamated Engineering Union
Boilermakers Union
Coopers Union
Iron Moulders Union
Machinists and Blacksmiths Union
Tinsmiths Union

Miscellaneous
Knights of St. Crispin (3 locals)
Bakers Union
Cigar Makers Union
Bookbinders Union
Dry Goods Clerks Early Closing Association (referred to in minutes for 1871)

2. THE NINE-HOUR MOVEMENT. 1872

Printers' Strike; Ten Great Days; Victory:

1872 is the year Canada's workers first demonstrated their identity as a class. The issue was the 9-hour day, and Toronto was the pacemaker. On January 19, the Trades Assembly adopted a motion that "55 hours be a legal week's work".[19] To this end, it held a mass meeting on March 15. This was a great success. Then the unions began to present "memorials" for the 9-hour day to the employers.[20] One of the first to do so was the Iron Moulders Union.[21] There were similar actions at Sarnia, Guelph, St. Catharines, Hamilton, Oshawa, Ottawa, Perth, Montreal.[22] Hamilton was an important centre, with a vigorous Nine-Hour League. Unions there presented memorials "for the shortening of the hours of labour", and in the middle of March some went on strike.[23] Oshawa was another centre for this type of action, notably at the Joseph Howe Works.[24] At Perth, the Journeymen Shoemakers Union joined in the fight. At Montreal, a Nine-Hour League led strikes of brass workers (at the Robert Mitchell Company) and also of workers in other trades.[25]

The union which led the way at Toronto was the Typographical Society. It now had 28 years of continuous existence behind it, and its membership was 130. Early in 1872, the Society decided on the following demands: "A week's work to consist of 54 hours, $10 per week; 25 cents per hour overtime for job printers."[26] On March 13, a membership meeting was informed that the master-printers had rejected the 54-hour demand.[27] The meeting decided: "Be it resolved that all union men quit work." Strike pay was fixed at $3 per week for single men, and $5 per week for married men.[28]

The man who led the fight against the union was again, George Brown ,of the *Globe*, "the prince of Reformers, the paragon of anti-labour employers", as the strikers called him. In his newspaper, he said shorter hours were bad for Labour. The men would have more time to spend at home, and would make a nuisance of themselves. A striker's wife replied that she did not know how the upper class lived but working women were glad to have their husbands an extra hour:

"Working men's wives, don't let your husbands rat it! I wouldn't live with such a creature for the world. When the trade at which your husband works is compelled to strike, don't let your man go back on the union. Take my word for it, the extra hour will do good to all concerned, and will not, as some have said, be spent in the tavern or in idleness."[29]

The printers faced difficulties aplenty. George Brown hired "detective from Ottawa to shadow them". Strikers were arrested on a vagrancy charge. Some were tried on a breach of contract charge and found guilty. Printers were brought in from the country to take the jobs of strikers

Then came 10 great days, April 15-24. A great event was the Queen's Park demonstration, April 15. This was organized by the Toronto Trades Assembly, and the aim was to rally the population against the employers who wanted "to crush the grand principles of unionism". The Assembly decided on the demonstration at a meeting held April 12, and printed 1,500 handbills. On Monday evening, April 15, detachments of union members gathered at the Trades Assembly Hall on King Street, and formed a procession in the following order: Iron Moulders, Bricklayers, Masons, Cigar Makers, Coopers, Coachmakers, Blacksmiths, Machinists, Bakers Union, Varnishers and Polishers, Knights of St. Crispin, Typographical Union, the Bookbinders Union, the Toronto Trades Assembly. Headed by a number of bands, including the Queen's Own and the Young Irishmen, the trade unionists began to march. They moved east along King Street to Yonge Street, north up Yonge Street to College, west along College to Queen's Park. On the sidewalks, thousands of spectators cheered them on, and more cheers came from thousands in the windows above.

At Queen's Park, 10,000 gathered. One speaker said: "They are bringing in labour-saving machinery. Who is to benefit by it? The men or the masters?" Another said: "Let them double their police force, we are not ashamed. We are fighting for the Nine-Hour Day. That's a great principle, and we fight in the light of day!" E. K. Dodds called for labour political action. The time had come when working men "should select those who would go and fight their battles in parliament". A snow storm began. But the men on the platform looked at the assembled thousands and found that for all the cold, "there was a gleam of cheerfulness shining over the scene, and the manifesting of warmth and enthusiasm in every countenance".[30]

The next day the employers struck back. They secured the arrest of the Printers' Vigilance (strike) Committee—24 in all. Those arrested included John Armstrong, vice-president of the Toronto printers local, later international president of the union; J. S. Williams, Toronto Trades Assembly secretary; Edward F. Clarke, later Mayor of Toronto and M.P. for York West; and union members Edward Ward, J. C. McMillan, and William Lovell.

What had happened? The employers were using the common law against the workers. In England, after two generations of struggle, the unions had gained statutory relief from those clauses in the common law which were interpreted by judges as rendering illegal, combinations for higher wages and lower hours. In Canada the common law prevailed without the relieving legislation. And so Magistrate McNab of Toronto had issued warrants for the arrests.

Against the employers' master-move, the trade unionists rallied their forces. That day, some of them hurried about Toronto raising bail for the committee, threatened with imprisonment in Don Jail. News of the arrests spread like wild fire. In the evening, 4,000 gathered in the Market Square. A procession of union members marched from the Trades Assembly Hall on King Street West to the Market Square. The speakers mounted a platform set up on the steps leading to the city council chambers. Excitement was high. From the crowd came the cry: "Down with Brown and the Bow Park Bulls!" (a reference to the police). The gathering was peaceful, but at one point, it surged towards a policeman. He took to his heels and reported: "There is a riot. I have had to run for my life!"[31]

From the speakers came rousing calls for action. E. K. Dodds renewed his proposal for political action: "Events of this last day prove the need for labour representation!" John Hewitt condemned the arrests:

"Generations yet unborn shall rise up in condemnation of this ignoble action. This transaction shall be recorded on the pages of Canadian history. Working men of Toronto, the eyes of toiling millions throughout the world are on you this day!"[32]

The gathering then adopted the following resolution:

"Be it resolved that this meeting views with indignation the outrage that has this day been committed upon this peaceful community, by the arrest of twenty-four highly respected working men, and pledges its determination to support them under all circumstances; and be it further resolved that it shall use all available means for the repeal of any law that might exist to warrant such unjustifiable interference with the rights of the people."[33]

Then came Thursday, April 18, a great day for labour. The *Ontario Workman* began publication, a pioneer labour newspaper, with J. S. Williams as editor. The inaugural issue contained the following extract from Marx's *Capital:*

"Listen, Mr. Capitalist, you are constantly holding forth to me the gospel of economy and continence. Very well, like a rational and prudent husbandman, I shall economize my only wealth, my power of work. I shall abstain from foolishly wasting it. By excessively prolonging the working day, you can consume a greater portion of my working power in one day that I can restore in three days. The *use* of my power of work, and the *robbing* of it, are two entirely different things. I demand a working day of normal length, and I demand it without appealing to your feelings, because money matters are not matters of affection, and business is soulless. You may be a model citizen, perhaps a member of the Society for the Prevention of Cruelty to Animals, you may even have the scent of sanctity and piety. But no heart beats in the bosom of this thing you represent towards me. What seems to be pulsating therein is MY OWN HEART BEAT. I demand a normal working day because I demand the value of my article like every other dealer!"[34*]

On that same day, the arrested printers appeared in court. The Defence pleaded the Typographical Union had been accepted by the community for over 25 years and was not illegal. The Crown argued that the common law forbade combinations of labour, and Canada had no exempting legislation. Magistrate McNab ruled that the arrested men were guilty of being members of an illegal body, a combination.

But on this Thursday, April 18, great events were unfolding at Ottawa. The Prime Minister was Sir John A. Macdonald, a great Canadian, a man for swift, decisive action. Federal elections were due in several months and government prospects were not too bright. The bold plans laid down at Confederation were slow in being realized. The Liberals were making inroads. Traditionally, Labour had inclined more to the Liberals—through earlier associations in the fight for responsible government. But here was a leading Liberal, George Brown, threatening to destroy the workers' movement. And here was an insurgent labour movement talking of going into politics itself. Sir John decided to move. That day, he introduced emancipating legislation modelled on the British Act of 1871. It provided that the mere fact of combining to increase wages or to lower hours was not a conspiracy and did not violate the common law.

The employers were furious. That evening some gathered at the Agricultural Hall in Toronto, with George Brown as foremost speaker. He cried: "Crush out the aspirations of employees! Stamp out the movement! Ostracize the union men and drive them from Canada!"[36]

Thus ended Thursday, April 18.

The next evening delegates gathered at the Trades Assembly Hall to ponder the week's events. They decided to hold a new demonstration. At 7.30 p.m., Wednesday, April 24, 4,000 gathered in the East Market Square. The meeting denounced "a dishonourable and unmanly character", and adopted a resolution protesting the arrests. John Hewitt spoke, and in measured words affirmed the principles of trade unionism:

"So long as capitalists try to take advantage of labour so long will the need of organization exist. Trade unions are a product of the age. The working men have found it necessary to combine in defence of their

---

* Marx says he secured the idea for this passage from a manifesto put out by building trades workers in London, England, in 1861, during their battle for the 9-hour day.[35]

rights against capital. Working men are losing their local and sectional feelings. Throughout the world they are becoming connected. What the combined efforts of capital throughout the civilized world have failed to do, George Brown and his satellites have now undertaken, but they will fail!"[36a]

The meeting concluded with "Three cheers for the 9-hour movement!" Thus ended ten great days for Labour.

The events in Toronto encouraged workers elsewhere. But the employers fought back. George Brown said: "If this agitation for shorter hours continued, let employers shut their works and starve the men in submission." Against the unions, the employers used the document and the blacklist. The document was a 19th century version of the "yellow dog agreement"—an employee's commitment, secured by pressure from the employer, not to join a union. The blacklist was a listing, written or oral, of union members. It would circulate among employers and be used to cut off union supporters from employment. For example, at Oshawa, the owner of the Joseph Howe Works discharged a union member and then wrote companies producing the same item across the Dominion, asking them not to hire this man—an action which excited this comment from an Oshawa union member: "A boss who could be guilty of such a despicable action goes far to prove the correctness of the Darwinian theory!"[37]

Also, employers put out anti-union propaganda. They argued that "ten hours in manufacturing is consistent with the normal condition of the operative", and denounced the 9-hour day as "communist levelling". The working class could do with less pay if they did with less luxuries", said an Oshawa employer, while a Hamilton employer declared: "Any man who can put money in a savings bank or build himself a home has too much already!"[38]

However, the trade unionists resisted. They fought the red-baiting —saying that it was opposition to reform that engendered revolutionary feelings. The struggle against the 9-hour movement was being conducted by "persons to whom gold is all and the future of our country nothing. These are people who have sacrified their patriotism at the shrine of selfishness". The workers forged their solidarity in action. When a Montreal newspaper discharged 6 printers, members of Typographical Local 97, the Nine-Hour League sent out the following appeal: "Let workers assemble in their halls through the length and breadth of the Dominion, and back up their brethren in Montreal!"[39]

The 9-hour fight went forward at Hamilton, St. Catharines, Toronto and other cities. At Hamilton, the Nine-Hour League planned a "grand demonstration" on May 15, "in honour of the 9-hour system". Some workers there left their jobs sooner than sign the "document".[40] A Hamilton trade unionist wrote:[41]

> "Arise ye men of Canada, ye sons of freedom rise!
> Proclaim the Nine-Hour Movement 'til its echoes reach the skies!
> Be earnest, truthful, prudent, but firmly take your stand,
> Ye are the wealth-producers, bone and sinew of the land . . .
> And ere thou sign the document our masters now propose
> Let the world forget the Shamrock, the Thistle and the Rose!"

At St. Catharines, towards the end of April, there was a large demonstration for the 9-hour day. A speaker said: "The nine-hour question is now a matter of social and physical necessity!" At Toronto, carpenters struck on May 1 and demanded an increase in their daily rate from $1.75 to $2. On May 17, the Toronto Trades Assembly considered what may have been a general strike—a "grand demonstration of all the trades" to be held on June 1.[42]

This fighting stand brought victory. At Hamilton, printers won the 9-hour day, and so did some workers in other trades, such as the machine shops. The Great Western Railway granted an agreement for "54 hours a week at 58½ hours pay". At Brantford, foundry workers won a strike. At Montreal, the Grand Trunk Railway instituted the 9-hour day and granted a general pay increase. The Nine-Hour League there reported hopefully that other large firms "are prepared to grant the 9-hour principle if it becomes universal!" At Toronto, strikes were won by printers, bookbinders, painters, iron and brass workers, and Grand Trunk Railway workers.[43] From Hamilton came this poem of victory written May 15, by trade unionist, Alec H. Wingfield:[44]

"The Nine-Hour Pioneers

> Honour the men of Hamilton,
> The Nine-Hour pioneers,
> Their memory will be kept green
> Throughout the coming years.
>
> And every honest son of toil
> That lives in freedom's light
> Shall bless that glorious day in May
> When might gave way to right.
>
> Your cause was just, your motives pure,
> Again, again, again,
> You strove to smooth the path of toil
> And help your fellow-men.
>
> And Canada will bless your name
> Through all the coming years,
> And place upon the scroll of fame
> The Nine-Hour pioneers."

3.   TRADE UNION STRUGGLES.   1873-1879

The Canadian Labour Union, 1873:

Out of the 9-hour fight came Canada's first trade union centre, the Canadian Labour Union. Hamilton trade unionists pioneered. On May 3, 1872, they were hosts to a conference of union delegates from Toronto, Brantford and Montreal. That conference decided on an organization to be called the "Canadian Labour Protective and Mutual Improvement Association", and with the following program: Union "of all classes of workmen for their mutual benefit"; repeal of "oppressive laws"; labour legislation by Dominion and Provincial legislatures; establishment of branches in the principal centres of industry; organizing of libraries and reading rooms in the industrial centres; fostering of the labour press.[45]

John Hewitt attended the Hamilton gathering. On his return to Toronto, he told the Trades Assembly that the Hamilton meeting was "Canada's first labour convention". He then proposed that "there be a grand convention of labour to be held in Toronto after the new year ... in conjunction with the meeting of parliament". The Assembly agreed, and sent a circular to unions across the Dominion proposing a national labour congress. Unions responding favourably included lodges of shoeworkers at Barrie and Orillia, the Jacques Cartier lodge of the Typographical Union at Montreal, and iron moulders local at Cobourg, Ontario.[46]

On September 23, the inaugural convention opened at the Trades Assembly Hall, Toronto. Gathered were capable, hard-working union officers like J. W. Carter of the Toronto Painters, John Hewitt of the Trades Assembly, William Joyce of Toronto Printers Local 91, and William Magness, a St. Catharines tailor. Delegates came from Toronto, Hamilton, Ottawa, St. Catharines, London and other centres. They represented 35 unions including the Shoemakers, the Operative Tailors, Toronto; the Iron Moulders, Hamilton; Stone Cutters, Limestone Cutters, Ottawa; Tailors Union, St. Catharines; Shoe Makers Union, London.

The convention came to order 9 a.m. September 23. In the chair was J. W. Carter of the Toronto Painters. He declared:

"This is one of the grandest events in connection with the labour movement that has ever taken place in the Dominion of Canada. The workers in this country have determined to centralize their energies and establish a Canadian labour union. Its necessity is beyond doubt."[47]

The delegates adopted a constitution whose preamble stated:

"The working men of the Dominion of Canada, in common with intelligent producers of the world, feel the necessity of co-operation and harmonious action to secure their mutual interests and just compensation for their toil, and such limitation of the hours of labour that may tend to promote their physical and intellectual well-being."

The preamble went on to say that it would be the function of the Canadian Labour Union to "agitate such questions as may be for the benefit of the working classes, in order that we may obtain the enactment of such measures by the Dominion or local legislatures as will be beneficial to us, and win the repeal of all oppressive laws now existing. The new organization would seek to unite "the energies of all classes of labour in this Dominion of Canada".[48]

Organization of the unorganized was a prime objective. The convention pledged "to help Canadian workers form themselves into unions whenever practical". Existent unions would be aided in their organizing work. Where there was no chartered organization in a trade, workers would be chartered by the Canadian Labour Union. Another task undertaken was mutual aid in strikes. When a union could not settle a dispute peacefully, it would report to the central organization which would then circularize its affiliated unions for financial aid "sufficient to sustain the labourers who were striking".[49]

Shorter hours, immigration, convict and child labour were other problems taken up. The convention demanded the 9-hour day, and condemned overtime as a practice "calculated to defeat the benefits accruing from shorter hours". Abuses in immigration were protested—bogus claims of immigration agents about Canada being a land of sunshine and plenty. Contract labour was condemned as a practice which enriched "capitalist speculators". Also, the delegates demanded legislation to control child labour—a ban on "employment of children under ten years of age in the factories and mills and other manufacturing establishments where machinery is used". Finally, they called for a Dominion bureau of labour and statistics, and for labour political action.[50]

The rules of organization provided for annual meetings of the Congress, with delegates elected direct from the unions. Per capita to the CLU was fixed at 5 cents quarterly per member in the case of a directly-chartered local, and 50 cents per member per year for affiliated unions. The executive elected included J. W. Carter of the Painters Union, John Hewitt, D. J. O'Donaghue of the Ottawa Typographical Union, William Magness of the St. Catharines Tailors, Hodges of the Hamilton Iron Workers; and MacMillan of the Toronto Amalgamated Engineers. The founding of Canada's first trade union centre was celebrated at a banquet in the Trades Assembly hall. The room was decorated with appropriate banners. Toasts were drunk to the success of Canadian Labour, and there were rousing speeches by John Hewitt, J. S. Williams and A. McCormack of the Toronto Bricklayers and Masons Union.[51]

Strikes, 1872-1879; Growth of Unions and Central Councils:

The 1872 strike movement reached its height in May, declined thereafter but did not stop. In the summer of 1872, furniture workers were on strike at Toronto, seamen at Port Hope, glass workers, plumbers and coppersmiths at Montreal. Sometimes there were setbacks, and hard lessons were learnt. At Hamilton, during a strike at the Wunzer Sewing Machine plant, some committeemen caved in and signed the Document. This led to loss of tne strike. Then the company cut the wages of committeemen who had broken ranks. That was a lesson. At Toronto George Brown brought in printers from the country to take the jobs of the strikers, but after the strike was over he treated the country printers poorly. That, too, was a lesson.[52]

As time went on, it was clear the bright prospects of spring 1872 would not be fulfilled. The employers were still too strong, and there was economic depression—one began in 1872 and lasted to 1879. "We are suffering all from a dullness in the trade", stated the Toronto Printers' Minute Book in 1876. Employers took advantage of these conditions to wipe out wage gains and wipe out unions, while unions fought to keep their gains and organizations. Strikes and lockouts developed. At Ottawa, an employer locked out the printers. "Comply with the rules," he said, "and you may come back!" Hard-pressed the Ottawa printers received financial help from the Toronto Society— $200. At Toronto, there were strikes of printers, bricklayers, iron moulders, tailors, plasterers and stonecutters.

The Toronto stonecutters strike of 1875 was important. In its sixth week strikers were arrested and brought before the police magistrate. He found them guilty and sentenced them to jail—a decision assailed by the Trades Assembly as "unlawful and unjust". The employers aimed to destroy the Stonecutters Union. They failed. In the middle of July 1875, the President of the Stonecutters Union told a meeting of the assembly: "Our trouble is over. We won!" A lesson was the role of the courts. It cost the union $500 to fight the cases in court—a staggering amount for those days.[53]

Another notable strike was the Toronto printers' strike of 1877, directed against the old foe of the printers, the *Globe*. In April that year the *Globe* wanted to cut wage scales to 28 cents per thousand M's. The printers struck and stayed out for 4 weeks. The next winter the *Globe* pressed again for a wage cut. The management put up a notice saying: "In future you shall be paid $11 per week of 60 hours." Times were hard, so the Union complied, but within a month it struck back. The members gathered at a meeting and adopted the following motion: "This firm shall be closed until such time as the proprietors comply with the scale of prices and recognize 54 hours as constituting a week's work."[54]

All in all, then, the years which followed 1872 were difficult. The President of the Canadian Labour Union stated in 1877: "A real conflict is going on between Labour and Capital."[54a] Despite these hardships, the pioneers persisted. Sometimes, unions scarce born died a quick death, and sometimes there were setbacks. Still, a distinctive movement was taking shape. A report in the Trades Assembly Minute Book for 1875 provides a clue to Toronto union forces at the time. 18 affiliate unions are listed with a total membership of 745.[55]

There were also early steps toward general unions—as distinct from isolated local unions. In 1872, the Toronto Painters Union corresponded with sister unions in Ontario, with the aim of establishing a single organization. A union with close-knit organization was the Knights of St. Crispin—an industrial union of shoemakers which originated in the United States. In the early 1870s it flourished in Canada, and had a provincial grand lodge—an early equivalent of the Canadian Conference of local delegates—which elected its own Canadian officers. At its fourth annual meeting in 1872, there were representatives from Barrie, Brampton, Chatham, Guelph, Hamilton, London, Orillia, Stratford, Brantford, Toronto, Montreal, Quebec City, St. Hyacinthe and Three Rivers. This union did not survive in either the U.S. or Canada.

Central city councils developed. Ottawa was a leader. Here, building trades unions had been organized in connection with the construction of the Parliament Buildings, also a Typographical Union, and in 1872 Ottawa stonecutters had gone on strike. Out of all this activity came a meeting of union delegates at the St. Lawrence Hotel in December 1872, at which the Ottawa Trades Council was organized.

Conventions of the Canadian Labour Union, 1874-1878:

At the inaugural convention of the Canadian Labour Union in 1873, delegates had been fired with the prospect for organizing workers across the country.[56] But increasingly, the reality was wage-cuts, unemployment, lock-outs, hostile employers and legislators, and prosecutions in the courts. When delegates gathered at Ottawa for the second convention in 1874, they found their numbers had declined, but as against this, some new unions had joined. Their prime concern was how to go ahead with organization. They considered a proposal for a full-time organizer but did not decide anything definite.[57]

The third convention was held at St. Catharines in 1875. Again, depression and employer attacks had taken their toll. Only 17 delegates were present—from Toronto, Montreal, Kingston, Oshawa and St. Catharines. Represented were the stonecutters and printers of Toronto; also unions of iron moulders, shoemakers, tailors, coopers, and a few other bodies. In the chair was William Magness of the St. Catharines Knights of St. Crispin. The meeting considered the CLU's scope and functions. The CLU could not substitute itself for local bodies like the Trades Assembly, or for the unions. Everybody agreed on this. What then should be its function? Some said it should be "a parliament of the trade unions of Canada", which battled through the year for legislation, and they suggested a parliamentary committee be set up for this purpose. Others felt this was too confined. The CLU should be "a central body for all unions in the country... should watch and guard the position of the various unions... keep up a continual agitation ... nurse and instruct the unions newly born ... rally the workers at public meetings".[58] A legislative centre or a full-scale operative centre? Here was the seed of a great issue to agitate the movement in decades to follow.

At the fourth CLU convention, held in Toronto, 1876, 25 delegates were present.[59] The fifth and final convention also met in Toronto. The big problem was the depression. Delegates said the way out was shorter hours and higher wages. One said: "I believe in the Four 8's— eight hours work, eight hours pay, eight hours sleep, and eight shillings a day!"[60]

4. TRADE UNION RIGHTS. 1872-1879

The Problem of Legal Status:

The legal status of the movement remained a major obstacle. The Trade Union Act of 1872 had been a step forward. However, the Government gave but also took. Along with the Trade Union Act, it put on the statute books another measure, the Criminal Law Amendment Act. This provided penalties for violence or intimidation during the organizing campaigns and strikes. Also, it stated a union contract was not enforceable in a court of law. Trade unionists complained it was discriminatory since it enumerated offenses arising from union activity, which were already punishable under other sections of the Criminal Code.

How did Prime Minister Macdonald defend his position? He looked to Britain as the model. In justifying the emancipating Trade Union Act, he had pointed out there was no reason "why operators in Canada should not have the same freedom of action and right to combine as those in England". But, he also used Britain as the model for the enslaving Criminal Law Amendment Act. The trade unionists' position was superior, more Canadian. They said legislation should be based on Canadian social needs. British legislation should be a pattern, not a strait-jacket.

Meanwhile, the Machiavellian tactics of Sir John, in coupling a bad Act and a good Act, presented the union men with a serious problem. They resolved it with a counter-Machiavellianism of their own. They recognized the pressing need was to win the 9-hour fight, to lift the threat of jail from the strikers, to win a measure of legal status, however inadequate. So they decided to let the Trade Union Act go through, and then fight the Criminal Law Amendment Act which accompanied it. At a meeting of the Toronto Trades Assembly on May 21, a motion was adopted that the law be accepted without protest for the time being, although it had "deficiencies of great importance": "Moved that we take no steps of recognition at present, but allow the Bill to pass."[61]

Union fears proved well-grounded. In 1873, when the Knights of St. Crispin went on strike, a striker was arrested on a conspiracy charge laid under the Criminal Law Amendment Act. Later years brought more arrests and jail sentences. The Criminal Law Amendment Act must go! The Toronto Trades Assembly took up the call. So did the Ottawa Trades Council and the Canadian Labour Union. In autumn 1874, the trade unionists contacted a reformer M.P. for Hamilton, Aemilius Irving. He agreed to sponsor a motion for repeal; and in support of this move, a mass meeting was held in Toronto. In March 1875, Irving introduced his bill. The M.P.'s were not too friendly. One who supported the bill said later: " I have never delivered a speech in the House which seemed of so little interest to the members, though so large a portion of their constituents are working people!" The bill got as far as second reading. Then Liberal Prime Minister Alexander MacKenzie said: "I will not support this." Irving was worried. Union men urged him not to back down, to "press for total repeal", to press the bill to a division. But he hesitated and thought it might be better to await the action of the Imperial Parliament at London which was then considering an amendment to the Criminal Law Amendment Act. Finally, he withdrew the measure.[62]

Later that year, the Minister of Justice, Telesphore Fournier, introduced a bill which improved a clause in the Criminal Law Amendment Act, relating to watching and besetting. This did not go far in satisfying trade union demands. In July 1875, the Toronto Trades Assembly re-affirmed the demand for total repeal. To this end it renewed pressure on the politicians. That fall, a by-election was due to take place in West Toronto. The Assembly struck off a committee to question candidates on the Act. What followed is related in the Assembly's Minutes: "We attended a meeting and questioned Mr. Turner publicly on the matter of the Criminal Law Amendment Act. Mr. Turner replied that he was in favour of, and if returned, would support a measure for its repeal."[63] Then the Committee turned its attention to the Federal Minister of Justice, the Hon. Edward Blake. Blake was due to address a public meeting in Toronto, November 4, 1875. The Committee used thorough measures to pin him down. It sent him a letter, arranged for an interview, and then, just to make sure, it despatched a delegation to the Minister's public meeting, with instructions "to question the Hon. gentleman on the Act if he failed to refer to it in the course of his speech". The Assembly also set up a special parliamentary committee to conduct the fight at the session due to open.[64]

This struggle ended with a legislative victory. In March 1876, the Minister of Justice, the Hon. Edward Blake, a Liberal, brought in an amendment to the Act, which restricted the clauses on violence and molestation. Watching and besetting was still an offence, but this modifying clause was added: "Attending at or near or approaching a house or other place in order merely to obtain or communicate information, shall not be deemed watching or besetting within the meaning of this section." Then some employers and employer-minded politicians made a last ditch effort to defeat the amendment. On its second reading, a number of M.P.s moved amendments aimed at cancelling the concessions. The trade unionists rallied to save Blake's legislation. They sent out the alarm that reform legislation was "meeting with the opposition of the capitalist classes of the Dominion". The Toronto Trades Assembly printed "dodgers" (leaflets) summoning the membership to a protest meeting. On March 14, 1876, the trade unionists won. Blake's liberating amendment was adopted.[65]

Then came the battle to erase from the statute books another evil law, the Masters and Servants Act. Under this Act, the simple decision of a worker to quit one job to another could be deemed a criminal offence—"breach of contract". Again and again, workers were brought before police magistrates on a charge of "deserting employment", and sometimes were sentenced to jail, as happened to a Hamilton glass blower in 1875. Moreover, the Act was discriminatory since it made breach of contract a criminal offence for workers, while it remained a civil offence for other citizens. If an employer did not pay wages for work done, he was subject only to court action under civil law. But if a worker moved from one job to another, he could be condemned to prison. Again, the Act provided that a worker charged with breach of contract could also be charged under the conspiracy sections of the Criminal Code. In 1875, the CLU convention condemned the Act as "despicable class legislation".[66]

In 1876, there was a step forward. The Act was amended to provide the penalty of $100 fine as an alternative to imprisonment. In 1876, there was another forward step. The Hon. Edward Blake introduced an amendment that breach of contract was a civil offence only. Blake exaggerated the significance of such concessions. He said Labour's troubles are now over. No longer are there class distinctions under the law. The trade unionists were doubtful. In 1876, CLU president, J. W. Carter feared this new legislation "would be twisted by prejudiced men who may have to decide on cases coming before them, placing a different construction on wordings of the Bill, than was the intention of the framers".[67] Still, against the bitter opposition of the "capitalist classes", Labour had won yet another reform.[68]

5. THE LEGISLATIVE STRUGGLE

Factory Legislation; Other Demands:

The movement fought not only for repeal of bad laws, but for enactment of good ones. The long fight for state measures to curb exploitation was opening up. An early piece of social legislation, the Ontario Mechanics Lien Law of 1873, provided that when work was done and wages not paid, a "lien" or seizure could be put on the employer's capital. This seems a small matter. But involved was a chronic problem of the time—"birds of passage" employers who hired men, worked them, and took off without paying wages. The Act's original provisions were inadequate. One defect was that it was operative only where unpaid wages exceded $50. In 1874, some good amendments were enacted, but still the Act contained loopholes for crooked employers. In 1875, a Toronto Trades Assembly delegation interviewed an Ontario cabinet minister called Crookes. He promised more amendments, but, reports the Assembly's Minute Book: "The result of this interview was that nothing further was heard of the amendment."[69]

This much is clear. To quite a degree a reform such as the Mechanics' Lien Law came about as a result of a persistant legislative struggle conducted by the trade union movement, combined at times by direct action. For example, at Ottawa, in the summer of 1872, a church building was being erected. The contractor obtained his money, then vanished, leaving the masons and stonecutters unpaid. The masons and bricklayers gathered at a mass meeting and decided they would not work for the new contractor until they got a hundred cents on the dollar for wages owed by the previous contractor.

Another reform sought was *control of child labour*. Exploitation of children was developing. In trades like tailoring and carpentering, apprentices hardly of school age were being brought in. A carpenter said: "If a boy can drive a nail, he is given a job." Another said: "These boys are like flies in summer time. First you see them, then they are full-sized and ready for action." This was not genuine apprenticeship. The employers were using the children as a reserve of cheap labour. Trade unionists complained that the young people were not kept on long enough to learn a trade. At the fourth CLU convention in 1876, demands were made for Government control, and a Board of Examiners, composed of employers and employee representatives, whose task it would be to check on conditions of employment of apprentices. One variant of child labour was connected with immigration—the bringing in of pauper children from Great Britain. A century earlier, Jonathan Swift had submitted his "modest proposal" for disposal of pauper children—cook them and eat them. Canada's capitalists were more practical. They put them to work, and profited from their work.[70]

Prison labour—another evil. An example is an agreement signed in 1872 between the Ontario Provincial Government and the Canada Car Company. This provided that the entire convict supply of the Toronto Central Prison was to be made available to the Company. The convicts were to be paid between 55 and 65 cents per day, and of this amount, it appears, the larger part was to go to contractors. The Toronto Trades Assembly fought these practices. It told the government: "The mechanics of Ontario ... are not going to stand by and see prison labour compete with free labour." But only in the early years of the 20th century was this use of prison labour eliminated.[71]

Immigration—a boon for Canada, but used by employers again and again to further their interest. In the 1870s, while Canadians walked the streets, the Government set up immigration agencies who beguiled immigrants into the country with the myth of good times. An immigration practice which especially aroused trade union resentment was the "bonus system" or "assisted immigration"—grants of money to immigrants for items such as transportation. The CLU condemned this in 1874 and 1875. In 1875, it won a concession from the Liberal Premier of Ontario, the Hon. Oliver Mowatt—a promise to cut the staff of immigration agents and reduce immigration by one-half.[72]

A Bureau of Statistics and a Department of Labour—today this is a standard part of the Federal Government apparatus. Organized labour helped win this reform. Its demand for a Dominion Labour Bureau goes back to the 1873 CLU convention. Twenty-seven years later, in 1900, this reform began to be enacted. For this, Canada's first Deputy Minister of Labour, Mackenzie King, is often given much of the credit. Yet in 1876, at the fourth CLU convention, J. S. Williams presented a brilliant document sketching the outline of a Federal Department of Labour.[73]

The Franchise. Because of property and income restrictions, many workers did not have the vote in municipal, provincial and federal elections. A reform—the "ballot bill", introduced by Sir John A. Macdonald in 1872, provided for the secret ballot, and extended the vote to more workers. But it fell short of universal manhood suffrage, and it granted multiple votes to property owners. Labour began its long agitation for reform. In 1876, Minister of Justice Edward Blake admitted that "the franchise that presently exists is logically indefensible". That same year, the CLU convention demanded extension of the franchise to every man who had free-hold property of at least $100. The delegates really wanted full manhood suffrage, but decided to move cautiously, for "they were not sure the country was ready". In 1878, CLU enlarged this demand to complete manhood suffrage in municipal, provincial and federal elections.[74]

Canadian independence—the trade union movement began to take a stand. In the 1870s, the promise of Confederation was fading. During much of the decade depression prevailed. This was part of a world cyclical crisis, but had other ramifications connected with Canada's colonial status. Whereas in Western Europe, Britain and the United States, the period between 1867 and 1900 was generally one of economic expansion, in Canada the prevailing trend was depression. Historians speak of this as "the long depression". It is reflected in the statistics of population. Between 1871 and 1901, 1½ million immigrants came to Canada. This figure, combined with an indigenous increase of 2 million, should have made for a total population increase of 3½ million. But in 1901, the increase of population over 1871 was only 1 million.[75] What happened to the extra 2½ million? Many went to the United States. And indeed, at this time, U.S. economic pressures were increasing, along with continuing pressures from Britain. Canadian resources were beginning to be used as raw material for U.S. industries, Canadian labour as a man-power source for U.S. industries, the Canadian market as a dumping ground for U.S. manufactured goods. At the CLU convention of 1874, the secretary stated:

"If there is anything calculated to make this country more dependent than it is now, it is the passage of the proposed treaty (the Reciprocity Treaty between Canada and the United States then being negotiated by the Liberal government which had replaced Sir John A. Macdonald's government in 1873). It is high time this Dominion laid aside swaddling clothes and became self-sustaining. Let's manufacture our own iron, wool, etc. I do not think we ask too much when we claim the right to set a foothold upon our own soil without being pushed down by foreigners."[76]

In 1877, J. S. Williams linked the depression to U.S. pressures. He told the fifth CLU convention: "To a very great extent, the present depression of trade in Canada results from the excessive importation of foreign manufactured goods. In order to remedy this evil, protective tariffs should be the policy of the country . . . The closed market of the United States and the open market of Canada is unfair to Canada. Both should be on an equal footing."[77]

CLU policy adopted that year was along the lines proposed by J. S. Williams. Some delegates, including Alfred Jury, doubted that high tariffs were the remedy, and feared this would foster monopoly and high prices.[78] This was the echo of what had now become a countrywide issue—"reciprocity of trade or reciprocity of tariffs!" Aggressive U.S. policies made reciprocity of trade out of the question, and this cleared the way for the National Policy. Adopted in 1879, it imposed new duties on American goods, and aimed to foster Canadian industry.

In the labyrinth of arguments about tariffs, what was true must be distinguished from what was false. Under conditions where capital was master, the fear that tariffs could foster monopoly and high prices was well-grounded. But there was no inherent connection between tariffs and high prices. A truly Canadian policy was conceivable which prohibited entry of foreign goods, or imposed quotas, but also prohibited price increases in Canada. How could the industries of a young country be fostered if they were not protected against foreign competition? The 19th century had shown that rising nations must shore up their defence against powerful neighbours. The complaint of Canada's Minister of Finance, Fielding, that "we have become a great milch cow for the United States, a hewer of wood and drawer of water",[79] was to remain the irrepressible fact of Canadian-American relations through the years.

6. POLITICAL ACTION

The Election of 1872; the Problem Posed:

When the workers began to build a central labour movement, the more advanced were already thinking beyond economic to political action. One of the first acts of the Toronto Trades Assembly, in 1871, was adoption of a motion for the registering of all parliamentary and municipal voters. Another motion by the Assembly, in 1872, stated: "Be it resolved that we form labour reform leagues in each ward in the city under the jurisdiction of this Assembly, to be composed of working men, to discuss matters pertaining to them as working men, and using their united efforts to advance the interests of labour."[80]

In 1872, "The Workingmen's Progressive Political Party", organized at London, Ontario, had a program demanding abolition of property qualifications for candidates in provincial elections, an elective Senate, a liberal land policy, and the vote for low income groups.[81]

In the federal election of 1872, Labour acted to influence events. Some trade unionists said: "Let's use our power to advance the masses." A Montreal worker pointed out: "The two political parties are fishing for the support of the working class." It seems that most trade unionists did not believe they were strong enough to enter the foray independently, and decided their best course was to defeat the Liberals, and help Sir John A. Macdonald who had helped them.

With the election just 4 weeks away, the outcome uncertain, the Toronto Trades Assembly arranged a public meeting for July 11, with Sir John A. Macdonald as guest of honour. This sent the *Globe* into convulsions, and it howled about interference in politics. But John Hewitt explained: "If the politicians are out to make political engines of the working men, we in return can use the politicians to gain our own ends."[82] The day came—a notable occasion. A few years ago, Organized Labour had been a scattered group, meaning little in Canada's destiny, but today the country's leader was coming to its home. The meeting hall was decorated with banners saying: "Trade unions guarantee the safety of the working man!" In opening the meeting, the chairman said Labour was not supporting Sir John because of his party, but because he had brought in a true reform. Another speaker, Andrew Scott of the Engineers, declared: "This meeting proves that the industrial masses of the country are fast becoming conscious of their own destiny." Putting aside subtlety, Scott turned to Sir John and said: "When your government is returned to office, the Criminal Law Amendment Act must go!"[83]

In his address, Sir John referred to the Trade Union Act of 1872, and described how difficult it had been to convince some members of parliament that "the trade unions were not like the Communes of France".* As regards more changes in legislation he was flexible, did not commit himself to very much but said he would welcome suggestions, and he did promise to extend the franchise. He expounded his theory of capital: The capital of the workingman consisted in the use of his hands and "this is as valuable as the same labour hoarded up in the chest of the capitalist!" He said modestly he was something of a worker himself. He was a "joiner"—look at the Confederation Act. And he was a "cabinet-maker".[84]

In the weeks that followed, trade unionists went about calling for defeat of the Liberals. At one meeting called by a Liberal candidate, union members arrived in force and secured adoption of a resolution favouring his opponent. At Hamilton, Andrew Scott, of the Amalgamated Engineering Union, asked: "Where was Mackenzie (the federal Liberal leader) when the Toronto Printers were arrested? Dodging in and out of George Brown's office, instead of being at his place in parliament to reform the barbarous law."[85] As for Sir John, he was a great campaigner. He went to the industrial constituencies and said the National Policy was a boon for labour and capital alike. He insisted Canadian industry must be fostered, and reminded workers how he had helped defeat George Brown's efforts to destroy their movement. August came, and with it the election. The Conservatives won. The Liberals lost. Triumphantly, the *Ontario Workman* wrote: "The result proves that the working men want no party in office that opposes the people."[86] In the years that followed, until 1896, save for one term in the 1870s, the Liberals were in the opposition.[87]

In this way, in the federal election of 1872, trade unionists helped shape politics. In a concrete situation where they were not strong

* A reference to the Paris Commune of 1871 which alarmed employers everywhere.

enough to provide an effective, winning labour alternative, they swung their weight, to a degree, to a standard party partly friendly to them, against another standard party hostile to them. However, the more far-seeing union members saw they had not solved the big problem. Not Labour's own were in office, but business-oriented politicians who had to be cajoled, prodded, pressured. John Hewitt said:

"Let us remember that neither of the existing parties are parties of labour, and neither will give reforms the workers need, except in compliance with the tactics and with the demands of a well-directed and united agitation. And that is why workers should not appear with the Grits or Tories."

More and more, the pioneers believed the solution was Labour's organization as an independent political force—"direct labour representation"—as the Canadian Labour Union called it. The CLU inaugural convention of 1873 proposed that workers "elect their own representatives to the Dominion Parliament", and that "a working man's platform be put before the industrial classes of the country.[88] At that convention, William Joyce of the Toronto Printers made a classical contribution. He said that in politics Labour was not attaining the united action to which it aspired in industry: "There is the sticking point". The workers' aim should be election of their own representatives to Parliament:

"The general who takes a poorly trained and equipped army into the field against an enemy perfect in all that appertains to war, is foolish indeed and invites defeat. And so it is with working men. Workers must build their army to fight manfully in the battleground of the polls. Let the enemy know that election funds shall be of no avail against men who refuse to sell their birthright for a dollar."[89]

The CLU's political orientation seems to have been to action based directly on the trade union organizations themselves. In 1875, it elected a parliamentary committee to check on federal and provincial legislation. This committee also assumed the function of an executive of the CLU. In 1876, the CLU proposed that this standing committee "embrace every opportunity to bring forward labour candidates wherever there is a large constituency".[90] This policy was further elaborated in this motion adopted by the 1877 CLU convention:

"Whereas it is impossible to secure adequate representation of the working class on the floor of parliament, until we are represented by men of our own class; therefore be it resolved that this Congress pledges itself to use all legitimate means in its power to secure the election of working men to parliament, and supports any working man's candidate nominated by the parliamentary committee or a local labour organization of the locality in which they reside."[91]

Another forward step by Labour on the political front was that it began to present candidates of its own. It was an uphill battle, for the movement was still weak and there were restrictions on the franchise. In 1872, H. B. Whitton was elected to the House of Commons from Hamilton. But, though a trade unionist, he ran on the Conservative ticket, and did not prove to be a reliable parliamentary spokesman of the movement. In 1874, D. J. O'Donaghue was elected to the Ontario Provincial Legislature from Ottawa. He was Canada's first labour political representative. Much of the credit for his success goes to the Ottawa Trades Council which nominated him and campaigned for him. Labour also entered the municipal field. In 1873, Hamilton Labour made a bid for office. The property qualifications made open worker candidates impossible, so the workers resorted to the strategem of nominating "gentlemen" pledged to back them. The employers were furious, and on voting day some gathered at the polling booth. Their intimidation proved effective, the pro-labour candidates were defeated, but so were a number of anti-labour councillors. That year, Oshawa Labour also sought municipal office, and here, too, some employers intervened. "'It's no use voting against the powers that be!'", said a factory manager to a worker. One labour candidate was elected.

7. TRADE UNION DEMOCRACY

The Printers; the Trades Assembly:

"The members run our union!"—trade union democracy. This was a quality of Canada's pioneer trade union movement. Important is organization on the job, democracy on the job. The Toronto Printers helped lead the way. In the 1870s they organized the "Chapel"— a grouping of the union membership at a particular shop. A function of the Chapel was to hold meetings on matters concerning the workers in that shop. The senior officer was the Father of the Chapel—a kind of shop chairman.

The printers placed much emphasis on discipline. Hence their "guardian committee", a secret committee which acted against unfair employers and unfair men. When discipline was violated, strict action was taken. An entry in the Printers' Minute Book for December 2, 1876, says: "S. F. Claus is expelled from the union for working on a job vacated by two other members who refused a reduction of the rate of wages."[92] Also, they developed the procedure of "being ratted". In January 1874, they voted funds "for a book to enter the names of rats". They had a "rat list"—a list of men who worked on jobs vacated by union men or who accepted wages lower than the prevailing union rate—and a "rat circular" which passed from local to local in the various centres. When charges were laid and sustained, the member's name was put on the permanent rat list. He had been ratted.

They believed in the membership meeting and looked to it as the fountain of the union's life and wisdom. Sometimes the issue before a meeting was difficult; in which case, unless it demanded immediate action, it might be referred to another meeting. Discussion seems to have been free and spontaneous, but without too much idle talk. There was constant check-up on decisions. Sometimes sharp differences developed, but over the years the printers had mastered the art of resolving disagreements within the organization, with the minority submitting to a majority, something better than berserk bolting into the arms of waiting employers.

At times the rafters shook with the force of the argument. This happened at a meeting held November 11, 1876. The Society, hard-pressed by unemployment, had accepted a wage cut at a Toronto newspaper, the *Mail*. At the meeting, some members tried to upset this decision. There was great excitement. A member arose and said: "I move that this meeting go into secret session!" The motion was carried. Another member asked for the floor, but "he could not be heard owing to hisses, cheers and general disorder". Then the president said: "If the members refuse to maintain order, I refuse to go on with the business." The vice-president took the chair. The meeting proceeded. Next came a motion asking the president to resume the chair. This was adopted. The time approached for the vote on the main question—should the decision to accept the *Mail's* wage cut be rescinded? Here an alert treasurer did his duty. The minutes state: "A recess took place caused by the flow of coins into the treasury from those members indebted to the union who desired to vote." The Ayes and Nays were called for. The motion to rescind was defeated.[93]

This trade union democracy inspired also the proceedings of the Toronto Trades Assembly. It was not just a deliberative body, but a working body, that is, it not only discussed and decided but implemented decisions and checked on results. All business was transacted by motion, and procedure was strictly adhered to. When some point of business required particular attention, delegates would go into "committee of the whole", consider the matter, then report to the Assembly. Special attention was paid to finances. In the struggle against the British Crown in the 17th century, parliament asserted its power through control of the purse strings. In the Assembly, delegates exercised a similar control over finances. Every expenditure, even a small one, was approved by motion. An entry in the minutes for October 1874 states: "Moved and seconded that the gas bill be paid and that an order be drawn for that amount."[93a] Officers were close to the membership. "The officers stand instructed"—this phrase appears in the Minute Book again and again. The position is clear. It was the members who made decisions and the officers' job was to carry them out

Here is an example of the Assembly in action—a meeting held February 9, 1878. The problem is a bill on the electoral franchise just introduced into the House of Commons. The Assembly delegates are up in arms about it. They decide to hold a public protest meeting. *Moved* and *seconded* that 3 delegates prepare resolutions for the meeting. *Carried.* Publicity is needed. That's a job for the printing committee. *Moved* and *seconded* that the committee print 2,000 "dodgers". *Adopted.* Who will get the dodgers out? That's the secretary's job. *Moved* and *seconded* that he see to this, and to 100 posters as well. In addition, the secretary is instructed to place advertisements in the *Mail, Globe* and *Telegram,* and ensure that copies of the "dodgers" get into the hands of members of parliament. Has everything been attended to? Wait! Who is going to sponsor the resolutions at the meeting? *Moved, seconded and adopted* that Alfred Jury move the first resolution, A. Lennox the second, and J. S. Williams and Goddard of the Stonecutters, the third. Two hours have gone by since the meeting began. Tomorrow, the delegates must get up early for work. Adjournment moved and carried.[93b]

8. TRADE UNIONISM AND SOCIAL CHANGE

Growth of Labour Consciousness:

In the trade union struggles of the 1870s, consciousness was growing. Labour consciousness, what is its source? Above all, practice—billions of experiences in wage movements, strikes and political action; the process of production itself, and the fight for conditions at the point of production; the tendency to solidarity among workers, and antagonism to employers, engendered in production; the experience of grievances, negotiations and strikes; discussion and debate at membership meetings; not least, constant interchange with workers in other lands, with the world workers' movement.

This is the process—the constant transition of labour and the fight for conditions, into knowledge. An example is a letter written by a Montreal worker, published February 4, 1873, in the *Ontario Work-*

man. The writer considers the 9-hour movement of 1872 and asks why it did not succeed. He says that one mistake was being too precipitate —lack of preparation. A second was abandoning the fight once the initial assault failed. The trouble was that the workers had not prepared for a prolonged battle. He compares them to a crowd attacking a fort. The crowd is unorganized, poorly armed, poorly prepared, while the fort is filled with veterans armed to the teeth, knowing how to fight, ready to open fire on the attacking party. "Nobody should go on strike unless he is prepared to stand out for a long period ... In struggle, as in military warfare, it is our duty to make ourselves so powerful that our enemies will be afraid to encounter us. We must make every provision for emergency, and when the time for action comes, strike as one man."

Precipitatedness and lack of preparation were some mistakes. Another one was giving up the fight once the initial assault failed, and sliding into "moody inactivity". The Montreal writer then considers the problem of leadership: "What if your fellows desert you, what then? Bestir yourself like a man and breathe into them the fire that fires you!" Finally, he proposes a study of strikes: "Their cause and the cause of their failure must be fully ventilated."[94]

The problem dealt with here is strategy and tactics, the principles underlying the effective conduct of Labour's day-to-day battle for conditions. However, the thought which came from the 9-hour movement went beyond that to take up the social question as such. The crux was the "surplus". Whence profits and rent? Whence the wealth of the capitalists? How to explain the anomaly that though the social order is founded on production, the producers remain poor, while the owners get rich? This problem engaged the Pioneers. John Hewitt declared:

"We increase our material wealth over and above our living requirements 3 per cent, while we pay for the medium of exchange at 7 to 12 per cent. Money is the power which swallows up and centralizes all, snatching from the labourer 4 to 9 per cent of his actual subsistence allowance. That is why wealth centralizes. Two per cent of our population possess half the wealth. In any community 100 of the leading capitalists possess as much as all the rest put together. Have they contributed more labour, physical, intellectual or moral to the community? A wrong has been committed somewhere in the distribution of production. Labour is the operative source of all wealth. No man can exist independent of labour, but many do exist on the labour of others."[95]

Hewitt is referring to money here, but links this to private ownership of the means of production. This same idea was expressed by a Toronto militant, John McCormack, in 1872:

"The line of the ruling class everywhere is—Property first, Man afterwards. We say: 'Man first, Property afterwards!' . . . The moneyocracy says: 'You shall not enjoy the fruits of your labour, only what we allow you. The balance of the value of your labour we will keep ourselves!' That's why we have trade unions and strikes!"

This bold line of thinking shook the complacency of employer circles. One newspaper, the *Leader,* hoped that the socialist and revolutionary element would be excluded from the International Workingmen's Association, and that workingmen in Canada would "confine themselves to legitimate agitation".[96] Another newspaper, the Toronto *Globe,* said after the fourth CLU Congress: "There must be the surrender of the dream of injustice and communism cherished by so many workmen."[97] This problem, the social system as a whole, was reflected also, though more sympathetically, by a leading intellectual figure of the time, Goldwin Smith. Smith did not challenge capitalism, but, like most first class 19th century thinkers, he had his doubts. At a meeting in the Montreal Mechanics' Institute in 1873, he stated:

"Why should one man spend on himself the income of 600 labouring families? Whatever the rich man desires, the finest house, the biggest diamond, the reigning beauty for his wife, political power is readily at his command. If the labour movement, by transferring something from their profits to that of wages, stops by any measure the growth of these colossal fortunes, it will benefit society. Communism as a movement is a mistake. But there is a communism which is deep seated in the heart of every man, which makes him feel that the hardest of all labour is idleness in a world of toil, and the bitterest of all bread that eaten by the sweat of another's brow."[98]

How can Labour be emancipated? Some said the solution was "co-operative ownership". The CLU took this up. The fourth convention, 1876, adopted a resolution for co-operative ownership as against private ownership.[98a] At the 5th convention, 1877, Alfred Jury said producer co-operation was most important rather than distributor co-operation. The principle adopted by the convention was "co-operation in production and distribution".[98b] For the pioneers, co-operation meant something more than piece-meal reform, a limited co-operative enterprise. This becomes clear in an elaboration by John Hewitt. He asks: "What shall be the governing principles of the new system? This I cannot say. It remains to be worked out by the experience of those who shall engage in the progress of the movement." Then he traces the outlines of a new social order:

"The system of employer and employees would be superseded. Labour would be lightened individually. Men would enjoy the fruits of their labour and not the dregs of their production. The kind of unjust system that gives men undue advantage over men would cease to exist."

This, then, was the aspiration to a new social order, as entertained
by some of the trade union pioneers. In turn it fused with internationalism—the recognition that Labour's struggle in all countries was
indivisible, that the struggle for shorter hours in Canada was bound
up with the struggle for shorter hours everywhere. An article reprinted
in the *Ontario Workman,* in 1873, put it this way:

"Men sometimes say to me, 'you are an internationalist'. I say I do
not know what an internationalist is, but if there is a system by which
working men from London to Gibraltar, from Moscow to Paris, clasp
hands, then I say, God speed to it. I do not care whether it calls itself
trade union, Crispin, international or Commune; anything that unites
labour in order that they may put up a united force to face the organization of capital—anything that does that, I say, honour to it!"

The Labour Press; Immigrants; The Problem of Class Collaboration:

The evolution of Canadian Labour has always been connected with
the labour press. The 1870s had a great model—the *Ontario Workman.*
It was exemplary in its clarity, forthrightness, the way it recorded the
workers' struggles and gave expression to their faith. The *Ontario
Workman* asked for shorter hours—"more of God's sunlight for the
workers". It wanted to know why employers and politicians shut their
eyes to "trade combinations, whiskey combinations, provision combinations, all kinds of combinations", and "yet they oppose working
men's combinations". It led the way in Labour's early efforts for
political action; and it brought to the movement news about struggles
of working men in other countries. The *Workman* seems to have succeeded in setting up a network of worker correspondents, and often
printed letters from readers in Montreal, Toronto, Hamilton, Oshawa
and other centres. Also, it carried progress reports from unions.

One of its prime qualities was a concern for conditions. A worker's
hand severed by a circular saw, a child drowned in the Cornwall canal,
a sawmill worker's head caught in unprotected belting, his neck
pressed against the whirling saw, the head severed—the *Ontario Workman* exposed such facts. Also, it carried poems on conditions, not perfect but poignant. One was called "A Factory Girl".

"Ten hours a day of labour
  In a closely lighted room
  Machinery was her music
  Gas her sweet perfume."

In this way, the *Workman* practiced the truth that a concern for the
people's conditions is a prerequisite of progressive politics and integral
culture. But it did not have enough money. Some workers tried to
help. One reported: "We were out canvassing for the *Workman*." The
Grand Lodge of the Knights of St. Crispin gave some financial sup-

port. However, in 1874, the *Workman* suspended publication. The Trades Assembly came to its aid, set up a committee, and asked unions to vote a subsidy. The suspension of publication was an issue at the 1875 CLU convention. Delegates said failure to support the newspaper was "a disgrace to working men". The convention decided:

"Believing that the education of the working men of the Dominion in matters affecting relations between labour and capital is the surest way of awakening their interest in co-operation in the cause of union and labour reform, and believing that the establishment of a labour newspaper is the best means of obtaining that object,

"The Canadian Labour Union pledges itself to use every legitimate means in its power to support any newspaper that may be established to reflect the views of the masses of our working men in matters affecting their welfare, by agitating for the repeal of those laws which bear heavily and unfairly on trade unionists as a class."[99]

We turn now to immigration. This has been an important factor in Canadian labour history, so much so, that some believed that the labour movement in Canada is non-Canadian in origin. The truth is that the immigrants' contribution, immense though it was, was part of and subject to, the internal evolution of Canada and Canadian Labour. An immigrant fighter of the 1870s was the Hungarian, Mark Szalatnay. In Hungary, during the revolution of 1848, he fought for freedom. After the defeat of that revolution, he migrated to Britain, and connected with the Chartists. For 6 years he was Secretary of the Miners Union of South Wales, took part in many strikes, and was often arrested. In 1855, he suggested that British unions endorse the *Communist Manifesto* of Marx and Engels. Later, he was deported as an undesirable alien, and migrated to the United States. There he became a member of the Cigar Makers Union of Baltimore. In 1860, while organizing a counter-demonstration against slave-owners, he was shot and wounded. Later, he came to Canada. Hungarian immigrants were then active in the cigar industry, and were helping build cigar makers' locals in Montreal and Toronto. Szalatnay became secretary of the Toronto Cigar Makers' local. In 1872, that local went on strike. The strike was defeated and Szalatnay was sentenced to 4 months' imprisonment. Then he was deported to the United States, where he dedicated himself anew to Labour's cause. In 1875, while serving as a functionary of the National Labour Union in Los Angeles, a strike broke out at a bread factory, and he was killed by a police bullet.

Some served, fought, starved and paid the supreme penalty. A few vaccilated. Most labour leaders of the 1870s were militants. John Hewitt of the Coopers Union, J. S. Williams and John Armstrong of the Toronto Printers, Andrew Scott of the Amalgamated Engineers, Leavesley of the Toronto Machinists, Ryan of the Hamilton 9-hour

League—had much of the integral working class organizer and thinker in their make-up. However, in the career of D. J. O'Donaghue, there was a shoot of that historic trend in the labour movement which stands opposed to militancy—class collaboration. During the 1950s, the leadership of the Trades and Labour Congress of Canada fostered the idea that O'Donaghue was the "father of the Canadian Labour movement". We have discovered no evidence that the pioneers considered O'Donaghue their father, and sometimes they wondered if he was their brother. The truth is that O'Donaghue was a bit of an opportunist. He contributed, but this should not be exaggerated. In his home town, Ottawa, when the first executive of the Ottawa Trades Council was elected in December 1872, his post was assistant secretary. His statements during those years do not have the substance of those made by John Hewitt or Andrew Scott. He became more prominent in 1874 when he was elected to the Ontario Legislature. As the years went by, the feeling grew that he was not carrying out his mandate, that he had to be pressed too much to do something, and was disposed to settle too low. For this, trade unionists criticized him. At the fifth CLU convention in 1877, Alfred Jury said: "The labouring classes have only one man in Parliament and we have only half of him!" Another delegate said: "D. J. O'Donaghue was no longer a representative of the Labour Party."[100]

His vacillations had a bad effect. Some asked if labour political action could succeed. One delegate at the CLU convention of 1877 said: "Until we can get a labouring man who will faithfully attend to the interests of his class, it is no good sending a man to Parliament!" However, more far-seeing labour leaders defended the principle. J. S. Williams said: "Even supposing a working man does not come up to the views of supporters, that is no reason why we should not have working classes candidates."[101]

Dissatisfaction with O'Donaghue reached a high point in the winter of 1878. The Toronto Trades Assembly and the CLU Parliamentary Committee decided to send a delegation to O'Donaghue and ask "for an explanation of his conduct in the legislature". An entry in the Assembly Minute Book for February 20, 1878 reads: "Moved and seconded that the Secretary be instructed to inform D. J. O'Donaghue

---

* In later years, O'Donaghue was active in the Trades and Labour Council of Toronto and the Trades and Labour Congress of Canada. After the turn of the century, William Lyon Mackenzie King, Canada's first Deputy Minister of Labour, secured his appointment as Canada's first fair wage officer. The data above refers to negative aspects in the work of O'Donaghue. Some of the positive aspects are covered in materials issued by the Trades and Labour Congress of Canada and the Canadian Labour Congress.

that the Assembly feels dissatisfied with his conduct with regard to the Lien Act.*[102]

O'Donaghue was not alone in his vacillations. In 1874, some members of the Toronto Typographical Society wanted the union to disaffiliate from the Trades Assembly, and they doubted the value of the CLU. The membership defeated them. In the Trades Assembly, a conservative group wanted to confine that body exclusively to wages and working conditions. Thus came a clash in 1875. Speculators moved in to take over Queen's Park and convert it into a site for building. Progressive-minded Toronto citizens rallied to save the Park, asked the Assembly for support, and secured it. When conservative elements in the Assembly objected, J. S. Williams replied that the Assembly's constitution permitted it to act on all matters affecting labour directly or indirectly. Again, in 1877, conservative trade unionists demanded dissolution of the Assembly. The Assembly rejected this.[103]

●

This was the condition of the organized workers' movement in Canada in the 1870s. They were difficult years. As the decade neared its end, prospects seemed dark. But distinctive labour organization was developing. The movement was being built.

CHAPTER 3

CONSOLIDATION OF A PERMANENT MOVEMENT
1880-1890

1. CONDITIONS OF LABOUR

Tobacco and Textile:

The central labour movement which emerged in Canada in the 1870s became consolidated only in the 1880s. A transforming factor was large-scale production. In textile, tobacco, shoe—in Ontario, Quebec, New Brunswick—industrial enterprises arose, enterprises employing not just 30, 40 or 50, as in the past, but 300 and even 500. Between 1881 and 1891, the number of establishments with a capital of $50,000 and over, increased by about 50%; and gross value of production increased from $153,000,000 to $260,000,000.[1]

With large-scale capitalist production, came the discovery that a road to riches was exploitation of women and children. Three generations earlier, British capitalists had shown the way. Now, Canadian capitalists took up the torch. Marx suggested in *Capital* that the exploitation of women and children was the negative expression proper to capitalism, of the positive fact that machinery could increase production and reduce reliance on skilled labour; that, as is said nowadays, "machines could replace men", not because the machines were bad, but because they were monopolized by a wealthy clique and used for profit rather than expansion of production and service to Canada. With proper controls, factory labour for women and young people would have been a boon. But it was only through years of struggle that curbs were put on the rapacity of the rich. Meanwhile, the mills were filled with women and children working in miserable conditions at miserable rates. In cotton and tobacco factories there were children, many children, some 10 or 11 years old, some 8 or 9.

A child of 8 was found toiling in a cotton mill, his wages for the year—$92.[2] Children worked the same hours as adults, from say 6 a.m. to 6 p.m., with an hour or so for lunch. Often they worked around unprotected machinery. In Montreal, boys toiled the night through in a glass factory. Concerning the women, Cardinal Taschereau declared:

"I've heard parish priests in my diocese say that the majority of persons, especially girls, who leave their families to go and work in factories, returned run down by work, and consumptive for the want of ventilation in these factories."[3]

As workers fought these conditions, and as elements in other classes came to their aid, government bestirred itself, to a degree. Thus came about two Royal Commissions of enquiry in labour conditions, one in 1881, another in 1887. The second Commission, the Royal Commission on the relations of Capital and Labour, 1886-1889, was important. One commissioner was John Armstrong, the printers' leader arrested in 1872. Its proceedings and report are a classic of Canadian social history.

Tobacco was a typical industry, with Montreal as the chief centre. Cigar makers, the skilled workers in the trade, earned between 80 cents and $1.25 per day, and children earned as low as $1.00 a week. At times, the children were manhandled by foremen. A cigar maker testified before the Royal Commission that a boy under 11 had been cracked across the head by the foreman's fists when he cut the leaf wrong. Here is a further extract from his testimony:

Question: "Have you seen little girls whipped?"

Answer: "Yes, sir."

Question: "Why were they whipped?"

Answer: "Because they talked among themselves while at work."[4]

Beatings were not only brutal but beyond reason. At one plant, while a lad was sweeping the floor, the foreman ordered: "Pick up the tobacco leaves." The apprentice went on sweeping. The cigar maker who witnessed this incident testifies:

"The foreman then took the boy by the ear, bent him down to the ground, and said to him: 'Why did you not pick up the tobacco?' He was only a child of twelve or fourteen and did not reply. Then the foreman made him get up by slapping him in the face."[5]

In history books we were given when we were young, we were told about the Black Hole of Calcutta during the Indian Mutiny of 1857, when British soldiers were jammed into a little cell and suffocated. But we were not told about the Black Hole of Montreal, imposed not by a brutalized colonial population on foreign imperialists, but by

Canadian businessmen on fellow-Canadians. The Black Hole was located in the tobacco factory of J. L. Fortier—an exploiter and labour-hater of the period. It was a kind of coal box in the basement which served as a prison cell for rebellious young workers. On the door was an iron bar. Apprentices told the Commission* a foreman had struck them, and thrown them into the Black Hole for hours in the winter, when the basement was unheated.[6]

Here is more testimony from a witness about a beating to a boy:

"It was after working hours. The foreman asked a boy to sweep. He refused. The foreman seized the cover of a mould and threatened to strike him. (The mould was a plank about 2½ feet long and 6 inches in width). Then the foreman took him by the arm and gave him a blow, saying: 'You will sweep!' Still the little fellow said: 'No!' Then the foreman struck the boy on the loins. After, he took him by the arm and ran him into an alley handing him a broom. Still the little fellow would not take the broom. When the foreman saw this, he took the boy by both hands on the hips, and sat him down on his knees. Then the little fellow lay on the ground for 2 or 3 minutes without stirring. He had lost his senses. He did not know what he was doing. I took him and led him to his mother."[7]

One witness testified he had seen a girl of 15 beaten:

"The overseer asked her to sweep. She refused. Then he seized her and sat her on the floor. He held her down on the ground with one hand and his knee. With the other he took a mould cover and struck her several times on the body. The young girl wept. When the overseer let her go, she was so weak she had hard work getting up."[8]

The owner, J. L. Fortier, took a hand in beating one of the young women there, Georgiana Loiselle, aged 18. She stated under oath:

"Mr. Fortier asked me to make one hundred cigars. I refused and he beat me with the mould cover. I was sitting, he seized me by the arm, threw me to the ground and beat me with the mould cover."[9]

When Fortier appeared before the Commission, he denied maltreating his employees. He said the foremen were instructed "to treat the apprentices as if they were his own children". A foreman acted "like a school master . . . lightly touching the children with the ruler or with his hands to correct them". He did not reply when the Commissioners asked him: "Would you correct your child with a mould such as this?"[10]

Some tobacco factories employed vicious special constables. At times they would haul the children off to the police station to appear before the Recorder of the City of Montreal. In the Fortier plant, the con-

---

* Royal Commission on the Relations of Capital and Labour, 1889. Where the term "Commission" is used in this chapter, the reference is to this Royal Commission, unless otherwise stated.

stable was especially vicious. He would tour the plant, terrorize children, search them for tobacco, and sometimes take them to the Recorder.[11]

When the Recorder appeared before the Royal Commission, he justified all this brutality in the name of "positive law", "civil law", "natural law", and "divine law". He told the Commission: "The master has the right of correction on the person of his servant, more particularly on his apprentice." The only limit he imposed was that there should be no permanent injury:

Commissioners: "If the defendent in a case before the Recorder admitted that an individual had thrown down a young girl of eighteen years of age and had then struck her, would you hold this individual guilty of assault?"
Recorder: "It all depends on the circumstances, on the manner in which she was struck, on the way in which she was thrown down on the floor, generally on the manner in which she was treated, in short it depends on a host of circumstances."[12]

Fortier was not alone among tobacco employers in maltreating workers. A boy of 13, employed at Tasse and Wood, testified an overseer had hit him with a steel punch. The Grothe Cigar plant had a chamber of chastisement matching Fortier's Black Hole, the "hot room". Here tobacco was placed to sweat, and so were apprentices, at times.

Fines were another evil.[13] They were sums deducted from wages for alleged violations of factory regulations, and might amount to quite a part of the earnings, particularly when the earnings were low. The ultimate was reached at one tobacco plant when a lad of 14 worked 40 hours for $1.60, but was fined $1.75, and so ended up owing the company 15 cents. The boy's father saw no future for his son in this business, and demanded the fine be returned, but to no avail.[14]

On Ontario Street east in Montreal today, is located the plant of the Macdonald Tobacco Company. Since World War II, it has been organized by the TWIU—Tobacco Workers International Union (CLC). During the 1880s, about 500 or 600 were employed there, some as young as 11. A youth of 11 told the Commission his work hours were from 7 in the morning to 6 at night, with an hour off for lunch. His salary was $2.00 a week. Sometimes, when he talked he was fined. The general range of wages for children was from $1.50 to $5.00 per week. The men's labour rate ranged from $6.00 to $8.50 per week.

When the owner, William C. Macdonald appeared before the Commission, he taught a lesson in capitalist economics, particularly with reference to the way the rate of wages was set. He said his practice in the past 30 years had been to cut wages in the winter. The Commissioners were struck with the anomaly that in winter when living costs went up, wages went down. They asked why, and Macdonald explained that in winter, there was more surplus labour.

Commissioners: "You do not work for charity?"

Macdonald: "No sir, I am in business for the purpose of business."[15]

Conditions were bad also in the textile industry. In our day, the largest company in this industry is the Dominion Textile Company. An antecedent of the 1880s was Hochelaga Cottons. It employed about 1,100, of whom about half were women, and 200 children. The men earned from 80 cents to $1.00 per day, the girls about 75 cents a day. Most employees were on piece-work. The basic work week was 60 hours—11 hours per day and 5 hours on Saturday. Sometimes, the hours went up to 17 per day. The families of many workers came from rural Quebec. The company would send an agent to the Saguenay district to bring in whole families to work in the factory.

At the Hochelaga Cotton Mill, fines were prevalent for "bad work" or other reasons. One girl received a pay envelope of $12.60 for 2 weeks work, with $1.00 deducted for a fine. A young worker with a pay envelope of $6.30 for 2 weeks work had 40 cents deducted.

Another company practice was to make its employees sign an agreement to work on holidays, save Christmas and New Year's. If an employee did not work on a religious holiday, he would be dismissed, and his 2 weeks' salary or whatever amount was due would be confiscated. Of the 200 children in the plant, some were 8 years old, and earned 25 to 30 cents a day. They toiled without a minute's rest from 6 in the morning until 6, or at times, 9 at night—the same hours as the men. The company's motto was: "When some work, all work!" If a child did not turn up for work in the morning after working until 9 o'clock at night, he was fined. From the little workmen's dwellings lining the streets ending on Notre Dame east, the tiny toilers, aged 8, 9 or 10, arose in the wee hours of the morning, trudged barefoot to work, and in the evening they left, the same time as the adults. In this way, glory was built for the textile millionaires. Here is testimony by Andrew F. Gault, president of the Hochelaga Cotton Manufacturing Company, and his Superintendent, before the Royal Commission:

Commissioners: "Do you think it right to employ children of twelve years at all?"

Gault: "I think that at twelve years a child should be able to work."

Commissioners: "Do you believe a child of ten is capable of judging exactly as to the work that is required of him?"

Superintendent: "Yes."[15a]

Again and again, workers took their jobs in their hands to fight the brutality against children. A worker stated:

"I saw a foreman beating a child of ten. I took up a stick and knocked the foreman down." Another worker said: "My own child was mistreated last year (1887). He came to me at noon and said: "Papa, the foreman has given me kicks in the rear." I went out and . . . told the foreman: 'If you beat my boy again, I will knock you down!' "[16]

About half a mile west of the Hochelaga Cotton Mill along Notre Dame Street was the St. Anne Cotton Mill, still an active producer today (1967). In the 1880s, hours were from 6.30 in the morning until 6.15 in the evening. The employees included children of 10 and 11. In 1887, the company's book listed an employee aged 9, another aged 10. When work was done, at 6 p.m. or sometimes 9 p.m., the men, women and children would huddle together, and jam against each other at the foot of the staircase. Sometimes, female employees were humiliated by the manager and superintendent. Attendance was forced on religious holidays. Once, employees were absent on Annunciation Day, and were fined.[17]

The Merchant's Cotton Mill, located on St. Ambroise Street, in the St. Henri district of Montreal, is today another major link in the Dominion Textile chain. It was then owned by the Merchant's Cotton Manufacturing Company. About 500 were employed there, including "a smart little girl of ten and a smart boy of eleven". Working hours were from 6.30 a.m. to 6 p.m. with three-quarters of an hour off for lunch. On Saturday, working hours were till 3 p.m. Testimony of manager before the Royal Commission:

Commissioners: "Do you think that cotton companies paying a 23% dividend could afford to be more liberal towards their operatives?"
Manager: "I think I will not say anything about that question, if you will pardon me."[18]

Textile conditions were bad in other provinces too. In Ontario, Cornwall was a centre for the cotton industry. Here, at the Canada Cotton Mill, working hours were slightly over 60 per week.[19] Further west, along-side the canal at Cornwall, was the Stormont Cotton Mill. (It continued operations until 1954.) In the 1880s, it employed about 400, including children who worked for 11 hours a day.[20]

In Moncton, New Brunswick, there was a large cotton mill, since gone out of existence. Here, along with adults, some 65 children worked. Hours were from 6.30 in the morning till 6 in the evening. The level of the women's wages is indicated by the testimony of one woman: "I think I can get about $6.50 a fortnight if I work like a real good winder." Young girls were paid $1.25 or $1.50 a week.[21]

Another cotton mill in New Brunswick employed about 425, of whom one-third were children. The children were paid 25 cents per day and up.

Other Industries; Accidents; Wages and Living Standards:

Exploitation prevailed also in other industries located in the Maritimes, Quebec, Ontario and British Columbia. In the baking and garment industries, there were many sweat shops at Toronto, London and other centres. In *Capital,* Marx contended that these sweat shops were not so much a continuation of domestic industry, as the result of large-scale capitalist production—a domestic extension of the factory system. At the Royal Commission, it was testified there were bakeshops in Toronto where men toiled "in underground places not fit to store coal in".[22] In one sweatshop, girls sewed shirts and overalls in a room 12 feet square, and earned starvation wages—as low as 80 cents for a 60-hour week.[23] In the garment industry of London, Ontario, there were "slaves toiling in the shape of women".

In the shipping industry, the men were often treated callously. A major employer was Hugh Allan, owner of the Allan Steamship Lines. He was a Knight, but not of the Round Table. A leader in the Canadian Pacific Railway group of financiers, he was involved, during the 1870s, in the alleged purchase of cabinet ministers in the Federal Conservative Government—amounts handed over are said to have been on the scale of a quarter of a million dollars. Among those working for him in the 1880s were the longshoremen of Montreal. Conditions were bad. Sometimes they worked almost beyond endurance, for a 35-hour stretch. One of them completed 30 hours and wanted to leave, but was called back by the foreman. When he objected, he was told "his services are no longer required". During an inhuman stretch such as this, the longshoremen would keep awake by running to the tap and sprinkling water on their faces. Some used alcohol as a stimulant.'[23a]

Coal mining was developing, also steel manufacture. One centre was Cape Breton. At Springhill, boy miners earned 60 to 80 cents per day. At the Nova Scotia Steel Works in Glasgow, about 200 worked at wages of $1.10 to $4.00 per day for a 10-hour day and a 60-hour week.[24]

In many industries, safety was neglected and accidents were frequent —on the railroads—wrecks, in the coal mines—cave-ins and other calamities—90 lives lost at Stellarton in one such accident. In factories, fire escape facilities were often poor. In the building trades, properly-secured scaffolding was lacking. Again and again, scaffolding collapsed and workers plunged to their doom.*[25]

What of wages and living standards? Workers who appeared before the Commission said there had been little or no improvement in their wages. Some insisted they were no better off in 1888 than they had been 15 years earlier, in 1873.[26] Some wages did improve. In the skilled trades, in Ontario, average annual earnings of blacksmiths, carpenters and machinists increased from $416 to $434 per annum between 1884 and 1886.[27] How slow progress was, even among the skilled workers who were beginning to organize in unions, is indicated by the wages of printers in Toronto in 1882—$11 a week—just $3 more than almost 40 years earlier.[28] This lack of progress in wages was connected with the long-term and short-term cycles of the capitalist economy in Canada—the depression of the 1870s, the upswing of 1879-1883, the downswing thereafter. Wages were too low, rents too high. The Royal Commission was told that in Montreal, between 1879 and 1888, rents had increased 20% and 25%.[29] This was caused partly by growth of industry and urbanization which gave the land and buildings an added value—a profit the landlord put in his pocket. Dwellings were often wretched but workers could not move to better ones because they could not pay higher rents. The Royal Commission said that in fact the tenants' liberty to move did not exist.

These then were conditions in the 1880s: Exploitation of women and children, low wages, accidents, poor living conditions.

Attacks on Trade Union Rights; Strikes:

Combined with bad conditions was coercion by employers and the state: blacklists, firings, "iron-clads", fines, jail sentences, anti-labour legislation. In 1882, in London, Ontario, cigar makers who organized, were locked out and blacklisted—the employers joined in agreement not to employ for 3 years those locked out.[30] In 1882, locomotive engineers who joined a union were dismissed by the Intercolonial Railway. Sometimes employers engaged private company police—even armed police. On occasion they used the "iron-clad": The *Toronto Mail* imposed this agreement on its employees:

"I will not belong to the Typographical Union, Knights of Labour, or any trade organization whatsoever, so long as I am employed in said office."[31]

* Testimony given to the Royal Commission revealed that in Montreal there existed a bylaw concerning scaffolding, but no building inspector had been seen by some of the men for 20 years.

Another company tactic was to prosecute union members in the courts. Sometimes this was co-ordinated with anti-labour legislation. This two-pronged attack was directed on one occasion against the Ship Labourers' Society of Quebec City. A court ruled that the Society was a benevolent body and so had no jurisdiction in working conditions; and at the same time the House of Commons considered legislation which would have adversely affected the Society. It seems that with the help of other unions, the Society partly defeated these moves.[32]

The workers fought back against this combination of bad conditions and employer-state coercion. In Nova Scotia, New Brunswick, Ontario, Quebec and British Columbia, they engaged in strikes. In *Nova Scotia:* strikes of coal miners at North Sydney, Stellarton and Acadia; of bakers, painters and sailmakers at Halifax.[32a] In *New Brunswick:* strikes of "raftsmen" and printers at St. John. In *Quebec:* strikes of shoe lasters, stove workers, cigar makers, cotton workers, printers, railway workers, ship labourers, gas works employees—at Montreal; a ship labourers' strike in Quebec City; a textile strike at the Granite knitting Mills in St. Hyacinthe.[33] In *Ontario:* A furniture strike at Chatham; strikes of moulders, stove mounters, telegraphers at Hamilton; strikes of female shoe operators, freight labourers and carpenters in Toronto; a strike at the Canadian Locomotive Works in Kingston; a cotton workers' strike at Cornwall.[34] In *Manitoba:* Printers' and tailors' strikes at Winnipeg. In *British Columbia:* A coal miners' strike at the Wellington coal mines on Vancouver Island.*

Three important strikes of the 1880s were the Toronto streetcar strike, 1886; the Toronto building trades strike, 1887; the Quebec City printers strike, 1887.

The streetcar strike was a stirring event. In the evening of March 9, 1886, streetcar workers joined the Knights of Labour, and each paid $1 initiation. The next morning, when they reported on the job, they found out the superintendent had taken their names off the employees' list. It was a lockout. As the news spread, many Toronto citizens demonstrated their solidarity. When the company tried to run streetcars, they were removed from the tracks, and their progress barred by slow-moving carts which, in friendly coincidence, appeared in front of them. On the third day, the company tried once again to get the cars going. This time large crowds surrounded the cars. Police, present in force, including mounted police, moved in on the crowds, swinging

---

* The mines, owned by the Dunsmuir family, employed about 700 to 800 workers, white and Chinese. The white workers' pay was $2.00 per day, the Chinese's pay was half this amount.

batons. It seems the crowds persisted, and the cars did not get very far.

The outcome was that the company promised to rehire unconditionally the discharged men, and then the strikers went back to work. But the company did not keep its word, and insisted all over again that its employees must not belong to a union. In April, the streetcar workers went on strike again. Now their demands were shorter hours, higher wages, and reinstatement of employees dismissed for joining the union. The strike was bitterly fought, and the strikers' difficulties many—the police magistrate of Toronto imposed heavy fines on some of them. However, the strikers won the support of other Toronto unions, and they also tried to solve their problems by organizing a co-operative bus line.[36]

In 1887, between 1,200 and 1,500 carpenters in Toronto were on strike almost 3 months.[37] The Quebec City printers' strike, also fought in 1887, affected newspapers and print shops. The printers were then earning $7 per week, some as low as $5—wages they described as "near starvation". They demanded $8 per week for day work, $10 per week for night work, the 54-hour week (the 9-hour day), and overtime of 20 cents an hour. Another problem was safety and sanitation. When the foreman of the Quebec *Chronicle*—Quebec City's historic, English-language newspaper—appeared before the Royal Commission in 1887, he was asked: "How often are the floors cleaned? Have they been cleaned the past 15 years?" He replied: "I do not think it." During the strike, 4 printers were arrested.[38]

2. GROWTH OF THE UNIONS

Central Provinces, Maritimes, the West:

Amidst these difficulties, the movement was growing. Unions defunct since the 1870s were reviving, and new ones were being built. The movement was taking on more of a cross-Canada character, spreading from Quebec and Ontario into the Maritimes and British Columbia.

Ontario was the largest centre. In southwestern Ontario, there were unions of agricultural implement workers, cigar makers, bricklayers and carpenters at London; and craft unions of carpenters and coopers at Windsor. In Hamilton, organization extended beyond tradesmen to take in workers in boot and shoe, cotton and tobacco factories, and also labourers in the building trades. In Toronto, during the early 1880s, there were at least 25 unions grouping bricklayers, carpenters, building labourers, plasterers, printers, seamen, longshoremen, bakers, tailors, shoemakers and cigar makers. In eastern Ontario, there were unions of carpenters, bakers and seamen at Kingston; textile organization at Cornwall; and a development of unionism at Ottawa based on the printing and building trades.[39]

In Quebec, Montreal and Quebec City were the main centres. Montreal had 2 ITU locals—one French-Canadian, the other English-Canadian. Another active union, the Cigar Makers, organized at least several hundred of the 1,300 workers in Montreal's tobacco industry. The Cigar Makers greatest foe was the employer, J. L. Fortier. On one occasion workers went on strike at his factory because some had been searched before going out. Fortier would say the Union was behind his troubles: "The union men about the factory were agitating everything." He charged that the union was instigating all the cases of brutality to children being brought before the Recorder. Once he took court action against the union aimed at putting some union members in jail.[40]

Quebec City has always been an active centre for trade unionism. Three important unions in the 1880s were ITU Local 160, the Ship Labourers' Society and the Longshoremen's Union. The Ship Labourers' Society helped increase wage rates from 75-80 cents per day to $4 per day — high wages for those times. The Longshoremen's Union brought wages up 50% higher than those in Montreal. The ship owners complained: "This Society takes away our freedom!"[41]

In the Maritimes, the coal mining industry was a major base for unionism. In 1879, the Provincial Workmen's Association was founded at Springhill, Nova Scotia, and from there spread to Glace Bay, North Sydney and other centres. In Western Canada, unionism developed in B.C., and here, too, coal mining was a main base—at Nanaimo, Vancouver Island.[42] Not just unions but central labour councils were being organized: In 1881, the Toronto Trades and Labour Council, successor to the Toronto Trades Assembly; in 1884, the Guelph Central Council; in 1886, the Montreal Trades and Labour Council.

The Knights of Labour:

During the 1880s, the Knights of Labour swept across Canada. Their first Assembly (the name given to their basic local organization) was founded at Hamilton, Ontario in 1881. By 1886-87 they had at least 158 Assemblies in Canada with about 1,200 members. This was unionism of a new type, geared to the unskilled and tending to organize on a *plant* rather than *craft* basis.

Ontario was a stronghold. At Toronto there were several thousand members. Hamilton had some 2,000 members among iron and steel workers, woodworkers, shoeworkers, tailors and cotton workers; at St. Thomas—about 1,700 members; at Windsor—about 600; at Cornwall there was a Knights organization at the Stormont Cotton Mill.

In Western Canada, membership was smaller. At Winnipeg, in 1887, there were about 400 members in 5 Assemblies—one at the CPR shops. In British Columbia, Local Assembly 3017 at Nanaimo on Vancouver Island was a flourishing body in the middle 1880s.[43]

The Knights' greatest impact was in Quebec. One of their first Assemblies was organized at Montreal in 1882. By 1887 they had 38 Assemblies in Montreal with a membership of 2,500. Their success alarmed the Roman Catholic hierarchy. On April 18, 1886, Cardinal Taschereau issued a "Mandement", or interdict on the the Knights. Basing himself on a Vatican decision of some years earlier, he told Catholics to leave the Knights on pain of being denied sacraments of the Church.[43a] However, it seems most members stayed with the Knights—at the height of the crisis a Montreal body of the Knights said "hundreds of new members were joining".[43b]

At this time, while French-Canadian workers were fighting for their right to stay in the Knights, Terence V. Powderley, the U.S. leader of the Knights was vacillating. Powderley's problem was that he was a conservative heading a movement which surpassed him, one powered from below by the unskilled workers, and helped by socialists and other radical elements. In his heart of hearts, he feared the workers, and more particularly the French-Canadians—an attitude which has played quite a part in Canadian labour history and in the relation of U.S. labour bodies to Canadians. He said:

"There are so many anarchists in Canada, they have reason to be suspicious. The French are much harder to manage than other people. We have some anarchists in the United States, but not of the dangerous class. The French are of a very different temperament. We can take our people and pack them in a solid mass from one end of Market Street to the other and there will be no horror. But take an equal number of Frenchmen, and the result will be serious."[44]

A situation where the hierarchy called on the workers to leave the Knights, and where many stayed with the Knights, had something untenable in it. Some Catholic leaders had their misgivings, and Cardinal Gibbons, an American, went on a mission to Rome. Soon there came a decree from the Vatican cancelling its interdict of some years earlier. Cardinal Taschereau then lifted his ban—Catholic Knights could now partake of the sacraments. However he insisted they must confess their sin in remaining members when the ban was in force; and he went on opposing the Knights:[45] "I advise all Catholics not to join the Order," he said in 1888.[46] Still, the Knights went on flourishing. In August 1887, the Mayor of Quebec presided at one of their meetings.

In the latter 1880s, the Knights declined. One reason was that the leadership lagged behind the membership. In the U.S. and Canada, the workers looked to the Knights as an instrument for organization and better conditions. U.S. membership alone swelled from 100,000 to 700,000 in a single year, 1885-6. But the leaders feared this mass membership. Also, they feared strikes and frowned on them save as a last resort. Under the banner of the Knights, many a militant strike was fought. But the leaders' lack of confidence in the strike—that decisive weapon of Labour—caused vacillation when crisis came, and affected adversely the conduct of strikes. Again the leaders declared their support for labour political action, and this attracted many workers. But in good measure—and this was characteristic of their inexperience and opportunism—their call to politics was not grounded in positive faith but was largely a counterpose to their fearfulness on the economic front. When the time came for political action, they would talk vaguely about "education for political action". Once, the General Assembly (convention) of the U.S. Knights even pronounced itself against the formation of a working class party.

The year 1886 was a major test for the Knights, perhaps a turning point. The 8-hour movement swept the United States. Events reached a climax in Chicago on May 1, when 38,000 workers there went on strike for the 8-hour day. One company, McCormack Harvester, brought in strike-breakers and Pinkerton guards. On May 3, police fired on the strikers, killed 4 and wounded 20. On May 4, a great protest meeting was held in Haymarket Square. The police attacked this meeting, killed several persons and wounded about 200. Then persons unknown threw a bomb. Later, several strike leaders were arrested, charged with the bomb outrage, and executed—they included August Spies and Albert Parsons.

How did Terence Powderley react? On May 8, 1886, he said: "Parsons, Spies, Fielding, Most, and all their followers should be summarily dealt with. They are entitled to no more consideration than wild beasts."[47] Now, Chicago was a Knights' stronghold and across the U.S., Knights were being active in the 8-hour movement. So when Powderley took this kind of position, he was putting a knife not only into the Chicago strike leaders and the 8-hour movement, but into his own organization. Thus the 8-hour movement which helped make the American Federation of Labour, unhinged the Knights.

Another mistake of the Knights was to get drawn into a conflict with the craft unions. In the middle 1880s, some national craft unions had joined the Knights. After the AFL was formed in 1887, most of these unions quit the Knights and joined the AFL. Towards this decision, the Knights' leadership adopted a nasty, negative attitude; and this in turn played into the hands of developing opportunism in the AFL. Gompers* and Powderley locked in dubious battle, each upholding his variant of opportunism which engendered its countervariant in the other; whereas had they combined their energies to unite the workers, skilled and unskilled, craft and industrial, into a single powerful body, they might have helped give a progressive impetus to American trade union history.

These were mistakes the Knights made in the U.S.A. Their performance in Canada was superior, to a degree. Here their attitude to political action was better, as was their response to the Haymarket case. Concerning the latter, a Hamilton paper close to the Knights, the *Palladium,* wrote: "It must never be forgotten that it is only the turning of the crushed worm, the revolt of the ignorant and degraded against their intolerable oppression and injustice."[48] However, the mistakes of the Knights and craft union leaders in the U.S.A., the civil war into which they entered, did harm in Canada. In 1884, a Toronto carpenters local (an international union affiliate) opposed—unsuccessfully—Knights' representation on the Trades and Labour Council. Two years later, the Canadian Knights combined with the craft unions to establish the Trades and Labour Congress.[49] So, from its inception, Canada's oldest, continuous labour centre was an all-in movement; whereas the U.S.' oldest, continuous centre, the AFL, was from its outset, exclusive, since it barred the Knights.

Two centres: The Canadian—all-inclusive, the U.S.—exclusive. One would think that in Canada, the Candian centre's pattern would prevail. But built into this centre from its outset was dual power: it grouped *Canadian* organizations, but they were mostly *international union* locals. In this way the Toronto Carpenters' move of 1884, though unsuccessful, was the advance signal of tragic splits to come.

The decline of the Knights has been noted above, their mistakes. But most important was their contribution to Canadian Labour's progress. They organized the unorganized—particularly the semi-

---

* Samuel Gompers, a founder of the American Federation of Labour and its first president.

skilled and unskilled. They were pioneers of industrial unionism, and led important strikes—the Toronto-Hamilton telegraphers' strike of 1883, the Toronto street railway strike of 1886. They speeded political action, and contributed to emergent progressive unionism in Western Canada. They were co-founders of the TLC and helped blaze the trail for unionism in Quebec. Not least, they fought for Canadian unionism—of this more in later chapters. In all these ways, they contributed immensely to trade union development in Canada.

The TLC, 1883:

In Canada the Knights were mainly a union and to a degree a movement. The Trades and Labour Congress, by way of contrast, was a full-fledged *centre,* a successor to the Canadian Labour Union. On August 17, 1883, the Toronto Trades and Labour Council adopted a motion that a "labour congress" be held in that city in December.[50] It sent out a call to all labour organizations in Canada. During Christmas week, 1883, the conference convened. Fifty delegates were present. Although the conference did not set up a permanent body, it decided on one in principle and laid the groundwork for it. Now all this was four years before the founding of the AFL. Indeed if the TLC's continuity with the Canadian Labour Union is taken into account, the organization of a Canadian trade union centre predates the AFL by 14 years.

The chairman at the 1883 convention was Charles March, president of the Toronto Trades and Labour Council. In his introductory remarks, his main point was solidarity. The "disturbed conditions of the trade ... and strikes" demanded a closer cementing of Labour. With reference to the "trade union" (the craft unions) and the Knights, he said:

"As between these two bodies, antagonism should not, and I am glad to find, does not exist, and between them no section or class of wage earners need be without organization and consequently protection."[51]

The convention of 1883 took up shorter hours—the demand not yet won for the 9-hour day: "Don't cut hands or wages", said Alfred Jury, "cut hours." The government immigration policy was criticized, in particular, exaggeration of job prospects by immigration agents. The delegates also turned their attention to women in industry. John Armstrong of the Printers (International Typographical Union), demanded equal pay for equal work, and urged women to be active in unions: "Women conduct business as well as most men."[51a] Finally, the conference turned over the calling of further meetings to the Toronto Trades and Labour Council.

In 1886 the Congress reconvened. Most delegates were Knights, while some represented craft locals of plasterers, building labourers, painters, plumbers, steamfitters and printers. The convention decided to establish the Congress as a permanent body which would hold annual meetings; and it elected an executive board with Charles March as president. The operative resolution establishing the TLC stated:

"(Be it resolved) that an organization be formed of Trades Unions and Knights of Labour Assemblies for the Dominion of Canada under the name of Trades and Labour Congress for the Dominion of Canada."[52]

In 1887, the TLC convention met at Hamilton, Ontario. The number of delegates had declined. Most came from the Knights. In all they represented about 5,000 members. The convention decided on the 8-hour day as a basic policy and demanded that the government provide for this in its contracts.[53] Another decision was to consolidate organization: A per capita payment to the Congress was fixed—it was estimated this would give the Congress a revenue of $318 per annum. Also the convention elected a parliamentary committee to function alongside the executive committee decided on the previous year.

The fourth TLC convention—the 1883 meeting counts as the first—met at London, Ontario in 1888. Times were hard, the unions weakened, and only 33 delegates attended. Trade unions represented (craft locals) included the Painters, the Brotherhood of Decorators, the Amalgamated Society of Carpenters (affiliated to the British union), the Iron Moulders, and the Bricklayers. The Knights of Labour were also present but their proportion had declined. The convention hammered out a more definite policy on the 8-hour day—the government was asked to enact 8 hours as the legal work-day for all branches of industry. Alfred Jury moved an amendment for a "general refusal" to work more than 8 hours, but this was not adopted. Another decision was a demand that the Dominion Government enact Labour Day as a national holiday.[54]

The fifth TLC convention was held at Montreal in 1889, in the city council chambers. Many delegates came from Quebec unions, particularly Knights' Assemblies. Craft unions represented included ITU Locals, the Montreal Cigar Makers, and the Montreal Plasterers Society.[55] Three members from Quebec were elected to the executive committee and a French Canadian was elected president.[56]

This completes the round of TLC meetings for the 1880s. Later pages will outline this body's progress and problems, what it did and what it failed to do.

3. SOCIAL LEGISLATION, POLITICAL ACTION, SOCIAL RECONSTRUCTION

Social Legislation:

A previous chapter on the 1870s had shown that as the workers organized, they turned their attention not just to employers but to government—the demand for social legislation, to begin with—factory legislation. Toronto trade unionists were trail blazers. In 1881, the legislative committee of the Toronto Trades and Labour Council appeared before a Royal Commission and proposed the following measures: A ban on employment of children under 12; a maximum 9-hour day for women and young people; the regular publication of information on industrial conditions by government ; the enactment of safety and sanitary regulations including protection against fires, shielding for gears and shafts, regular inspection of engines and boilers, and a staff of inspectors to enforce these measures;[57] the regular publication of information on industrial conditions by government.

Another step forward was the Royal Commission on the Relations of Capital and Labour, 1886-89. The Commission's report in 1889 recommended:

1. Maximum hours of 10 per day and 54 per week for child and female labour.
2. A ban on employment of children under 14, and night work for children under 16.
3. Abolition of fines.
4. Appointment of female family inspectors.[58]

Progress in the implementing of these recommendations at the federal level was small. One reason for this had begun to be clear 6 years earlier. In 1883 the Federal Government had considered a Factory Act, but decided not to introduce it in Parliament. The reason it gave was lack of jurisdiction. This problem—the division of federal-provincial powers continued to bedevil legislative progress through the years. Had the various agencies of government at both federal and provincial levels put the people's welfare first, not private enterprise, they would have found the constitutional formula which facilitated uniform social legislation, and protected both federal and provincial rights. Indeed, as early as 1887, the TLC proposed that the constitution be amended, and so did the Royal Commission in 1889.[59] But the federal authority which handed over hundreds of millions to the CPR* and other corporations, and later spent billions in 2 world wars

* Canadian Pacific Railway Company.

—a course not opposed by the provincial governments—did not acquire the powers to enact adequate legislation for the jobless, aged and infirm. Over half a century went by before—during World War II and its aftermath—there was a greater expanse of Canada-wide social legislation. Thus was callousness written into Canadian social and constitutional history; and for this the pattern was being set in the period under review.

In the circumstances, a major responsibility fell on the provincial governments, but they were slow in responding. In 1880, Ontario adopted an Act regulating hours of labour, and in 1883 a Factory Act as such.[60] This was progress, but the Act did not cover shops with fewer than 20 people. So, many sweat shops were left untouched. Another defect was insufficient enforcement. Two years after enactment of the Act, inspectors had not been appointed; and when they were appointed, another 2 years passed before a single case of violation was brought to the courts.[61]

In Quebec, progress was slower still. In 1884, legislation was adopted providing a degree of workmen's compensation, and in 1885, a Factory Act. This prohibited labour for women and children beyond $12\frac{1}{2}$ hours per day or 72 hours per week; and employment of boys under 12, or girls under 14. Provision for inspection was inadequate, and the regulations often violated.[62]

Political Action:

As Labour consolidated, it renewed its interest in political action. The Canadian Labour Congress convention of 1883 decided:
"... The working class of this Dominion will never be properly represented in parliament or receive justice in the legislation of the country until they are represented by men of their own mind and opinion."[63]

The inaugural TLC convention of 1886 re-affirmed this policy and asked its affiliates to do their best "to bring out candidates at the ensuing local and dominion elections."[64]

Labour's political effectiveness was tested in the Ontario provincial election of 1883. On January 19, 1883, the Toronto Trades and Labour Council adopted the following motion:
"Moved and seconded that the council proceed to nominate candidates for the coming elections to the local legislature and submit them to the public meeting for adoption."[65]

Later, Labour candidates were nominated for East Toronto, West Toronto, and one in a Hamilton riding. They were not successful. The East Toronto candidate won only 308 votes. The Hamilton candidate was also defeated but his vote was higher—about 1,200. The partisans of labour politics were not discouraged. The Hamilton *Palladium* wrote: "The 1,200 votes are a nucleus to rally the labour party of the future."[66]

In the Quebec provincial election of 1886, Labour's showing was more successful. On July 17, 1886, a hundred union delegates met in Montreal's Webber Hall and nominated three candidates—W. Robertson, a saddler, Edouard Gravel, a stereotyper, and W. Keyes, a Knights of Labour organizer. All three had the support of the Montreal Trades and Labour Council, and went to their constituents with an electoral program which included a demand for the protection of children working in factories. Much enthusiasm was generated among Montreal's working population: 4,000 attended a labour meeting in Chaboillez Square, and 3,000 came to another in St. James Market. The labour candidates were defeated, but won a good vote—6,054 out of 18,051 votes cast in their constituencies. A precedent had been set. Robertson said: "We will have a party of our own, faithful to our country and faithful to the working man."[67]

The federal election of 1887 was another test. The Trades and Labour Councils of Toronto and Montreal nominated or endorsed some candidates. A sign of Labour's strength was the way Sir John A. Macdonald of the Conservatives and Edward Blake of the Liberals vied with each other to woo the workers. They took up the demands of the trade union movement. Blake criticized Macdonald for not bringing in labour legislation, while Macdonald pointed to his legislation of 1872 which had legalized unions.[68]

This was political action on the modest scale of the 1880s. One of its qualities was directness. As conceived and operated by the pioneers, political action came from the unions themselves. This did not exclude formation of a party, and the pioneers were working on this. Meanwhile, results were slim, for the movement was small, its resources meagre. Still, a beginning had been made. In 1887, a trade unionist, Thomas Webb told the TLC convention:

"The only thing to do is to keep on agitating. The 9-hour system was secured in Toronto after 18 years hard work. Straight labour representation will be secured if it is agitated for all the time."[69]

Social Reconstruction:

Labour evolution in Canada as elsewhere is a chain of development. Vital links are: 1. Concentration of the workers in large-scale production under conditions of exploitation. 2. Development of wage struggles, strikes, unions, legislative and political action. 3. The encounter in these struggles of the hard realities of the social system. 4. The cycle of victory and defeat, of correct decisions and mistakes, of solidarity and disunity. 5. Through all this, the gradual emergence of a distinctive labour consciousness. This consciousness confines itself largely to the here and now, the urgent problems of the day—that is decisive—but begins also to concern itself with the social system as a whole, its reconstruction.

In the decade under review, this chain of development was being forged, link on link. After the Ontario provincial election of 1883, the Hamilton *Palladium* said:

"Those who see the injustice of a system in which many toil to enrich the few, will not be discouraged. The ultimate object is not merely to tinker and patch a rotten and corrupt system but to replace it by a better and juster one."[70]

In 1883 a Canadian labour newspaper published a poem:
"The Men Who Killed My Child"
". . . And I'll preach it and I'll preach it,
Till I set our people wild
Against the heartless, reckless, grasping
Of the men who killed my child."[71]

This reflected rising consciousness. So did testimony by working class witnesses at hearings of the Royal Commission on the Relations of Capital and Labour, 1886-89. One said: "We do not benefit from cheapened machinery production, because all the improvements in machinery are competitors for our labour under this system."[72] Another was asked by the Commissioners: "Do you think the tendency to centralize capital has anything to do with the material prosperity of the working class?" He replied: "It has to do with their *want* of prosperity."[73]

Decisive was the problem of the surplus product: How much went to the owners over and above the cost of production, and how much to the workers? The *Hamilton Palladium* took this up. It said that the return on capital seems to be just about equal to the cost of wages. An investment of $1,000 yields $386 profit, as compared with $425 in wages. This, said, the *Palladium,* was robbery and swindling—the worker was being robbed of half the product of his labour.[74] John Hewitt also concerned himself with surplus product or profit. When he appeared before the Royal Commission of 1886-89, he said wealth in Ontario was increasing 3% per annum, but profits were between 6% and 12% per annum. His conclusion was that Labour was giving 3% to 6% to people who didn't work.[75]

The emerging labour consciousness of the 1880s did not confine itself to the economic foundation, but probed into the superstructure.

The feeling was that big money was corrupting all society, and seeking to bend all to its will; that the money power, as the *Palladium* put it had transformed politics into a cauldron of corruption: "The orator, the statesman and the editor ... have become the mere puppets of the money-bags and stock exchange wire-pullers."[76]

Against workers who looked to a new social order, some cried "communism". This tactic was used against a Hamilton labour candidate, a locomotive engineer, in the Ontario provincial election of 1883. On February 10, 1883, the *Palladium* said:
"If we denounce and oppose this rotten system, if we look to the dawn of a brighter day, equal conditions and opportunities where men's work shall be rewarded according to their value to society ... if this be communism, we have no desire to disclaim the accusation !"[77]

This was some labour thinking in the 1880s. Perhaps John Hewitt epitomized the best in it, because he plunged himself into the *here* and *now*, he concentrated on the fight for immediate results, but he gripped the causes of the *here* and *now*, and thus saw into the future. He said: "Monopolies will become so oppressive in the not distant future, that the masses will rise up and wipe them out."

CHAPTER 4

THE TRADE UNION MOVEMENT
1890-1900

1. GROWTH OF UNIONS. STRIKES,
LEGISLATION

Growth of Unions; Strikes:

In the early 1890s, industrial growth was slow. The "long depression" was continuing. After 1896, economic expansion began. The overall result for the decade was modest progress. In 1900, total manufacturing capital was $447,000,000 compared to $353,000,000 in 1890; and population was 5,371,000 compared to 4,833,000 at the beginning of the decade.[1]

Along with growth of capital came centralization of capital. "The big fish were consuming the little ones", said labour supporters at the time. In 1890, the Hochelaga Cotton Company and St. Ann Cotton Company, in Montreal, joined the Dominion Cotton Association, a syndicate of 11 mills. Capital was accumulating and concentrating. But wages stayed low. Even in a skilled trade like printing, Toronto union members were earning $12 a week for a 54-hour week in 1890, and Montreal printers $11 a week.

The movement grew slowly. About 250 new local unions were organized during the decade. Much of this new organization came after the expansion which began in 1896. Also, many unions built in the 1880s were still functioning; so, in sum, the movement was taking on stability.

Montreal was an important union centre. Unions found there in the early 1890s included Local 74 of the Brotherhood of Painters and Decorators, and Lodge 111 of the International Association of Machinists. The Cigar Makers were active. Also, there were moves to organize stone-cutters, plumbers, stone masons, roofers, glass blowers and leather cutters.

Toronto was the largest centre. Its unions included: the International Brotherhood of Painters and Decorators, the International Association of Machinists, the Cigar Makers International Union, the Blacksmiths' Helpers, the Journeymen Tailors' Union of America, the Journeymen Stonecutters, the Bricklayers, the Carpenters, and the Builders' Labourers.

At Winnipeg, a plumbers' local and machinists' lodge were organized. Unions also developed in British Columbia: in 1895, the Western Federation of Miners was founded—parent body of to-day's (1967) International Union of Mine, Mill and Smelter Workers.

The Knights of Labour were still active. They had Assemblies at Levis, Quebec, Montreal, Cornwall, Toronto, St. Catharines, Prescott and Windsor.

Along with unions, central labour councils were being built in key cities: Quebec City, 1890; Winnipeg, 1894; Halifax, 1898. By 1900 there were more than 20 of them.

The struggle for organization and conditions gave rise to strikes. In *Quebec:* Valleyfield cotton workers and Hull lumber workers in 1891, and Montreal cigar makers in 1894 and 1898. In *Ontario:* many strikes at Toronto involving bricklayers, moulders, printers, glove makers, gas works employees, tailors, cloakmakers and shoemakers ; a streetcar strike at London. In *Manitoba:* a series of bitterly fought strikes in the latter 1890s.

The Hull lumber strike of 1891 moved many trade unionists across Canada. The workers were then earning between $6.50 and $8.50 per week—this was after a $1.00 cut in 1890. With the help, it would seem, of the Knights of Labour, they combined to demand improvements: a wage increase of 50 cents per week and a cut in hours from 11½ to 10 per day. Management refused. On November 14, 1891, 2,000 walked out. As the employees left one mill, they marched to the next and called out their fellow workers. All lumber mills in the Ottawa, Gatineau and Hull districts seem to have been closed down. The indications are that not long after, at least one firm granted the 10-hour demand.[2]

The London streetcar strike of 1898 was another battle which stirred the movement. This strike's intensity and duration reflected Labour's rising strength, but also the employers' rising determination to crush the unions. In 1898, London's street railwaymen were being paid 12 cents an hour. Their union, the Amalgamated Street Railwaymen of North America asked the company to raise the wage rate to 16⅔ cents per hour, and reduce hours to 9 per day. The company replied: "We refuse to receive you as a union committee." On Thursday, October 27, the union struck. The cars were run into the barn. By 10 p.m. the strike was completely effective.

On Friday, October 28, the company tested the strike's effectiveness by running car No. 76 along the streets. Large crowds gathered, and the car did not get by. That evening, motormen and conductors gathered at the Labour Hall, and paraded to the Princess Rink. 5,000 London citizens were there to greet them. On Saturday, October 29, the company moved again to· break the strike. Strike-breakers were brought into London, and one flashed a revolver. Indignant crowds stormed the car barns; and for over a mile, Dundas Street was a seething mass of humanity. On Monday, October 31, the Riot Act was read, but still the crowds gathered. The London Trades and Labour Council helped by printing tens of thousands of cards with the slogans, "We Walk" and "no surrender to monopoly".

The company backed down. On November 11, the strike ended. The settlement provided an increase in wages to 15⅔ cents per hour, the 9-hour day, the right to join the union and no requirement to sign the "Document". But the company was biding its time. It did not live up to its word. On May 22, 1899, the workers went on strike again. A major issue now was the right to join the union. This second strike became a marathon battle extending into the 20th century. Such was the company's desire to break the strike that, so it was reported, it sought to purchase a union leader. A company agent allegedly contacted J. D. Marks, an officer of the London Trades and Labour Council and asked him: "What is there in this strike for you?" Marks, it was said, rejected the bribe. Meanwhile the strike was prolonging from month to month, and the strikers' privations were acute. But the London public showed that solidarity with Labour which is one of this city's proud traditions. Many citizens refused to use the streetcars; and on May 1, 1900 London workingmen joined in a mile-long parade to support the strike. Nine months after the strike began, the union said:

"Our front is unbroken. Our men have hardly the necessities of life, but having raised the banner of organized labour, we consider no sacrifice too great to carry it on to victory."[3]

Trade Union Rights and Social Legislation:

Hunger and state coercion—a formidable combination. Employers used it constantly against the unions. In 1894 when the employees of

J. D. King and Company, a Toronto shoe firm, organized in the Shoe Workers Union, the company brought in spies. When the union went on strike, 5 girls and a man were arrested on a charge of intimidation. At Valleyfield, when cotton workers struck in 1891, militia were brought in, and 3 strikers were killed.[4] During the lumber workers strike at Hull in 1891, the companies called out 4 companies of militia who were issued 2,000 ball cartridges.[5]

Against these sanctions, the unions sought relief in legislation. But progress was difficult, and defeat followed victory in diabolic succession. In 1890, parliament amended the Criminal Code to provide that a clause prohibiting conspiracy in restraint of trade would not apply to combinations of workmen. This was progress. But in 1892, when the Criminal Code was consolidated, a clause enacted in 1876 was omitted. The clause provided that attending at or near a factory gate to communicate information was not watching and besetting. So in this respect the unions had been dragged back to 1876. Such callous disregard of the most basic human and social rights outraged the organized workers. In 1891, the TLC convention was demanding that anti-labour employers be put on the "free list"—meaning that government lift tariff protection for their products.

Progress in social legislation was slow. In 1894, Labour Day was established as an annual statutory holiday. In 1891, a TLC committee met Prime Minister Sir John A. Macdonald to present the movement's legislative program. This practice—the "annual presentation"—has gone on to this day—annual meetings between the Federal Government and the Canadian Labour Congress, Confederation of National Trade Unions, Railroad Brotherhoods and Independent unions. In 1898, the Winnipeg convention of the TLC adopted a platform of principles. With various amendments, and in one variant or another this platform lasted through the years and became part of the standard program of the Canadian Labour Congress and other union bodies. Its main points were:

1. Free compulsory education.
2. The 8-hour day.
3. Government inspection of all industry.
4. Public ownership of public utilities.
5. Abolition of the Senate.
6. Abolition of child labour under 14.
7. Abolition of property qualifications in all public offices.
8. Abolition of prison labour.[6]

In the provinces there was a measure of progress. The Ontario Conciliation and Arbitration Act of 1894 provided for union representation on the Board administering the Act. In Ontario and B.C. some workmen's compensation legislation was enacted. In Ontario, the Factory Act was improved to provide for inspection of shops with fewer than 20 people. But some manufacturers continued to disregard provisions in the Act. In B.C. and Quebec, the Factory Acts were amended to include smaller factories.

During this period, Labour's legislative program continued to extend beyond union rights and factory conditions to demands such as: abolition of non-elective bodies (the Senate and Quebec Legislative Council), the vote for women, a ban on the handing over of federal public domains to companies.

Canadian independence was one prime issue. If in the first 3 decades after Confederation, progress in Canada was disappointingly slow, while it was swift in the United States, Britain and Western Europe—one cause was the continuing pressure of British capital on Canada, and Canada's continuing subordination to Britain in foreign and military policy. A further cause was constant pressures from the United States—the Hull lumber strike in 1891 and the London streetcar strike of 1898 were against U.S. companies. In short, the problem of Canadian independence was developing. The movement's concern was expressed in a resolution adopted at the TLC convention of 1893. This called on the Federal Government to hold the following plebiscite:

"1. Do you favour maintenance of Canada's present colonial status?
2. Do you favour imperial federation?
3. Do you favour Canadian independence?
4. Do you favour political union with the U.S.A.?"[7]

2. UNITY, CANADIAN UNIONISM, POLITICAL ACTION

An All-In, Effective Canadian Centre:

A great idea of the pioneers was that Labour should combine and come forward as an independent, cross-Canada force in economics and politics. To this end they built the Canadian Labour Union and TLC. "This Congress is the workingman's parliament!", said a delegate at the TLC's 1892 convention. And indeed, the way this body met and considered its problems in fraternal unity, pointed to great things ahead. The Congress was growing. It was sinking roots in the provinces and organizing provincial legislative committees—the nuclei of the later provincial federations. Such committees were established in Ontario and Quebec, 1891; in Manitoba and British Columbia, 1896; in

New Brunswick, 1899. But the Congress was still small. At the 1895 convention 39 delegates were present from 27 organizations. In 1891, TLC revenues were $539.80, but due to considerable expenditure, the balance on hand was $5.90.

With $5.90 on hand, prospects for organizing workers across Canada were limited. In 1897 the Congress' officers said they could not afford a single full-time organizer. The real problem was not just meagre membership but lack of concentration—a constant drainage to the U.S.—the international union link. During this period, more locals of international unions were being established in Canada; and more Canadian unions were joining U.S. bodies. For instance, in 1890 the Stonemasons Union met in Toronto "to consider uniting" with the International Stonemasons Union.

This expansion of international unionism in Canada, it must be stressed, was the *appearance,* the *mode.* The *substance* was Canadian unionism.

How did Canadian unionism manifest itself? Consider the London Street Railway strike. It was led by an international union—the Amalgamated Street Railway Employees. But it was the London Trades and Labour Council which helped the workers organize, and it was through the Council's initiative that application was made for a charter from the Amalgamated. At that time, the Amalgamated in the United States did not have much money, and the larger part of funds for the strike came from workers in London and other parts of Canada.

We see, then, that direct action by Canadians in building their unions and conducting their battles was one way Canadian unionism manifested itself. Another way was the struggle of international union locals in Canada for greater freedom of action—a struggle which sometimes reached the point where the members demanded a completely Canadian union.*

Still another manifestation of Canadian unionism was the Knights of Labour. The Canadian Knights were affiliated to the U.S. Knights, but this link was becoming less important because the U.S. Knights were ceasing to be a union—after 1893 they switched from unionism altogether. In contrast, the Canadian Knights continued to be a union. The practical result was that they were beginning to be a totally Canadian or "national" union (as distinct from international union). This was the more so because they were based mostly on Quebec; and

---

* In 1890 and 1892 Jacques Cartier Lodge 145 of the International Typographical Union in Montreal, and an ITU lodge in Quebec City, adopted a motion for a Canadian union of printers.

this enhanced their distinctness from foreign connection—the French Canadian fact. Urban Lafontaine, TLC president-elect in the 1890s was a French Canadian and a Knight; and most delegates at the 1890 convention were Knights. As the years passed by, their power at TLC conventions declined, but continued to be significant through to the turn of the century.

These are some ways Canadian unionism manifested itself. Another expression was the work of the TLC and its members in international union locals and national union locals. The Congress' aspiration to organize the unorganized has been noted above, and also some difficulties—inadequate membership and funds, lack of concentration, drainage to the U.S. How to bring unions not in the Congress into the Congress, how to centralize the resources of the movement in Canada, how to overcome dispersal to the south—that was the question. In short, the problem was unity *and* Canadian unionism. The issue was beginning to be posed: was the Congress to be an effective centre for organization, mutual aid and legislative action. Or, was it to remain a loose association of local unions—many looking southward to their U.S. headquarters—a weak association which met annually with government and won some promises but few results?

This issue emerged at the 1894 convention of the TLC. Two delegates from the Knights of Labour in Montreal, Darlington and Metcalfe, moved this motion.:

"This Congress having outlived its usefulness, as proven by its inability to obtain even a moiety of justice from either provincial or federal governments, be it resolved that before adjourning, we reconstruct the Congress in conformity with the advanced ideas of the generation and upon such lines as we will be in a position to issue charters for the purpose of organizing all toilers of any occupation . . ."

Two other delegates moved a motion along similar lines. This asked the Congress to assume the functions of a "Canadian organization, with full powers of organizing, issuing charters, levying per capita and such other duties as pertained to a national union". An organization of this kind, the motion went on to say, would further the cause of unionism by the "institution of new unions under a Canadian head".[8]

These motions were not accepted. However, the convention did decide that the Congress could charter unions, and this was confirmed in an amendment to the constitution adopted the following year. *But* the amendment specified that the Congress would not charter a union in a jurisdiction (trade or industry) occupied by present Congress affiliates, be they international or national. That meant that the intent of the motions cited above had been rejected. At a TLC convention some 2 years later, some delegates tried all over again to get the Congress to take on the title and function of a full-scale Canadian Federation of Labour. They failed. What did happen was that the Congress leaders conducted discussions for several years with American Federation of Labour leaders in the United States. The year 1899 brought the fruit of these discussions—an AFL commitment to grant the Trades and Labour Congress of Canada $100 per year.

A hundred U.S. dollars was not the answer to what ailed the TLC. The problem posed by international unionism—a basic problem of trade union evolution in Canada—was developing.

Political Action:

Political action was another problem. Significantly, the Darlington-Metcalfe motion of 1894, cited above, had said that a congress reconstructed along the lines it proposed, would better be able "to concentrate forces for political action". In 1899, the TLC convention adopted a strong motion on political action:

"Be it resolved that this Congress recommend that the various central bodies of labour in Canada take steps to form themselves into political parties. Where possible, candidates should be placed in the field. We should endeavour to have direct representation in the various Houses of Parliament, on lines similar to organized workers in Great Britain, etc. Hereafter the members of labour organizations found on platforms advocating the interests of the old political parties, should be regarded with suspicion as decoys of the wage earners and should be regarded as opponents to the advance of the labour movement."[9]

The Congress also decided to submit the political action problem to its affiliates in a referendum vote whose terms were:

"1. Are you in favour of independent political action?
2. If a majority of all unions vote in favour, will you assist morally and financially after candidates are chosen?"[10]

Meanwhile concrete electoral work was being done. The Trades and Labour Councils of Toronto, Montreal and Ottawa nominated candidates for the federal election of 1891. In the Ontario provincial election of 1894, the Toronto Trades and Labour Council had a candidate in East Toronto. Towards the end of the decade, a Labour party was established at Winnipeg. In 1899 Ralph Smith, a coal miners' leader at Nanaimo—later a TLC president—was elected to the B.C. provincial legislature. Also, there were beginnings of farmer-labour unity. In 1891, the Ontario TLC executive stated:

"The interests of the farmer, as relating to the encroachment of monopolistic tendencies, are identical with the artisans of the city. Any action that will tend to the harmonious alliance of the farm and city artisans will be hailed with delight and hope by organized labour throughout the length and breadth of our Dominion."[11]

The Patrons of Industry were a leading farm organization of the day—they were represented on the Toronto Trades and Labour Council, and a delegate attended the TLC convention of 1895. That year the convention spoke of the "brother toilers of farm and factory". In 1896 the Patrons were proposing to the TLC a joint convention of the workers and farmers of Canada.

3. TRADE UNIONISM AND SOCIAL CHANGE

Socialist Ideas of the 1890s:

The trade union movement's progress in the 1890s, outlined in the previous two sections, was part of a larger process. That process had two ingredients: 1. Growth of Capitalism and its contradictions. 2. Formation and organization of the working class.

From these two ingredients, and along with them, came a third: The continuing evolution of labour consciousness. As noted in the previous chapter, this consciousness was primarily directed to the practical problems of the day—the fight for conditions, the building of unions, the struggle for an *effective* labour movement. These matters have been covered in the previous two sections of this chapter. In addition however, this consciousness focussed on the deeper discontents of the social system—its reform and regeneration, or its abolition to make way for a higher social system.

All this gave rise to the socialist current in the organized workers' movement. In the United States, AFL president Samuel Gompers furiously fought the socialists in the trade union movement. He counterposed socialism and "pure and simple" unionism, the winning of better conditions day by day. Practice proved him wrong, for the socialists were among the most dedicated builders of the unions both in the U.S. and Canada. *Solidarity was the key*. There was room in a single trade union movement for adherents of all the various groupings: those who wanted the movement to advance to objectives such as political action, sweeping social reform, even general social reconstruction; those who thought the movement should confine itself to day-to-day economic action for better conditions; and those finally who stood somewhere between these two standpoints. All these groupings could be combined in a single movement, providing: *firstly,* no single grouping socialist, non-socialist, or anti-socialist—tried to substitute itself for the movement as a whole, and exclude others; *secondly,* all the groupings united around the primary aim — a strong trade union movement along lines desired by the large majority.

Now in Canada, as distinct from the United States, there was always greater solidarity between these various trends in the trade union movement; and if this solidarity was disrupted on occasion, this was due not only to pressures from social forces in Canada—parallelling those in the United States—but also to the *direct intervention* of the AFL and U.S. international headquarters into Canadian trade union affairs—the constant export of U.S. disunity and intolerance to Canada. Meanwhile, the evidence indicates that in the 1890s, socialism, and the trend to socialism was operating as *one* significant current in the trade union movement. To this current we now turn.

"Socialists stand for the overthrow of the competitive system. They seek abolition of private ownership of the means of production, including land, capital and machinery. They seek the organization of an industrial commonwealth in which the government will control the production and the people control the government."[12]

This is how the Toronto *Labour Advocate,* organ of the Toronto Trades and Labour Council, put the case for abolition of capitalism in the early 1890s.

The objective was socialization of the means of production. What was to be the link of transition? The fight on immediate issues, reforms which could be won in the here and now, but advanced the struggle for a new social order. In 1891, 119 miners were killed in an explosion at Springfield, Nova Scotia. The *Labour Advocate* reacted by demanding *firstly* that violation of mine safety rules be made a criminal offense, and *secondly* by charging the miners "had been victims of capitalist selfishness." It added: "The time of redress must come. All such sources of natural wealth must cease to be private property and be owned by the nation."[13] A Toronto girl found dead of starvation and exposure, a dock worker dying of hunger and exhaustion — the *Labour Advocate* exposed these tragedies. So the point was leadership in reform, and exposure of what was considered to be an unjust social system.

What kind of reform? One was public ownership of certain industries. Public utilities was an obvious beginning. The socialists said that if an industry was under federal, provincial or municipal charter, if its profits came from the public domain, then it should be publicly owned. In 1891 the *Labour Advocate* denounced capitalist opposition to this reform:

"Their (the capitalists') acquisitive instinct and selfish fears are aroused by the thought that whatever can be done by the people's representatives better than can be done by private monopolists, ought so to be done. They feel their investments and privileges are in danger."[14]

The socialists recognized that nationalization of an industry did not mean abolition of capitalism, but said it was a step in this direction. "Every successful experiment in the working of public services by the community educates workers into what can be done in diverting the profits from the swollen hoards of manipulators and speculators to the pockets of the actual producers."*[15]

From public ownership of a particular industry like municipal transport, through ownership of a number of industries, to the final goal—socialization of all large-scale means of production—this transition is indicated by a writer in the Labour Day Souvenir program of the Toronto Allied Printing Trades Council, 1898:

"Public necessities ought not to be controlled by private individuals for their personal profit."[16]

Another reform proposed was the initiative and referendum. The *initiative* meant that any sizable group of voters in a municipal ward, or provincial and federal constituency, could initiate a petition for a new law, or amendment in a present law. It would then be the duty of the legislative body to draft the proposed measure and submit it to a vote of the people. The *referendum* meant that a legislative body on adopting a bill must submit it to a popular vote if enough electors asked for a vote.

Why did Canadian trade unionists, at least those who were socialist, take up this idea? This was because they had seen their legislative bodies fall more and more under the influence of business interests.

Usually this happened indirectly—the normal process of business ties of dependence, and business domination of the economy. Sometimes it happened directly through purchase of Members of Parliament, as in the CPR scandal of 1874 which led to the fall of Sir John A. Macdonald's Conservative Government.

This was the problem. The classical solution of socialism was legislative bodies of a new type—adaptation of present ones or institution of new ones; bodies impregnated with the spirit of democracy; mainly working bodies not talking bodies, with debate cut down to the essential issues; bodies whose members could be recalled and replaced by new ones whenever a majority of their constituents wanted it that way. Moreover, parliamentary institutions even at their best were not enough. Democracy—and the lack of it—sprang from the economic foundation. If the economy was totalitarian, if the main industries were owned by a wealthy minority, if most of the public was exploited and discouraged from participation in public life, then, said the socialists, it was hard for parliamentary institutions to fulfil themselves,

* Statement by the *Labour Advocate*.

and their progress could only be the fruit of prolonged struggles by the people. To a degree at least significant, trade unionists of the 1890s must have looked at matters in this light. In 1899, the TLC convention adopted this motion:

"The present representative system of government is fast assuming the form and essence of dictatorship. It has led to the almost complete control of legislation in the interest of the wealthy capitalist class. The power of the electorate is solely confined to the quasi-annual choice of one individual who may represent anything or nothing, who during his term of office may deliberately act contrary to previous promises, without forfeiting his position as representative. The initiative and referendum is the means best calculated to obtain government in the interests of the whole community and the abolition of class legislation, class privilege. The aim of democratic government should be the fullest expression of the public will with regard to the laws which govern them."[17]

Sources of Socialism; Internationalism, Peace, the Labour Press:

A few words on the sources of this socialism emergent in Canada. In the 1890s, concentration of capital was developing. Increasingly society was polarizing into two classes, Capital and Labour. Strikes were increasing in impact and intensity. These strikes demonstrated the economic power of Capital, but also of Labour: the power of capitalist ownership—to hire, pay, wait—*versus* the power of the workers—production, the collective cessation of production, the strike. That was the conflict. The workers' way of resolving it was organization—first and foremost for conditions, then for all other demands. In turn this became a source of socialism in Canada.

A second source was economic crises, unemployment. In 1894, the Toronto ITU Local 99 minute book said: "Unemployment is serious among our men ... 30% of our people are unemployed ... this is due to the introduction of machinery." That same year the minute book of the Montreal Jacques Cartier ITU Lodge reported that members, after working years in their trade, were walking the streets.

The workers began to fight back against this unemployment, and they used every weapon they could lay their hands on—economic and legislative. Sometimes they took direct action. In Toronto, on February 11, 1892, 300 unemployed labourers gathered on St. Andrew's Square and formed a procession headed by a black flag—on the flag the motto—"Work or bread!" The procession advanced to the city hall, where a large crowd had gathered, and a delegation met with Mayor Clark (one of the printers arrested in 1872).[18] The city council later voted $15,000 for public works. A modest success like this raised the workers' confidence in victory through solidarity and action.

The third source of socialism was the world socialist movement. Socialist parties, many influenced by Marxism, were being established in western Europe and Britain—in 1889 most of them grouped in the Second International. In Canada also, socialist bodies were being built—the Socialist Labour Party; the Canadian Socialist League (Toronto); the Industrial Brotherhood of Canada (London); a Nationalist Club in Toronto (it called itself nationalist because it stood for nationalization). A socialist press was beginning—the Winnipeg *Voice*, London *Industrial Banner*, Toronto *Labour Advocate*. The mass movement was growing. In 1891 the Second International, moved by U.S. workers who had fought for the 8-hour day on May 1, 1886, proclaimed May 1 the international workers' holiday. Canadians participated in this rising movement. On Labour Day 1891, 15,000 marched in Montreal, and 1,500 in Ottawa.

These then were sources of socialism in Canada. The crux was Canadian workers' solidarity in the struggle for conditions and a better life. But this same struggle was going on across the world. How natural then that these two processes should fuse—the fight in Canada and across the world: internationalism. This *oneness* of the world workers' cause had been felt by Canadian workers as long ago as 1833. In the 1890s the Toronto *Labour Advocate*, a typical spokesman of Canadian socialism, gave it expression and leadership. Its columns reported events then moving the international workers' movement—a major strike in Russia in 1890; celebration of the 20th anniversary of the Paris Commune in 1891; the killing of 20 workers during a demonstration in France on May 1, 1891. All this was internationalism, world labour solidarity. It became a distinct, constituent source of socialism in Canada, one which fused with the other sources.

Labour's socialist wing also stood for peace. "Only lords and swells, capitalists and office holders, profit from war," said the *Advocate*. This journal looked back to the Crimean War (1853-54) and asked what interest can a British worker have in fighting a Russian worker: "... The workers are duped into butchering each other ..." Now, it just so happened that at Christmas 1890 a British veteran of the Crimean War died in a poorhouse. He had been a member of the Light Brigade celebrated in Tennyson's poem, "Charge of the Light Brigade". And now, said the *Advocate*, he was making his last charge into the poorhouse and slow death from starvation.[19]

Finally, the socialists, along with many trade unionists, fought for the labour press, and were hostile to newspapers owned by wealthy private interests. In August 1891, the *Labour Advocate* carried this declaration by a New York journalist—made, so it reported, at a gathering where his colleagues had asked him to toast the press:

"I am paid $150 a week to keep honest opinions out of my paper. You are paid similar sums to do similar things. Any journalist who wrote his own honest opinions would be out in the street looking for a job. The business of a leading journalist is to distort the truth, to lie outright, to pervert, to vilify, to fawn at the feet of mammon, to sell his country and his race for daily bread. We are the tools and vassals of rich men behind the scenes. We are jumping jacks. Rich men pull the strings, we dance. Our time, our talent, our possibilities, all are the property of other men. We are intellectual prostitutes. Gentlemen, I give you—the press."[20]

This was plain speaking. And this direct attitude was a quality of the labour and socialist press springing up then—the Winnipeg *Voice,* London *Industrial Banner* and Toronto *Labour Advocate.* All three newspapers were advocates of social reconstruction. All three were organs of the Trades and Labour Councils in their cities of publication. The *Advocate* was a model. It conducted campaigns for reform and social reconstruction. Also, it paid careful attention to trade union affairs. Its weekly issues carried a full page of the proceedings of the Toronto Labour Council. The proceedings of TLC conventions and other union gatherings were also reported in painstaking detail. Another *Advocate* feature—in the tradition of the *Ontario Workman*— was the printing of novels as serials—serious but popular novels with a labour and social content.

Unionism and Socialism:

How could the trade union movement be built? What was its best course? This constant concern of the socialists expressed itself in a variety of ways:

First. The socialists were active in the day-to-day building of the movement and conduct of its struggles.

Second. They advanced proposals aimed at making the movement more effective. For instance, the Knights of Labour delegates at the 1894 TLC convention who called for the transformation of the Congress into a full-scale Canadian Federation of Labour, were members of, or inclined to, the Socialist Labour Party.

Third. The socialists said the unions should advance to political action. The rise of the trusts and their increasing power in government proved that the purely economic struggle no longer sufficed. When Labour confined its battles to the economic base, it tended to be outmanoeuvered by capital which operated not only from its own powerful economic base, but also from the reserve political base of government and the state. The solution was that the workers should marshal their forces on a Canada-wide scale and constitute themselves as an independent force in Canada-wide politics. If this was done, the day would be speeded when, as a Canadian socialist put it in 1891, the "politics of the wealth-makers... stands foremost in the parliament of nations".

Fourth. The socialists tended to oppose class collaboration. A previous chapter has outlined the beginnings of class collaboration—that objective trend in the trade union movement which seeks reconciliation with employers as a substitute for independent working class struggle around independent working class objectives. The case of D. J. O'Donaghue has been cited—and vigorous trade union reactions to his conduct have been noted. Now, in the 1890s, O'Donaghue was still active. In 1891, Toronto trade unionists and socialists were fighting for public ownership of the municipal transport system. When the city council, dominated by pro-employer elements, moved to renew the charter of the private company which operated the street railway system, the *Labour Advocate* took out an injunction to block the council. O'Donaghue—then active in the Toronto Trades and Labour Council—convinced the Council to deny any connection with the injunction. Infuriated, the *Advocate* accused O'Donaghue of playing capitalist politics and berated "O'Donaghue and his rabid following of Grits (factionists)... Mr. O'Donaghue's course in this action was prompted by that petty malignancy and jealousy which constantly inspires his actions." That same year O'Donaghue opposed proposals for a workingman's political party. In 1894 he fought affiliation of the Patrons of Industry to the TLC.

Opposition to class collaboration in the trade union movement—this then was a further manifestation of the socialists' concern for the future of that movement.

Fifth. The socialists' concern for the union expressed itself in the way they got to grips with the problem of *wages,* the wages system. This point is absolutely decisive. We will elaborate on it.

In 1898 a Canadian trade unionist said:

"Let's keep up the fight until our wages rise to the level of our earnings and not a single parasite is left to rob us of the fruits of our labour."[21*]

Here is a case of a Canadian getting to grips with the *wages question* —the meeting point of trade unionism and socialism. He is picking up a thread reaching as far back as Robert Owen's Grand National Con-

---

* Extract from an article appearing in the Toronto Allied Printing Trades Council Souvenir Program of 1898.

solidated Trades Union, 1833. Owen's point had been later taken up and developed by Karl Marx and Frederick Engels. And here was the gist of the wages problem as they posed it. Should the workers confine themselves to seeking higher wages and shorter hours? In other words, should they merely seek a bigger slice of the pie? Or should they go for the whole pie, because they were the ones who baked the pie, and made the materials that went into the pie?

Now, even if workers believed the whole pie was rightfully theirs and acted on that belief, that was not good enough. For the pie belonged to the capitalist. He aimed to sell it on the market and get the best price for it. And he was going to make sure that at the end of the cycle of production and marketing, after the costs of materials, wages, machinery and buildings had been met, there was still a fair slice of the pie for him—*profit*. This was capitalist free enterprise. And all the forces of practice, accumulated habit, ownership, economic and political power, the various dominant social institutions and ideas were there to ensure that capitalist free enterprise operated unimpeded and unchallenged—at least, not frontally challenged, not basically and consistently challenged.

However, the workers had another alternative. On the market was not just the pie they had baked—commodities in general, but a commodity of a special type: their power to work, labour power. Therefore, the best course was to do what the capitalists did: Go out on the market and get the best possible price and condition for their commodity—labour power. Go out and get higher wages, shorter hours, a more tolerable workload, a better life for themselves and their families.

The way to do this was—combination. Organize! *But,* when a union won the best price for labour power—the highest wages, shortest hours, best conditions—it did something else as well: It generated a new and distinct force—working class solidarity. This meant that within the womb of the free enterprise system of production for profit, the elements of a higher society were forming—one based on production for use, on the union of the producers.

Thus arose the conflict of Capital and Labour. As this conflict developed through years, decades and even generations, Labour would learn its lessons in defeat and victory, would ever strengthen its organization, and eventually it would overthrow the domination of Capital. This victory of Labour was inevitable because the combination of labour and production was essentially *compatible* with modern large-scale production, while capitalist private ownership, though transitionally fostering production, was essentially incompatible with it.

Capitalist free enterprise tended to confine production to the movement of profit, and to block the natural, imminent power of production itself. It followed as surely as day followed night, that sooner or later the private ownership of the large-scale means of production would be replaced by their common or social ownership.

Finally, let all this be granted, and two conclusions followed.

First. The workers should realistically recognize their status as commodities on the market. They should go out and get the best price they could for their commodity, their power to work. They should aim for the best conditions in the here and now.

Second. The workers should press forward to abolish a system which confined the improvement of their conditions to the limit set by capitalist production for profit rather than to the boundless possibilities of large-scale production itself.

This was how Marx and Engels approached the *wages problem,* and this was their solution. These ideas were then beginning to have an impact wherever there was a labour movement. Certainly in the Canada of the 1890s, the indications are that socialists were inclining to this kind of thinking. An example is the way the Toronto *Labour Advocate* reacted to the single tax theory of Henry George. This theory was then widespread among workers and farmers in the United States. Its starting point was: Why progress and poverty? Why does poverty follow on progress? Henry George said this was because progress — meaning economic expansion, the growth of industry—tended to raise the value of land. In turn the landlords pocketed this increase—an unearned increment. In other words the fruit of progress—the annual surplus product—was taken over by the landlords. Hence poverty for the mass. Henry George's solution was: Put a 100% tax on the increased land values. Do that, and no other taxes will be necessary. This was the single tax—a tempting dish, though not for the landlords.

In Canada, socialists disagreed with Henry George. They said his ideas were a "halfway house".[22] In this respect once again they were inclining to the Marxist view. In *Capital* Marx had stated that in a capitalist economy, the landlords, like the bankers, are just another wing of the capitalists. What is absolutely basic is *not* land or money, but *material production*—the processing of materials *through the simple fact of work,* and the consequent increase in their value. So far as land was concerned, it was just another means of production. It became capital the same as buildings, machinery, and the money fund for wages. Capital moved indiscriminately from industry to finance to commerce and service to land, and back again—attracted where profits were higher. It followed that a single tax on landlords was not the answer. The solution was the social expropriation of all *large-scale* means of production — in industry, finance, commerce, service and land.

This then is how socialists in Canada, and socialism generally, oriented itself to that decisive question—the wages problem, the wages system. And this was the socialist solution—socialization of the large-scale means of production. The Canadian socialists of the 1890s recognized that this more basic change might be a long time coming. Meanwhile the unions must win improvements in the here and now. However, the socialists appealed to the trade union movement that it should recognize, in the words of the Toronto *Labour Advocate*, that this more basic change was the "one it has in view" and "should demand such legislative measures as tend in that direction".

The socialists' concern for the trade union movement has been outlined above—as expressed in:

First.   Their day-to-day work in building the movement.

Second. Their proposals for a more effective movement.

Third.   The call for political action.

Fourth. Opposition to class collaboration.

Fifth, and most important. The orientation to the wages question.

What was the response of the trade union movement?

One indication is what happened in Toronto in 1891, when two trade union bodies—the Trades and Labour Council and the Knights of Labour—combined forces with the Nationalist Club and *Labour Advocate* in a campaign for municipal ownership of the street railway system. Again, in 1894, the Toronto Trades and Labour Council charged that the Consumers' Gas Company was a monopoly endangering the public. That year the Council adopted a sweeping program for municipal ownership of the street railway company, telephone services and the power and gas works.

At the all-Canadian level, the movement also responded positively. In 1891, the TLC convention endorsed federal ownership of railways and telegraphs, and municipal ownership of public utilities. It also approved the initiative and referendum. The TLC convention of 1893 endorsed the principle of co-operation at both the producer and distributor levels, and called on municipal and provincial governments to implement it. This convention also decided to conduct a vote among Congress affiliates as to what social system they favoured. Here were the choices:

1. "Do you favour the present industrial system?
2. Do you favour the co-operative system of production, distribution and exchange?

3. Do you favour a communist system of government?

4. Have you any other system other than those suggested above?"[23]

Plainly socialism was having an impact on the trade union movement. However, this should not be exaggerated. Socialism was but one of several tendencies in the movement. Moreover the unions were beset by the daily problems of the *here* and *now*. Again, in numerical terms, the socialist forces were slender. In 1895 one of their parties—the Socialist Labour Party—was reported to have 150 members! True that the trade union movement's forces were also pitifully small, probably well under 50,000 members—scarce the size of a single large union today (1967). Plainly the labour movement as a whole was still in the preliminary stage where it was just gathering its forces, and these forces were modest. But from the standpoint of the future, a decisive durable of Canadian history was slowly evolving—working class economic organization; and not just economic organization but consciousness: check-up on results, the formation of clearer, more precise and more general ideas about these results, the working out of more effective plans for a better to-day and a better to-morrow.

●

This then was the condition of the trade union movement as it rounded the bend of the 19th century and approached the 20th. We see a young movement increasing its numbers and consolidating its ranks; a growing movement unfolding its wage, strike, legislative and political struggles; a struggling movement beginning to concern itself with Canada's problems as a whole and with the social system.

CHAPTER 5

TRADE UNION STRUGGLES
1900-1914

1. GROWTH OF CAPITAL AND LABOUR

Expansion of Production; Condition of the Workers:

The opening years of the 20th century brought the economic expansion envisioned at Confederation. Between 1901 and 1915, manufacturing capital increased about fivefold, from $446,916,497 to $1,994,103,272.[1] Between 1900 and 1910, total capital invested in industry increased from 2⅓ billion to 5 billion dollars.[2] Annual wheat production rose from 25 million bushels in 1900 to 200 million in 1911. Between 1890 and 1910, primary iron and steel output went up fivefold. The accumulation and concentration of capital also increased. In 1871 average capital per manufacturing establishment was $1,889, in 1915—$93,594.[3] In 1871 fixed capital per worker was $415, in 1915—$3,873.[4]

So, for business, times were buoyant. But not for the workers. Their lot was hard labour, low wages, long hours, accidents, unemployment. Money wages went up, but so did living costs. The statistician, Jurgen Kucynski, states that in 1900-14 the increase in real wages was nil.[5] Firestone, a Canadian economist, calculates that between 1900 and 1910, annual real wages (in terms of 1935-1939 dollars) actually declined: $726 in 1900, $618 in 1910.[6] At the turn of the century, annual wages in manufacturing was $333, in 1910—$458. But this increase tended to be cancelled by rising costs—in 1900-13, rents went up 36%.[7] In 1915, at 14,887 establishments, over half the workers were earning under $12 per week.[8]

The entry of women into industry was continuing, but so was their exploitation, and also the exploitation of children. In 1901, women numbered about a fifth of the labour force. In 1915, at 14,887 factories, 57,000 women were employed, of whom only 4,097 earned over $12 per week; and 8,411 children were employed, of whom only 115 earned over $12 per week.[9]

Labour was developing — in numbers, organization, struggle. Between 1900 and 1910 the number of workers employed in manufacturing rose from 339,173 to 515,203*[10] Between 1900 and 1913, union membership increased from about 50,000 members in about a thousand locals in 1900,** to 175,799 members in 2,017 locals in 1913. The rising struggle for conditions is reflected in strike statistics. Between 1900 and 1915, 377,234 workers were involved in 1,519 strikes, with a total time lost of 1,712,262 man work days.[11] The increasing impact of strikes is shown in this table:

Period	Time Lost in Working Days
1901-1905	2,461,199
1906-1910	3,280,524
1911-1915	4,969,739[12]

2. RAILWAY STRUGGLES

Trackmen's Strike, 1901; Canadian Northern Strike, 1902; UBRE, 1903:

A major sector of capital was the railroad industry. Here owners grew rich at the expense of the public and their employees. The largest company was the Canadian Pacific Railway. Swollen with millions in cash and land handed over gratis by the Federal Government, the CPR savagely resisted its employees' efforts to unionize and win better conditions. In 1900, CPR shopmen struck. Two units affected were the Winnipeg and Calgary shops where machinists, blacksmiths and boilermakers walked out. In 1901, CPR trackmen (maintenance-of-way-men) went on strike. Their key demand was a 10 cent increase—that is that their daily wage be raised from $1.15 to $1.25—trackmen were then among the most exploited of CPR employees. The strike lasted two months and affected the company's operations across the country. A striker-poet wrote:

"Listen to the voice of honest labour
  Coming from the din and strife,
  Coming from the iron pathway,
  Where the world's busy traffic is rife."

* The 1910 figure is for establishments with 5 hands and over.
** An estimate only. The Federal Department of Labour regular statistical table of membership goes back only to 1911.

The wealthy classes were nervous. In July 1901, it was reported that Indian labourers were holding a council of war and thinking of joining the strike. An alarmed newspaperman at Winnipeg stated: "In a few days, several thousand well-armed Indians could descend, and the government has no arms or ammunition here in Winnipeg.*

The strike ended August 1901. The men won about a quarter of a million dollars in wage increases. This was good, but there were charges of skulduggery. The dominant unions in the North American railroad industry were then the standard railroad brotherhoods—the Order of Railroad Conductors, the Brotherhood of Locomotive Engineers, the Brotherhood of Locomotive Firemen, and similar bodies. They were dominated largely by conservative leaders disposed to balance the interest of the more skilled workers against the less skilled; and disposed to balance both against the companies. These leaders had defeated the attempts of Eugene Debs and other militants to build a militant, united, industrial movement of railroad workers. They showed their hand in this strike. They criticized the trackmen's demands. Significantly the company agreed to Brotherhoods' chairmen as arbitrators (chairmen were Brotherhoods' heads for the various districts). And that was how the strike was settled: by an arbitration board made up mainly of the Brotherhoods' chairmen. Soon after, the *Voice,* organ of the Winnipeg Trades and Labour Council, said the railroad workers suspected the company had "tampered with the heads of the Brotherhoods"; and a senior officer of the Trackmen's Union charged that "the general chairmen had allowed the CPR officials to use their (the chairmen's) prestige against Maintenance-of-way-men".[13]

In 1902, Canadian Northern Railway workers went on strike. The owners, Mackenzie and Mann, were typical railroad buccaneers—it was said they had won control of 10,000 miles of railroad without investing scarce a dollar of their own. Also, they were ferociously anti-union. The strike began on May 16, with Winnipeg as a chief base. It involved skilled workers—machinists, boilermakers, sheet iron workers. But what gave it impact was the unskilled. They had been organized in a new union, an industrial union, the United Brotherhood of Railway Employees. Between 1901 and 1903 this body flashed like a star across the western horizon. Organized in the United States in 1901, a product of the struggle for industrial railroad unionism, the UBRE said the answer to increasing trustification on the railroads was one industrial railway union. It bitterly opposed the standard railroad

* This was just 16 years after the second Métis revolution of 1885.

brotherhoods, condemned them for neglecting organization of the unskilled; and it hated Samuel Gompers, President of the American Federation of Labour—it looked on him as an employers' agent. A union which collaborated closely with the UBRE was the Western Federation of Miners. Both unions were members of a new trade union centre in the United States, the Western Labour Union.

The UBRE president, Estes, seems to have been an excellent organizer. In 1902, he came to Winnipeg and won the support of the Trades and Labour Council. A lightning campaign of organization began. By July, the UBRE had grown to about 1,000 members including freight handlers, clerks, switchmen and brakemen. These newly-organized workers went out on strike alongside the skilled workers. This was solidarity. On July 15, 10,000 Winnipeg workers demonstrated in support of the strike.

Then came a stab in the back. Representatives of the standard international unions—the railway Brotherhoods—came to Winnipeg and proceeded to the head office of the Canadian Northern Railroad. Soon after a settlement was announced. It covered the skilled workers only. The unskilled were left "holding the bag". Later that year, the Manitoba executive committee of the Trades and Labour Congress of Canada was to state:

"It is thus clear that the trainmen, conductors, engineers and firemen entered into a common understanding to defeat the men who had legitimately combined and struck for laudable ends; and had done this at the instigation of the grand officers of the leading railway brotherhoods ... The action of the brotherhoods in thus disregarding the broad principles of co-operative action between unions as well as individuals, is sincerely deplored, and will constitute the blackest page in the history of trade unionism in Manitoba."[14]

Despite this reverse, the UBRE continued the strike and it terminated in February 1903, having lasted 7 months. A few months later, the UBRE began a still bigger battle, this time against the CPR. The main base was British Columbia. Here the UBRE had built quite an organization, particularly in Vancouver. CPR wages were then among the lowest in the North American railroad industry. The Company opposed the UBRE's industrial unionism, which grouped all the trades and crafts in a single organization. On February 2, 1903, CPR superintendent Beasley is reported to have said: "The CPR is ready to spend a million dollars to break the United Brotherhood of Railway Employees."[15]

The strike began in Vancouver among the railroad clerks. They were then working long hours and earning about $40 a month. They walked out February 26, and were followed by other office workers and baggage men. Then the freight-handlers went on strike, then the longshoremen, and seamen—the latter, members of the B.C. Steamshipmen's Society. Two weeks later, UBRE locals at Revelstoke, Nelson and Calgary were on strike. Early in March, freight-handlers and clerks struck at Winnipeg. The strike reached as far east as Montreal—on March 18, 8 clerks at the Windsor Station were dismissed for being UBRE members. Now the strike was in its fifth week, and the UBRE was claiming that CPR freight business between Winnipeg and Vancouver had come practically to a standstill. Moreover, not only CPR employees were on strike but employees of other companies including blacksmiths, carpenters, boilermakers and others.

Now came the turn of the coal miners. On March 8, miners at Ladysmith, Vancouver Island, gathered at a meeting and joined the Western Federation of Miners. In retaliation, the employers (the Dunsmuir family) discharged the key men and locked out the working staff, whereupon 600 miners struck. In April, miners at Cumberland, Vancouver Island—employees of the Wellington Coal Company—also organized in the WFM. Here, too, the company retaliated by discharging some key union members. On May 2, the Cumberland miners went on strike.

In this way, the UBRE strike against the CPR had become a general battle of the B.C. working class. Solidarity was at a high. Trades and Labour Councils—TLC chartered bodies—at Victoria, Vancouver, Calgary and Winnipeg were endorsing the strike. Then the Canadian Northern pattern repeated itself—a stab in the back by the conservative, international union officialdom in the United States. A later chapter will show that at this very time, when B.C. workers were fighting the battle of all-Canadian labour, international union officials in the U.S., combined with some officials in Canada, were taking action leading to a split in the orgnized workers' movement of Canada —something scarce likely to help the strike struggle in B.C.

More direct and plain to see was the role of senior officials of the standard railroad brotherhoods in the United States. The *Trainmen's Journal,* organ of the Brotherhood of Railway Trainmen, carried an article savagely denouncing the UBRE and the Winnipeg *Voice* (organ of the Trades and Labour Council of Winnipeg). Such was the favour this article aroused from the CPR, that its secret service—so it was reported—circulated it as a pamphlet during the strike. Again, from Kansas City, the grand president of the Boilermakers' Union issued a directive to Canadian boilermakers on the CPR that "under no consideration will we allow any of our members to violate the contract", that if any member went out in sympathy, "we will immediately annul their card", and that if any lodge encouraged the men, "we'll have to call in its charter".

So, in this concrete situation, decisive international union leaders in the United States acted in a way which helped big business and harmed a major Canadian trade union struggle—although this struggle was being led by an international union, the UBRE was being supported by Canadian locals of international unions, and had been endorsed by TLC-affiliated Trades and Labour Councils in major cities.

This was one adverse circumstance. Another was the orientation of the Federal Government. Towards the end of April it set up a Royal Commission. The secretary of the Commission was the Deputy Minister of Labour, William Lyon Mackenzie King. Its other members were a B.C. judge and a clergyman. They showed their bias from the outset. "Why not return to work, pending the Commission's report", they asked miners at Ladysmith—a suggestion which was rejected.[16] The Commission's dominating idea seems to have been that solidarity was a sin, and that a sympathy movement of workers—a strike by one group of workers in support of another group—was a conspiracy. Dramatically, at one of the sessions of the Commission, Mackenzie King produced the following exchange of telegrams between the officers of the WFM local at Nanaimo, and a leader of the organization in the United States, William Haywood: From Nanaimo to Denver, Colorado: "Ladysmith asks Cumberland out in sympathy". From Denver, the reply by William Haywood and Charles Moyers: "We approve of calling out any or all men necessary to win at Ladysmith. Organize Japanese and Chinese if possible."[17] In order to prove that the coincidence of the rail and coal strikes was collusion, King said the aim in the coal strike was to cut off the CPR's fuel supply. Now if this was so, then from a union standpoint, it was commendable. However, the Commission's own evidence indicated that it was the coal owners who had provoked the strike. For instance, there was the provocative action of the Wellington Colliery Company in posting a notice that, as of April 1, the mines would be closed.

But the Commission made it a trial of motives. There were facts, it said, and there was "the true inwardness of the facts ... The actual occurrences are the demonstration that there has indeed been conspiracy". Bitterly, the WFM leader in the U.S., William Haywood, said in May, 1903: "It seems that the Western Federation of Miners is on trial in Canada, but our members will keep the union banner flying!"

Then came the Commission's Report. It proposed that unions be incorporated, and that the Federal Government be empowered to stop strikes and refer issues to courts whose decisions would be binding for one year. These were proposals which, in the words of a committee at a TLC convention held somewhat later, "could strike a severe blow at all labour organizations".

The Commission's Proceedings and Report are documents throwing a powerful light on Canadian labour history. They are skillfully produced. The Mackenzie King hand is at work: diligent, methodical, scholarly. Almost certainly his is the hand which wrote, at the close of the Report that "the machine should be the servant of man, and not man the slave of the machine".[18]

Here is the first elfin note of *Industry and Humanity*.* The ineffable strategist of capitalism in Canada, Mackenzie King, is serving his apprenticeship here on the backs of the railroad workers, and developing those qualities later to stand him in good stead—a roving eye for conservative labour leaders; an alertness to the possibilities of reactionaries at U.S. headquarters; roseate sentiments; a devious type of employer-employee mediation which sometimes leaves the union enervated and a strike petered out to a loss; an intellect strong but cluttered by the constant impulse to dissemble employer aims; a man pining for the shades of his grandfather, William Lyon Mackenzie, but lacking the grandfather's quality. For, the grandson has decided early in life that he will not lead a struggle for Canadian independence and basic social progress, but will reconcile himself to the domination of big business and imperialism.

However, beyond the person Mackenzie King, is the employer class policy he helped fashion, and whose necessity he was intelligent enough to perceive. It was a policy which sprang from Canada's social reality, and was devised to solve a problem posed by that reality—how to contain an advancing labour movement in the condition of advancing monopoly capitalism. And here were the main points of the policy: Make some concessions, reforms. Keep them to a minimum. Time and funnel them so that conservative labour leaders and conservative-led international unions get the credit, while the mass of the trade union membership, and along with them the militant trade unionists who had sacrificed themselves to get these concessions in the first place, take a back seat. Finally, combine these concessions with coercion when that is absolutely necessary, but avoid too strong reprisals if possible.

That was the policy. It worked. Combined with such factors as the overall weakness in the forces of the trade union movement; the

---

* Title of a work published by W. L. Mackenzie King in 1918.

constant pressure of big business, domestic and foreign; the problem of craft union fragmentation as opposed to organization by industry; the tendency to domination by international unions based on the United States—it played its part in producing an inclination to class collaboration, which to a given degree, affected a section of the trade union officialdom, and continued to be one significant factor in Canadian trade union evolution down through the years.

This was the Royal Commission of 1903, and this its role. Combined with other adverse circumstances—a CPR powerful and hostile, a Dunsmuir coal ownership hard-set against trade unionism, sabotage by the standard railroad brotherhoods—there was a resultant force, and in the concrete circumstances, that force overcame another powerful force—the workers' economic power, solidarity and will to win. The CPR workers returned to their jobs without the union recognition and wage increases they had sought. The UBRE did not succeed in establishing itself. A great opportunity was lost for Canadian rail unionism in particular, for trade unionism in general.

CPR Shopmen's Strike:

The year 1908 brought another battle against the CPR—the Shopmen's strike. It involved 8,000 mechanics at Montreal, Winnipeg and other centres. The causes were — first, the CPR's refusal to recognize the union, a "mechanic's federation"; and second, the company's desire to change established rates. Through August and September the battle raged. At Montreal, hundreds of strikers picketed the Angus Shops gates on Rachel Street East near Davidson Street. Sometimes strikers and their wives gathered in the vicinity of Masson and Papineau Streets, met strike-breakers and chastised them. A Montreal *Star* issue of 1908 describes one battle at the company gates: "Going off at the double, they (60 police) charged the crowd, truncheons swinging." At Montreal's Monument National, trade unionists met to raise funds for the strikers. An entry in the minute book of the Montreal Trades and Labour Council for September 1908 states: "A hundred non-union men joined the walk-out."

Winnipeg was another major centre. Here, 500 mechanics walked out; and the CPR shops took on the appearance of a fortress, with newly erected gates closed tight, and fences patrolled by special police.

The CPR fought the strike with everything it had. It secured warrants for the arrest of strikers in Montreal. It brought into Montreal "strike-breakers armed to the teeth with revolvers"—so a union lawyer charged. It used British and U.S. immigrants as strike-breakers.

The strike was defeated. One reason was insufficient solidarity and united action. But this was no Greek fate. It was the product of the craft and class collaboration policy pursued by conservative trade union officials based mostly on international headquarters in the United States.

There was vice-president Morrissey of the Brotherhood of Railway Trainmen. During the strike he came to Montreal. How much heart he had in this struggle whose success meant so much to railroad union-ism is indicated by what he said: "My visit had nothing to do with the strike!"

Again, the terms of settlement were engineered with the help of pro-employer politicians, and were not good. They included a vague promise by the company "to use all reasonable means to find employ-ment" for the strikers.

Finally, the strikers were not properly consulted. When the Mont-real strikers heard about the settlement, they would not believe it. Assembled at St. Joseph Hall on Ste. Catherine East, they cried: "No surrender! The strike goes on!"—and sang "The Maple Leaf". Next morning, 1,000 were out at the Angus Shop gates, picketing all over again.

At Winnipeg, the hue and cry from the rank and file was such that the rail unions set up a committee of enquiry. The committee's report was a damning indictment of class collaboration. It criticized the western strike leaders for "calling off the strike—without having ob-tained a definite satisfactory term from the company" and proposed that from now on a referendum vote be held before a strike is settled. However, it cleared the strike leaders from charges they had been bribed by the company.

Like the UBRE strike of 5 years earlier, this strike was another opportunity lost, another defeat where there might have been victory. But it had positive repercussions too. It stimulated moves to federa-tion among railroad shop unions; and it set union men to thinking about industrial unionism, political action and social reconstruction.

3. STRUGGLES IN COAL, TEXTILE, CLOTHING

Coal Mining:

Canadian history should be approached from a coal miner's point of view. That would give us something basic. In 1900-1914 there was politics aplenty—politics at Ottawa and the provincial capitals. But there was also the politics of the people—their daily struggle. The coal miners were foremost exponents of this latter politics. They conducted prolonged strikes, sometimes lasting more than a year: stubborn battles in the face of callous companies, pro-employer legislators, military-scale operations by police and army, prosecutions in courts. Between 1901 and 1915, 78,000 coal miners were involved in strikes. This was the largest number for any industry. Total time lost as a result was 43% of total time lost for all strikes in Canada in this period.[19]

The Cape Breton coal strike of 1909-11 was one such battle. Led by the United Mine Workers of America,* it involved about 1,500 miners mostly employees of the Cumberland Railway and Coal Company. The main demand was higher wages and union recognition. Such was the miners' spirit that when the strike ended, out of the original 1,500 who went on strike, only 34 had broken ranks and of these only 8 were miners. The strike leader, J. B. McLachlan, later told the 1911 TLC convention: "The company admitted it could not work the mines. For 17 months they tried to start the mines and failed."[19a] But again, there were formidable obstacles. Militia was dispatched to the strike scene. And immigrants were sent in to work the mines. So, the miners decided to retreat, but did so in an orderly way and ended the strike with all re-hired and no wage cuts.

Apart from Cape Breton, Nova Scotia, the other coal-mining centres were in Alberta and B.C. Here, too, unionism developed. As early as 1891, a union contract was negotiated on Vancouver Island, between the Mine Labourers' Protective Association and the New Vancouver Coal Mining Company. Coal miners' unionism progressed more rapidly after the Western Federation of Miners entered the field—in 1901 it led an important strike at Rossland, B.C. By 1903, the WFM was implanted at Nanaimo, Fernie, Michel, Morrissey and Crow's Nest Pass. Later WFM headquarters in the United States conceded its coal jurisdiction to the UMWA, and confined itself henceforth to hard-rock mining. So subsequent coal battles were fought under the UMW banner. In 1906 there was a coal strike at Lethbridge, Alberta—Mackenzie King helped settle it. In 1911, 7,000 coal miners at 18 coal mines in the Crow's Nest Pass went on strike. The strike lasted 7 months and ended with a partial victory for the union.[20]

---

* The original union of the Cape Breton coal miners was the Provincial Workmen's Association, founded 1879. By the turn of the century its leadership had declined in militancy. A move developed to join the United Mine Workers of America. The company, for its part, was not disposed to break its relations with the PWA and extend recognition to the UMW—which, in the given circumstances, had emerged as an instrument of the Cape Breton coal miners' militancy. A referendum was held among the miners to decide which union they wanted. The UMW won, but the PWA did not accept the result. Then the miners went on strike under the UMW banner.

Then came the biggest battle of all in 1912. 4,000 Vancouver Island miners went on strike. They faced immense difficulties: militia—"half-clad Welsh barbarians"; judges who declared picketing illegal and sentenced miners to jail; a provincial Minister of Labour who sided with the company. For two years they fought on. They did not win but the battle blazed into their minds and became part of their manifold contribution to pre-World War I trade union struggles—against compulsory arbitration and use of militia in industrial disputes, for conditions, industrial unionism, and world peace.

Textile Unionism:

Textile strikes account for about 10% of the total time lost in strikes between 1901 and 1915. There were strikes at Cornwall, Ont., 1901; at Milltown, N.B., 1903; at Windsor, N.S., 1905.[21] The biggest movement was in the Quebec cotton industry. Between 1900 and 1908 there were 40 strikes and lockouts at Montreal, Valleyfield, Magog, Montmorency and other centres, of which about half were won.[22]

Valleyfield was a storm centre. Three strikes were fought here in 1901-1902. The first, in October 1901, was a sympathy strike. Labourers engaged in construction struck for an increase. When troops were sent in, 3,000 cotton workers walked out in a protest strike. Mackenzie King arrived on the scene. He showed skill. The troops were withdrawn, and the cotton strikers went back to work.[23] In 1902 there was another strike involving 2,500 workers. This time the cause was discharge of a worker. The strike ended 10 days later, when the worker was reinstated.

The big development in organization came in 1906. Cotton workers organized in 14 locals affiliated to the United Federation of Textile Workers of America—an international union. Soon after, the Canadian members decided to cut their U.S. connections. Thus came about the Federation of Textile Workers of Canada, established September 1906. It grew fast. Most cotton workers in Montreal joined—at the Hochelaga, Merchants and Cote St. Paul mills. So did workers at Valleyfield, Magog and Montmorency. The union spread to Ontario—a local was set up at Paris, probably at Penman's, where organization had developed a few years earlier.

In this its heyday, the FTWC fought major battles. In 1907 it led a strike at Valleyfield, which involved 2,000 workers and lasted 10 days. It also led a strike at Magog. This was caused by a company attempt to bring in a "yellow dog" agreement. 300 workers refused to sign. They were joined by 350 more, and also by employees at the Cotton Printing Works. The strike was settled after 3 weeks.

The overall result of the 1907 strike movement was a wage increase of about 10%.[24] This was the prelude to the still bigger strike movement of 1908. On Saturday morning April 25, workers arriving at the Montreal Mills of Dominion Textile and at the Montreal Cottons in Valleyfield, found the following notice posted up:

"A reduction of 10% in wages to all employees will go into effect on the 4th of May, 1908. Signed, Dominion Textile Company Limited."[25]

The company, it would appear, had decided to revenge itself on the workers for their victory the year before. At Montreal, Valleyfield, Magog, Montmorency Falls, 6,000 Dominion Textile workers went on strike. They fought for a month, but did not win. However, such was the magnitude of their battle, that a Royal Commission was set up by the federal government.* The Commissioner was Mackenzie King.

From the Commission came a huge volume of proceedings, and a report. These too are documents throwing a precise, powerful and prejudiced light on Canadian labour history. In the report, Mackenzie King criticized the strikers, and said their strike was "unwise and ill-timed". True the company was also at fault, but mostly it was the workers' fault. The trouble was that Dominion Textile workers were in the grip of an illusion. They believed that the *cause* of wage increases was organization and struggles, and were the more inclined to believe it because this had been the sequence of events in 1907. As King put it: "It was a *post hoc ergo propter hoc*** sort of reasoning which unconsciously filled their minds."[26] There must be some way to prevent these dangerous clashes between Capital and Labour. King said that at Fall River, Mass., the United Textile Workers of America, AFL, had found a way. It had concluded a sliding scale agreement with the employers under which wages would vary with the cost of cotton and the price of cotton products. The result by May 1908 was a disastrous reduction in wages.***[27] King proposed this type of agreement

---

* Royal Commission to inquire into Industrial Disputes in the Cotton Factories of the Province of Quebec (1908).

** "After this therefore *because* of this."

*** Rank and File revulsion against the practices of the UTW-AFL—a typical international union of the AFL—brought about the famous Lawrence, Massachusetts strike of 1912, led by the Industrial Workers of the World. Among the IWW leaders were William Haywood and Elizabeth Gurley Flynn. During one of the great demonstrations which marked the strike, a women textile worker carried a sign which read: "We want bread but we want roses too!" Thus came about the Labour song: "Bread and Roses":

"As we go marching, marching, in the beauty of the day,
A million darkened kitchens, a thousand mill-lofts grey,
Are touched with all the radiance that a beauteous sun discloses,
For the people hear us singing—Bread and Roses! Bread and roses!"

for the Canadian industry. He also proposed "Labour partnership"—an arrangement under which, he said, the joint interests of the employers and employees would become "apparent to both parties". These were doubtful remedies. But he also recommended a "limitation of the total hours of labour"; and that meant the textile workers were beginning to win from government at least preliminary recognition of the need for shorter hours. So, the logic of their struggle was proving superior to King's logic, and it was not they but he who was in the grip of an illusion.

Clothing Unionism:

Developments in the clothing industry prior to World War I is intermingled with the immigrants who came in thousands to Canada. Light on the conditions of these immigrants is thrown by this entry in the Minute Book of the Montreal Trades and Labour Council in 1901: "Shiploads of Europeans are being put to work at scandalously low wages at the Markman's Clothing Factory in Montreal." The industry was located mostly in Montreal, Toronto and Winnipeg. It was largely owned by Jews, and many workers were Jews. The Jewish owners paid the Jewish workers wages as low as those they paid the Galicians, Poles or French Canadians—and demonstrated thus their freedom from race prejudice.

Around issues such as abolition of sweat shops, child labour, "home work", the clothing workers began to organize. Unions in the field then included the Journeymen Tailors Union (a fore-runner of the Amalgamated Clothing Workers of America), the United Garment Workers of America, and the United Hat and Cap Workers. The National Trades and Labour Congress also tried its hand at organization. In 1904 it was considering hiring "two Hebrew organizers to better organize the Jewish working people".

An important reform affecting this industry came early in the century —the first Dominion Government Fair Wage legislation. One of its clauses aimed to deny government orders for articles such as postal uniforms to factories where subnormal conditions prevailed.

In their battle to improve conditions, the clothing workers fought many strikes. Between 1900 and 1914, 40,000 of them took part in 158 strikes. The time lost in these strikes was 10% of total time lost for all strikes in Canadian industry between 1901 and 1915. In 1913 4,500 clothing workers at Montreal were involved in a 6 weeks strike, and 1,000 clothing workers at Toronto took part in a strike which lasted a year. At Hamilton 2,000 were on strike, at Montreal 1,000 operatives were on strike for 7 months.[28]

CHAPTER 6

TRADE UNIONS AND PUBLIC LIFE
1900-1914

1. TRADE UNION RIGHTS

Role of Employers:

As the trade union movement grew, the employers combatted it, and they used weapons such as dismissals, misuse of immigrants, blacklists, labour spies, detectives, private police.

Tens of thousands of immigrants were then coming to Canada. Sometimes employers gave them false information and brought them into strike situations. During a strike at the T. Eaton Company in Toronto, the company brought in a cloakmaker from Europe, Alexander Redder. When Redder discovered why he had been brought to Canada, he told the T. Eaton agent: "Give me some fare money so I can get back to New York." The agent refused. In despair Redder took his own life.[1]

Not every immigrant chose to fight this lonely way. During the Canadian Northern Railway strike of 1902, the company tried to convince Doukhobors to act as strike-breakers. They refused and demanded their return fare. A trade unionist wrote in the Winnipeg *Voice:* "The Doukhobor does not live on the moral plane of a railroad exploiter. His philosophy and humanity are pitched in too high a key." During the 1903 UBRE strike, CPR officials haunted the immigration hall at Winnipeg and sought to engage immigrants as strike-breakers. The officials were rebuffed on at least one occasion by a group of Galician immigrants. In the Grand Trunk strike of 1907, the company brought in British machinists to break the strike. However, they were members of the British Amalgamated Society of Engineers, and refused to let themselves be used this way. In this misuse of immigrants, the Salvation Army played a role at times dubious. It helped bring immigrants and said they were bound for the farms, but sometimes they turned up in the cities. The "Army's" practice prompted the *Industrial Banner* to complain in 1907 that "mechanics are more profitable than beef or mutton". During a dispute at Victoria, B.C., in 1907, Scottish immigrants said Salvation Army advertisements had encouraged them to come to Canada. But the "Army" had not told them they were to be strike-breakers. They charged the "Army" with deception and each demanded $250 in compensation.[2] The Canadian Manufacturers' Association was also heavily involved in similar abuses of immigrants.[3]

The trade union movement protested these practices and demanded improvements in the Immigration Act. In 1905 it won a partial victory —an amendment banning the bringing in of immigrants under false representations. The Deputy Minister of Labour, Mackenzie King, contributed to the adoption of this legislation, and this should be remembered, but so should the immigrants who refused to let themselves be used against their fellow-Canadians in time of trouble, the Jews, Scots, Doukhobors and Galicians, the man Alexander Redder who took his life sooner than be a strike-breaker.

So much for abuse of immigrants. Employer and police violence in strikes were another acute problem. In 1903 during the UBRE strike, CPR Special Police killed Frank Rodgers, a fishermen's union leader in Vancouver.[4] In the CPR Shopmen's strike of 1908, a strike breaker at Winnipeg shot Robert Kirk, a member of the Machinists' Union.[5] During a coal handlers strike at Port Arthur, police shot 2 strikers, the Deprenzo brothers. One was shot 7 times, the other 5. Then they (the Deprenzo brothers, not the police) were charged with attempted murder, convicted and sentenced to 10 years in jail.[6]

There were the blacklists. Early in the century a CPR official sent a letter to a railway company official in the U.S. advising him about the union connection of a worker.*[7] That was the blacklist in operation. It was not an isolated case. And yet, through the period under review and indeed, through a century of Canadian labour history, this writer does not know of a single employer who went to jail because he blacklisted a union member, although, from a moral and human standpoint, such an offence is probably much graver than a striker punching a strike-breaker on the nose in a picket-line encounter.

Another device was the labour spy. In 1900, the J. B. King Shoe Company of Toronto hired spies who worked alongside the regular employees. As union members were "fingered", they were "fired"

---

* A copy of the letter is contained in the proceedings of the Royal Commission on Industrial Disputes in the Province of British Columbia, 1903.

(dismissed). The CPR was a master in labour espionage. "... Paid hirelings of the CPR had worked their way into the union, taken a leading part in its deliberations, initiated new members and duly reported all that had taken place to their masters." So it was testified at the 1903 Commission.*[8] The CPR Secret Police succeeded in corrupting a lesser UBRE official — of weak character, in poor health, with financial difficulties, uneasy about past wrong doings—in short, suitable bait. CPR detectives met him, and threatened to expose him. He then signed this statement: "I ...., organizer of the UBRE, do hereby offer my services to the Special Service Department of the Canadian Pacific Railway Company."

There were the private police. In 1912, TLC president Watters went to Cape Breton to help J. B. McLachlan organize at the Dominion Iron and Steel Company. When he came to the union hall, he saw company police lined up in front. That year the TLC convention condemned "hirelings of the companies used as tools to pressure their fellows".[9] In 1912 the TLC demanded that company police be outlawed.

There were the hated private detective agencies. Many, like the Pinkertons, had been organized in the United States—another of the union-smashing techniques highly developed in that country. One was the Thiel Agency. In 1911, the Montreal Trades and Labour Council minute book reported that a Thiel detective had hounded a Montreal union offical who was organizing the street railway workers.[10] In 1914 the TLC demanded action leading to an end to employer use of private detective agencies in industrial relations.[11]

The State:

So far employer coercion has been considered. There was also the state: courts, police, militia, legislative bodies.

First the courts. In the Criminal Code there were laws against conspiracy and watching and besetting. Judges would sometimes use such laws to hand down decisions harmful to Labour—for instance, bans or limitations of picketing. This happened during strikes at Brantford and Hamilton, and also during a strike at the Toronto Massey-Harris plant. The trade union movement complained that laws did not precisely define offenses, and that different judges interpreted the same law differently.

Injunctions were a constant trouble. In 1908 a Winnipeg court ordered members of the Plumbers Union to restrict activities with

* Royal Commission on Industrial Disputes in the Province of British Columbia, 1903.

regard to "persuading or inducing working men to leave the employment of the plaintiff and not enter his employment" and also with regard to watching and besetting.[12] This was in connection with a building trades strike which began in Winnipeg in 1907. There was the injunction in operation. One celebrated case in the early years of the century was the injunction against the Moulders Union boycott of Gurney Stoves across the country. Another was the injunction at Winnipeg in 1907 during a strike at the Vulcan Iron Works.

This was the role of the courts. There was also the police—municipal and federal. The Royal Canadian Mounted Police (Royal Northwest Mounted Police) was then beginning its dubious career—dubious in matters labour. The RCMP is "an annex to corporations and companies" said the TLC in 1906. That was in connection with the Force's part in a coal strike that year in Lethbridge, Alberta.[13]

More serious still was the use of the army. In 1906, militia armed with Gattling machine guns took over the streets of Winnipeg in the course of a street railway strike. In 1909, militia went down to Cape Breton during the coal strike there, and on one occasion confronted the strikers with fixed bayonets—an action taken over the protests of the mayor. "Coal barons own the government," protested the *Industrial Banner*. Later a TLC convention demanded a Royal Commission investigation into this use of militia at Cape Breton. In 1909 the TLC executive committee stated:

"It is a matter for serious consideration that soldiers can be called out without apparent excuse but simply at the behest of some capitalistic organization to oppress and intimidate wage earners who happen to be on strike."[14]

In later years the movement demanded that the use of militia in industrial disputes be halted.*

Finally there was anti-labour legislation. The Industrial Disputes Investigation Act of 1907 was a major departure. The Act outlawed strikes in public utilities, mining and railroads until a conciliation board had submitted a report. Basically this was coercive legislation, since it curbed the right to strike. But the Act also provided for mediation. In this way the Act had two decisive aspects—coercion and mediation. Now *there was no necessary connection* between these two aspects. However, the government chose to connect them in the same law, and place thereby the *stamp* of a *real and necessary connection*, on what was an *arbitrary* connection. That *is to say, the connection was* real enough once it was in the statute books, became incorporated in

---

* This demand was largely won in the 1920s.

management-labour relations, and through the accumulation of precedents—even became incorporated in people's minds as the fixed idea: This is the way things are, this is the way things must be! But, in the more *durable* sense, there was no necessary connection between mediation *and* coercion—between government assistance in solving disputes through conciliation and arbitration, on the one hand—*and* curbs on strikes on the other.

These were some of the deeper problems involved in the IDI Act of 1907. The plain facts are that from the outset, *many* trade unionists opposed the Act, but probably *most* supported it. This was because the Act seemed to provide a way of preventing or postponing long and costly strikes. Also, the Act catered to those trade union officials —often of international unions in the United States—who were inclined to soft settlements rather than hard negotiations and strikes when need be. Again, there was the illusion that arbitration would be fair and square, and that the "third man" or chairman of an arbitration board would be neutral. But this chairman—in practice often appointed by the government—would swing his weight frequently to the kind of settlement which pleased the companies rather than the workers.

Gradually the results began to come in. During the Grand Trunk Railway strike of 1907, the workers at the Montreal Pointe St. Charles shops (to-day called the CNR shops) wanted to strike in solidarity with their fellow workers in the Ontario shops. But that would have meant violating the IDI Act. They did not do it. So the Act helped break the strike. Then there was the CPR shopmen's strike of 1908. The chairman of the Western Strike Committee said at the time that the effect of the Act was to stop a union from striking when striking was timely.[15]

These harsh experiences engendered a change of heart in the movement. The cycle of change, from approval to disapproval, is registered in votes taken at successive TLC conventions: In 1907, a majority of 81-19 turned down an amendment seeking restoration of Labour's right to strike in industries affected by the Act. In 1911, the majority defeated another resolution demanding the Act's repeal, but this time by the narrow margin of 5 votes. Finally in 1916, the majority adopted a resolution demanding the complete repeal of the Act. So now the majority were saying the minority had been right! But 9 precious years have passed by—9 years of heart-break and defeat—when there could have been victory, and the Act, now embedded in law and practice, was not to be dislodged by a vote at a trade union convention.

2. THE LEGISLATIVE STRUGGLE

At the Federal Level. In the Provinces:

In the period under review, there was some legislative progress. First, the federal level. In 1900 there was a breakthrough: adoption of the Dominion Fair Wage legislation; establishment of a sub-department of Labour, monthly Labour Gazette and labour library; the beginnings of a statistical service for industrial relations and conditions. In 1909, the sub-department of Labour was converted into a full-scale department, and William Lyon Mackenzie King—appointed in 1900 as deputy minister responsible for Labour—became Canada's first Minister of Labour. Another forward step was that the annual meetings between union representatives and government—begun in the previous decade—were now regular. In his new capacity as Minister of Labour, Mackenzie King participated at one such meeting in 1910. The TLC executive committee commented later: "King said that he could not say yes or no, but would further the workers' interest in every legitimate way."[16]

Despite this legislative progress, many demands were not met. In 1910, Alphonse Verville—a labour member of Parliament from Quebec and member of Plumbers Local 144—introduced a bill for the 8-hour day in government works. Four years later the bill had not reached second reading.[17] Legislation for old age and widows pensions existed scarce at all. "Every day the police courts of the cities are full of citizens arrested as vagrants, their offence being that they are too old to get a job," said D. J. O'Donaghue—TLC solicitor and son of the trade union pioneer—in 1911.[18]

In 1912, Mrs. Evans, residing at 1460 Des Ecores Street, Montreal, wrote the TLC convention and proposed that the government provide an allowance for each child of a widow and that the widow "should be allowed so much per week to keep her family from starvation . . . Do you think a woman can save enough of her husband's pay . . . what with the high cost of living, and the rent and clothes we buy . . . Please read my letter to the men at the convention".[19] The trade union movement adopted the demand for widows and old age pensions. On the eve of World War I, prospects for enactment of this legislation had brightened. Then the Government became involved in war. Pensions were shelved.

Why was progress not greater? One reason was that not only the unions but also the employers were developing their legislative initiative. In 1903, the Canadian Manufacturers Association was established. From its inception it showed drive and energy—commendable qualities. The CMA blocked a union label bill, and a conciliation bill introduced into the House of Commons by a labour M.P. from Winnipeg, A. W. Puttee. In 1907, the CMA dispatched to its member employers this moving appeal for solidarity:

"If you have ever endeavoured to fight a bill singlehanded you will appreciate what a tremendous task it is to produce results. As an individual manufacturer you have neither the time nor the money to devote to work of this kind ... The Association needs your assistance. A successful campaign against the 8-hour bill alone has saved the price of your membership fee a hundred times over. This is but one of a long list of items which go to make a splendid record of parliamentary achievements."[20]

So much for the federal sphere. In the provinces too, progress was slow. As late as 1906, prison labour was still in effect in Ontario. In all the provinces legislation for school attendance was inadequate. In 1908 there was a forward step in Ontario. The Legislature adopted an amendment which prohibited employment of workers under the age of 14 in factories, and under 12 in retail establishments. This was a reform but was far from meeting the demand then being pressed by the unions—total prohibition of employment under 16.

The year 1914 brought a victory of greater sweep, one significant for all Canada: the Ontario Workmen's Compensation Bill. A previous chapter has outlined how Workmen's Compensation legislation began in the latter years of the 19th century—inadequate legislation. In 1910, Ontario unions opened up the fight for a more effective workmen's compensation law. A key demand was that only employers pay to the compensation fund, not employees. The employers opposed this. "Employers and workmen should pay", said the CMA. The CMA also stood for "contributory negligence"—meaning that when an employee was injured, and it was established that he was at fault or partly at fault, he should be paid less compensation. Another point of contention was—how much compensation. The CMA proposed that the maximum disability payment be $20 or $25 a month.

As the deadline approached for adoption of the Bill, employer feelings rose to fever pitch. "Socialism of the worst kind ... a vicious measure!" exclaimed Senator Edwards, a member of an employer delegation—during a CMA presentation to the government January 1914. Sir William Meredith, the commissioner appointed by the Ontario Government, commented: "I cannot think any employer ever consented to increase his liability, unless he saw it coming".

The unions persisted. The Bill was adopted. It provided for a permanent total disability payment amounting to 55% of the average earnings of the worker during the 12-month period prior to injury.

Employers were obliged to take out insurance, so that their ability to make compensation payments would be guaranteed. Payment to the compensation fund was to be by employers only. Finally, protection was provided against employer action in courts to block payment of compensation.

A great principle had been won—co-responsibility of employers and government for injury on the job. This kind of victory helped convince the union rank and file their movement had a future.[21]

3. POLITICAL ACTION

Experiences, 1900-14:

"Little or no result achieved" in social legislation—the TLC executive committee would report to conventions year after year. Rebuffs from employers and government, rebuffs in efforts to secure the union's legal status—this was the pattern. What was to be done? The more far-seeing trade unionists said the first thing was to strengthen the unions and build a united, effective, Canadian, industrial-oriented trade union movement. This side of the question shall be outlined in the next chapter. They also said the movement must go into politics—initially to curb the growing power of capital in government, eventually to substitute for that power, the power and leadership of the class they deemed most numerous, productive and essential—the working class.

The reader will recall that the 1899 TLC convention had decided to submit to its affiliates a referendum on political action. This was done. The result showed a large majority for political action. The 1903 TLC convention reaffirmed the policy:

"Resolved that this parliament of labour declare for political action to be taken by the working people of Canada, in nominating and electing labour candidates for parliament, along the lines of independent politics, apart from either of the existing parties."[22]

To a degree — and this is indicated in the motion just cited — the movement was considering *direct* political action by unions and union centres. J. D. Marks—prominent in the affairs of the London Trades and Labour Council, told the 1903 convention: "The various organizations are hereby advised to place independent labour candidates in the field wherever possible".[23] Soon after, the Trades and Labour Councils at Vancouver and Berlin (Kitchener) were calling meetings to select candidates for the 1904 federal election.[24]

Winnipeg Labour helped blaze the trail. A labour party had been set up there in 1900. In 1902 the Winnipeg Trades and Labour Council elected a political action committee and instructed it to add to its numbers from other groups in the labour movement.[25] The resultant body was called the Labour Representation League. In 1903 the League participated in the Winnipeg municipal elections, and in 1904 it campaigned to re-elect one of Canada's first labour M.P.s., Arthur W. Puttee, member for Winnipeg Centre and editor of the *Voice*. Puttee's main campaign issue was a publicly-owned railway. He was supported by two lifelong friends of Labour and servants of the Church-Rev. Ben Spence and Rev. A. E. Smith. The League's funds were scanty, so it cut rents to the bone by meeting in the open air. The campaign song was Ebenezer Elliott's hymn, "When Wilt Thou Save the People?":

"When wilt thou save the people,
O God of mercy, when?
The people, Lord, the people
Not thrones and crowns, but men!"

The hymn was good but Puttee lost. At Nanaimo, B.C., Ralph Smith was more fortunate. He was re-elected, but meanwhile he had switched to the Liberal ticket. He taunted Puttee for losing, but Puttee said—better to lose on a labour ticket than win on an employers'.[26]

British Columbia was another leader in labour political action. In 1903, the Vancouver Trades and Labour Council resolved:

"Be it resolved that any member of a labour organization found on a capitalist platform be regarded with suspicion as decoys of the wage earners."[27]

In 1904, two Socialist Party members, Kingsley and Hawthornewaite, were sitting as members of the provincial legislature.

Labour political success in the municipal and provincial fields strengthened the desire for more sweeping central action, and the more so because of breakthroughs in Western Europe and Great Britain—election of 35 British Labour Party Members of Parliament in 1906. Thus came about the political action debate at the 1906 TLC convention. The progressive and socialist delegates at this convention —particularly from Western Canada—pressed for a labour party, a disciplined party, they said, whose representatives in legislative bodies carried through party decisions.

These delegates might have succeeded had it not been for James Simpson—a leading Toronto trade unionist and member of ITU Local 91. Simpson said that as a socialist he could not support another party, not even one sponsored by the unions; and he called on the convention to endorse the Socialist Party of Canada. In words this was socialist, in practice it blocked the advance of the whole trade union movement to political action. Now the conservative trade union officials in the United States and Canada were also opposed to a labour political party. So, in the result, Simpson's policy coincided with their's. In later years, Simpson became a reliable servant of conservative international unionism in the United States and its counterpart in Canada.

In this way the political action debate at the 1906 convention became a battleground of 3 trends: *First,* support for a labour party based on the unions. *Second,* opposition to such party—from the standpoint of "pure and simple" "business unionism". *Third,* the splitting, simon-pure socialist doctrinairism of Simpson. The outcome was that the delegates adopted a compromise resolution drafted by TLC secretary-treasurer, P. M. Draper—a dedicated, shrewd, conservative trade unionist. The motion endorsed "sending representatives of labour to parliament or to local legislatures", and instructed the provincial executives of the Congress to convene conventions of trade unionists and other groups to set up a labour party.

The Convention also adopted a model constitution for a Canadian Labour Party (it was attached to the 1906 proceedings of the Congress).[28] The constitution's preamble said the Labour Party opposed all types of politics that conflict with the working class, and would seek to replace the present political system "with a social and co-operative form of government". Also, a model constitution was laid down for provincial units of the Labour Party. It provided for labour clubs in the constituencies, and city committees consisting of 5 delegates from each labour club and 15 delegates from the local Trades and Labour Council. Attached to these model constitutions was the TLC Platform of Principles—to serve as a guide for the party organization.

This was the 1906 decision. It had a more questionable side. The motion said that after the provincial founding convention for a party had been convened, "the functions of the political executive in this regard shall cease" (the political executive was the name given to the trade union committee in each province which would initiate the political action). The motion also stated that "Congress has been and must continue to be the legislative mouthpiece of organized labour in Canada, irrespective of and independent of any body engaged in the effort to send representatives of the people to Parliament".[29]

This meant the Congress was going backwards at the same time it went forward. It was yielding to the demand for a party, but backsliding from the idea of Canada's trade union pioneers in the 19th century that the unions should be the direct continuing basis for such a party. Also, it was avoiding a clear commitment to the organization of a party at the federal level—and yet convention after convention of the Congress ever since 1883 had been pressing towards just this objective.

In the passage cited above, the operative word is "independent". Independent of what? Of employers or Labour? When the 19th century pioneers used the term "independent" political action, they meant independent of parties dominated by employers. But now the Congress leaders were saying this also meant independent of Organized Labour. Thereby they were initiating an idea, later to be a fixed dogma in the movement, that the unions' continuing, active commitment to political action was incompatible with their freedom in the economic, organizational and legislative fields. This was a confused idea which sprang from the confused realities of the time; and one such reality was the international unions' opposition to political action, and the tendency of Congress leaders to balance between this attitude in the U.S. and the demand of many trade unionists in Canada for political action.

Some progress there was. In the municipal field, by 1914 labour representatives sat on city councils at Montreal, Toronto, Fort William and other centres. In the provinces, there were labour parties in Quebec, Ontario and Manitoba. Federally, a labour M.P., Alphonse Verville was elected to parliament from the Maisonneuve constituency in Montreal. Still, the partisans of political action were dissatisfied. In 1908, the Quebec executive committee of the TLC demanded that the political labour movement be "under the direct guidance of the Congress". At the 1910 TLC convention, some delegates reminded their colleagues that "many conventions of this Congress have urged upon the wage workers of Canada the absolute necessity of seizing the federal and provincial law-making powers".[30] These appeals were largely unheeded. That was tragic. Canada was still young, its politics plastic. A more vital trade union movement would have made a greater impress on events.

4. TRADE UNIONISM AND SOCIAL RECONSTRUCTION

Continuing Growth of Labour Consciousness:

What should be the movement's orientation to the social system as a whole? This was being considered more actively. Strikes were having a profound effect—the 20th century was ushered in by a wave of strikes. In 1901, a writer in the Winnipeg *Voice* said these strikes were "but ripples before the storm": If the workers could shut down a single industry, then the day was coming when across the country they "would federate in one grand union and strike for the emancipation of labour". When that day came, "the Pinkertons and Strathcona Specials* would be seeking the shade of some dark alley. Men would cease to work for less than the full profits of their labour" and Canada would enter the era of the "great trust of the people".[31] Again, after the 1901 Trackmen's strike, some union members said that if workers could tie up a big company like the CPR,** then Labour must be prior to Capital. The CPR Shopmen's strike of 1908 made a particularly strong impact on union minds. The Winnipeg strike secretary said the strike proved that workers must take over the state: "So long as we allow governments, courts and the means of livelihood to remain in the possession of capital, so long will this unequal struggle continue."[32]

The trend to class consciousness in trade union thinking is also reflected in the attitude to strike-breakers, "scabs". The reader will recall how the Toronto printers looked on this in the 19th century. Now the problem was being considered more generally. In 1902, the president of the Winnipeg Labour Party related scabbery to the general problem of labour solidarity. In 1903, a freight handler told a Royal Commission*** how he felt about it:

Commissioners: "So there are not only scab freight, but also scab bills?"

Freight Handler: "Yes."

Commissioners: "Scab bills would infect the labour men?"

Freight Handler: "Yes."[33]

Behind "scabbery", behind the gnawing fears and economic pressures which made a working man break ranks, was the power of the employers. The nub of the social question in Canada then—as understood by socialist trade unionists was: Who owns the fields, forests, mines, factories, stores and banks? In 1903, David Halliday, a coal miner from Cumberland, B.C., gave his views to the Royal Commission:

Commissioners: "What is socialism?"

Miner: "It is the scientific analysis of human society and capitalist production... It is the emancipation of the working class. Under

---

* The Pinkertons: a U.S. private detective agency used by employers in industrial relations. The Strathcona Specials: a force of Canadian police also used in industrial disputes during the period under review.

** Canadian Pacific Railway Company.

*** Royal Commission on Industrial Disputes in the Province of British Columbia, 1903.

socialism ... the working class will control the machinery of wealth and production."

Commissioners: "Supposing the socialists get a majority of people to think that way, how are they going to effect it?"

Miner: "By capturing the reins of government. It means that the people will be the government, and all natural resources will be controlled by the people."

Commissioners: "I suppose the government would be a committee of the people?"

Miner: "It might ... if you want to obtain the scientific analysis of the situation, you could procure a copy of Karl Marx' *Capital* ... that is the groundwork of modern socialism ... the scientific analysis of capitalist production."[34]

This is how socialist ideas evolved. Organization also grew. Parties were founded in a number of provinces. In Manitoba a socialist party was functioning in 1902—its program demanded "socialization of the means of production". In 1905 the Socialist Party of Canada was established at a convention in British Columbia.

A labour and socialist press developed. In 1894 the *Voice* was established. It survived until 1923 and during most of this time, along with its successor *Western Labour News,* it was the organ of the Winnipeg Trades and Labour Council. The *Voice's* columns before World War I are impressive: agitation on overcrowded streetcars and other immediate issues; reports on urgent problems of the international workers movement—like the debate on the significance of the general strike; articles on the Marxist doctrine of historical materialism. Also it reported in detail the proceedings of the Winnipeg Trades and Labour Council, Trades and Labour Congress conventions, and the debates in the House of Commons. It brought classical literature to the workers by printing works such as Tolstoy's *Resurrection* in serial form; and it helped make known the internal problems of socialist organization by placing one of its columns at the disposal of the Socialist Party.

Other notable labour papers were the Regina *Realm* and the *Industrial Banner.* The *Realm,* organ of the Regina Trades and Labour Council, published articles explaining the basic principles of Marxist economics—the labour theory of value and the theory of surplus value —principles it deemed valuable for the labour movement. The *Industrial Banner,* a monthly founded in 1892, was published at London, Ontario and endorsed by the London Trades and Labour Council. Later it moved to Toronto, became a weekly and was endorsed by the Toronto Trades and Labour Council. In its heyday, its editor was J. D. Marks.

Internationalism:

As in the 19th century, the labour movement of Canada was developing in interaction with the world labour movement. There was a lively awareness of events in Europe, Britain, the United States—a sense of solidarity. One expression of this was Canadians' sympathy with the Russian revolution of 1905. Why did many Canadians support the revolution? Hatred for the Tsarist autocracy drenched in the blood of the Russian peoples; the strength and sweep of the Russian revolution as a genuine mass movement of workers and farmers; the memory still bright of Canada's own battle for liberty between 1837 and the end of the 19th century; finally, Quebec's struggle for its freedom and the independence of all Canada—a totally free Quebec in a totally free, totally united Canada—these were some of the motives which moved Canadians to support the Russian revolution. In November 1905, as the revolution was reaching its climax, Prime Minister Sir Wilfred Laurier addressed a mass meeting at Ottawa. He appealed for subscriptions to a relief fund set up for the victims of the Tsarist pogroms. The Prime Minister said:

"Russian autocracy was only reaping the fruits of what it had sown for many years during which it had refused to lend an ear to the cries of the people for more liberty and a greater share of justice. With the refusal of the Tsar to grant much-needed reform, he had invited revolution and revolution had come."[35]

On December 12, 1905, *Le Canada,* organ of the Liberal Party in Quebec, stated: "It is feared that many priests are secretly revolutionaries."[36] Two weeks later, at the height of the armed struggle in Russia, a Montreal *Gazette* editorial stated:

"The Tsar is reported to have refused absolutely to grant universal suffrage to the Russian people. What the Russian people are taking for an alternative seems likely to be far worse . . . It may make exiles of the Royal Family."[37]

The Revolution was defeated. Certain of the revolutionaries who were being hunted by the tsarist police fled the country, and some came to Canada. Thus arose the Federenko case. In August 1910, Sava Federenko, a Russian political refugee, was arrested in Winnipeg on the instigation of the tsarist authorities. A Winnipeg court ordered his extradition. That meant almost certain death. The labour movement organized a great campaign for his release, and won support from the Winnipeg and Toronto municipal councils. The Mayors of Montreal and Toronto served as trustees for the Federenko Defence Fund. Large gatherings were held. At Vancouver, thousands assembled at one of the greatest progressive meetings hitherto held in the city. At Winnipeg there was a meeting of 2,000. At Toronto, a meeting of 4,000 was addressed by the Mayor. In December 1910, Federenko won his unconditional release.

All this was the interaction of Canadian and world progress. It was a general law. There were factors which slowed it down. These included: Canada's distance from what was then the main theatre of labour struggle—Europe; also, the greater strength of capitalism in North America, and the weakness of the labour movement in Canada. However, there were factors which speeded up the development of this law. One was immigration.

At this time, hundreds of thousands of immigrants were coming to Canada, among others—English, Scots, Irish, Russians, Ukrainians, Hungarians, and Jews. They were coming from countries dominated by capitalists and landlords, bringing with them the experience of the fight, and taking their place in Canada as exploited workers. Often they were among the most exploited — it was only during and after World War I, that immigrants began to get better jobs. In other words, they were a source of super-profits for monopoly capitalism developing in Canada.

Inevitably, the struggles and progressive ideas of these immigrants fused with the developing labour movement of Canada. Again and again, in Montreal, Toronto, Winnipeg, Vancouver, it was the immigrants—Scots, English, Ukrainians, Jews, Russians—who took the lead in building the unions in the mines, lumber camps and factories. When the Swift Packing plant was being organized in Toronto, a Russian immigrant, Sayarnuk—a sailor revolutionary of the battleship Potemkin in 1905—helped lead the way. When a carpenters' union was built in Toronto in 1913, another Russian immigrant, Kochar, took the lead. At a meeting held at Massey Hall in 1913 to organize the unorganized, a Russian immigrant, Artum, was one of the speakers.[38] In battles to organize the hard rock miners at South Porcupine and Cobalt, in coal miners' unionization in Western Canada—Ukrainians and Slovaks were among the most active.[39] One of the builders of the Amalgamated Clothing Workers of America in Toronto, in the years before World War I, was a Ukrainian, John Boychuk. He was a committee member of the local which won the first Amalgamated contract.

The Jews played an important part. They brought with them the liberating ideas of the Russian revolution, combined with progressive Yiddish culture—the intellectual tradition of a crushed people who would not give up. In Montreal, Toronto, Winnipeg, they were builders of the garment unions, and contributed many activists to the labour movement. A Russian Jew, Alamazov, was killed by the Royal Canadian Mounted Police during the 1919 Winnipeg general strike.

The Finns were also a dynamic factor. In 1912, John Ahlquvist was an officer of the Journeymen Tailors' Union of Toronto. Carl Lindalla was a mayoralty candidate of the Social Democratic Party of Canada in a Toronto municipal election held before World War I—he won 12,000 votes.

Much the same applies to the other immigrants: the English who brought with them the experience of the great trade union movement and labour party of Great Britain; the Scots who became a vital factor in centres such as Winnipeg; the Irish with their blazing hatred of imperialism.

In sum, the labour struggles and advanced ideas of these immigrants did much to build Canada. Primarily this was a matter of internal Canadian evolution, a specific thread in that evolution. However, as it turned out, it was also internationalism in action.

Unionism and Socialism:

The inter-relationship of trade unionism and socialism was a continuing vital problem. In the period under review, socialists were influencing the organized workers' movement. Many union builders among both the rank and file and leadership were socialists. This influence was reflected in policy. In 1912 the Trades and Labour Congress platform of principles included a demand for public ownership of railways, telegraphs, telephones, water works, lighting plants.

However, such was the *organic* link between the *total* labour movement and the *specific* movement for social reconstruction, that the pressures and problems which weighed on the former reproduced themselves in the latter. The crux was the emerging power of big business, and Labour's ability to build the kind of movement which could stand up to that power. So far as Labour did this, it succeeded, and this success reproduced itself in the movement for social reconstruction. Reciprocally socialist progress heartened and mobilized the total labour movement. So far as Labour did not build the kind of united militant movement which was possible in the concrete circumstances, it was inviting defeat; and this weakness reproduced itself in the socialist movement. Reciprocally, weakness in this latter movement reacted back on the labour movement as a whole. In sum, what we are dealing with here is the living, complex, highly-interactive process of development, of victory and defeat, which constituted the labour movement, as it was then.

It is in this context that mistakes in the ranks of the socialists must be considered. What were these mistakes? One was dogmatism. For instance, some socialists believed that with the advent of the trusts and their increasing power in the economy and the state, and with the advent of anti-labour legislation, the chance for success on the economic front was now slim, as was the prospect for winning strikes. These socialists inclined to the view that the role of the unions had become rather confined, that the unions could no longer be looked on as the prime lever in Labour's struggle for emancipation, that the way out was through the ballot box rather than the strike. "Socialism has superseded trade unionism as a dominant factor in the working class movement." This is how a member of the Manitoba Socialist Party put it in 1902.

These socialists were making the mistake of balancing the trade union movement against the socialist movement. They were jumping too quickly from the one to the other, and were overlooking the creative possibilities of the unions for growth and adaptation. This was a mistake. As the years went by it tended to harden into doctrinaire snobbishness, a kind of socialist looking down on the rank and file. "It is more dignified to enter socialist ranks after an unbiased study of socialism than to be kicked in through economic pressure". This is what M. D. Armstrong, a Social Democratic Party organizer said in 1913.

This was dogmatism. A worse mistake was opportunism. In the debate on political action at the Trades and Labour Congress convention of 1906, James Simpson had said:

"The best interests of the Congress will be served if we continue as a legislative body, looking to either socialists or an independent labour party to promote such legislation as this Congress shall determine at that convention".

Now, to begin with, this was dogmatism and sectarianism, Simpson was substituting the narrow political action of the Socialist Party for the political action of the trade union movement as a whole. But more important and basic was the opportunism behind this. What Simpson was saying was that the Trades and Labour Congress should confine itself to legislative action rather than develop as an effective trade union centre which furthered industrial, economic action and also fostered political action. But this policy of Simpson's *was precisely the policy of Samuel Gompers,* of international union headquarters, of business unionism-minded officials in Canada. They said: Let the AFL and international unions take care of the industrial side of things, and let the TLC serve as the international unions' "legislative mouthpiece" in Canada. Also, let the Congress keep out of political action. So in the result, Simpson's policy, though seemingly socialist, *coincided with* Samuel Gompers' anti-socialist and business union policy. Here then was one case of opportunism at work in the trade union movement of Canada.

More generally, opportunism as a trend in the labour movement, had two aspects, *economic* and *political*. On the economic side, it expressed itself in the lack of combativity to the employers, the failure to mobilize the maximum resources of the movement to meet the challenge of the employers, the failure to do what it was realistically possible to do. On the political side, opportunism expressed itself firstly in the tendency to *counterpose* trade unionism and politics; secondly, so far as political action *was* pursued, the tendency to substitute electoral objectives for the total economic and political progress of the movement—narrow parliamentary activity instead of economic and political mass action of the broad labour movement—action which could be greatly furthered by maximum use of the possibilities on the parliamentary front.

This opportunism made the rank and file uneasy. "We protest his posing as a labour leader when he is not!" This is what delegates of Montreal Painters Union Local 49 said in 1910 at a meeting of the Montreal Trades and Labour Council.[39a] They were referring to Gustave Francq—a well-known, astute trade union leader of those years. Francq was a Quebec version of Samuel Gompers, and in practice he was a stout advocate of *Gomperism*—international unionism, business unionism, and class collaboration. We shall hear more of him and James Simpson—the Ontario counterpart of Gompers—in later chapters of this book.

The Painters' delegates were opposing opportunism. Against dogmatism, voices were also raised. In 1910 a socialist at Stouffville, in eastern Ontario, wrote a letter to the *Voice*. In a bitter protest against dogmatism, he insisted that wage demands *do* have positive results. One reason the German and French socialist parties had become mass organizations, was that they *combined* the fight for immediate demands with the long-term socialist goal.[40] He went on to cite from the classical Marxist works, the *Communist Manifesto* and *Value, Price and Profit* in support of his policy.

Another who protested against dogmatism was Kier Hardie—an outstanding leader of the British Labour Party. In 1908 he went to Canada, addressed the TLC convention, and expressed his dismay at socialist dogmatism. He called it "Pharisaism". He laughed at those who believed in organized labour pure and simple apart from socialism, and those who believed in socialism pure and simple apart from organized labour. Socialism, he said, was a "process of evolution, to which the union of the working class is a step".[41]

In 1912 Hardie addressed the TLC convention once again, and made a classic statement on the strategy and tactics of the movement. He criticized one aspect of both dogmatism and opportunism noted above—the tendency to believe that political action is a cure for everything. In this connection he pointed to the importance of strikes. At that time a massive strike movement of railwaymen and miners had developed in Britain. Struggles of this kind, said Hardie, were "a great stimulus to the political side· of the movement". This was because they helped convince the workers that "the old parties are primarily capitalist parties". True, these struggles could not of themselves resolve the basic problem of the social order—only "the conquest of political power can do that". But they were an indispensable preliminary step to the conquest of power. He went on to say that the British Labour Party had shown what could be done, for it had combined the unions into a force for political action; and in turn, the workers thus politically combined found their combination "for industrial purposes" likewise enhanced. He concluded:

"The workers are learning that unity is the secret of success, and that while they have a whole world to gain, they have nothing to lose but their chains."[42]

Some of the dangerous trends then emerging in the socialist and broad labour movement have been noted above—dogmatism and opportunism. They must have played their part in producing a split within Canada's socialist movement. In 1907, a number of socialist clubs at Vancouver split away from the Socialist Party and founded a Social Democratic Party. In 1910 the split widened. A Social Democratic Party was also set up at Winnipeg. This new party, the Social Democratic Party of Canada, had a program inclined to Marxism. In 1914, a principal point in this program was the condemnation of the monopoly of the means of production by the capitalist class, a monopoly which, the program said, was being defended by the state apparatus. The SDPC program went on to say that the party's aim was "to organize the workers into a political party, to seize the reins of government and transform all capitalist property into collective property". The result of the split was that the socialist and labour political movement before World War I came to group a diversity of bodies such as the Socialist Party of Canada, the Social Democratic Party of Canada, the various labour parties and other bodies.

This, then, was the socialist movement. The preceeding pages have dealt with mistakes that were made. These mistakes were serious and held back the progress of the labour movement. However, they were only one side of the socialist movement. Moreover, this latter movement, important as it was, *must be grasped in the aggregate of total labour evolution.* Certain that the socialists' shortcomings were grave. But historically most decisive was the dedication, hard work and sacrifice of workers who were fired by the ideal of social reconstruction. In wage and strike struggles, in day-to-day building of unions, in the fight for labour political action, perhaps on a pleasant sunny Sunday afternoon on a picnic in Winnipeg where good cheer might be mingled with a lecture on the class war—on all the fronts of the labour movement's battle, these socialist pioneers were at work. Something of their attitude, their faith in the labour movement, their forebodings about leaders who might betray, is communicated in William Morris' poem *"The Voice of Toil",* reprinted in a 1902 copy of the *Winnipeg Voice.*

"I heard men sing, leave hope and praying,
    All days shall be as they have been;
    Today and tomorrow bring fear and sorrow,
    The never-ending toil between.

When earth was younger, midst toil and hunger,
    In hope we strove, and our hands were strong;
    Then great men led us, with words they fed us
    And bade us right the earthly wrong...

Who now shall lead us, what God shall feed us
    As we lie in the hell our hands have won,
    For us are no rulers, but fools and befoolers,
    The great are fallen, the wise men gone...

Come shoulder to shoulder, ere earth grow older—
    The Cause spreads over land and sea;
    Now the world shaketh and fear awaketh—
    And joy at last for thee and me."

CHAPTER 7

UNITY, INDUSTRIAL UNIONISM,
CANADIAN UNIONISM
1900-1914

1. PARADISE LOST

The Split in the Trades and Labour Congress, 1902:

Unity, industrial unionism, Canadian unionism—much of the trade union history in the 20th century has rotated around these three issues. How did they come into being? The movement which entered the 20th century was still a united one, but there were signs of discord. The previous chapter has referred to the developing conflict between trade unionism in Canada and the international unions. For this conflict there might have been a harmonious solution, but the leadership of the American Federation of Labour in the United States and those of kindred mind in Canada decided that matters should be regulated otherwise. Samuel Gompers, president of the American Federation of Labour, was a principal engineer of destruction, and Quebec an important battlefield.

Quebec was then the main base of the Knights of Labour; and the Knights' assemblies, along with locals of the international craft unions, were co-members in the Montreal Federated Trades and Labour Council, established 1883. Tragically, in 1897, the council was split. Delegates from a number of international union locals withdrew. Later a second trades and labour council was set up. Gompers had a hand in this: A golden jubilee history issued by the Montreal Trades and Labour Council some years later refers to this 1897-1900 period as one in which there took place the "development of internationalism and the disorganization of the Knights under the able and adroit Gompers whose engaging eloquence completely conquered Montreal."[1] This brutal way of dealing with the Knights had important implications both for Canadian unionism and for the relationship between the trade union movement and Quebec. This was because the Knights had developed, in effect, into a virtually Canadian and largely Quebec detachment of the movement.

At the 1901 TLC convention, matters were coming to a head. The incumbent president, Ralph Smith, said "the results of our work are not as extensive as we would desire", and proposed transformation of the TLC into a Canadian Federation of Labour:

"A federation of American unions represented by a national union and a federation of Canadian unions represented by a national union, each working with the other in special cases, would be a great advantage over having local unions in Canada connected with the national unions of America."

This part of the president's address was referred to a committee which was instructed to report at the convention of the following year.

Then came the Berlin (Kitchener) convention of the Trades and Labour Congress, held September 1902. Here the evil deed was done, the movement split. Present were delegates from Canadian unions such as the Knights of Labour assemblies at Montreal, Toronto and Ottawa; also locals directly chartered by the TLC, Trades councils, and national (non-U.S. affiliated) unions such as the Canadian Federation of Boot and Shoe workers. Present also were delegates from locals of international unions, such as the United Brotherhood of Carpenters and Joiners. The latter were in the majority. There was discord from the start. The Convention refused to seat delegates from the Montreal Federated Trades Council, lifted that council's charter, and seated instead delegates from the Gompers-approved council. This embittered the "nationals". Then came debate on the key issue—to adopt or not adopt an amendment to the constitution that "no national union be recognized where an international union exists". Against the advice of leading Congress figures like P. M. Draper and D. J. O'Donaghue, the delegates adopted this amendment by a majority of 89 to 35. International union power was stamped further into the Congress by the election to its presidency of John Flett, a paid officer of an international union.

Adoption of this amendment meant automatically the exclusion of the Knights of Labour. In turn this meant a counter-revolution in the Congress, a reversal of the basis on which it had been founded, as a united movement of the Knights of Labour and international unions. And so, in this almost casual way, the delegates to this historic convention were fooled and intimidated into selling their Canadian heritage for a mess of U.S. pottage. But for this they had some compensation. One was a promise by the AFL that henceforth it would pay the TLC $500 per annum.[2]

In the Home Base of the International Unions:

Canadians there were who consoled themselves with the idea that the new power of international unions in Canada meant closer connections with a progressive country, the United States. But U.S. progressiveness was in good part a myth: Technologically—yes; in living standards—yes; but in social legislation, management-labour relations, respect for minorities and human rights—no. By 1908, old age and widows' pensions had been adopted in Britain, New Zealand and Australia, but they were not adopted in the U.S. until decades later. Another indicator was frequency of industrial accidents. A U.S. newspaper wrote in 1913: "With every 16 ticks of the clock a worker in our country is injured. Every quarter of an hour a worker is killed." In 1913, the *Industrial Banner* declared that life "is much better protected" in England and Germany than in the United States.[3]

There was also the attitude to unions and strikes. The capitalist rulers of the United States were then among the most brutal the world has ever known. At Ludlow, Colorado in May 1914, soldiers and company guards burst in on an encampment of strikers' families and killed 40. The *Industrial Banner* wrote at that time: "Men, women and children were shot attempting to escape or were roasted alive."[4]

For Organized Labour in Canada to be connected with, and subordinate to, Organized Labour in a country whose working class was subject to such brutal pressure, had its dangerous side. Reaction in the United States, the power of monopoly capital there, heightened the power of reaction and monopoly capital in Canada. A symptom was the way the employers in Canada availed themselves during those years of union-smashing, labour-baiting techniques developed in the U.S. In 1904, machinists striking in London, Ontario, charged that "Yankee detectives and labour spies are being imported from Chicago".[5] In 1914, the Montreal Trades and Labour Council denounced the U.S. Burns Detective Agency as a "foreign agency" used by employers in Canada to create discord.[6] "Small wonder there are no annexationists", wrote the *Industrial Banner* (London Trades and Labour Council organ) in 1910, "the people of Canada fear the prospect of rule by injunction judges . . . They fear a corrupt judiciary . . . Where once the stars ruled, there is now just the dollar sign."[7]

What of the trade union movement in the United States? In good measure its progressiveness was also a myth. The U.S. movement was lagging behind the movement in other countries. One reason was the extraordinary weight of capital in the U.S. relative to Labour. Another was the swollen development within the dominant echelons of the U.S. trade union movement, of class collaboration. This expressed itself in bureaucracy, craft union backwardness, callous lack of concern for Negro and foreign-born workers and for the unskilled in the unorganized, mass production industries. True, many of the founders of unions in the United States had been progressives. But, in the early years of the 20th century, a rapport began to be established between some craft union officials and big business. This was connected with the switch from competitive to monopoly capitalism and imperialism in the United States after the turn of the century. The crux of this rapport was that minor concessions and recognition were granted at times to the craft unions—although they too were hard-pressed by employers and often had to fight difficult strikes. In return, the craft unions did not bestir themselves sufficiently to organize the bulk of the workers, the semi-skilled and unskilled. This helped produce a situation in the United States where in 1913 only 10% of the workers were organized as compared to 22% in Britain and Germany.

Backward also was the AFL's policy on political action. Gompers' motto was "reward your friends and punish your enemies". In practice this meant "reward the employers and punish the workers". It contributed to the situation which prevailed in 1914: In England, France, Germany, Australia, New Zealand, even in tsarist Russia, dozens of labour members were sitting in the legislatures; but in the United States, there was scarce a labour representative in Congress.

Another characteristic of the dominant U.S. trade union leaders was that they tended to agree with their Government's foreign policy. "We are proud of our institutions, we would fight and die for them!", exclaimed the AFL fraternal delegate when he spoke to the 1908 TLC convention. Many Canadian trade unionists were bound to be repelled, for they were much more independent of their government's foreign policy, as is shown by resolutions they adopted at central union gatherings in the period under review.

All this was but one aspect of the U.S. trade union movement—not its *labour* and *union* side, but its *business union, craft, class-collaboration* side—caused by the ability of U.S. big business to grant, from its super-profits, concessions to sections of the U.S. workers, and thus create among them a privileged strata. Always there was the opposition, the progressives, who identified themselves with the mass of the exploited workers. These progressives combatted the AFL policy. They organized the unorganized, fought great strikes, and led great campaigns. One sign of their strength, as far back as the 1890s, was the defeat of Samuel Gompers when he ran for re-election as president of the AFL. Another was support at the AFL 1912 convention, for a resolution endorsing socialism—it won almost half the votes. The American Railroad Union of Debs, the Western Labour Union, the American Labour Union of Eugene Debs and William Haywood, the Industrial Workers of the World of William Haywood and Joe Hill, also the constant progressive struggle within the AFL—all this testifies to the progressive trend in the U.S. trade union movement. But it never became the dominant trend. And, even if it had, *this did not cancel the problem inherent in international unionism,* inherent in a situation where Canadians became dependent on the ebb and flow of events in a foreign country. True, that a progressive U.S. trade union movement would have been quicker to pronounce its blessing on the Canadian trade union movement, bid it be sovereign, help it along the way, and build solidarity between two sovereign movements—genuine internationalism. But, not progressivism but *business unionism* retained the hegemony in the U.S. trade union movement, and as applied to Canada, this meant *labour imperialism.*

This labour imperialism was closely connected with the sell-out of the U.S. workers themselves. In the period under review, and through to the present (1967), the "great" U.S. trade union movement failed to organize the majority of the U.S. workers. It did not organize the workers in the South ; and yet this would have gone far to solve the problems of the Negroes—and white workers too. It lagged in the organization of Negroes, and it tolerated Jim Crow policies in its ranks. In šum, the U.S. trade union movement was one which did not fulfill its obligations to its own membership in the United States, but found time and money for something which was none of its business —the affairs of the Canadian trade union movement.

2. CONSEQUENCE OF THE BERLIN SPLIT

Coal Miners, Carpenters, TLC:

What did the Berlin split mean for Canadians? Here is how coal miners were affected. At that time, their principal union was the Provincial Workmen's Association in Nova Scotia,· then among the larger unions in the country. The next logical step was its entry into the Trades and Labour Congress, but this could not be done because of a clash of jurisdiction with the United Mine Workers of America, an international union. Yet at the turn of the century, this latter union had no membership at all in Canada, while the PWA was one of Canada's senior unions—established in 1879, it pre-dated even the TLC. In 1904, when this matter was being considered, the Nova Scotia executive reported piteously: "Since the PWA is a provincial association, it is impossible for them to affiliate with the Congress."

Consider now the fate overtaking the Amalgamated Society of Carpenters—a union dating back in Canada to the 1860s. In order to facilitate integration of their American locals into the trade union movement of this continent, the British headquarters of the ASC came to an agreement with the AFL, under which this latter body extended recognition to ASC locals. In 1911, the AFL abruptly terminated this agreement, and in 1912, the United Brotherhood of Carpenters and Joiners, AFL, asked the Trades and Labour Congress to take similar action—to terminate recognition of the ASC. This request the 1912 convention of the Congress rejected, but subsequently the TLC executive committee cancelled the convention's decision, and returned the per capita payments to the ASC, in other words, it terminated that body's affiliation to the Congress—an action which Congress Secretary-treasurer P. M. Draper justified as follows in a letter to the ASC written in 1913: "The international trade union movement ... as understood in Canada ... recognizes as its supreme head the AFL and this for all trade and jurisdictional matters." William Young, an ASC leader in Canada, sent Draper an indignant reply that "the disguise has been ripped from the Congress. The Congress was "truckling to institutions officered by men whose allegiance is to another country". He added:

"It is to be sincerely hoped the time will soon come when we shall see the Canada Trades Congress take a firm stand for its independence while keeping friendly relations with the workers in other countries."[8]

Then there was the effect on militant unions in Western Canada, like the Western Federation of Miners and the United Brotherhood of Railway Employees. Up to now they had been seated on the Trades and Labour Councils at Victoria, Vancouver and other cities. Now they had to withdraw: a new schism, a new tension between the standard movement and militant-led unions—likewise to persist through the years.

Most serious of all was the impact on the TLC itself. First there was the loss of membership. The loss of 30 or 40 locals with a few thousand members may not seem too serious, but Congress membership was then scanty, scarce 13,000 and its revenue meagre—in 1902 only $2,342. An immediate consequence of the split was the establishment of a new trade union centre in 1903, the National Trades and Labour Congress, based on the 27 Knights of Labour Assemblies expelled from the Congress. Thus was engendered a persisting duality, a multiplicity of trade union centres in Canada, which has persisted down to the present (1967).

A further grave consequence was a qualitative change in the character of the Congress. Though the matter was never clearly defined in the proceedings of the Canadian Labour Union and TLC in the 19th century, the general intention was clear: the all-around development of the Congress as an active and sovereign centre. This was ripped asunder by the 1902 decision. More and more the Congress stultified itself and tended to become an instrument of the international unions. This was reflected in the constitution of the Congress, in particular the clauses governing affiliation of unions. As the years passed by, one restrictive clause after another was jammed into the constitution. Their general effect was to close Congress doors to all *national* as distinct from international unions. The constitution became a strait jacket, a network of prohibitions. True, the Congress could charter local unions—but "in no case where international or national unions existed". Again, a national union could not be chartered "where there is in existence an international union of their craft". Two further clauses were an insult to Canadian trade union sovereignty. One said that an organization expelled or rejected by the American Federation of Labour would be automatically excluded from membership in the Trades and Labour Congress.[9] Another said that a local union which was part of a national body which had broken with the international union in its jurisdiction or was challenging the jurisdiction of an international union recognized by the Congress, would not be permitted to have delegates "at any central body chartered by this Congress".[10]

In sum, increasingly the condition of membership in the Congress was becoming membership in an international union. The Congress, founded as an organization of *both* national and international unions, was tending to shrink to an organization of the latter only. In 1913 the decline was almost complete. Credentials submitted to the Congress convention that year show little or nothing in the way of directly-chartered locals or national unions.[11]

This was the result, then — the denigration of the Congress, the thwarting of its fulfilment as a Canadian trade union centre, a tendency to convert it into an instrument of the international unions in Canada; in short the *narrowing* of the Congress. "Congress is the legislative mouthpiece of the international unions", said TLC president John Flett in 1903. The main job of the TLC was to uphold "the legislative interest of the great international labour movement in Canada", said the TLC executive council that same year.[11a]

From the AFL labour imperialists, the Congress' surrender of sovereignty and character aroused—contempt. TLC pleas for more Canadian rights would be given short shrift. For instance, when in the period prior to World War I, the TLC executive council proposed that Canada's trade unionists be directly represented in the executive council of the International Federation of Trade Unions—a world trade union centre of those years—the AFL curtly dismissed the suggestion with the reply that no Congress representative was needed, that the AFL representative on the IFTU executive spoke for Canada as well.

Thus was the Congress humiliated. On its emblem still the maple leaf and beaver, but closer to reality, to a degree, the American flag bedecking its 1905 convention: The official explanation was that the U.S. flag was there as a mark of "recognition of the international character of all the unions".[12]

Some Further Justifications for the U.S. Connection:

The denigration of the Congress has been outlined above. A decisive cause had been noted—the power and aggressiveness of the international unions, their grip on key unions in Canada and on the leading councils of the TLC. A further correlate cause was the influence of business unionism and class collaboration in Canada's trade union movement. However, the orientation of the Canadian rank and file must also be considered. The denigration of the Congress was caused also by their genuine, sincere confusion—illusions. The AFL and international union leaders used this confusion to divide and dismay many Canadians who in their heart of hearts wanted an active, all-in, industrial, Canadian trade union movement.

The AFL leaders would put forward ideas which had the ring of truth. One such idea, and it became one of their favourite slogans through the years was—"international unions for international business". Like every first class lie or illusion, this one had a foundation in reality—it was a tangent from reality. Through the 19th and into the 20th century, the workers of the world had learnt the value of international solidarity. To this end they had done two things: Firstly and primarily, the workers in each country had built strong, active national centres. Secondly, they had given these national centres an *international* orientation; and this international orientation had expressed itself organizationally in the *voluntary* grouping of the various *national* trade union centres into *world* bodies or regional bodies. *But in no important industrial country of the world had it ever happened that the workers should organize in unions based in a foreign country*. That had absolutely nothing to do with internationalism! Indeed, such a development was bound to bear within it the danger of the very antithesis of internationalism—imperialism—the domination of workers in one country by bodies located in another country.

The adage has it that there is an exception to every rule. Could it be that Canada was the exception? That might have applied, had there been a genuine agreement among Canadian trade unionists that their movement should be one of international unions. But there was no such concensus. The pathway to international union domination in Canada was division, expulsion, and reprisal.

Consider another aspect of the argument. Was it true that when a country was dominated by the capitalists of another country, then it was best for the workers of the *dominated* country to join the unions of the *dominating* country? Once again world labour experience is an invaluable though not inexorable guide. This writer does not know of a single significant case where the workers in a colonial country based their movement on membership in the unions of the colonizing country. The reverse has been the case—and for obvious reasons! In practically every colonial country, the workers, who have absolutely nothing, and are doubly degraded because their employers are foreigners, are the more concerned that they should control the one thing they do possess—their power to combine—their unions—in short, that they should be "master in their own house". This does not mean that the unions and trade union centres of both the colonizing country and the colonized country should confine themselves to narrow nationalism. On the contrary it is desirable that they should have an international orientation—both with regard to the world's workers at large and to relations with each other. And this is exactly what has happened. For instance, the most progressive and most vital sections of the British trade union movement have always solidarized themselves with the unions of India. They have felt that was their international duty. Likewise the most intelligent and alert sections of India's unions have sought active relations with the British workers. But at no time did they offer to join British unions! The same applies to unions in the rest of Asia, Africa and Latin America.

So much for the hoary argument engendered in the period under review and persisting through the 20th century—"International unions for international business". Another argument was money, lots of money at international headquarters in the U.S.A. Here, too, practice is a good guide. Could union funds in another country be a substitute for working class solidarity? Would not the cross-Canada solidarity envisioned by the founders of the Canadian Labour Union and the

Trades and Labour Congress have been a power vastly greater than the "hoarded gold" of international union headquarters? And in any case, as every experienced trade unionist knows, money is but one item in the aggregate—one which is indispensable but which reflects in the final analysis Labour's total fighting fitness. Here is an example. In 1904 the Provincial Workmen's Association, which was a national union, fought and lost the steel strike at Sydney, Nova Scotia. The AFL leaders said the PWA lost because it did not have enough money. However, when the United Mine Workers of America, which was an international union, moved in some months later and in turn tried its hand at organizing the Sydney steel workers, it also encountered ferocious resistance from the company—and lost.

There was a further argument pressed by the international union leaders. This one was particularly attractive to the rank and file in Canada because it was so *close* to the truth—so directly and diabolically a tangent from a vital *reality*. In 1903, a B.C. coal miner was asked why he favoured connections with the U.S. He replied: "Local organization is no good; we have tried that in this country!"[12a]

What were the circumstances? The miner was a member of Western Federation of Miners. He was defending his organization, under attack by employers and government because of its part in the British Columbia strike movement of 1903. But he was not just doing that. He was also defending the principle of general unions as against isolated locals. So far he was right. But then—and this was the jump—he was *confusing* the *necessary* progress from local organization to general unions—something which happens in every industry and every country sooner or later—with the accidental *appearance* of *general* unions as *international unions*.

General unions and international unions: In practice often identical, but in practice also, totally distinct, two distinct items. General unions: *common* to every country. Their *appearance* as international unions—*peculiar* to Canada! Was the B.C. coal miner right in joining the WFM in 1903? Probably. So were many other workers in that period and in later years who joined international unions. The plain facts are that one reason the international unions became rooted in Canada was because they *merged* with the natural, spontaneous progress then going on in Canada as in every other country, to general unions. *They helped fulfill the function of general unions for Canadian workers.* But there was no *intrinsic* connection between international unions and general unions. There was no natural, long-term, historic *inevitability* in such a connection. Indeed, there was a contradiction. For international unions were not just fulfilling the function of general unions in Canada. They were also *dominating* Canada's unions, and they were blocking the progress to general unions in Canada. One reason was that international unions were mostly craft unions, and thus brought to Canada not just general unions but the chaotic isolation inherent in craft unions. Another reason was that international unions used aggressive tactics against national unions in Canada. Examples have been given in previous pages, and more will be provided in later ones.

In sum, this seeming identity between general unions and international unions was an illusion, the confusing of two distinct processes which *seemed* to coincide in real life, and to a degree, *did*. This illusion we call the *fetishism of international unionism*.

But beyond this illusion, so deep-rooted in the Canadian rank and file, was something else dark and dirty: The cruel manipulation of the illusion by the AFL and international headquarters: the way they merged this honest though erroneous idea of the rank and file with the brutal facts of their power, strength and aggressiveness. The international unions were then being most active in taking over Canadian unions or supplanting them. They were telling the Trades and Labour Congress in no uncertain terms that they expected the trade union movement of Canada to be a continental movement. They were succeeding in the conversion of the chief trade union centre of Canada, the TLC, into their own vehicle and agency. That meant that it was becoming more difficult to be a member of the central, official, labour movement unless one was a member of an international union. For instance, in 1903 a trade union officer was asked whether the Trades and Labour Council of Victoria, B.C. would admit delegates from a national union. He replied: "No. We would bar them from joining if there was an international, and they refused to join". Again, that same year another trade unionist was asked what would be the status of union members who sought to establish an exclusively Canadian body. His answer was that they would have to "withdraw from the labour council at Vancouver" and organize a separate council.

Again, there was now the problem of protecting contracts and pension funds at international headquarters in the United States. For Canadian union members to break loose from their parent international unions might endanger these.

Finally there was the problem of solidarity. In a situation where international unionism was becoming the chief mode of union organization, and where it was difficult to obtain the co-operation of the Trades and Labour Congress unless one was in an international union; and in a situation where employers were often attacking international unions—not mainly because they were international unions but because they were *unions*—the specific instruments of struggle of the Canadian workers at that time—in this situation, many trade unionists felt they had no alternative but to support and join international unions — despite their misgivings about organizations located in a foreign country.

These, then, were the problems, confusions and illusions connected with U.S. domination; and this is how it merged with and reinforced the basic process of domination itself. In sum, this was the result: In the years following the Berlin decision of 1902, an unwholesome and unhealthy situation was developing in which Canadian workers could join with each other only through the external mediation of membership in a foreign organization. And what is more, this situation, so *alien* to the principles of world and Canadian trade union development alike, and so *distant* from the deep-going needs and desires of Canadian trade unionists, was assuming the mask of consent, was becoming *a deep-going, mass ideological trend* within the Canadian organized workers movement. Trade unionists, even those who were active and conscious ones were coming to *accept* international unions as natural and necessary. True, their consent could only be seeming and transitional, for it rested on illusion. How else to explain the periodic explosions, revolts against international unions, erupting now in this industry, now in another? Still, amidst the vicissitudes of such struggles — the ebb and flow of the fight for Canadian trade union autonomy and sovereignty — a situation was being engendered which was to have the most far-reaching, crippling effect on the evolution of organized labour in Canada, and to a degree, on Canadian political evolution as a whole — given the decisive significance of Labour and labour organization in the life of the country. Worse still, though the problem was being tackled in *practice,* as it arose in this or that concrete struggle, it was not being continuously and consistently gripped in *principle. The decisive significance of a sovereign Canadian trade union movement was not being systematically understood and pursued on a cross-Canada basis.* Hence this antithesis persisting through the years: On the one hand, the *reality,* the deep-going antagonism between the progressive laws of Canadian labour evolution, *and* international union domination; on the other hand, the failure to *know* this, and the attendant result, a movement baffled, dismayed and crippled, when — at crucial cross-roads of Canadian politics and trade union history — the cruel reality of foreign union domination asserted itself. Of all this more in later chapters.

Orientation of the Companies and Government:

Thus far we have considered Labour's orientation to the U.S. connection. What of the companies and the government? Where did they stand? Sometimes they played both ends against the middle—using international unions against the workers, and the workers against the international unions. Certain that the deed done at Berlin reinforced the employer cry about "alien labour agitator". That cry was partly hypocritical, because the employers often meant not so much alien to Canada as alien to their class interests. At that time, some of them were busily importing strike-breakers, spies and detectives from the U.S.A., and were busily trafficking with British and U.S. capital. The alien cry was something they were reserving for the workers.

Confusion must also have played its part in the shaping of the employer attitude — for example the *fetishism of international unions.* Given that Canadian workers were then largely conducting their battles under the banner of international unions, was it not understandable that some employers would believe that trade unionism came from the United States, and would be the more prone to believe it, because it suited their interest?

Another factor shaping the employer attitude was patriotism — at least, that transitional, fluctuating but highly-significant point where the profit interest of businessmen begins to coincide with the national interest, and awakens their natural, deep-seated, but slumbering patriotism. For instance, some employers entertained the fear — and to a degree it was a well-grounded fear — that a labour movement whose headquarters were located in a foreign country — and at that a labour movement of a *special* kind, whose leaders were often too friendly to the very, foreign employers who were competitive to Canadian business—was a danger to Canada, and more particularly to their interests.

These were some motives—mostly selfish, anti-labour and profit-seeking, but with just that touch of the historically objective, the *problem of Canadian independence and prosperity* — which contributed to moves to outlaw international unions in Canada. In 1904, Senator Lougheed introduced legislation which made it a penal offence for a non-British subject to enter Canada and counsel Canadian workers to seek an increase in wages. The bill was not adopted. Another bill along similar lines brought in by Senator Belcourt in 1910 was likewise not adopted.

Why the rejection of these measures? The basic reason was that they were aimed not just at *international unionism* but at *trade unionism.* And the employers and government feared this would sharpen labour-management relations. Thus, the anti-labour motive behind these measures defeated other motives perhaps more worthy of consideration.

This was one reason. Another was that the employers and government gradually came to recognize that the basic problem was not *international unionism* but *trade unionism*. Now, if trade unionism was inevitable, and with it the attendant danger of *militant* trade unionism close to the Canadian workers—then why not scotch the danger by realistically recognizing some merits in the *international* variant of trade unionism? One such merit, increasingly plain to see, was that international unions, inclined as they often were to business unionism and reconciliation with the employers—a "soft" approach—and oriented as they were to friendly relations with the government of the United States, brought with them an element of *stability* in labour-management relations—at least the kind of stability the employers and government wanted.

Mackenzie King was one who helped set the homespun profit-makers wise, and enlightened them on the difference between militant, grass roots unionism and the conservative business unionism of standard international unions. In other words, he contributed to the employers' understanding, and advanced them to greater flexibility and realism. He did them a favour. He did it operatively, in the heat of actual industrial disputes—rather than by any coherent statement of principles and motives. An instance is his orientation during the proceedings of the Royal Commission on Industrial Disputes in the Province of British Columbia, in 1903. At that time, he expressed misgivings about the merits of foreign union interference in Canada. But he was directing his fire against *specific* international unions, and in *specific* circumstances. The unions were the United Brotherhood of Railway Employees and the Western Federation of Miners. The circumstances were that these unions were engaged in a battle against the CPR and the colliery owners. Moreover the UBRE and WFM were not *typical* international unions. On the contrary, they were the product of the U.S. workers' revolt against *typical* international unions. As noted in an earlier page, both these unions were not in the AFL, and were antagonistic to AFL business unionism and class collaboration. How natural, then, that Mackenzie King should later inform TLC president Flett that "the findings of the Commission are no reflection on the AFL". In other words, Mackenzie King did not pursue the principle of Canadian unionism to the hilt, but *adapted* it to the needs of the employers, and of social stability as he conceived it. And that was the hallmark of his life. He never pressed an honest principle to a fighting finish. He always compromised. His suppleness was a virtue, but not the forfeiture of principle, and not the *end*—the kind of stability which left the workers a degraded class, save so far as they combined and endangered the social order, at which time the necessary concessions would be made. That was a vice.

The CPR's orientation at this same Royal Commission is also significant. Against the UBRE it raised the "foreign union" cry. How wrong that the UBRE based on the United States should have the power to call Canadian workers out on strike! But, what of the standard railroad brotherhoods who were *also* "foreign" unions? Here, the CPR's attitude became: See no evil, hear no evil, think no evil. And why? Because the standard brotherhoods were strike-breaking, were ordering their members on the CPR to cross the picket lines of the UBRE. That was the pattern: manipulation of genuine public feeling for *trade unionism* and *Canadian unionism;* the denunciation of any union conducting an honest fight, be it national or international, and to this end, the use, on occasion of the "foreign union" cry; but behind it all, systematic trafficking with international unionism—in particular the Gompers "business union" variant—in order to confuse, divide and dominate the workers. In the years that followed, this became the pattern for big business in Canada.

This, then, was the emerging employer and government orientation to international unionism. And this orientation *combined* with the various trends in *Labour's* orientation to produce the given result: Increasing domination by international unions. Natural? Of course! It *happened*. It was the product of the given relation of forces. But it was not *intrinsically* natural, no more than the subjugation of a weaker country by a stronger one is *intrinsically* natural. In the most *abiding* sense, international unionism was *unnatural*—contrary *to the basic positive laws of Canadian trade union evolution.* Hence the constant struggle against international union domination and all it represented; the constant struggle for a united, militant, industrial Canadian trade union movement. Structurally, for the period under review, this struggle assumed two forms:

1. The emergence of a new, wholly Canadian centre.
2. The continuing battle within the TLC.

To this we now turn.

3. THE NATIONAL TRADES AND LABOUR CONGRESS

Its Program and Policy: Why It Did Not Succeed:

In 1903 the National Trades and Labour Congress of Canada was founded, as a sovereign Canadian trade union centre dedicated to "organization along national lines",* and removal of "the octopus of taxation without representation".** The NTLC's founding bodies were mainly the national unions and Knights of Labour Assemblies ousted from the TLC in 1902. The new centre's intention is plainly stated in its title. Obviously it aimed to substitute itself for the TLC, to lift up the banner of an all-inclusive Canadian trade union centre which had been dropped by the TLC in 1902. This is confirmed by what the NTLC said some years after its founding—that it aspired to be the nucleus of a "great national federation of Canada".[13]

The accent here was on Canadian unionism, but this was combined with a certain element of class consciousness and Canadianism—concern about the danger of U.S. imperialism to Canada. In 1908, a report submitted by the NTLC executive committee for Ontario denounced "paid officers of internationals" who are seeking "to retain the allegiance of Canadian workers to a cause which is at best bound to keep Canada in a position of subservience and is preventing its working class from adopting a more progressive and modern policy". It went on to suggest measures which would help Canada "avoid the mistakes which have allowed the United States to become the plutocracy and oligarchy which at present it represents socially and industrially".[14]

Other legislative demands and procedures of the NTLC were not too different from those of its competitor, the TLC—factory legislation, fair wage clauses in federal government contracts and annual meetings with the federal cabinet—begun by the NTLC in 1904, and paralleling those of the Trades and Labour Congress. There was this distinction, however: The NTLC placed a greater emphasis on tariffs and measures aimed at developing Canadian industry. It put forward the slogan of "Canada for Canadians", and proposed tariffs on imports that could be made in Canada. In 1904, the NTLC was protesting the import of boots and shoes from the United States, and in 1906 it demanded a Canadian ship-building industry.

A few words now on the new centre's organizational progress. When the inaugural convention met in Quebec City in 1903, the main force was the Knights of Labour Assemblies ousted from the TLC in 1902. There were also delegates from national unions like the Canadian Federation of Shoemakers and from local unions of Cigar Makers, Painters and Carpenters. At the 1904 convention, representation increased. Delegates were present from 45 unions, including 26 national

* Extract from the preamble to the constitution of the NTLC, 1908.
** Extract from a statement made in 1906 by John Mee, President of the National Trades and Labour Congress of Canada.

unions. In 1905 representation dropped—there were delegates from only about 30 unions at the convention held that year. In 1906 the NTLC claimed a membership of 20,000—a sizable number for those times. In 1908 it changed its name to Canadian Federation of Labour and made a new bid for expansion. This failed. At the 1911 convention only 17 unions were represented—13 from the Province of Quebec, the balance from lodges of the Provincial Workmen's Association of Nova Scotia. By the beginning of World War I, the CFL was a very weakened body.

Why did the new centre not succeed? Ferocious opposition by the AFL, the loyalty of trade unionists to their established organizations— these were two reasons. A third was doctrinairism. The NTLC did not place sufficient emphasis on organizing the unorganized and building industrial unions. Instead it often sought to build by winning over members in the international unions. In this way the NTLC was duplicating the mistake of the TLC. The TLC had shut the door on national unions. The NTLC was shutting the door on Canadian locals of international unions. This was the more tragic because, as noted earlier, in its formative, plastic phase, the NTLC had seemed to understand that the only way to build a united trade union centre was to do just what the Canadian Labour Union and TLC had done in the 19th century—open the door wide to all unions, international and national.*

This, then, was the third reason for the NTLC's failure—doctrinairism. Needless to say it played right into the hands of the AFL and it angered many trade unionists who otherwise would have been sympathetic to such NTLC objectives as Canadian unionism.

This doctrinairism was closely connected with a tendency to *class collaboration*. This was the fourth reason for the NTLC's decline. An example was the fear of strikes. In 1905 the NTLC said strikes could be avoided or reduced through meetings with the Canadian Manufacturers Association. In 1912 CFL (NTLC) president Moffatt condemned "industrial ferment" in the west—meaning the great Vancouver Island coal strike of 1912-1914. The CFL leaders were duped also by the Industrial Disputes Investigation Act of 1907. They believed the Act rendered strikes less important. In 1909 they proposed that the Act be applied to all industrial disputes.

Another example of class collaboration was the NTLC's insufficient combativity in relation to employers and government. For example,

---

* At the 1903 convention, the president of the NTLC said the new centre would admit international union locals, even if they continued their connection with the United States. But the NTLC did not pursue this policy.

the NTLC leadership cultivated the illusion that the Federal Government would back up Canadian unionism, perhaps by statutory action. In this way the NTLC was once again duplicating the business unionism and opportunism of the TLC and the international unions— the very force which had brought about the split within the Canadian trade union movement, and the subsequent establishment of the NTLC. In 1908 the NTLC leaders were hopefully proferring words of praise to Minister of Labour Mackenzie King present at their annual convention.

These were some reasons for the NTLC's decline. In sum, the NTLC's development, its rise and fall, was determined by this contradiction: on the positive side—Canadian unionism and Canadianism; on the negative side—dogmatism and class collaboration—the duplication within the NTLC of these reactionary trends which had had such destructive results in the TLC and had made necessary the organization of the NTLC. In the outcome, this dogmatism and class collaboration blocked the fulfilment of the NTLC's Canadian unionism and Canadianism.

However, despite this drawback, the NTLC was a moment of the historic struggle for a united, militant, Canadian trade union movement. This is shown by subsequent development. One shoot from the NTLC leads to the All-Canadian Congress of Labour—established in 1927 as a centre for exclusively national unions. In turn the ACCL was a co-founder of the Canadian Congress of Labour—also a product of the struggle for Canadian unionism. Still another shoot of the NTLC leads to the Confederation of National Trades Unions—a centre which has persisted to this day (1967) as an organization of exclusively national unions. Of all this more in later chapters.

4. THE FIGHT FOR PROGRESS IN THE TLC
1902-1914

Canadian Unionism, Industrial Unionism, United Action:

The fight for progress went on in the TLC too. One issue was Canadian unionism. Already at the Berlin convention, the demand was put forward that the Congress should have greater powers, that AFL-chartered central councils and federal unions should be obliged to join the TLC—21 central councils were then not affiliated. The TLC executive council pressed this demand after the Berlin convention. The outcome was that the American Federation of Labour did not relinquish its right to directly charter central (city) councils in Canada, but conceded that these councils must also take out a charter with the

TLC—a concession fenced in with the careful proviso that the affairs of these central councils "shall be transacted along the lines of international trade unionism". Moreover, the AFL refused to transfer its directly chartered federal local unions in Canada to the Congress.* How the international unions showed contempt for the TLC and starved it, is shown by their per capita payments to the Congress in 1908: With 50,000 members in Canada, they were paying for only 20,000.[15]

This is how the fight for Canadian unionism went forward in the TLC—slowly, all too slowly, because the basic position had been surrendered in 1902.

A second issue was industrial unionism. This was connected with Canadian unionism. The reason was that most international unions were craft unions, and committed to craft unionism, as opposed to industrial unionism. In 1901 the AFL had adopted Samuel Gompers' policy of "craft autonomy". This meant that the AFL would not interfere in the jurisdiction of its craft union affiliates. For instance, it would not accept industrial organization of the steel workers unless the craft unions in that industry, like the Amalgamated Steel and Tin Workers, agreed. Now, in effect, the TLC was committed to international unions as the prevailing form of organization. This meant that in practice it was committed to craft unionism, that generally it could not organize workers into industrial unions, and for that matter, into any kind of unions. Nor was this merely a matter of practice but of express provisions in the Congress constitution. If there was any doubt the AFL put it plainly in 1911. It agreed that the TLC had priority in matters legislative, but said sternly that "autonomy of international unions in trade matters (must) be maintained as heretofore".[16]

However, counterposed to the reality of domination by U.S. craft unions was the reality of working class struggle in Canada. After the CPR Shopmen's strike of 1908, Canadian railroad workers began to say that what they needed was a great federation of all railroad workers. This was the only way to beat the CPR. "The time has come when every railway union and brotherhood from the engineers to trackmen should confederate for mutual protection!" said the *Industrial Banner* in September 1908.

Canadian unionism and industrial unionism—these, then, were two

---

* It was only in 1956, with the establishment of the Canadian Labour Congress, that this transfer finally took place. In turn, many of these federal unions, now directly chartered by the Congress, were merged with Congress' international union and national union affiliates—in short, in at least a number of cases, a transfer from the AFL to the CLC and a transfer back from the CLC to the international unions.

issues. They merged with a third: united action. After the Cape Breton coal strike of 1909, the miners asked why they had been defeated. Many believed the reason was lack of united action. Subsequently, two officers of the United Mine Workers of America, District 26 in Cape Breton — J. B. McLachlan and William Watkins — went to the UMW international convention and submitted a resolution proposing a meeting of all international union representatives, for closer relations in strikes. The UMWA referred this to the forthcoming AFL convention. There it was buried.

McLachlan was not a man to be stopped this way. He took his case direct to the TLC. In a moving letter he called for industrial unionism and united action. What's the point in miners striking if rail and ship unions "scab" on them, bring in coal and take out coal? What's the point in rail workers striking, if other organized workers supply goods for imported "scab labour" and rolling stock? What's the point in one union striking, if another union stays at work? The miners of Cape Breton had been beaten because "international unions in this country were not prepared to take a course they were justified in taking to maintain the principles for which all working men organized". Finally, the letter asked the Congress to "marshall their craft organizations into line". If this was done—the employers would learn once and for all that any attempt not to negotiate with a union, or break a strike, would bring about a cessation of work by all sections of labour affected. In short, "the grievance of one is the grievance of all".[17]

The fight for industrial unionism has been mentioned above. This was stimulated by the jurisdictional chaos imported into Canada by international unions. For example, at Edmonton, Alberta, trade unionists complained that the building trades craft unions were warring with each other, and being ineffective in their dealings with the Builders Exchange. In 1911 the Alberta provincial executive of the TLC submitted the following resolution to the TLC convention:

"We are of the opinion the time has arrived in the history of the Canadian labour movement, when in order to justify its continued existence as the head of organized labour in Canada, the Trades and Labour Congress must declare for absolute supremacy, not merely on legislative matters alone, but also in all economic questions which concern the welfare of Canadian trade unionists as a whole."[18]

At this convention there was a promising result—adoption of the following motion by Victor Midgeley of the Vancouver Trades and Labour Council:

"Whereas craft unions have proved inadequate to successfully combat present-day aggregations of capital; and whereas the activities of the craft unions are almost entirely obscured by jurisdictional disputes, causing an internal warfare that prevents any continued successful co-operation of crafts in any given industry, therefore be it resolved that this convention endorse the principle of industrial unionism."[19]

From the AFL convention which met shortly after, this resolution excited apoplectic opposition. At the 1912 TLC convention, delegates aligned with the AFL tried to knock out the Midgeley resolution. They failed. But in the process the Midgeley decision was softened to a pulp. It was now pronounced to be "only of an educative nature". Moreover, the TLC leaders opposed a resolution submitted by United Mine Workers of America, Local 2388, Ladysmith, Vancouver Island. The resolution called on the Congress to "endorse the industrial form of organization", and asked "the affiliated unions to at once get the machinery in force to have this completed". Congress secretary-treasurer P. M. Draper objected, saying the TLC could not interfere with the character of its affiliates—mostly international unions, and the resolution was tabled.[19a]

What was happening? The Congress leadership was backing down, and continued to do so through the years. This is how trade union history was made in Canada. But another part of this history was the constant struggle for a progressive Canadian movement. This went on in unions across the country, exploded on the floor of TLC conventions, and though it never became official policy, it persisted to a point which alarmed the AFL. For instance, at the 1911 TLC convention, a shocked AFL delegate said:

"I thought today and yesterday that I was not attending the convention of a legislative body. I imagined I was attending the convention of the American Federation of Labour, where all sorts of disputes are expressed and acted upon."[19b]

Moreover, the situation must be viewed as a whole. The period under review was one of mass immigration and economic expansion. Great strikes were being fought. Union membership was growing. By 1908 the TLC had 620 locals in affiliation, and its total membership was 40,728. This is scarce the size of a medium-membership union to-day (1967), and reflects the lag in trade union and TLC development. Still it was a sizeable increase over the TLC's scanty forces at the beginning of the century.

The basic process, then, was trade union development—propelled forward by working class struggle, by the historic drive to a united militant Canadian trade union movement; blocked by the *external* opposition of big business and governments oriented to big business, and the *internal* conjoint reactionary force of craft unionism, international union domination and class collaboration. The play of these opposite forces determined the cycle of defeat and victory in the trade union movement for the period under review. Grief there was a-plenty, but joy too, and cheerfulness kept breaking through. "The infernal fraternal delegate"—this is how delegates to a TLC convention once described the AFL fraternal delegates—an epithet historically precise, though its immediate purport was obscure. Again, the TLC convention of 1903 at Brockville, Ontario, concluded this way, so the proceedings tell us:

"The labours of the representatives of the sons of toil being concluded, they linked their brawny arms and horny hands in each other, formed an oval-shaped chain around the hall; the merriment began by all singing Auld Lang Syne. Then came exclamations of 'Brockville is all right' and 'there will be a hot time in the old St. Lawrence Hall tonight!' "[19c]

CHAPTER 8

LABOUR, CANADA, PEACE,
1900-1914

1. MONOPOLY CAPITAL — DOMESTIC
AND FOREIGN

A Double Burden:

Labour, Canadian independence, peace, these three issues flowed harmoniously into each other to form a great progressive force; and confronting that force was monopoly capitalism and imperialism. In the period under review the iron laws of economics were at work. Centralization of industrial capital was increasing. In 1901-1915, average capital per manufacturing establishment went up three-fold:

Year	Number of Establishments	Total Capital	Average Capital Per Establishment
1901	14,650	$ 446,916,487	$30,506
1905	15,796	846,585,023	53,595
1910	19,418	1,247,583,069	64,912
1915	21,306	1,994,103,272	93,593[1]

Centralization of banking capital was also increasing. In 1902-1916, the number of chartered banks declined from 36 to 22, but the number of bank branches increased from 747 to 3,198.[2]

Centralized industrial and banking capital tended to merge to form monopoly capital—big business, the trusts. One pathway was *mergers* of business enterprises. In 1900-1914, 73 mergers absorbed 345 concerns. In 1901-1911, 41 mergers absorbed 196 firms with an aggregate capital of $125,000,000.[3] Thus were born such typical monopoly capital enterprises of our day as Canadian Johns-Mansville, Canada Cement, Imperial Tobacco, Steel Company of Canada, and Dominion Textile.[4] Here are three examples:

Canada Cement: Established 1911. Combined 11 companies with a total capital of $17,750,000.

Steel Company of Canada: Established 1909. Led the way in a group of mergers in the steel industry—others being Canada Car and Foundry, and Cockshutt Plough. All told, these mergers in the steel industry brought together 40 firms with a total capital of $95,711,500. Genuine competition in the industry was abolished.[5]

Dominion Textile: Founded in 1904. Its founder was not a weaver but a banker, Sir Charles Gordon, father of its president in later years, Blair Gordon. This is how it was organized. Sixteen capitalists provided amounts totalling $1,000,000 to set up the new company, in return for which they received stock worth $5,000,000—which meant an original, modest profit of 400%. Thirty-two years later, an enquiry into the textile industry headed by Mr. Justice Turgeon, revealed that as a result of accumulation in this original capital, the profits on the original investment, over a period of 31 years, from 1905 to 1936, averaged 98.4% per annum.[6]

This is how monopoly capital fastened its grip on Canada. It did it with little or no productive work, by the brute fact of ownership of capital and manipulation of ownership — and at times with a surprisingly small amount of original capital investment. In 41 mergers between 1901 and 1911, the initial outlay was $125,000,000 but the authorized capital was $334,000,000—something approaching a tripling of the initial outlay and representing promoters' profits exceeding $200,000,000.

In this its path to power, monopoly capital was aided by generous assistance from federal and provincial governments and also by its ability to use the stock exchange and other institutions to channel unto itself the credit of the country. It was benefitting from the centralization of production, a desirable process — but not desirable, though for the time being effective, was the centralization of ownership in the hands of a few monopoly capitalists, trusts, based on Toronto and Montreal, their domination of the workers, the farmers of western Canada and the peoples of the Maritimes and Quebec.

More serious still for Canadians—this rise of monopoly capital at home, coincided with and to a degree interlinked with monopoly capital domination from abroad. All in all, this meant imperialism— *a double burden of oppression for Canada.* Canada's domination by foreign capital was nothing new. This dated back to the 18th and 19th centuries. However, both before and after Confederation, a counter-process had been at work—the formation of Canadian capital. Now, in these opening years of the 20th century, a major world transformation was going on which tended to enhance the initial factor—domination by foreign capital. In principal industrial countries of the west, competitive capitalism was passing into monopoly capitalism, imperialism; and as part of this process, the alienation of the world by the wealthy capitalists of the west was quickening. Moreover, a new imperialist power was coming to the fore, located in North America, and with a long-standing, specific relationship to Canada-U.S. imperialism.

Until now, the U.S. capitalists had confined themselves to the exploitation of their own land and its people, white, Negro and Indian. Now they jumped on the wave of the future. The Spanish-American War (1899-1902) was a turning point. It ended with U.S. annexation of the Philippines. Then came the seizure of Puerto Rico. Restless and rapacious, U.S. imperialism looked north. Canada—a fine prize! Thus came about the Alaska Boundary Dispute of 1903. The U.S. government demanded Canadian territory on the Pacific coast north of 54° 40'. The Canadian government protested that Canada would lose every serviceable harbour on the Pacific north of 54° 40'. The dispute was submitted to an international arbitration board. The U.S. and British representatives on the board upheld the U.S. claim, while the Canadian representative was left in a minority—an outcome which Canada's Prime Minister, Sir Wilfrid Laurier denounced as a sell-out.

In the main however, U.S. imperialism's drive on Canada was not so much territorial as economic. American companies such as Ford and General Motors where then opening up branch plants in Canada. By 1914 the U.S. had invested a billion dollars in Canada. Also, U.S. exports were hammering on the Canadian market. In 1903, Prime Minister Laurier called the United States "an ever vigilant competitor": "Heaven grant that whilst we tarry in disputes, the trade of Canada is not deviated into other channels, and that an ever vigilant competitor will not take to himself the trade which properly belongs to those who acknowledge Canada as their native or their adopted land."[7]

Finally, there was the entry of international unions into Canada, the absorption of Canadian labour organizations. This too reflected the pressure of U.S. imperialism, not necessarily in the *intention* of the unions concerned, but in the *result*—the tendency to surrender of Canadian labour sovereignty. Moreover, for key AFL leaders, it was not just a question of result, but to a degree, of intention. They tended to identify themselves with the objectives of U.S. imperialism, and one such objective was North American integrationism under the hegemony of the United States. They endorsed the seemingly appealing but dangerous idea that the line of demarcation between Canada and the United States was—in the words of a speaker at the 1906 AFL convention—purely imaginary.

Coinciding with this North American integrationism, and almost certainly connected with it, was the AFL leaders' insistence on North American trade union hegemony. For Samuel Gompers, president of the AFL, the very idea of a sovereign Canadian trade union movement was anathema, and his denunciations were bitter for those who, in his words, sought "to divide the organized workers in the Dominion from those of all America".

In sum: branch plants, pressure of U.S. exports on the Canadian market, and pressure from international union—these, in the result, were three prongs of the U.S. imperialist economic drive on Canada. In this way, Canada, like Latin America, began to be a hintherland for U.S. imperialism, but Canada's degradation was the greater because though still in a dependent economic and political relationship to Great Britain, Canada—unlike the countries of Latin America —had a relatively modern industrial base and potential.

2. CANADIAN INDEPENDENCE
AND PEACE

Developments, 1901-1914:

Monopoly capital domination from at home and abroad — imperialism — fused with war. The Boer War of 1899-1902 was a signal. Trade unionists across Canada opposed it. So did the people of Quebec. Henri Bourassa, elected to parliament on a Liberal ticket, resigned his seat in protest, and was re-elected on a program of non-participation. In 1902, the Trades and Labour Council of Montreal protested "participation in any of England's debts caused by military or naval action as same is contrary to the interests of Canada"; and the Winnipeg Labour Party denounced militarism as "an inevitable offspring" of imperialism. The headline in the *Voice* (Winnipeg Trades and Labour Council organ) for June 1902, reads: "Peace in South Africa, Social War in Winnipeg!" Below a large cartoon shows Capital seated in the chariot of Empire, while in harness is a weary worker. The caption to the cartoon reads: "But the chap in the shafts is growing a little weary. He is beginning to think."

The trade union movement was taking up the fight for peace. In 1901 the TLC convention recommended that trade unionists should not join a military organization unless Canada was invaded.[8] Five years later the Congress called for a halt to the armaments buildup.[9]

This was part of a gathering struggle for peace in the world workers' movement. In 1907 this struggle was given dynamic impulse. The Stuttgardt Congress of the Second International of Socialist Parties adopted a motion that the duty of international labour was to do all possible to prevent war, but "should war result nonetheless, it is their (the working classes) duty to intervene in favour of a speedy termination, and do all in their power to utilize the economic and political crisis caused by the war, to rouse their peoples and thereby hasten the abolition of capitalist class rule".[9a]

Three years after this decision, the TLC executive council proposed that the Congress call "a convention of all peoples and citizens of Canada for the purpose of presenting Parliament with the views of those opposing militarism".[10] In 1910 the Congress convention instructed the executive to "communicate with all national and international labour congresses and federations to arrange an international peace conference, in order to establish a universal policy of opposition to international warfare among the working class throughout the world".[10a]

Then came the historic federal election of 1911. Peace was one great issue—Canada's freedom from involvement in imperialist entanglements and imperialist wars. In 1909, the TLC executive council charged that both the Liberal and the Conservative parties "are liable to be committed to great expenditures for military purposes".[11] The following year, 1910, the council warned that the naval issue "may some day involve Canada in wars, in the making of which it has no choice". The warning was well-grounded. That same year, the Laurier Liberal government had introduced a Naval Service Bill, whose principal provision was an appropriation of $10,000,000 for a Canadian navy. Many Canadian were dubious and felt this was a step to war.

Canada's independence was another great issue. In 1910 the Government had negotiated a reciprocity agreement with the U.S.A. On the surface this involved merely a mutual reduction of tariffs on agricultural and other commodities, but many Canadians were uneasy. It was charged that the initiative for the agreement had come from the U.S. Moreover, some U.S. political leaders were plainly declaring their desire to take over Canada. "I hope to see the day when the American flag will float on every square foot of the British North American possessions," said the Speaker of the U.S. House of Representatives. The Congressional representative from New York State had proposed to President Taft that he negotiate with Britain for the annexation of Canada. President Taft himself had exuberantly stated: "Canada is at the parting of the ways ... It was attached to the Empire only by a light and imperceptible bond !" It was not surprising then, that many Canadians should look on the Reciprocity Treaty as the "thin edge of the wedge" for taking over Canada.[11a] This hostility was heightened by the fear that the Treaty would undermine the National Policy, endanger Canadian manufacturing, and open the sluice gates to the inflow of cheap American goods.

Then there was the labour issue. Working class wrath was mounting against the Liberals. The Government had been too slow in bringing in social legislation. Dissatisfaction was increasing with the Industrial Disputes Investigation Act. There had been too many "sell-outs", too many instances where Federal Department of Labour mediation combined with pliable class collaborationist leaders and anti-labour companies to do damage to the workers' cause.

Finally there was the problem of Quebec, of French Canada in general. The Nationalists, led by Henri Bourassa, were then condemning the Naval Service Bill and charging that it was inspired by the imperialist war-making alliances of Europe. In 1910, Bourassa had founded the newspaper *Le Devoir* as an instrument in the fight for recognition of Quebec and French Canadian national rights.

Peace, Canadian independence, Labour, Quebec—their fusion—this was a prime issue in the federal election of 1911. A magnificent opportunity for labour leadership! But where was Labour? Weak, still, its forces meagre; what forces it had, disunited; its veins pumped full with the poison of Gompers' North American integrationism; feeble also in independent political action—without a national labour party, with just a few scattered provincial parties, and even these paltry efforts undermined by labour leaders who appeared in an unprincipled way on the platforms of the established parties. In sum, Organized Labour was not able to give Canada leadership at a time when this was sorely needed. This was due not just to its material weakness relative to big business—though this was exceedingly important. It was also due to its moral weakness, its internal problems: disunity, craft isolation, business unionism, domination by international unions. Labour's weakness led to lack of adaptability in a time of crisis. In 1911 the trade union movement did not see the situation as a whole. It did not systematically expand its interest to include Canadian independence, peace, the rights of Quebec. In short, it did not *combine* Labour and Canada.

True that in the heat of encounter this was difficult. Here is an instance. In 1911 the Winnipeg and Montreal Trades and Labour Councils endorsed reciprocity. This was understandable, for the labour and farm movements alike often opposed tariffs as a big business instrument. Partly they were right. But how was Canadian manufacturing to progress in the face of U.S. competition? That was what was worrying Canadians in 1911. Could the issue be posed merely in the single dimension of free trade versus tariffs, when free trade became the channel for U.S. economic aggression? Had the trade union movement not been entangled, to the degree that it was, by craft isolation, class collaboration and international union domination, then almost certainly it would have been speedier in finding the formula which worked, the correct combination of the social and national questions, one which advanced both these causes and assured the workers maximum allies.

What of Labour's left, the socialists? They also were often confused about the national question. In the United States, even a dedicated socialist like Eugene Debs, though warmly sympathetic to the Negroes, downgraded this as a decisive issue and believed the Negro workers' problem was basically the same as that of the white worker. In the same way—though the problem was distinct and much less acute—some socialists in Canada had a nihilist attitude to the *national question* as it affected Canada in general and Quebec in particular. In March 1911, R. A. Rigg, a Manitoba TLC leader said: "Trade unionists are international... and glory in it... We have no conflicting interests with the U.S. workers."[12] "Why worry about U.S. annexationism," asked a writer in the Winnipeg *Voice* about this same time, "the workers are already annexed in every way!"

With Labour weak and disoriented in this way, with the Liberals discredited and neutralized in Quebec by the upsurge of nationalism, the Conservatives came to the fore. They went about Canada warning about the U.S. danger. When election night came, they stood at the head of the polls. In the whirling maelstrom of events, the floodtide of popular passion for peace, Canada's independence and prosperity, Labour and French Canada—these great durables of Canadian progress—had been diverted into a reactionary channel, because there was no unity, no *coalition* of all the patriotic and progressive forces of Canadian society.

Once in office the Conservatives forgot their promises. In December 1912, Prime Minister Sir Robert Borden brought in a Naval Bill which provided for an appropriation of 35 millions to build 3 battleships which were to be handed over to the British Navy—much worse than anything the Liberals had proposed. Some charged that powerful corporations had inspired this—at Montreal the Vickers shipyards had just been built, and at Sydney, Nova Scotia, a subsidiary of the John Brown shipyards—both British firms. "It is significant that the Canadian government made its ship offer the year Vickers announced opening up the yard at Montreal!", said the Winnipeg *Voice* in 1913.[13]

However, though the Conservatives had abandoned the issue which brought them to power, the issue persisted—Canadian independence and peace. In the House of Commons Sir Wilfrid Laurier and Henri Bourassa gave expression to it. Sir Wilfrid Laurier denounced the imperialist arms race as "a circle of power worse than any described in Dante's Inferno"; and Bourassa charged the war scare was being created by the munition makers. In Parliament there was a furious debate on the government's Naval Bill, and tension rose to fever pitch. One session lasting continuously for 2 weeks until the government shut off debate by closure and jammed the Bill through.

The growing war tension was felt in the trade union movement as well. In 1911, the TLC convention called for a general strike in all countries planning war, and it instructed the executive council to propose this to all countries with a trade union centre, including the United States, Britain and Germany.[14] In 1912, the British Labour Party leader, Keir Hardie told the TLC convention:

"If every means fails in avoiding war, we are prepared to organize a revolutionary general strike, which should necessitate the presence of the armies at home, and prevent them being sent out to slaughter each other in a quarrel which is not theirs."[15]

In its report to this 1912 convention, the executive council said a way must be found to counter "the jingo fever of those who do the shouting but leave the fighting to the common people". The only object of war between Germany and Britain would be "deeper degradation of the toilers". Contact should be made with the British Trade Union Congress "to find out what action was being contemplated there".[16]

Shortly after, the Congress of the Second International convened at Basle, Switzerland. The Congress re-affirmed the Stuttgart "war against war" policy, and warned employers that an imperialist war would be followed by a people's revolution. Such was the depth of anti-war feelings at this Congress, that opportunist labour officials voted with the majority, and the resolution was adopted unanimously.

Hand in hand with this struggle for peace went an increasing hostility to capitalism as such. Economic and political tensions were mounting. Living costs were increasing, and so was the impact of strikes.* Rage was mounting against a system which—so, many Canadian workers felt—exploited them at home and threatened them now with physical extermination abroad. This radicalization was reflected in the TLC executive council's message to the 1912 convention. The

* Between 1911 and 1914 there were more workers on strike in Canada than any other period since the beginning of the century.

council spoke of the "gathering momentum of labour's forces, the awakening in the minds of the workers... of the reasons for their present position in society". It predicted that the present system was "doomed to severe changes in the near future", and called for a united labour front against the "profit-hunting labour-exploiting interests of this country".[17]

Radicalization was even more pronounced at the 1913 convention. One motion adopted urged the common people to act together in the political field "until they won their industrial freedom". Another decision was that officers and members of the Congress "inform themselves of the commodity nature of labour power, the labour theory of value and the Marxist theory of the process of surplus value". A message of solidarity—its terms bitterly denouncing "the despotic ruling class"—was sent to the B.C. coal miner Pettigrew, imprisoned in a Vancouver Island jail. Also, the executive council put to the delegates the idea of "a general strike to stop any commercial war".

In numbers present, members represented and forward-looking policies adopted, this 1913 convention marked a highwater point for the movement. As the 345 delegates looked back 4 decades to the beginnings of a central labour movement, they could take pride in the progress made. From the 18,000 or 20,000 members of the 1870s and 1880s, or the approximately 50,000 members at the turn of the century, the trade union movement had become an army of 175,000 members, and had shown its power in wage, strike and legislative struggles. Struggles and difficulties there were a-plenty — employers powerful at home, abroad the threat of war. Still there was the mounting strength of Labour in Canada and across the world. Beyond darkness then, the vista of a brighter day. As the convention concluded, the delegates joined hands and sang *Auld Lang Syne*.[18] Then came the thunder-bolt.

CHAPTER 9

THE TRADE UNION MOVEMENT
IN WORLD WAR I
1914-1918

1. LABOUR AND THE WAR

The Problem of the Trade Union Policy:

On June 28, 1914, Austrian Archduke Francis Ferdinand was assassinated by a Serbian nationalist. Four weeks later Austria invaded Serbia. On August 1, Germany declared war on Russia. Within 3 days, France and Britain declared war on Germany. World War I had begun. The immediate reaction of many union members in Canada was to denounce the war. On August 7, the *Industrial Banner*, Toronto Trades and Labour Council organ, wrote:

"The workers of the world will unite and repudiate all obligations imposed upon them by their selfish rulers... they will break forever the chains that have so long enslaved them... the bankruptcy of the capitalist class is approaching."[1]

However, as against these anti-war feelings, there was the powerful fact that high-placed labour leaders in the western belligerent powers had put aside the "war against war" policy decided at the Stuttgart and Basle congresses of the Second International. In Germany, classical country of social democracy, with seemingly the most powerful labour movement in the world, the majority of the trade union and socialist deputies in the Reichstag, voted their approval of the war. They said this was not the capitalist war they had anticipated, but a just war against Tsarist despotism. In France and Britain, most senior trade union leaders and labour members of parliament also voted support for the war. They said this was not the capitalist war envisaged, but a just war against Prussian despotism. For those who doubted it was a patriotic war, the dominant labour officialdom in the western belligerent powers offered a further explanation. They said solidarity had broken down, and shifted blame one to the other. The French leaders said they wanted to stand by their pledges at Basle, but the German leaders had caved in. The German leaders said the same in reverse.

This was the attitude of the Western labour leaders. Their failure to stand by the "war against war" policy sent a shock wave through the world labour and peoples' movement. "Is it a lie that the proletariat of all nations are one?" asked N. J. Ware in the *Industrial Banner* of August 14, 1914. Concerning this crisis of faith in 1914, Manitoba TLC vice-president R. A. Rigg was to state 3 years later:

"My great lament is that the international working class forces were so overwhelmed by the shock of the sudden onslaught and with the potent appeal of press and pulpit subservient to capitalist interests..."[2]

The orientation of the labour officialdom in Britain and Western Europe was matched by that of the AFL. Since the U.S. was neutral, the AFL was in a favourable position to take a peace initiative aimed at stopping the war or shortening its duration. However, the AFL leadership was one inclined to U.S. big business—certainly in foreign policy—and peace was not the foreign policy of big business. Neutral it was, but not to win the war, rather to profit from it by selling armaments to both sides and loaning money to both sides. In the result, the AFL's policy paralleled the big business policy. A resolution adopted by the AFL convention of November 1914, instead of calling on the world's workers to act now, asked them to ponder how they would act later, when the war was over:

"Be it resolved that this convention of the American Federation of Labour, in view of the general peace congress which no doubt will be held at the close of the war for the purpose of adjusting claims and differences, holds itself in readiness, and authorizes the executive council to call a meeting of representatives of organized labour of the different nations to meet at the same place, to the end that suggestions may be made, and such action taken as shall be helpful in restoring fraternal relations, protecting the interests of the toilers, and thereby assisting in laying the foundations for a more lasting peace."[3]

So this was the situation. Canada was now at war. Automatically this put the trade union movement to a severe test. It now faced the classic problem—how best to serve one's country in an hour of crisis, how best to serve Canada. But there were other factors too. There was the dependent relationship in which Canada tended to stand both economically and politically to Great Britain and the United States. Also, there was the dependence of most of Canada's unions on the U.S. unions. Another factor of the utmost gravity was the orientation of the official trade union movement in Great Britain, France and the United States. Again, there was patriotism—concern for the security of Canada; the bond of affection between many Canadians and the land they looked on as their mother country—Great Britain. In Quebec, there was friendship for the people of France. Among Canadians at large there was revulsion when they heard about German atrocities in Belgium.

These were some of the factors which combined to produce the result — the trade union movement's cancellation of its anti-war commitments. A signal of the change of course impending was the TLC's submission to an emergency session of Parliament held August 18-22, 1914. This submission did not condemn the war but pleaded that Labour not bear the burden alone. The plain facts are that in 1914 the trade union movement of Canada was not ready to take on its own government and employers, as well as the official trade union movement of Western Europe, Britain and the United States. Indeed the very idea that Canadian trade unionists could consider such a course would seem unthinkable. But the record shows that some did. They looked on the TLC's anti-war decisions of 1912 and 1913 as binding commitments. They believed that if the world's organized workers stood by the "war against war" policy, then the lives of millions would be spared.

This feeling was evident when the TLC convention opened at St. John, New Brunswick, soon after the outbreak of war. One who expressed it was D. McNaughton, a Winnipeg trade unionist representing the Commercial Telegraphers Union (an international union). He said Labour should use all its powers "to effect the speedy termination of the war". Also, he called for a national general strike to free the coal miners imprisoned on Vancouver Island as a result of the 1912-1914 strike.[4] Another who expressed it was City Commissioner Potts of St. John. He declared that "federated labour had the power to stop work for 24 hours." Labour could take anti-war action now by tying up transportation and preventing the movement of troops.[5]

What was the line of the TLC executive council? On the one hand it expressed Labour's anti-war feelings: "The awful struggle in Europe was a standing indictment of the management of great nations by the ruling class... There was no quarrel between the working people in the different countries..." The Council recalled resolutions adopted at earlier conventions that since "the capitalists of the world cause all war, they be allowed to do all the fighting". On the other hand, the Council did not support Delegate McNaughton's motion for action now to end the war; and in justifying its course, said that action was needed by workers "in all the countries": "The working class in one country alone cannot stop war." In other words, the Council pronounced itself against any independent peace initiative by Canadian workers.

Bitterness and disgust there must have been. In October 1914, W. R. Trotter—a B.C. trade unionist prominent in TLC affairs, wrote this poem:

"Brute force is king,
And rules the world with devilish glee,
Home, hearth, and happiness his prey,
Churning peace and joy each day,
As pagans feast.
Is there a God
Controlling with directing arm?
Is there indeed a Christian church?
Or has the sword replaced the torch
In lifted hand?"[6]

These feelings nothwithstanding, the movement's official policy had now become support for the war. But an undercurrent of doubt persisted. Significantly the 1914 convention's foreign policy resolution, while rejecting independent action by Canadians against the war, did hold back from fervent support for the war. In other words—a tacit acquiescence in the war, as distinct from the more outspoken pro-war policy of the British and French trade union movements. Statements made by the TLC executive council in later years of the war also communicate this shading of doubt. They are less belligerent than those of the British TUC or AFL leadership. At the 1916 convention of the TLC, President Watters said: "If there is any right in this war, we hope that right will prevail." And the executive council stated: "This hurricane of conflict that rushes over the world today is in no way near labour. On the contrary, it comes from a point that is as distinct from that occupied by the labour element, as the pole is distant and distinct from the equator."[7]

In 1918, the council said the war "was none of our doing but had to be accepted".[8] Some Congress leaders were more distant still. In 1917, David Rees—B.C. trade unionist and fraternal delegate to the convention of the British Trade Union Congress—told the British body he supported the project for a conference of socialist parties at Stockholm aimed at ending the war. At a mass meeting in London, England, Rees said:

"If ever the workers in Great Britain feel that time has arrived to declare war on the industrial barons they can rest assured that the Canadians will be heard from."[8a]

All this reflected the world situation as it was then. In World War I, Canada's allies were Britain, France, Belgium and Russia. What of

Britain? By 1914 democracy and reform had progressed there; yet Britain was then suppressing the liberty of hundreds of millions of people in Asia and Africa, and was tending to dominate Canada through investments, and through continuing controls over Canada's foreign and military policy. As for France and Belgium, they had also advanced in democracy and reform but were exploiting tens of millions of colonial peoples.* Russia was then the land of the Tsars, of pogroms and brutal suppression of workers.**

What of Canada's principal enemy, Germany? As distinct from the Germany of 1939, the Germany of 1914, though dominated by big business, landlords and militarists, more closely resembled the western parliamentary democracies. Ever since the 1800s its unions and socialist party had enjoyed legality; and when war was declared, 110 socialist deputies sat in the Reichstag.

Circumstances such as these help explain Canadian Labour's doubts, expressed cautiously on the surface but felt bitterly below, that the workers were being singled out, and Canada was being made a victim of big business and imperialism.***

On the Battlefields; In the Factories; 1914-1918:

In World War I, there were 225,000 casualties, and 60,000 were killed. Families were afflicted in Halifax, Montreal, Toronto, Winnipeg, Vancouver, in other cities and towns, also on the farms—this in a country populated by only 11,000,000. Canadian troops shed their blood at the Somme, Ypres, Vimy Ridge and Passchendale. At Vimy Ridge, casualties totalled 68,000; and at Ypres they were victims of the German's first chlorine gas attack.****10

At home, living costs rose rapidly. Between 1914 and 1917, the price of a 100-pound bag of sugar went up from $5.41 to $7.94; and by winter 1917 coal was selling at $11.03 a ton. Meat also went up in price, and philanthropic elements began an "eat fish campaign", with the result that the price of halibut increased by 4½ cents per pound.

* At the 1914 TLC convention, the Winnipeg Trade unionist, D. McNaughton said that people who talked about this being a war for little Belgium, should remember Belgian atrocities in the Congo.[8]
** In January 1917, the TLC leadership asked the Canadian Government to seek rights for Jews from "the despotic Russian rulers".
*** An echo of the imperialism then weighting on Canada was Federal Minister of Labour Crother's statement at the 1914 TLC convention: "We have done nothing to bring about this war!" There was some truth in this, given the dependent relationship of Canada to Britain, and pressure from the United States. However, big business was also developing in Canada, and was supporting the war.
**** In June 1918, a Canadian government recruiting advertisement declared: "There has been a heavy toll . . . the Allies still depend on Canada in order to maintain their fighting forces at full strength."

Profiteering was rampant—in 1917 profits of 40% on butter, 107% on cheese, 50% on eggs, and 130% on beef, were being reported. "Foodstuffs are plentiful, but are carefully stored away awaiting higher prices" complained Quebec's *Labour World*. Scandal piled on scandal. Production of the Ross rifle brought millions to its manufacturers, but soldiers at the front complained the rifle jammed. A wartime rhyme ran:

"It's pretty even betting,
These contractors have been geting
Quite a pile out of Tommy Atkin's soul."

Behind profiteering were the trusts. "Trusts are flourishing like a green bay tree", declared Mayor Church of Toronto in 1916. In September 1917, TLC president Watters charged that "profits have been a motive prompting manufacture of essentials". That year, the Congress demanded public ownership of all cold storage plants, abattoirs and canneries. The case for profit was boldly put. In 1916, the federal Minister of Railways said: "Munitions cannot be made without profit because that would interfere with private enterprise." In 1917, a government commission reported: "Eliminate the profit and you eliminate the enterprise." In August 1917, the Minister of Finance, Thomas White, said that capitalists should not be called upon to reveal "intimate details of their private business to their competitors".[11] In 1917, after much protest from the people, an excess profits tax was introduced, but this left untouched the bulk of big business profits.[12]

To stimulate businessmen's interest in the war, titles such as "honorary colonel" were bestowed. Some millionaires were knighted — for example, Sir Joseph Flavelle of Canada Packers and the Canadian Bank of Commerce—lampooned as "that eminent pork seller and conserver of dead chickens, Sir Joseph Flavelle", by Ernest Lapointe, in the House of Commons, April 1918.[13] "This attempt to create a Canadian nobility is ridiculous!" exclaimed the Quebec *Labour World* in March 1917.

In this way the large employers drew profits from the war, while Canada's sons—including their own—moved by love of country and the desire to serve her durable institutions and values—fought and died. In the factories, the employers lengthened hours and stepped up exploitation. At a Toronto munitions plant in 1917, the management increased hours from 13 to 14 a day. At least 7 women refused to work the extra hour. Of these, 2 had husbands at the front, one had lost a brother overseas, one had a brother on active service, and one had been awarded the munitions workers good service medal. The 7 went to the office of the Toronto *Daily Star*. "Look at our hands!" cried one, and she thrust out hands blackened with oil from which the skin had peeled in big patches. A member of the delegation said: "One of the girls was too sick to come with us. Oil in her system is killing her. Two have died!" Another said: "They are killing us off as fast as they are killing the men in the trenches!"[14]

The incident was not a lone one. At the Verdun Munitions Board plant, women worked 72 hours per week and upwards. At Nobel, plumbers worked 70 hours per week; and at Camp Borden, 200 building trades workers were housed in a single room built originally as a railway baggage room. At Thetford Mines, Quebec, in 1916, miners' wages were cut, despite a threefold increase in the price of asbestos.[15] When 200 of them enlisted, their places were taken by alien internees. When the miners, infuriated, organized in the International Union of Mine, Mill and Smelter Workers, and 1,000 went on strike in 1917, internees were brought in as strike-breakers.

All in all, employers took advantage of the war situation to eliminate the 8-hour day in many cases where it had been won, and substitute for it the 10, 12, 14, 16-hour day—even the 7-day week. In munitions plants, workers were often refused a voice in determining conditions—in the latter part of the war, the trade union movement won a partial change in this policy. Matching this was the cheap attitude to soldiers' pay—$1.10 per day. The trade union movement demanded this be increased to $2.00 a day, but to no avail.*

2. THE CONSCRIPTION CRISIS — 1917

Labour's Rising Struggle:

As death mounted on the battlefield, and exploitation at home, unrest deepened. "Our men die abroad and our children starve because of the war profiteers. I've lost every relative but one," said a Montreal labour militant, Rose Henderson. Unrest in Canada was heightened by events in Europe. Disgust with the war was mounting. In the midsummer of 1916, the Stockholm Peace Appeal was launched. In March 1917, revolution broke out in Russia. The throne of the Tsars went toppling in the dust.

In Canada, trade union fortunes revived. Membership—reduced in 1914-1915, rose to 204,603 at the close of 1917. This surpassed the 1913 high—175,799.[16] Strikes increased. The number on strike had also declined in 1914-1915. In 1916 it was 26,538—roughly equal to the aver-

---

* In 1942, Canadian soldiers enlisting were being paid $1.30 per day—20 cents per day progress in 25 years!

age for 1900-1913. In 1917, it was 50,255. This surpassed the pre-war high—42,860 in 1912.[17]

Involved in these strikes were miners at Drumheller, Alberta, and street-railwaymen in Toronto. At Hamilton in 1916, 1,500 machinists, toolmakers and helpers went on strike for the 9-hour day.[18] In Quebec, during 1916-1917, there were strikes at the Drummondville Powder Works and the Montreal Vickers shipyards. At Montreal garment and fur workers were on strike in 1917.

This rising economic struggle merged with the fight against conscription. The 1915 and 1916 TLC convention had condemned conscription. For its part, the Federal Government used dissemblance. After the 1916 convention, a cabinet minister told the Congress: "It will never be necessary to go as far as conscription. You can rest assured that whatever we do will meet with the approval of the labour interests in Canada"[19] However, in December 1916, the government took a long step to conscription. At a meeting in Ottawa, Prime Minister Borden and R. B. Bennett, Director-General for Manpower, informed the TLC that the government was planning registration of the country's working force. Later, the Prime Minister wrote the Congress a letter in which he said that this registration was "not connected with conscription", but added: "If conscription proves the only effective method for preserving the existence of the state, I shall consider it necessary and should not hesitate to act accordingly."[20]

Instead of heeding the threat in this letter, the TLC leaders comforted themselves with its re-assurance. In January 1917, they recommended that Labour co-operate with national registration.[21] This implicitly violated the anti-conscription decisions of the 1915 and 1916 conventions, and was protested by trade unionists across the country. At Winnipeg, the Trades and Labour Council adopted this motion: "The Dominion executive erred in judgment in recommending that registration cards be filled in. We move that action be repudiated." At Montreal, the Trades and Labour Council expressed its resentment. In the Manitoba provincial legislature, R. A. Rigg—an outstanding trade unionist—delivered a memorable address. "The interests of the nation are being subordinated to political patronage, political corruption and profit-making." Some high sources* were threatening that if he spoke his mind he would be shot, but he could no longer be silent. As Rigg went on, he sounded the depths of the conscription issue, and expressed Labour's protest against war in general:

"When people cry aloud for reforms and threaten capitalist profits, the capitalists start a war. When people cry for old age pensions,

* This was understood to be a reference to the Premier of Manitoba.

women's suffrage, workmen's compensation acts, the capitalists start a war. The working men of one country have no quarrel with the working men of another country. The common enemy the world over is the capitalist class."

During the months of spring, trade union resistance to conscription continued to mount. Across the country, more particularly in the western provinces, Trades and Labour Councils and provincial federations began to call for a general strike against conscription. The result was that the TLC executive council adjusted its position. In May 1917, the council asked the Congress' affiliate unions: "To prevent anything that savours of conscription, are you prepared to use the most effective and almost the only weapon within your reach?"

In June 1917 the crisis came to a head. The Conscription Bill was introduced in the House of Commons. Across Canada reaction was bitter. One worker said: "I am a wage slave here, and I have three brothers in France. That's conscription enough for me!" The Calgary Trades and Labour Council and the B.C. Federation of Labour called for a general strike. At Ottawa, in June 1917, a gathering of senior trade union officers called on the workers to fight the Bill "by every means in their power".

The storm burst into the House of Commons. Some M.P.s charged that while Canadians were being marched to the trenches, plans were being made to have their jobs taken by Americans. Advertisements in U.S. newspapers were cited which called for 50,000 workers to come to Canada—one U.S. newspaper had asked textile workers to come to the Dominion Textile Company plant at Magog. An Ontario farm M.P. charged that U.S. college students were summoned to Canada, to replace Canadian farmers joining the armed forces—all expenses were to be paid by the Canadian government and each student was promised 150 acres and "no compulsory service".[22]

On June 28, Alphonse Verville, a member of Montreal Plumbers Local 144, M.P. for Montreal Hochelaga since 1906 and a past TLC president, denounced conscription. "There were two major views on the War," he told the House of Commons, "that of the exploiter and that of the exploited." The autocracy of capitalism was becoming more and more a menace to Canada. He derided employers' talk of "patriotism":

"Is it patriotism to manufacture implements of war at scandalous profits?... Is it patriotism to speculate on the most vital part of the soldier's existence, that of foodstuffs?..." The next day he told the House that Labour stood for a general strike:

"When I say that organized labour will do all it can against conscription... I want this House to know what that means, it means a general strike... As for the French Canadians, they are prepared for civil war."

With motions pouring into TLC headquarters from across the country, early in July, President Watters proposed that the day conscription went into effect, every worker should refuse to work for private profit: "Let labour demonstrate their loyalty and patriotism, even if a general strike is necessary to bring it about..."[23]

At Montreal, between July 13 and July 17, there was a series of powerful demonstrations. On July 13, 15,000 Montrealers gathered in the east end, corner Logan and Champlain Streets. Mayor Mederic Martin—present by invitation of the Montreal Trades and Labour Council, told the crowd he was going to appeal to the Imperial authority against conscription. Alphonse Verville spoke of plans for a general strike. The meeting called for a referendum on the conscription issue, protested restrictions on freedom of speech, and sang "O Canada".

Three days later 16,000 gathered at Jacques Cartier Square in Quebec City. Armand Lavergne, nationalist M.P., called for a general strike. He said England was not fighting for Belgian freedom but to "prevent Germany from taking over British Trade".

On July 17, there was another demonstration at Montreal's Lafontaine Park. The speakers compared Quebec's lot in 1917 with Ireland's in 1916 (a reference to the Easter Rebellion). One proposed that Liberal members resign en masse from the House of Commons. From the crowd came cries: "Up Cartier and Macdonald! Up Chenier! Hurrah for Nelson and Riel!"[24]

In the House of Commons, debate was fast and furious. On July 19, the Hon. Rodolphe Lemieux charged Quebec had been betrayed. He linked Quebec's anti-conscription struggle to the Canada-wide struggle: "The first rumblings against conscription had to come from Winnipeg, Calgary, Vancouver, Hamilton, Toronto and Ottawa."[25]

In this way, in the trade union movement in Quebec and on the parliamentary front, the anti-conscription struggle was mounting and merging with the wage and strike movement and with radicalism. The Quebec *Labour World** denounced "invisible government piling up thousands and millions a year".[26] Some union locals increased their resistance to class collaboration policies. Also, labour political action revived. In 1917 an independent labour party was re-established in Ontario. In the midsummer of 1917, the Montreal Trades and Labour Council set up a committee to reorganize the Quebec Labour Party.

* In 1967 this newspaper was still being published as an organ of the Quebec Federation of Labour (CLC).

U.S. Imperialism; The AFL; Class Collaboration:

This mounting militancy in Canada was part of a world situation. In Britain, union struggles were sharpening—a wave of strikes, an outburst of shop stewards' rank and file action on the Clydeside. In Russia, the soviets of workers, farmers and soldiers were coming to the fore.

But, in this complex of circumstances, there was also the orientation and weight of the United States. During the first three years of the war, the U.S. was neutral. U.S. big business made huge profits from loans and arms sales to the belligerents. "The war was being prolonged to make billionaires!", exclaimed a UMW* delegate at the 1915 AFL convention. Now the U.S. was approaching a new turn—full-scale participation in the war. The attitude of the U.S. public must be understood. That is a distinct question. Certain that as in Canada, Americans were moved by love of country and the desire to foster her security, and sincerely accepted their President's assurance that this was a war for democracy. But certain also that U.S. big business had distinct motives of its own. The outbreak of revolution in Russia in the spring of 1917, the severe losses sustained by Britain and France on the Western Front had weakened the Allied position; and in turn this endangered the repayment of huge loans made by the House of Morgan and other U.S. financial groups. U.S. big business wanted to protect its blood money, to stabilize capitalism in Europe against the danger of popular takeover, and implant its own economic and political powers there. All in all, the result was that on March 14, 1917, the U.S. declared war on Germany.

In this course, the U.S. government was strongly supported by the AFL. At the 1915 convention, when UMW delegates protested against militarism, President Samuel Gompers opposed them, saying he had been a pacifist but now believed in preparedness and military training. During the critical years preceding U.S. entry into the war, Samuel Gompers painted rosy pictures about post-war possibilities, but did not put forward any concrete proposals for action now to end the bloodshed and misery. He told the workers to look forward to a post-war congress of the powers, at which the terms of peace would be established. That Congress would provide an opportunity "to democratize the countries and nations of Europe politically". And the U.S. was "peculiarly fitted" to contribute to this objective, for was it not the "land of freedom and democracy", the land which "had a conception of the possibilities to which men and women may grow?"[27]

When the time came for the U.S. to join the war, Gompers moved like an automaton. On March 12, just 5 days before U.S. entry into the

* United Mine Workers of America.

war, he convened a special conference of top union officers at Washington. That conference decided:

"Despite our endeavours and hopes, should our country be drawn into the maelstrom of European conflict, we... offer our services to our country in the field of activity of defence, to safeguard and preserve the Republic of the United States against enemies, whomsoever they may be."[27a]

With the U.S. now at war, AFL officials were not to be outdone by anyone in military zeal. At a mass meeting in London, England, sponsored by the British Trade Union Congress in September 1917, the AFL delegates told the Englishmen: "Kill the Prussian beast! Kill the German first then talk to him afterward! There should be no more Kaisers or Kings!"

U.S. entry into the war stepped up militarism in Canada. In this the AFL and international unions were a key instrument. They became most active in efforts to draw Canadians into their war plans. Some Canadian union officials were present at the Washington AFL conference of March 12, 1917—just prior to U.S. entry in the war. The tendency to colonial status by Canada's trade union movement is epitomized in the fact that these Canadians—citizens of a country which had poured out its blood in three years of war while the U.S. was neutral—stupidly signed the AFL statement cited above, which proclaimed dedication "to the Republic of the United States... against all enemies, whomsoever they may be"!

In Canada, TLC vice-president James Simpson assured union members that American entry into the war would help them in their fight against conscription—there would be so many Americans at the front that conscription would not be needed. The opposite was the case. On June 1, 1917—the day the U.S. Congress adopted a draft conscription law, the Conscription Bill was introduced into the House of Commons.

In this way, just when Canada's unions were contemplating a general strike against conscription, the AFL was committing itself to a policy of no oppostion to conscription. Automatically this introduced vacillation into the Canadian movement's struggle against conscription, because of *dual power;* on the one hand the Canadian membership and Canadian union structures; on the other hand, ties of dependence to international union headquarters which for the most part favoured conscription. It was not surprising, then, that even in Quebec, where anti-conscription feeling was particularly strong, already in June 1917, Gustave Francq—a key trade unionist and supporter of the international unions—was suggesting conscription should not be opposed.

The effects of U.S. international headquarters were felt on the wages front too. In September 1917, the Alberta executive committee of the TLC asked the Congress to notify the various U.S. headquarters that the "Canadian membership be not asked to continue to work for less wages than in several instances have been ultimately arranged by arbitrators". In June 1917, Federal Minister of Labour Crothers said "Gompers and William Green* are fine working class leaders".

The attitude of some socialist leaders was also a factor. In earlier years of the war, they had inclined to an anti-war position, though not a strong one. In the Winnipeg *Voice* of 1915, a writer had charged that the "refined capitalist class" had plunged the world into war "for profits", that Britain was in the war "to retain economic and financial control of colonial territories against Germany... We appeal not to the present rulers of society but to the working class to stop the war!" However, some socialist leaders moved away from this anti-war policy. They said the workers could not take anti-war actions because they were not "yet in office". They suggested that since "war was inevitable under capitalism", the workers "must accept all the consequences of capitalist rule... (which) includes the horrors of war". The pro-war position of the British socialist leadership should not be condemned, because in this wartime period "these socialists had accepted the temporary community of interests with other classes". Also their attitude to Quebec was dubious. They tended to counterpose Labour's struggle to the patriotic anti-conscription struggle of the people of Quebec. In the early months of 1916, a writer in the Winnipeg *Voice* asked the government to look to "the seditious utterances of Bourassa and Lavergne, instead of hunting out anti-war attitudes in the Labour movement".

A further factor was the grinding campaign of reprisal and terror against those who opposed the war or conscription. They faced intimidation, perhaps loss of employment, or prison and internment. Sometimes troops, stationed in Canada, were incited by "brass hats" (senior army officers) and profiteering "honorary colonels" into attacks on meetings of progressive workers. What the labour movement had to endure is reflected in a proposal by Alan Studholme, a well-known Hamilton trade unionist, for years a member of the Ontario legislature. He said trade unionists should defend their meetings "with clubs" if necessary. One of those jailed for opposing the war was the union member John Reid. In January 1916 he was sentenced to 15 months in Lethbridge jail, but was released after a strong protest by

---

* William Green, Secretary of the AFL, and later its President.

the TLC and the Montreal Trades and Labour Council. In 1917 and the first 3 months of 1918, 3,895 people were arrested on charges connected with anti-conscriptionist activity.[28]

The TLC Convention of September 1917:

The TLC convention of September 1917 was the theatre for the clash of tendencies in the trade union movement. The more radical element spoke out with new boldness. Laura Hughes urged the convention to support the Stockholm Peace Conference then being sponsored by the left socialists in the various belligerent countries. She said the objective should be a world peace settlement without annexation or indemnities, and she called for support to the workers and peasants councils in Russia.[29] L. L. Pelletier, of the Order of Railway Conductors, an international union, declared: "Every wreath of smoke from the battlefields of Europe is weaving a rope that will hang every vestige of capitalism."[30] Cassidy, a delegate from Montreal Lodge 111 of the International Association of Machinists (AFL-TLC) charged that "someone is sitting on the lid telling us to hold off striking until the war is over"; and he called on the workers and soldiers of Canada to unite as they had in Russia: "We have only one enemy, and that is the international capitalist class!"[31] This rising radicalism was reflected also in the report of the Congress executive council:

"Kingdoms and empires will have passed away ... but through it there will be a conflict of the rich and poor, employers and employees, capital and labour".[32]

This was one trend. But there were opposing trends and pressures. Prime Minister Borden told the delegates the troops were fighting not just for Canada but for "Empire and Liberty". He spoke about the battle of Vimy Ridge. He was not sure how many Canadian casualties there had been. Someone had told him 13,000, someone else 18,000. Conscription was needed to make up for such losses.[33] When he finished, the chairman announced the next speaker, Emmanuel Koveleski, of Rochester, New York, fraternal delegate of the AFL—whereupon Sir Robert rose to his feet and cried: "I was not aware there was a delegate here from the United States ... Three cheers for the United States!"[34] Then Koveleski spoke—more Prussian than Labour. He said that war was "a fundamentally co-operative action of organic society. Co-operation for war must come from two primary sources, the possessors of creative labour power and the controllers of capital."[35]

Conscription was the main issue. Before the convention were resolutions calling for a general strike. One, from the Transcona Labour Council proposed "a general strike of organized labour from the Atlantic to the Pacific" if conscription of manpower was carried through without conscription of wealth and nationalization of all industries.[36] However, just 2 weeks before the convention, the Conscription Bill had become law. This meant that the labour movement had been presented with a tough fact. To overcome this fact, it had to face it, and react with facts of its own, tougher still. But this the more conservative element opposed. One delegate complained about "Bourassas in other provinces". Another, Gustave Francq, put the case for the pro-conscriptionists in these words:

"No matter if 99% of the people were opposed to conscription, I would be in favour of it, because we have to fight the battle of democracy against autocracy . . . When a law is passed, no matter whether we like it or not, we have to obey it."[37]

Between the right wing supporters of conscription, and its militant opponents, was the centre as represented by delegates like A. Martel of the Montreal Carpenters,* John Bruce of the Plumbers,** and R. A. Rigg, Manitoba TLC vice-president. They called for a legal fight against the Conscription law, aimed at securing its repeal, but they opposed a general strike. Their policy, in the result, regardless of intention, served as a buffer for pro-conscriptionists, since it provided an ineffective, legalist channel for mass anti-conscription feeling, as distinct from the more effective channel of a general strike.

Where did the executive council stand? It said the Congress could not "stultify itself to the degree of either withdrawing or contradicting carefully thought-out views on the question of conscription", but now that the measure was law, to oppose it meant to expose the movement to "heavy penalties", and this the Congress could not do:

"Under our representative form of government, it is not deemed right or patriotic, or in the interests of the Dominion or the labour classes, to say or do ought that might keep them (the government) from attaining all the results anticipated from enforcement of the law."[38]

This policy was expressed still more precisely in a speech by Congress secretary-treasurer P. M. Draper. It was all very well, he said, for delegates to come to this convention and call for repeal of conscription, "but if they go out and advocate repeal, and get arrested, what protection can we give them?" A lawyer had told him that to advocate repeal meant to oppose the law, and violate the law—and this had been confirmed by the government leader in the Senate, Senator Lougheed.***

* United Brotherhood of Carpenters and Jointers (AFL)
** United Association of Plumbers and Steamfitters.
*** The kind of pressure which weighed on the delegates at the 1917 convention is reflected probably in the reaction of the chair to one of them (Cassidy), who asked what protection there would be for those who spoke their mind, would they be subject to reprisals from the authorities? The chair did not provide him with the assurance he sought.

The executive council had yet another argument—the status of Canada's labour movement. James Simpson, Congress vice-president for Ontario said:

"It is just as well, at this time, that I should point out that the organized workers of Canada stand in a position that has no parallel in any other country of the world. This Congress can only exert its moral influence in the enforcement of decisions, and the economic power necessary to support legislative demands is not vested in our movement, but is under the control of the international officers of our representative unions. When the executive council of the American Federation of Labour reaches a decision, members of that council, being the heads of powerful international trade unions, can use their influence effectively. The same applies to the parliamentary committee of the British Trade Union Congress, but in Canada we cannot use our economic power without the sanction of the heads of our international unions ... In cases where our decisions are at variance with decisions taken by the American Federation of Labour regarding important national issues, it is difficult to secure that sympathy, that support in the exercise of our economic powers, as we otherwise would receive if the executive of the Congress were composed of the heads of powerful economic organizations."[39]

This was the leadership's second argument — the colonial status of Canada's trade union movement — note well, not the *struggle* against that status but *resignation* to it, and its use to justify departure from a course which had been suggested by Congress president Watters several months earlier — general strike. Some delegates were bitter. Of what avail Draper's talk about the Congress being sovereign when, as Simpson had said, "its hands were tied"? "It would appear that we are only a limited monarchy", said one.[40] Another said the position was clear — the only way to stop conscription was to have a general strike, but the Congress could not do this because AFL president Samuel Gompers was opposed: "President Gompers had committed the workers of the United States to conscription, therefore a general strike was not feasible."[41]

Under the impact of these arguments, the ranks of the anti-conscriptionists were broken. The executive council's policy was adopted by the slender margin of 30 votes (136-106). The council's majority was smaller still on an amendment moved by the "centre" forces — one which called for repeal of the conscription law but stopped short of a general strike, (111-101). Then by a large majority, the delegates adopted a motion affirming their opposition in principle to conscription.

The Khaki Election, December 1917:

Meanwhile popular discontent and radicalism continued to rise across the world and in Canada. On November 7, 1917, the Soviets took power in Russia. In Canada, rage was mounting against the employers, and against labour leaders whose policy tended to coincide in the result with that of the employers and government on issues like conscription. In the Jacques Cartier Typographical Lodge at Montreal, the members, angered by Gustave Francq's position on conscription, withdrew him as delegate to the Trades and Labour Council; whereupon Francq asked ITU international headquarters to transfer him to another local.

As against this mounting militancy, the AFL had now become hot in its support for the war. Its November 1917 convention was a flag-waving one. The TLC's fraternal delegate to that convention reported later: "The delegates and visitors marched to the hall in a body, carrying the American flag, led by a band of 100 pieces!"[42]

In Canada, a critical federal election was due to take place in December 1917, and conscription was the main issue. Just 3 weeks before that election, AFL president Samuel Gompers came to Canada and proceeded to Toronto to address a victory loan meeting at the Toronto Armouries on November 26. He told the crowd that a person who would not fight for free institutions was "a coward and poltroon". He explained that in his own case, "they will not let me fight", but, "people could fight with money too". That very day, crossing the border at Niagara Falls, he had subscribed to a $50 bond, and this showed "where my heart is". He said doubts about the war should be cast aside: "Neutral countries, neutral minds, there ain't no such animal: fish, or cut bait! Fight or buy Victory Bonds!" Scarce 3 weeks before this meeting, the Soviets had taken power. Gompers charged that the Bolsheviks were German agents who were "betraying the people of Russia to Imperial Germany. The officers of the general staff of the pretended new government are Germans..." He also referred to relations between the Canadian and U.S. labour movements. Efforts were being made to divide Canadians from U.S. workers. In favour of international unions, he cited a testimonial from Sir Charles Ross (the man who, it was alleged, had made money from the rifle that jammed). Since dealing with international headquarters, Sir Charles had found that "I never got such good service from my employees". Then Gompers turned to the main issue. He did not want to interfere in Canadian affairs, but felt "the people of Canada ought to stand united without regard for religion or any other difference to bring victory and glory to the Dominion". He advised Canadian workers to abandon opposition to conscription:

"I held it and shall hold it to be the duty of every Canadian and American citizen in time of war to obey that decision, rightfully and lawfully reached ... When the duly-constituted authority in time of war arrives at a conclusion, it is no longer a subject to discuss ... This is war, it is not a game. When the Congress or Parliament decrees a certain course, it is the duty of every man to stand by and see that policy is put into successful operation."[43]

This intervention by the AFL president into a Canadian situation, at a time when the conscription issue was before the electorate, meant assistance to both the U.S. and Canadian governments. How the Canadian government used it is indicated by this unscrupulous misuse of terms in a pro-government advertisement which appeared 10 days later in the *Industrial Banner,* organ of the Toronto Trades and Labour Council: "Put the union label on union government!"*

In this way, at a time when the leader of the Liberal opposition, Sir Wilfrid Laurier, was campaigning across the country against conscription; when the people of Quebec as well as trade unionists across Canada were pressing for defeat of the conscriptionists; when it would probably have been to Organized Labour's best advantage to march along with such a movement, indeed in its van, the trade union movement found itself divided, torn by conflicting loyalties, undermined by business unionism, class collaboration, and U.S. interference, and unable to act as a united force. Had the anti-conscriptionist movement then sweeping Canada, been reinforced by the decision to conduct a general strike, as had been proposed by some delegates at the TLC convention several months earlier, then the possibility for an anti-conscription victory at the polls would almost certainly have been greater.

As election day approached, the big business-government-conscriptionist coalition threw everything into the scales. Their policy was: Get the result. Maybe, make apologies later. But get the result. Some years later, a well-known Canadian public figure, W. T. R. Preston, was to write as follows concerning events before this election:

"Never can there have been such frauds, never an election such a travesty! ... Instruction came by letter and cable from the Cabinet at Ottawa, telling the number of fraudulent votes which must be allotted to ensure the return of the goverment candidates in their respective constituencies ... The votes were to be allotted fraudulently to constituencies where the qualified vote would not suffice to elect the government candidates ... There was a committee composed of senior officers ... which had the duty of finding out soldiers who were too frank in their Liberal tendencies ... These men were sent to the front at the first opportunity. To one officer who was getting cold feet at

* Prime Minister Borden was calling for a "union" government to consist of Tories and conscriptionist Liberals—something which had nothing to do with "union" in the labour sense.

the extent of the proposed fraud and feared an enquiry, the reply was made: 'Those likely to tell will be buried in France in six months.' ... Non-combattants in the Forestry Corps who spoke against the government were sent without compunction to the trenches. Two officers attached to general headquarters, Argyle Street, had authority to send to the front any soldier who was too-outspoken in his intentions to vote for Laurier's candidates. Twelve such men were sent out to No Man's Land. Not one of them ever returned... The brother of one of these, saying that he intended to vote for Laurier was told: 'Look out! You know what happened to your brother!' "[44]

December 17 came, election day. The result: 153 pro-government candidates elected, (including "Union" or conscriptionist Liberals) as against 83 Laurier (anti-conscriptionist) Liberals. The anti-conscriptionists had been defeated. The TLC leaders now said that it could do nothing about conscription in view of this "pronouncement at the polls". But they did not say that their policies had helped produce the pronouncement, and prevented the kind of mobilization which, just possibly, might have produced an opposite pronouncement. Here was Canadian history influenced—to a limited yet significant degree—by class collaboration *combined with* international union interference from the United States.

3. 1918: TRADE UNION PROGRESS VERSUS CLASS COLLABORATION

The Continuing Anti-Conscription Struggle;
What Class Collaboration Meant:

Despite the outcome of the Khaki election, trade union advance continued. By the end of 1918, membership had risen to 248,887—20% over the previous year, and 50% over 1916.[45] In 1918 79,743 workers were on strike as compared to 50,255 in 1917.[46] Government employees were an important factor: Organization by municipal police in some cities; a wave of strikes among public service workers in Winnipeg in May 1918; an important strike of postmen—terminated when the leadership decided to accept the government settlement over the protests of some in the rank and file. The movement's rising militancy was reflected also in a revival of Labour parties, in Ontario, Manitoba and Saskatchewan. The anti-conscription struggle continued. The B.C. Provincial Federation of Labour and the Vancouver Trades and Labour Council conducted a struggle on this issue, during which 2 trade unionists were killed by police—William Kerr and Ginger Goodwin. Goodwin had been an organizer with the International Union of Mine, Mill and Smelter Workers. In protest against his death, the Vancouver Trades and Labour Council conducted a 24-hour general strike.[47]

In this way trade union militancy was rising, and so was the anti-conscription struggle in Quebec. But there was no *combination* of these two great durables—Organized Labour and Quebec. This was ruled out because the dominant trade union officialdom in Canada and the United States did not put itself at the head of rank and file militancy but resisted it, and along with that, had an incorrect orientation to Quebec.

However, despite the lack of central co-ordination, the popular struggle continued. Quebec City became a storm centre. On the evening of March 28, 2,000 citizens gathered on the streets of Quebec. Dominion police present asked one to produce exemption papers—a request which was refused. The crowd became indignant, pursued a number of police, and burst into a police station where they had taken refuge. The government authorities charged later that in these incidents, 15 Dominion police had been assaulted. The next day there was a new demonstration. The director of the Dominion Government's Military Service Branch reported: "The Dominion police were in the face of a hostile attitude from practically every source."

In this situation, the general officer commanding the Quebec City military district, called for more troops. On Monday, April 1, he ordered that placards be posted up warning citizens not to attend unlawful assemblies, and to stay indoors. Despite this, a large crowd gathered on the streets that evening. They were confronted by troops ordered to the scene by the senior army officers, despite a demand from the mayor of Quebec that troops not intervene. Then came a new series of incidents. Thirty soldiers broke into a shop and bayoneted the shopkeeper. A student visiting in Quebec was killed. The troops fired on the police, and in turn a number in the crowd pelted the troops with bricks and stones and fired on them. In this latter clash, 5 of the federal forces were wounded, while in the crowd, 4 were killed and 60 arrested.

The Federal Government reacted vigorously to this unrest. It charged that Quebec City's police and municipal administration were not supporting the army. Also it announced it would get the Military Service Act amended to provide that all those of military age who opposed the Act would be subject to conscription.[48] In the House of Commons, Quebec Liberal Party members opposed this. On Friday, April 5, Ernest Lapointe said that "drunken brutes were being used" in Quebec City, "to enforce the Military Service Act"; and Sir Wilfrid Laurier charged that ex-boxers and degenerates were being thrown against the citizenry.

Plainly mass discontent was mounting. To counter it, the government used class collaboration. It named union officials to key posts. Gideon Robertson, a senior Canadian officer of the Commercial Telegraphers Union was given a seat in the Senate. Other union officials were appointed to government boards. They sat on these boards with representatives of business and processed the conscription of labour for farm and industry, national registration, enforcement of the Military Service Act—they did all this while union members were being shot, the right to organize often trampled on, and savage reprisals visited on the people of Quebec.

This class collaboration drive in Canada was interconnected with a parallel development in the U.S.A. In 1918, the AFL leaders concluded an agreement with the representatives of big business under which the situation in management-labour relations was to remain status quo—unaltered for the duration of the war emergency. In other words, the AFL leaders promised not to rock the boat, not to take advantage of the war situation to organize the mass production industries. In Washington, Samuel Gompers sat in state as chairman of the labour section of the Council of National Defense. At his side were the copper magnate, Samuel Guggenheim and the oil millionaire, John D. Rockefeller, Jr.—the latter had employed William Lyon Mackenzie King as his labour advisor some years earlier. Gompers had come home. If recognition of this kind was his aim in life, he had it. He used to say that such appointments meant that "organized labour is being recognized". This was not true. A few posts for a few labour officials on a few government boards could be no substitute for union recognition in the shops. And some employers who gave Gompers their friendly hand-shake at Washington dealt ruthlessly with the least move to unionism by their employees. The AFL leaders also claimed their collaboration had ended the commodity status of labour, or at least, the commodity theory of labour. The AFL fraternal delegate brought the good news to Canadians at the 1918 TLC convention: "The commodity theory of labour was officially repudiated by our nation when Congress enacted President Wilson's declaration of October 5, 1917."[49] The truth was that this declaration was just another of Wilson's pompous principles which never cost the U.S. capitalists 50 cents.

These AFL illusions were echoed in Canada. In 1918 the TLC leaders said: "We note with satisfaction that organized labour has arrived at the point where the government is forced to recognize our movements."[50] Samuel Gompers was active in winning over Canadian trade union officers to a class collaboration position. He invited some to an international labour conference at Washington, so that Canadians could get the benefit of U.S. experience on how to establish harmony between Labour and Management. On April 26, 1918, he came to Ottawa, addressed the House of Commons, and said the war was "the most wonderful crusade ever entered into by men in the whole history of the world."[51] Later that year he was in Canada again as guest of honour at a gathering of Canadian employers.

Unity, Industrial Unionism, Canadian Unionism:

This class collaboration was a hot point of dispute at the 1918 TLC convention. "There can be no confidence between labour and the class we work for," declared Kavanaugh, a delegate from British Columbia. Also there was a motion that the Congress' constitution be altered to bar from office all those who held posts with government. This was opposed by more conservative delegates, and defeated—as was another ingenious motion demanding abolition of interest on war bonds.[52]

Then came debate on the main issue: Trade union unity, industrial unionism and Canadian unionism. A motion from the Winnipeg Trades and Labour Council asked the Congress to take "a referendum vote on the question of organizing the Canadian labour movement into a modern and scientific organization by industry instead of by craft". Another motion from the Transcona Trades and Labour Council said that joint action in Canada was being paralyzed because it was "necessary for each craft to attain sanction from its international" before it could do anything. Yet another resolution from the Winnipeg Trades and Labour Council demanded the deletion of the destructive amendment inserted in the TLC constitution in 1912, under whose terms bodies banned by the AFL were also banned by the TLC.[52a]

These were motions backed by substantial forces at the convention —most of the western and some eastern delegates—motions whose adoption meant gradual conversion of the Congress into a sovereign, all-inclusive centre. But they were opposed by the Congress leaders and delegates aligned with international headquarters, and they went down to defeat. That was a tragedy whose consequences were to reverberate through the years, and whose immediate result it was to keep the Congress from doing what it had to do to solve the problems of this troubled period. None are so blind as those who will not see. Just a few minutes after the motions were voted down, a Congress vice-president arose on a point of privilege. He had a "matter of great importance" to bring to the attention of delegates. Then, so the Proceedings state, he went to the platform and "presented fraternal delegate Haywood of the AFL with a diamond ring".[53]

In this way militancy failed to break through at the 1918 convention. But down below at the grass roots level it continued to develop. In October 1918, Canadian Pacific Railway freight handlers went on strike from Fort William, Ontario to Vancouver, B.C. In their support, the Calgary Trades and Labour Council decided on a general strike. At Winnipeg, just 2 weeks before the Armistice, a number of affiliates of the Trades and Labour Council voted for a general strike.

The government countered with coercion. Towards the end of September 1918 it issued an order-in-council banning 8 left wing bodies, and in October another order-in-council aimed at preventing all strikes.

Miners in Le Roi Mine at Rossland, B.C., 1908

Rock drilling contest held in Centre Star Gulch, now Esling Park, with crowd watching from Spokane Street, Rossland, B.C. Before 1910.

From the Provincial Archives, Victoria, B.C.

Police and soldiers taking strikers to prison, Nanaimo, 1912.

Ruins of the residence of Mine Manager Cunningham, which was looted by angry strikers before the arrival of troops and burned after the temporary withdrawal of troops.

From the Provincial Archives, Victoria, B.C.

Notice Board depicting a meeting of striking miners. Flin Flon, 1934.

Striking miners going to polling station to vote on decisions of the strike. June, 1934, Flin Flon.

Striking miners at Flin Flon voting on strike at the Community Hall. June 30, 1934.

From the Manitoba Archives.

Winnipeg Street Car Strike, 1906.

Soldiers awaiting orders in the Winnipeg Street Car Strike. March 30, 1906.

From the Manitoba Archives.

A riot taking place on Main Street during the Winnipeg General Strike. June 10, 1919.

Angry strikers over-turning a street car on Bloody Saturday. June 21, 1919.

Crowd dispersing after parade was charged on by the RCMP and Specials, on Bloody Saturday. June 21, 1919.

The 8 arrested strike leaders of the Winnipeg General Strike at Stony Mountain Penitentiary, 1920. Left to right standing: J. S. Woodsworth, George Armstrong, Robert Russell, Fred Dixon, R. E. Bray, A. A. Heaps, Left to right seated: Wm. Ivens, John Queen. See Chapter 10. From the Manitoba Archives.

Regina Riot, July 1, 1935.

From the Archives of Saskatchewan.

See pages 256 - 258.

Valleyfield strikers and pickets of United Textile Workers of America (AFL) at Dominion Textile Company's Valleyfield plant, April 2, 1952. See pages 291 - 292.

Madeleine Parent, provincial organizer of the United Textile Workers of America, arrested again for her part in the strike at Lachute (P.Q.). On the right is her lawyer, Bernard Mergler. May 6, 1947. See pages 321-323.

From the Public Archives of Canada.

Strikers standing outside buses used to transport supporters, from the Canadian Labour Congress and Canadian and Catholic Confederation of Labour, who came to picket in solidarity, 1957. Murdochville Copper Miners Strike.

From Canada Wide Photo. See page 329.

Shipping strike of Canadian Seamen's Union: SCAB effigy being hung, April 12, 1949.

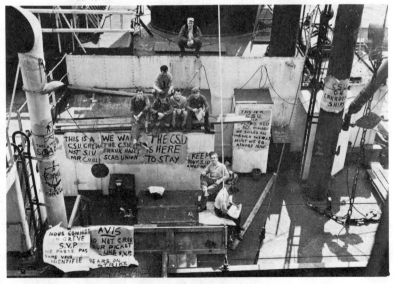

Shipping strike of Canadian Seamen's Union, April 12, 1949.

From the Public Archives of Canada.

See pages 280 - 284.

CHAPTER 10

THE WINNIPEG GENERAL STRIKE
1919

1. A STIRRING YEAR

Growth of Unrest and Militancy:

1919 was a great year, a molten year in which all things flowed. There had not been one like it before. When 1919 began, union membership was 248,887. When it ended, union membership had risen to 378,047—an increase of 130,000, or over 50%.

1919 was also a tremendous year for strikes—148,915 workers in 336 strikes and lockouts. This has since been surpassed. In 1943—218,404 workers on strike, and 1950—192,153. But the impact of the 1919 strikes, as measured by man-working days lost (a figure which combines number of workers involved and duration of strikes) was much greater: 3,400,942 man-working days lost—three times the number for 1943 and 1950. The 1919 figure is surpassed in turn by 1946—the year which followed World War II, just as 1919 followed World War I. In 1946 man-working days lost totalled 4,516,393.[1] But, as against this, in 1946 industry was much more developed than in 1919, and union membership much larger.

Again, in 1919, the greatest strike was the Winnipeg General Strike. And yet the number on strike at Winnipeg was but a quarter of the total for Canada. In short, the 1919 strike movement was a Canada-wide movement.[2]

What gave rise to all this? On Armistice Day 1918, Prime Minister Robert Borden and TLC president Tom Moore told the workers the world was going to be a happy place to live in. The troops began to come home at the rate of 3,400 per month. In Canada jobs were not too plentiful. By the winter of 1919 unemployment was increasing in Ontario and the West. Also, the cost of living was rising—workers were complaining it cost twice as much to keep a family as before the war. For their part, the employers and landlords were basking in the sun of big profits. Working class bitterness grew.*

A signal was demonstrations of returned men and soldiers. At Toronto several such demonstrations took place, and there were clashes with police. At Winnipeg and Halifax there were similar demonstrations. In Britain there was a mutiny in the Third Division, when orders were given that some of its members be put on police duty against British strikers.[4] Unrest grew greater still in 1918 when—Armistice scarce over—a Canadian military expedition was dispatched to Archangel.[5] This was too much. First the authorities asked Canadians to die in a war, with the Russian Tsar as a principal ally, and then asked them to die to defeat the government which had replaced the Tsar.

Meanwhile, the government had not released workers interned for anti-war activities, nor had it rescinded the ban on free speech and free assembly. Demands grew for government action to cut living costs, curb profiteers, impose heavier excess profits taxes. Unrest reached its pointed expression in wage and hour demands, in union organization and strikes.

All this reflected in turn a growing dissatisfaction with the social system. Soldiers wives, living in cramped quarters, contrasted their lot with that of the wealthy. The workers looked at their pay envelopes, and they were slender compared with the profits of the big business "patriots". The flames of wrath against capitalism began to flare, and the demand grew for a redistribution of wealth. Along with this, the concrete progress of the movement — the tens of thousands joining unions, fighting for wage demands, striking—heightened the workers' confidence and kindled their enthusiasm.

Clearly, a kind of native Canadian socialism was developing. Its primary roots were in Canada's present and past. But its growth was also being speeded by events in other parts of the world. The Russian revolution of November 1917 had captured the imagination of more radical Canadians. They read in the newspapers that the new government, within 24 hours of assuming office, had socialized the large factories, redistributed the large estates among the farmers, and enacted the 8-hour day.

* Something of the spirit of the times is communicated in a sketch written by Stephen Leacock entitled, "Why I Shot My Landlord". A landlord told his tenant he was *not* going to raise his rent. The tenant, astounded, concluded the landlord was suffering from softening of the brain and mercifully shot him dead.[3]

So, it was not surprising that Marxist ideas spread among trade unionists. On September 20, 1918, *Western Labour News*, organ of the Winnipeg Trades and Labour Council, carried an article predicting that "Bolshevism will not confine itself to Russia!" Soon after, it published another article suggesting that Canadian workers "should form a dictatorship".[6]

Then came a meeting at the Walker Theatre in Winnipeg, on Sunday, December 22, 1918, sponsored by the Socialist Party of Canada. One speaker, R. B. Russell, a leading figure in the Winnipeg organization of the International Association of Machinists, AFL, said: "Capitalism has come to a point where it is defunct and must disappear."[7] Another speaker, Sam Blumenburg of the Socialist Party, said: "Bolshevism is the only thing which will emancipate the working class!"[8] Between January and March 1919, similar meetings were held in Calgary.

By the spring of 1919, socialism was being discussed in the House of Commons. In a statement which sounded suspiciously like Karl Marx' theory of surplus value, the Hon. W. D. Euler said, concerning Sir Joseph Flavelle: "No man, no matter how able he may be, could earn a hundred million dollars, he is simply appropriating the product of the labour of others."[9] Another member, J. J. Pelletier, from Matane, declared:

"A new power has asserted itself and that power, which had overturned everything in certain countries, will soon make its influence felt in Canada ... This new power is that of the immense army of working men and the select battalions of farmers ... Let's remember that, in Russia, it is the soldiers, the working men and farmers that have taken the reins."[10]

In April 1919, a Liberal member, Hon. Rodolphe Lemieux, warned that the returned soldiers were "upset and angry", and asked: "Is the Government going to wait until there are soviets in every industrial centre?"[11]

The pace of events quickened. The Winnipeg Trades and Labour Council elected a more radical leadership to replace the previous one, inclined to conservatism.[12] In 1918 and 1919, conventions of railway shopmen and machinists voted for industrial unionism. Nervously, the Trades and Labour Congress leaders reassured the employers. In an address to the Canadian Manufacturers Association in March 1919, president Moore said: "The intelligent trade unionist was the capitalists' strongest bulwark ... The downfall of capitalism would mean idleness and starvation".[13]

Then came two major events: First, the convention of the B.C. Federation of Labour; then, the Western Canada Labour Conference, both held in Calgary, March 1919. The B.C. Convention decided on the 6-hour day, to be won by a national general strike effective not later than June 1, 1919. To this end a vote would be held among all Canadian local unions.

Some delegates felt the vote should include U.S. locals, because these locals along with Canadian locals were in the same international unions. This was rejected. Speaking for the majority, Jack Kavanaugh of the Vancouver Trades and Labour Council said Lenin had not waited for Western Europe to revolt, but had gone ahead on his own in Russia; and another delegate said: "We are seeking to break away from the bucket shop of the international officers of the AFL." The convention also endorsed this pro-socialist resolution submitted by Victoria Lodge 456 of the International Association of Machinists, AFL:

". . . Full acceptance of the principle of proletarian dictatorship is absolute and sufficient for the transformation of private property (into) public or communal wealth."[14]

Then came the Western Canada Labour Conference. Opening on March 16, it was attended by 250 delegates representing most of the important union locals between Winnipeg and Victoria—probably the largest trade union convention held in Canada to that date. The chairman was Robert Tallon—in later years an acting president of the TLC and an Unemployment Insurance Commissioner.

The Conference decided on a general strike to begin around June 1, 1919, for these demands:
1. The 6-hour day.
2. Complete freedom of speech and release of political prisoners.
3. Removal of restrictions on working class organizations.
4. Immediate withdrawal of allied troops from Russia.
5. Defeat of allied attempts "to overthrow the Soviet administration in Russia or Germany".[15]

The convention also called for "immediate reorganization of the workers along industrial lines". Also, it decided that disaffiliation from international unions be put to the Canadian membership in a referendum. The operative clause in the resolution stated: "This convention recommends to its affiliated membership severance of their affiliation with international organizations."[16]

Finally, these resolutions were adopted:
1. *Abolition of capitalism:* "The aims of labour are abolition of the present system of production for profit, and the substitution for it of production for use."[17]

2. *Working class rule:* "The system of industrial soviet control by selection of representatives from industry is declared superior to capitalistic parliamentarism". Working class rule (dictatorship of the proletariat) is endorsed as the instrument for abolishing capitalism and building socialism.[18]

3. *The November Resolution a Model:* The convention endorsed a resolution from the Alberta Federation of Labour (TLC), which said that the Russians, in socializing the means of production, had acted in the spirit of the Alberta Federation's constitution, for this constitution also stood for social ownership of the means of production. The resolution went on to express its "full accord and sympathy with the aims and purposes of the Russian Bolshevik and German Spartacist revolutions".[19]

2. THE WINNIPEG STRIKE — FIRST PHASE

Events Leading to the Strike; Its Early Days:

The militancy and radicalism which had reached a high point at the Western Canada Labour Conference, now pressed forward to a new climax, and Winnipeg was the place. Twenty-five years of labour struggle had prepared this city for the role it was now to play at this crossroads of Canadian history. Important strikes had been fought there. Its working ranks had been reinforced by Scottish, Ukrainian, Jewish and other immigrants, often with strong labour and socialist convictions.[20] Its Trades Council had risen in stature as a centre of labour authority, and was showing increasing independence from international headquarters in the U.S.

This was Winnipeg's past. And now its present—economic grievances fusing with socialist ideas: Many of Winnipeg's workers were earning only $12 or $15 a week, when—so it was reported—a dollar could buy only a quarter or third of what it bought before the war. Small wonder that workers began joining unions en masse. James Winning, president of the Winnipeg Trades and Labour Council, was to say somewhat later that during this period just before the strike, "more (people) had been added to the organized labour movement . . . than during the past 15 years".[21]

In the van of the movement stood the metal trades workers. To overcome their isolation in separated craft locals, they had organized a metal trades council. The employers—mainly the Vulcan Iron Works, Dominion Bridge Company and the Manitoba Iron Works—insisted they would not deal with this council, but only with shop committees from the individual shops. On May 2, the metal workers went on strike. They demanded:

1. Recognition of the metal trades council.
2. An 8-hour day and 44-hour week.
3. Double pay for overtime, a one hour premium for the night shift.
4. The following hourly rates: 85 cents for machinists, boilermakers and electric welders; 55 cents for labourers, 25 cents for apprentices.[22]

Meanwhile in the building trades, workers were earning about $900 per year when, so they claimed, the head of a family of 5 needed $1,500 per annum. To correct this condition, the building trades unions demanded substantial wage increases. These unions had also grouped themselves into a council and they demanded that the council be recognized. When the employers—the Builders' Exchange—rejected these demands, the building trades unions likewise decided on strike.[23]

Then the metal trades and building trades councils appealed to the Winnipeg Trades and Labour Council for support. The council responded by holding a general strike vote among its affiliated local unions. On the strike ballot were these demands:

1. A living wage.
2. The 8-hour day.
3. The right to organize—to be confirmed by signed agreement.

The result was a large majority for strike action.[24]

The strike began Thursday morning, May 15, 11 a.m. 12,000 organized workers walked out. They were followed by another 12,000 unorganized workers.[25] The metal trades plants were closed. So were the Canadian Pacific Railway shops. Construction came to a halt. Streetcars stopped running. Transportation froze.[26]

Swiftly the strike spread from industry to industry. Communications were cut off when telephone workers and telegraph workers walked out.[27] Hotels, banks and buildings became largely inoperative because the servicemen and passenger elevator operators stopped work. The supply of retail goods was cut off or sharply reduced as retail and wholesale clerks went on strike. The supply of food was likewise sharply reduced because bakery and dairy deliverymen joined the strike[28]—within 48 hours bread and milk were no longer being delivered.[29] Restaurant workers also walked out—thus cutting off a precious alternative source for food. Newspaper publication ceased completely. By Saturday, the third day of the strike, no newspaper was being published in Winnipeg save the strike committee's "Strike Bulletin". Finally, police, firemen and postal services, though not cut off, were jeopardized because the municipal policemen and firemen and the federal postal workers said they were ready to go on strike if called upon.

So here was the result within 48 hours after the strike began: 35,000 on strike in a population of 200,000.[30] Industry, transport, banking, finance, postal service, food supply, water and power supply, fire and police services—all paralyzed or operating by decision of the strike committee.[31] The Montreal *Gazette* later described the situation this way:

"Their orders (those of the Winnipeg strike committee) which were obeyed to an extent which is some cause for surprise, contemplated a complete tie-up of necessary public and private services. The post office, the street railways and municipal sanitary and protective services, as well as food distribution of the city were ordered to cease; and to an extent the order was enforced."[32]

Winnipeg now presented a spectacle never before seen in a Canadian city. On the streets, there were large crowds of workers. Concerning them the *Strike Bulletin* said on May 19: "There was radiant hope in every face ... The voice of every worker was filled with the passion of resolve."[33] Hundreds of workers were pouring into the Labour Temple (the strike headquarters) and asking to be organized. Many were joining unions of bakers, cooks, butchers and waiters. 1,500 new members were added to the rolls of the Retail Clerks. The metal trades unions reported an increase of 600 members as from April 1. The building trades and teamsters unions swelled in ranks.

This entire complex general strike operation was directed by the Central Strike Committee. It was composed of about 300 members— 3 delegates from each of 95 local unions plus 5 from the Trades and Labour Council.[34] The principal task of the delegates was to report back daily to their organizations. Also, the central committee struck off sub-committees for food, press, organization and other functions— these sub-committees were in constant session, save for a few hours after midnight.[35] Finally, the central committee elected an executive of 15, but retained in its hands decisions on basic policy.[36]

The central committee's sessions were lively. One task was to decide what industrial and civic activities would be allowed to continue. An extract from the committee's proceedings for Tuesday morning, May 21, reads:

"Delegate McBride informed the committee that he had been instructed to pull out all telephone employees in the province. He asked permission of operators to send necessary telegram. Granted."[37]

Here then was a committee concentrating in itself the power of Labour on a scale not before seen in Canada.

With the strike now at its height, the committee stepped up its demands. The original demand had been recognition of the building and metal trades councils, and granting of their wage demands. Now, in a resolution adopted May 22, the committee added two important demands:

1. All strikers must be reinstated without discrimination.
2. Employers and governments must recognize the right to organize.

In particular, the provincial and federal governments were asked to enact legislation obliging employers to recognize trade union bodies—be they craft or industrial, be they locals, councils or federations.[38]

Meanwhile Winnipeg's employers were not sitting by idly. Early in the strike they organized the "Citizens Committee". The committee said it wanted milk for babies, an uninterrupted supply of water, bread and milk for the public.[39] But, early in the strike, it organized between 3,000 and 5,000 "volunteers" into a militia body. Plainly, it wanted something more than milk for babies and food for the public. Towards the strikers, at least some of the committee's adherents harboured a hatred bordering on hysteria. The committee's newspaper organ said: "The would as soon breed rattlesnakes in their own beds, as permit this accursed thing, anarchy, to make its home in this fair land."[40] The committee's partisans also insisted that a "soviet regime" had been installed in the Labour Temple, and that Winnipeg was "under red rule". Nerves were jumpy. When the *Strike Bulletin* editor, Rev. William Ivens, casually said something about "the weather being good but a storm approaching", some Citizens Committee members thought he meant an armed uprising.[41]

What was the orientation of government? First the Winnipeg municipal council and the Manitoba provincial government. On the council sat a number of trade unionists—John Queen, A. A. Heaps and E. Robinson. They could be counted on for support and one or two other councillors were sympathetic. But the mayor and the majority were hostile. So was Manitoba Premier Norris.

What of the Federal Government—the Borden "Union" or coalition government of Conservatives and Conscriptionist Liberals elected in the Khaki election of December 1917? It was exceedingly hostile and said the strike was "an attempt at revolution".[42] When some members of Parliament asked Prime Minister Sir Robert Borden to state the government's policy on the strikers' demands for the right to bargain collectively, he replied that he did not think the term collective bargaining "has any definite and final meaning which is recognized in all parts of this country". Moreover, he felt this was a matter for the provinces, beyond federal jurisdiction.[42a]

Uncertain Borden might be on what collective bargaining was, and the federal power to implement it; but certain he was about the government's power to coerce. He said that "law and order shall be maintained",[43] and that public servants did not have the right to strike.

In keeping with this policy, the Government proceeded to take coercive measures. Early in the strike, it sent Royal Canadian Mounted Police to Winnipeg. On arrival at Winnipeg, the RCMP began, to a degree, to act like a private agency of the employers. For instance on May 21, RCMP Commissioner Perry appeared before the executive of the Saskatchewan Grain Grower's Association and denounced the strikers.[44]

Then came another strike-breaking move. On May 22, General Ketchem, the general officer commanding the Winnipeg Military District, wired Ottawa for help. The government promptly sent in a battalion of troops and 2 Lewis machine guns.[45] On May 26, the government took another strike-breaking move, still more serious, this time in conjunction with the provincial and municipal authorities. It told the postal workers they must go back to work and sign an agreement pledging never again to go on sympathetic strike or stay in affiliation with the Winnipeg Trades and Labour Council.[46] The provincial government issued a similar ultimatum to the telephone workers.[47] And the Winnipeg City Council told the firemen and policemen they must return to work or be fired. The policemen were called on to sign the following agreement:

"I further agree that I will not join or remain a member of any union or association with whose orders, directives or recommendations... we as members are obliged to agree... I will not take part in or support or favour what is known as a sympathetic strike... Upon a breach of the above conditions, I shall be liable to instant dismissal from the force..."[48]

3. THE STRIKE — MIDDLE PHASE

A Great Week, May 29 - June 5:

Confronted by these strike-breaking moves of the employers and government agencies, Winnipeg Labour mobilized its resources, and so did trade unionists across Canada. Thus came about the third week of the strike—May 29 - June 5, a historic week, with action following on action. Such intensity had not been seen since the 10 days of April 15-24, 1872—the 9-hour movement. But the range and impact were now vastly greater.

First the situation at Winnipeg. The Central Strike Committee stood steadfast by its demands. It rejected the federal-provincial-municipal ultimatums to the government employees. Further, the committee declared point blank: "Not a single worker goes back until all are reinstated."[49]

Meanwhile, major events were unfolding in British Columbia. At Vancouver, 60,000 workers walked out. Shipyards were closed, loading ceased on the docks, the streetcars ground to a halt.[50]

The strike wave spread into the prairies. In Alberta, railroad shop workers and expressmen walked out at Edmonton. Postal workers, street car employees and hotel and restaurant workers went on strike at Calgary. So did miners at Drumheller and Lethbridge.[51] In Saskatchewan there were widespread strikes, assuming at times the proportion of general strikes, at Regina, Saskatoon, Prince Albert and Kamsack. In Manitoba there was a general strike at Brandon.[52]

In this situation, Ontario, the key industrial province, became pivotal, and in particular Toronto. Initially prospects seemed promising—from a trade union standpoint. Forty-four unions in Toronto held a strike vote, and a general strike was called for Friday, May 30.[53] This strike did not assume the proportions anticipated—some reasons will be given in the next chapter. However, 15,000 workers did leave their jobs for the 44-hour week and in solidarity with the Winnipeg strikers. By June 1, 200 factories were closed down, including 50 garment plants, and work was halted on 50 buildings.[54] In sum, this was a serious situation, though far removed in quantity and quality from the "rebellion against capital" which some Toronto employers said it was.

Finally, there was the situation in Quebec—growing unrest among the workers, the beginning of a large strike movement.

Clearly, the Winnipeg Strike had now become an interlocked general strike movement based on Winnipeg but extending west and east across Canada. In this new situation, the secretary of the Vancouver Trades and Labour Council proposed that the strikes be co-ordinated around a single demand—the right to bargain collectively. If this was not granted, they should continue "until the present government resigns and places the matter before the electorate".[55] In other words, he was proposing that the general strike movement, though confining itself to its central economic objective, should become a national political strike aimed at a federal election in which the public would render judgment on the justice of the workers' demands. Quite possibly this was a realistic demand. Certainly it was far removed from the suggestions of "Soviet power" wrongly attributed to the strike leaders by the employers and Government.

We return now to the situation at Winnipeg. A new power had emerged—the returned soldiers. Thousands of them were then in Winnipeg—most of them workers; many, union members and some union leaders. The original idea of the opponents of the strike was to align the veterans with the citizens committee. On the first day of the strike, they invited the veterans to a mass meeting called by the committee. Their plan went awry. The majority at the meeting defeated an anti-strike resolution, and instead adopted one which declared "full sympathy with the purposes of the present strike".[56] Thereafter, delegates from the Great War Veterans Association sat on the strike committee,[57] along with 20 other returned men who were delegates from local unions. Towards the end of May, the Toronto *Star* reported: "The Great War Veterans Association and returned soldiers generally sympathize with the demands of the workers and approve the strike."[58] In the House of Commons, Major Power of Quebec City said: "The returned soldier is more apt to side with the workers than with the capitalists."

What the ex-soldiers' power meant when combined with the strikers' power was shown by a series of demonstrations in Winnipeg between Friday, May 30 and Monday, June 2. On Friday, 1,000 ex-servicemen demonstrated before the Legislature—demanding an immediate settlement of the strike, withdrawal of the ultimatum to the police, and enactment of legislation for compulsory collective bargaining.[59] On Saturday a still bigger demonstration was held. 10,000 ex-servicemen marched behind the flag down Kennedy Street, and reached the Legislature at 11 a.m. Then a delegation met Premier Norris and asked him to promise he would bring in legislation for collective bargaining. Premier Norris replied: "I must find out what my powers are."

"Soldiers: How about the postal employees?
Norris: That's a federal matter.
Soldiers: How about the firemen and policemen?
Norris: That's a municipal matter."[59a]

Asked to settle the strike, the Premier answered: "Call the strike off first!" The ex-soldiers were dissatisfied, and from their ranks the cry went up: "Resign! Resign!"[60] Then they paraded to the city council, and some entered the council chambers while the council was in session. The Mayor tried to address the crowd which had gathered outside, and again the cry went up: "Resign! Resign!" This demonstration seems to have had an effect. The municipal authorities suspended the ultimatum to the police until the Tuesday following.[61]

On Monday, June 2, the returned men were back at the Legislature. As they arrived at the government grounds, they were greeted by a tremendous crowd. Premier Norris was still evasive. The veterans told the Premier that if, as the federal government contended, collective bargaining was not its jurisdiction, then it must be in the provincial jurisdiction. Premier Norris replied that he wasn't sure the government had the authority to call a special session of the Legislature to enact right-to-bargain legislation. Disgusted, the ex-soldiers renewed their demands that the government resign, and they challenged the government to take the issue to the people by a referendum vote.[62]

Monday and Tuesday, June 2-3, were charged with lightning. On Monday, 10,000 ex-servicemen marched in Winnipeg, while in the House of Commons at Ottawa opposition members blasted the government. On Tuesday, 60,000 struck at Vancouver. At Winnipeg the central strike committee gathered at the Labour Temple. The delegates, bristling with energy, decided that workers sent back to their jobs "by permit", a gesture of co-operation with the authorities, were to be called out again. Included were bread, milk and ice drivers, motion picture operators, restaurant workers, stationery engineers, flour mill employees, elevator operators and musicians.[63] The committee officers also announced that representatives from unions across Canada were being called to Winnipeg, and a Dominion strike committee would be convened.[64]

Thus ended the third week in the strike.

Point, Counter-Point; June 5 - June 16:

In the fourth week, big business and government thoroughly alarmed, took counter-action. The Federal Government dismissed 190 postal employees at Winnipeg who had turned down the ultimatum.[65] Then, on the evening of June 9, the Winnipeg municipal authorities struck a cruel blow—they dismissed the regular police force. Down to practically the last man, this force had turned down the ultimatum—cited in a previous page.[66] Its place was taken by the "specials". This was a private force recruited by the citizens committee. The strike committee charged that some had police records, one convicted of stealing an automobile, another involved in bootlegging.[67] The municipal authorities swore in this strike-breaking force of 2,000.

On June 9, the specials made their first appearance on Winnipeg's streets. Many ex-servicemen were furious. One said: "Little did we know (that) men who had made money out of our sweat and blood would be ready to take up arms against us."[68]

A major clash developed at Main and Portage Streets. A large crowd of strikers and ex-servicemen had gathered there. The specials, mounted on horses, and supported by RCMP, charged into the crowd.

The crowd then surrounded the horses and caused some of them to bolt down towards Broadway. Also they hurled bottles, brickbats and ashcan covers on the specials, and some in the crowd hit the specials on the head with their own clubs.

In combat, the specials—many of them youths—were inferior to the strikers, toughened in the daily grind of industry and the blood-soaked trenches of Flanders Field. Some specials became confused, hit each other, and broke ranks, upon which a number were unhorsed and felt the force of the strikers' censure. One special, a youth of scarce 20, ripped off his police badge, jumped from his horse, handed over his baton to a striker, and cried: "That's enough police duty for me."[69]*

Three hours later, the specials and RCMP terminated their actions and dispersed. Later, it was announced that there had been 12 casualties and that 5 had been taken to hospital. The strikers and ex-soldiers remained victors in the field, and they had trophies—heavy chains loaded with bolts and covered with leather—"whoever made them had murder on the brain!" Towards the end of the day, the RCMP were ordered back into the barracks, and the specials withdrawn from the streets. Thus matters rested for the next few days, and there were no disorders.[70]

The battle of June 9 demonstrated that the strike-breaking moves had not had the effect anticipated. The strike was still in full vigour. Moreover there were factors which favoured its victory.

First, the situation in Manitoba. Here the primary factor was the solidarity and strength of the strike itself. And this was reinforced by impressive signs of public support. Farmers sent in resolutions of sympathy, and some offered to help feed the strikers. A member of the Manitoba Legislature, Captain John Wilkins, said the strikers were "fighting against the New Family Compact comprised of a thousand bankers, railroad magnates, industrial barons, stock brokers and government officials... This New Family Compact must be destroyed..."[71] Canon Frederick George Scott, best-known of Canada's army padres, went to Winnipeg, addressed ex-servicemen's gatherings, and branded opposition to collective bargaining as "unconstitutional".

A further factor in Manitoba was the ex-servicemen. They were still strongly supporting the strike and this was very important. Though they were no longer demonstrating before the legislature, they had not disorganized, but were meeting regularly in "Soldiers parliaments". A June 14 dispatch to the London *Times* said: "The gravity of the

* The details about the youth is based on an account in the *Strike Bulletin.*

situation is accentuated by the certainty a percentage of the returned soldiers are in sympathy with the strikers."[72]

There was this further favourable factor in Manitoba—the signs of a break in the employers' ranks. Until now, the ironmasters, bolstered by the attitude of the Federal Government, had refused to settle until the strike ended, but now they were uncertain. Also, it was reported on June 16, that Manager Tucker of the T. Eaton Company had withdrawn from the citizens committee. There was hesitation in government circles too. On June 15, Mayor Gray was said to be dejected, hesitant to declare martial law.[73] There were indications also that the provincial government was inclining to settlement.

This was the situation in Manitoba. It merged with the situation across the country—in particular the strike movement. This extended from Montreal to Vancouver. At Montreal, rubber workers were on strike, also glove makers, butchers, packinghouse workers, employees of Dominion Textile and Vickers. There was talk about a general building trades walkout.[74] At Vancouver the general strike was still on. Also there was growing tension on the railroads: On June 16, it was reported at Montreal that the executive committee of the railway shopmen had issued a strike order effective June 18. At Winnipeg, lodges of the Brotherhood of Locomotive Firemen and Brotherhood of Locomotive Engineers gave the municipal council an ultimatum that if the strike is not settled, we are "unanimously resolved to go on strike 6 p.m. June 13".[75] On Monday, June 17, the news was that firemen, engineers and switchmen employed by the Canadian Northern and Grand Trunk Pacific companies had gone on strike.[76]

These were some factors favouring a victory for the general strike movement at Winnipeg and across the country. But big business and the Federal Government were determined this must not happen.

4. CRISIS. END OF THE STRIKE.
JUNE 13 - 26

Arrest of strike leaders, June 17; Bloody Saturday, June 21:

Baffled thus far in attempts to break the strike, the authorities decided on more ruthless measures. On Thursday, June 12, word reached the central strike committee that 100 to 150 strike leaders were slated for early arrest.[77] On Friday, June 13, Minister of Labour Gideon Robertson wired Prime Minister Borden from Winnipeg and proposed that arrests be made. On Saturday, June 14, military officials at Winnipeg told Canon Frederick George Scott that his services were required elsewhere and that he should leave town on the 11:30 train—this was just a day after he had reaffirmed his support for the strikers.[78] On Monday, June 16, Robertson wired Borden again and told him that action would be taken "in the next 24 hours", and he was confident this would "result in speedy and satisfactory conclusion of the trouble here".[79] Also there was talk about exceptional activity at the Midland Barracks—an armoured car was being readied for action and 45 squads of machine gunners were being mustered.[80]

Then came a blow—arrest of the main strike leaders in the early hours of Tuesday, June 17. They included metal trades council Secretary R. B. Russell, *Strike Bulletin* Editor, Rev. William Ivens, ex-servicemen's leader R. E. Bray, Winnipeg Trades and Labour Council officers George Armstrong and A. A. Heaps, a number of strike and labour activists including a machinist Peter Herenchuk—an ex-serviceman wounded twice at the battle of the Somme, the socialist activist Sam Blumenburg, and a number of Slav militants.[81]

A measure of the ferocity used in the arrests was the treatment of Rev. William Ivens. Police descended on his home and dragged him away in the middle of the night, as his children stood by crying. Alderman John Queen was seized at A. A. Heaps' home. Here, the door was violently broken in, the desks and bureau drawers ransacked, the two aldermen handcuffed and taken away. The *Strike Bulletin* said: "They (the RCMP) came by night, hatred blazing in their eyes."

The arrested strike leaders were piled into automobiles which sped to Stony Mountain Penitentiary. Bail was refused.[82] Also, raids were carried through at the Labour Temple, the offices of the *Western Labour News,* and the Ukrainian Labour Temple. At the Trades and Labour Temple, the doors were burst open with crowbars, the office wrecked, and the files and records strewn over the floor.

If the authorities believed these punitive measures would paralyze the strikers and terrify them into submission, they had made a big mistake. What had happened was that the strike had entered a more acute phase. Victory or defeat—which was it to be? Across Canada, all that was most militant in the trade union movement rallied in defense of the Winnipeg strikers. At Toronto the metal trades council proposed a national general strike for release of the arrested men. The Toronto Trades and Labour Council demanded the release of the strike leaders, the dismissal of Gideon Robertson, and warned that refusal to grant these demands would cause a general strike across the Dominion. From Cape Breton the coal miners' leader J. B. McLachlan wired Ottawa: "We pledge ourselves to do all we can to bring about a general strike all over Canada".[83] At Montreal, Trades and Labour Council president J. T. Foster, said:

"There is something wrong with the government of the people, when it can enact legislation in 25 minutes to arrest labour leaders; when we cannot in five years secure legislation in the interests of Canadian working men."[84]

At Winnipeg the strikers refused to yield. The *Strike Bulletin* of June 18 described their mood as one of "quiet determination". Friday came, June 20, and with it an encouraging event. The nationwide protests had had their effect. The arrested strike leaders were released on bail, after being detained 72 hours. The hour of decision was approaching. So felt many of the strikers and ex-servicemen. Ex-Sapper J. W. Jones, Regimental No. 475120 said:

"Let us go over the top again if need be, for the emancipation of labour ... The returned men are true to the class which nurtured them ... Fellow soldier-workers, how long are we going to stand by while those sheltered behind our sacrifices of life and limb, prepare now to *imprison us* ... The worker has slept too long, allowing the master class to dictate to him the mode of life he is to lead ... The souls of our dead comrades echo the call from Flanders Fields ... If going to France was in law and order, why is it unconstitutional to hit straight from the shoulder against injustice in Canada?"[85]

Something must be done! The same idea was expressed in a poem in the *Strike Bulletin* on June 18: "They Shall Not Pass!"

" 'They shall not pass!' from Verdun's walls
    O'er shattered France the cry went forth —
    Whilst millions rushed to fill the breach
    And prove their nation's fighting worth.

'They shall not pass!' The scene has changed,
    But strife is rampant here as then,
    And this same purpose, firmly held,
    Spurs on the soldier-citizen."[86]

Thus was born the idea of a silent parade to protest the arrests and violence, and for this parade the returned men assumed full responsibility.[87] Saturday came, June 21, the day scheduled for the parade. In the morning the Mayor read the Riot Act and warned that those taking part in the parade did so at their own risk. In the afternoon, a large crowd of men, women and children assembled on the main street near the city hall, and the ex-servicemen began to line up.

Then came the first attack. About 2.30 p.m. in the words of the *Strike Bulletin*, "fifty mounted men swinging baseball bats rode down the main street, about half of them wearing red-coated (RCMP) uniforms, the others wearing khaki." This first attack by the RCMP and Specials did not succeed in breaking up the demonstration. The crowd opened its ranks, let the attackers through, and closed in behind them.

Then the mounted men wheeled around and charged the crowd again. From the crowd came hisses and boos, and some stones were thrown. Later two riderless horses were seen. The mounted men galloped up the main street. The RCMP reined in their horses and formed up opposite the old post office.

Then came the second attack. The *Strike Bulletin* reports: "With revolvers drawn they (the RCMP and Specials) galloped down the main street, turned and charged into the crowd on Winning Avenue, firing as they charged. That's not possible, a spectator told himself, the Mounties must be firing blanks." Suddenly, a person beside him dropped with a bullet through his breast. Then, lines of police, swinging clubs, were thrown across the main street. The officer in command of the RCMP during this incident was later to give this description of what happened:

"About 120 bullets in all were fired into the crowd of men, women and children. They were not marching round the streets but standing in front of the city hall. Many were running away when we fired on them. I didn't wait to see if they would run on our charge, but fired."[88]

Two were killed that day, about 30 injured. Winnipeg was declared under military control, khaki-clad men with rifles were stationed at the street corners, and about 100 people were arrested.[89]

The Strike Ends; The Unions Battle On; June 26 - July 10:

Winnipeg now was under military control. Continuation of the strike had become difficult. Public meetings in the city were abandoned—the strike committee explained that because of military control, meetings would be held outside city limits.[90] Then negotiations were resumed with the iron masters. On June 26, the general strike ended by decision of the central strike committee.

In the final days of June and the early days of July, the metal trades and building trades workers went back to their jobs—after 9 weeks of strike. They had won a partial victory: A reduction in metal trades hours from 55 to 50 per week with the same pay; and a commitment by the companies to deal with the shop committees· instead of merely the top local committees.[91] For building trades workers, a wage increase was left open for settlement by negotiation.[92]

However, the strike had ended without a victory in the main demands. These had been:
1. Recognition of the building and metal trades councils.
2. Recognition of all of Winnipeg unions by the employers.
3. A guarantee that all strikers would get their jobs back.

4. Legislation enacting the right to organize and bargain collectively.

As the strikers went back to their jobs in the final days of June and the early days of July, thousands were locked out, blacklisted, dismissed, or otherwise discriminated against. In the metal trades, it was reported that the Manitoba Bridge and Iron Works would reinstate only 70 of the 170 employees who had gone on strike. Reprisals were visited on the government employees. Members of the Municipal Firemen's Union were locked out, and some firemen and policemen lost their jobs. On July 8, it was reported that 119 provincial government telephone employees had been refused reinstatement. A number of postal employees were dismissed. On the railways, it was said that only 1 sleeping car porter out of 97 had been reinstated. The Church was drawn into the campaign of vengeance. The Methodist Church barred Rev. William Ivens from a post—the reason given was that he had refused a regular pastorate.[93] In sum, the situation seems to have been that thousands of the strikers' jobs were in danger but that the workers conducted a partially successful guerrilla warfare to avert this—many refused to go back to work until their fellow-workers were reinstated.

Hand in hand with the employers' economic sanctions went state coercion. In the early days of July, Dominion Government military police raided the Winnipeg Labour Temple, drilled into the safe, and carted away the Council's records, raided the Ukrainian Labour Temple; and, in the early hours of Tuesday morning, July 2, they raided the homes of E. Robinson, secretary of the Trades and Labour Council, Jacob Penner, and almost 50 other labour activists at Winnipeg.

At Calgary, Saskatoon, Brandon and Montreal, similar raids took place.[94] They went on practically every night. Police arrested scores of trade unionists and sympathizers on charges of sedition and criminal conspiracy. On July 3, the *Western Labour News* stated:

"If you have your safe cracked in the name of democracy, or your house raided by the representatives of law and order, please communicate the facts to *Western Labour News*. Let your light so shine before men that they may see your good works upon you to glorify the constitutional government which is in Ottawa."[95]

This was hardship—clubs, bullets, arrests, raids, blacklists, dismissals from employment. But Winnipeg Labour was undaunted, and in its bitterest hour, wrote an imperishable page in Canadian history. The authorities had banned union meetings in Winnipeg. However, union members and their families held meetings outside the city limits. At one, on Sunday, July 6, Rev. William Ivens, cheered the throng with these words from James Russell Lovell:

"Though the cause of evil prosper,
Yet the truth alone is strong."

The gathering then sang:

"Faith of our Fathers, living still,
In spite of dungeon, fire and sword—
Faith of our Fathers, holy faith,
We will be true to thee to death![96]

Re-organization began. On July 8, the Trades and Labour Council set up a committee to visit unions. Assistance was organized for unemployed workers, and a program of mass meetings arranged. Also, the employers were warned that workers would strike again if wages did not increase, hours decrease and discrimination stop. The *Western Labour News* stated on July 10:

"The spirit of labour was in no way crushed, it has but had a setback!"[97]

CHAPTER 11

HISTORIC SIGNIFICANCE OF THE WINNIPEG STRIKE

1. WAS DEFEAT INEVITABLE?

How Strong Was the Government?

The Winnipeg strike did not attain its main objective. In this sense, it was defeated. Was defeat inevitable? Was the success of government coercion pre-determined? Consider first the official justification for the coercion. In the heat of the fight, Justice Minister Meighen told the House of Commons:

"Consequently I say, and it is proved by the example of Winnipeg and indeed follows inevitably from the logic of the situation, that for a general strike to suceed or even be continued, it must result in the usurpation of governmental authority on the part of those controlling the strike. It was so in Winnipeg, it must ever result so."[1]

The same point is made to a degree, but not with the same animus, by the Canadian historian, D. C. Masters, in his able work on the Winnipeg general strike.*

"There is room for disagreement over the expediency of certain specific actions by the Government, yet it was almost inevitable that there should have been governmental intervention in Winnipeg. The reasons for this are inherent in the nature of a general strike. To such an extent does it shatter the texture of ordinary society that it must be followed by the assumption of political control on the part of the strikers or by the resumption of control on the part of the existing authorities.

"A labour critic of the strike described this dilemma with great cogency at the Trades and Labour Council on the twenty-fifth anniversary of the strike. He said that it is folly to attempt a general strike unless you are prepared to take over the state. The strike committee reluctantly assumed a few of the functions of government, i.e. in re-

---

* The Winnipeg General Strike (Toronto, 1950).

gard to food deliveries; but with society apparently on the verge of collapse in Winnipeg, they made no further effort at the assumption of political control. Faced with this crisis, the authorities, local and federal, were compelled by the logic of events to intervene."[2]

There is some merit in what Masters is saying here. He is pinpointing a weakness in the strike — the strikers' retreat from their original intention to make the strike total—withdraw police services, take over the supply of food to the population, and so on. However, to a degree, Masters is inclining to Meighen's view that a general strike is inseparable from a plan to take over the government: if the strike is to succeed, the workers must be ready to take power.

The operative concept here is "usurpation of governmental authority". As Meighen puts it—"for a general strike to succeed . . . it must result in the usurpation of governmental authority" by the strikers. But *what* is "usurpation of governmental authority"? And *was* the Winnipeg strike a "usurpation of governmental authority"? Meighen says yes: "It was so in Winnipeg . . ."

Meighen's stand is dubious.

Firstly, what happened at Winnipeg was far removed from usurpation of governmental authority. The strike was essentially defensive— a mass cessation of work.

Secondly, even if the strike had become more total—to the point that municipal authorities could not supply water, fire protection and police services, save by agreement with the strikers, this still would not have been a usurpation of governmental authority, but an internal extension of the strike, which was and remained essentially, a peaceful, voluntary, general withdrawal of labour services.

Thirdly, let it be assumed that the strikers had ceased their recognition of the existent municipal government, had established a new municipal government oriented to Winnipeg Labour, and had done this without an election—and none of this *happened*—that could be considered a usurpation of governmental authority. However, it would have been confined to a single city, and would not have extended to the total Canadian state power—the federal-provincial-municipal apparatus of army, police, courts of law, civil service, municipal councils, provincial legislatures and federal parliament.

In sum, Meighen and Masters are confusing a sweeping, revolutionary, social objective with the transitional defence measures which are inherent in every strike, particularly a general strike. One such measure is organization of a network of committees based on the rank and file, to ensure that jobs shut down stay shut down—particularly the vital ones—and are not manned save by the strikers' consent. Another is the development of an apparatus of internal control, again based on the rank and file, for food supply, strike relief, public relations, and not least, for protection against employers' economic sanctions and state coercion.

If the Meighen-Masters thesis were accepted, it would follow that Labour should not consider a general strike unless it is prepared to go through with a social revolution, and that if it does go out in a general strike, then the state is justified in using coercive measures to break it. For though the strikers' objective may be the winning of immediate demands, the logic of their action is social revolution. This thesis is false, a dangerous violation of common sense. Increasingly it will become incompatible with the Canadian social realities of our time (1967 seq.) when Organized Labour's strategy may well have to include a general strike if necessary—for 1 hour, 24 hours, or a more prolonged period.

This is the argument in theory, but for those impatient with theory, there is the unassailable argument of practice. Through the 20th century to the present (1967) there have been many general strikes in Britain, Western Europe, Asia and Latin America. Some were won and some lost; but almost all were not aimed at social revolution, and their outcome left the system intact.

Practice refutes also the suggestion of inevitability communicated in the Meighen-Masters thesis, though not explicitly stated—the idea that when a government decides to break a general strike, it can just go ahead and do it. As Masters puts it, "intervention by the Dominion Government smashed the strike".

The facts are that when the Federal Government took its coercive steps at Winnipeg, the economic and mass potential of the strike had far from reached the maximum. Had the strike become a national general strike; had the tie-up of services in Winnipeg been more total; had the massed power of the strikers and ex-soldiers been used more actively, but in a planned, organized, disciplined way, and in *defence* of these four basic rights: to work, not to work, to organize, to assemble —then it is conceivable the government's coercion could have been defeated, and this by action confined to the aim of victory for the strike —an aim well within the limits of the present social system and constitutional government.

This judgment is confirmed by events in the strike, and by the attitudes of those directly engaged in operations—strikers, employers, politicians and generals.

Consider the standpoint of Judge Robson—he headed a Royal Commission of Enquiry into the strike—set up after its termination, by the Manitoba Provincial Government. In his report, Judge Robson stated: "The loss occasioned by the strike was universal... a general loss to the community... The direct monetary loss was enormous... Business was diverted from Winnipeg." He went on to describe the consequences which had followed from a comparatively small strike of Dominion Express employees in western Canada during May and June of 1919. All told not much more than 500 expressmen quit work but the result was a halt in daily food supply of 400 cans of cream and 1,200 dozen eggs. Judge Robson concluded:

"It is not difficult for anyone to realize immediately the far-reaching effect this disruption of freight and transport would have on the community referred to."[3]

Again, consider the standpoint of General Ketchem, the officer commanding the Winnipeg Military District. In this situation—a mass movement of 35,000 people including thousands of ex-servicemen trained in the tough school of Vimy Ridge and Passchendale — he recommended caution. He was not even sure of his informers. It would appear he paid one informer $75 per week, and then paid a second informer $50 per week to inform on the first informer. This use of the taxpayers' money was reported to Ottawa by the General, and thus conserved for history.[4]

Consider also the action taken by Gideon Robertson at the end of the first week of the strike, when he secured the removal of a militia officer whom he considered unreliable.[5]

Machine guns, the outward mark of sovereignty, behind them—fear. The guns are delivered in secret. On May 23, General Hill was told an officer would report to him in Montreal and turn over 8 Lewis machine guns, packed in ordinary boxes marked "Regimental Baggage, 27th Battalion". The Federal Government report states: "It is the desire that these guns reach Winnipeg without anyone being the wiser."[6] When the 27th Battalion arrived in Winnipeg with the machine guns, only 2 of its members volunteered for service and the Battalion was disbanded.[7] Not long after the strike, Brigadier-General Kirkaldy stated:

"Military forces should as far as possible be kept out of such things as have recently occurred. We must keep the military popular and not send your son or mine to shoot down their own fellow countrymen. The military should be used only as a last resort."[8]

How significant also that Government "specials" and RCMP did not pass some tests of action with glowing colours, and yet, on Bloody Saturday, June 21, they had the advantage over the strikers who had been told by their leadership *not to fight back,* and had not even received a clear directive to demonstrate.*

Then there are the arrests: the misgivings they aroused in an intelligent antagonist of the strike—John Dafoe of the *Winnipeg Free Press;* the way the provincial government shifted responsibility for the arrests on to the federal government;[9] and how, within the federal government, Minister of Justice Meighen shifted the responsibility to Minister of Labour Gideon Robertson.[10] As the *Strike Bulletin* put it: "The authorities are afraid of the people!"

Finally consider this: The government which thus "corrected" Winnipeg Labour was itself "corrected" 2 years later. In the federal election of 1921 it was defeated and hurled into the opposition, there to stay for 9 years.

All this evidence points to the limits in the powers of big business and the federal government. And that *is* the point: The concrete *relation of forces* between the strikers and their antagonists. That's what decided the outcome. In the specific circumstances of 1919, the combination of big business hostility and state intervention did operate as a decisive cause for the defeat of the strike. But there was *nothing inevitable about it,* and generalizations are dangerous. As a matter of fact, when the situation is looked at more closely, a *second important cause* is found, one which *interacted* with the primary cause. To this we now turn.

2. ROLE OF THE CONSERVATIVE OFFICIALDOM AND U.S. HEADQUARTERS

Strike-Breaking:

In 1917, Prime Minister Robert Borden "recognized" organized labour by appointing Gideon Robertson, international vice-president of the Commercial Telegraphers Union, AFL, to the post of Minister of Labour. In this hard world, you don't get something for nothing.

---

* The *Strike Bulletin* declared at the time: "The returned men assume full responsibility for the silent parade, making a special request that the strikers should not join them." At the trial of the Winnipeg strike leaders after the strike, it was testified that "Winning (president of the Winnipeg Trades and Labour Council) tried to stop the parade but as he was not a returned soldier, he could not speak at a soldiers' gathering. On June 21, 1919, the General Officer Commanding wired Minister of Justice Meighen: "I believe the strike committee did all in its power to prevent the red soldier parade that started the riot." That same day, the Justice Department agent Andrews wired Meighen: "I think however if we had not admitted to bail, riots would have been precipitated by the Strike Committee who I believe did all in their power to prevent the red soldier parade which started the riot." In his report on the strike, Judge Robson said: "The leaders' policy was peaceful idleness, but turbulent persons affected by this extraordinary condition broke loose and were responsible for the demonstrations and violence that took place during the strike."

The time had come for Robertson to pay. Early in the strike he went to Winnipeg and promptly began to misrepresent the situation. He said the strike committee was seeking a revolutionary mode of collective bargaining, in which settlements by local unions must be approved by higher bodies—councils, central bodies and such-like.

This was sophistry. Robertson was counterposing individual and joint negotiations. Obviously joint negotiations did not violate a local union's autonomy, if the local union agreed to bargain this way. Patiently, the central strike committee explained that the objective was recognition for the metal and building trades councils, that this mode of bargaining was already in force in Division 4 of the AFL (the railway shopmen), and had been accepted by the federal government in negotiations with the Vancouver Metal Trades.[11]

This would have satisfied Robertson if he wanted the truth. But what he wanted was to smash the strike. So he went on weaving his web of intrigue. On May 29, he wrote AFL President Samuel Gompers:

"In my opinion, the prestige and authority of the international unions whose local membership is participating in the strike ... should receive the rather serious consideration of the executives of the various organizations concerned ... The motives are undoubtedly support of the One Big Union movement."[12]

Concerning this letter, a leading Quebec Liberal member of Parliament, the Hon. Ernest Lapointe, was later to say: "This is an appeal clamouring for help by a Canadian Minister of the Crown to a foreign labour leader."[13]

There was a response to that appeal. Certainly there was action. The U.S. headquarters of international unions began to oppose the general strike movement in Canada. At Toronto, when the street railway local union met on June 1, international representatives appeared and persuaded the men not to join the general strike planned for Toronto;[14] and that decision was likely a turning point in the Toronto situation. Again, when Canadian railway locals asked international headquarters what they (the locals) could do to help the strikers,[15] headquarters often replied that their constitutions forbade such strikes, and that in any case the locals could not strike unless headquarters agreed. At times, international headquarters even recommended strikebreaking. The U.S. headquarters of the Brotherhood of Railroad Trainmen at Cleveland, Ohio, sent the following order to their membership in Canada:

"In view of illegal strike of members of the Winnipeg lodge, resulting in terminals in that city being tied up, it is deemed necessary that our organization use every effort to furnish members of the brotherhood willing to accept positions made vacant by the illegal strikers, and that members of the organization be called upon to furnish such assistance as is needed (to) handle business of the road affected . . ."[16]

Canadian railroad unionists who disregarded such directives and supported the strikers were threatened by international representatives. On June 14, Geo. K. Wark, an international vice-president of the Brotherhood of Locomotive Firemen (AFL), and James Murdoch, a Canadian international representative of the Brotherhood of Railway Trainmen, denounced running trades locals at Winnipeg who had supported the strikers. A sympathetic strike could not be countenanced, they said. This was something "absolutely unauthorized". The laws of the organization "would be upheld by every means". Two days later, Murdoch said members striking in defiance of international headquarters would be taken off the membership list, and locals defying headquarters would have their charters revoked.[17]

This strike-breaking was coupled with manoeuvres from within. In the climactic days of the strike, in mid-June, senior railway running trades officials offered their mediation services to the central strike committee and the committee accepted. It is fairly clear, however, that the rail officials did not carry on this mediation in an honourable way, instead they substituted themselves for the committee, and entered into direct negotiations with the metal trades employers, without involving the committte or even keeping it properly informed. It is also fairly definite that Gideon Robertson took part in these negotiations.

Then came a surprise move. On June 16, *just 24 hours before the arrests,* the Winnipeg newspapers carried a joint statement by the metal trades employers and the mediation committee. The statement said the employers were willing to recognize the unions *on a craft basis,* as distinct from the metal trades council basis demanded by the central strike committee.[18]

This was a stab in the back, coinciding in the result and almost certainly in the intention with government coercion, and the more deadly the thrust because it came amidst indications that the employers and provincial governments were considering negotiating with the Central Strike Committee.

Then there was TLC president Tom Moore. On June 23, when government reprisals were being visited on the strikers—reprisals condemned by TLC members across the country—when the strikers had their backs to the wall but still a fighting chance to win, Moore wrote the Winnipeg Trades and Labour Council, and in so many words rejected its appeal for help; or at any rate, he set conditions the council could not accept—and he probably knew it—for they entailed abdication of the council's authority to international headquarters.

This is how international headquarters in the U.S. and senior trade union officers in Canada aligned with international headquarters sabotaged the strike in its crisis stage. Was it surprising then that some locals at Winnipeg should begin to waver?*

And why this sabotage? On May 25, 1919, Gideon Robertson wired the Federal Government:

"If it (the general strike) proved a failure, the One Big Union movement will, I think, also fail."[19a]

In 1926, the House of Commons conducted an enquiry into the 1919 events. The Hon. Peter Heenan, Minister of Labour in the Mackenzie King Liberal Government, went through a wealth of materials yielded by this enquiry, and he concluded:

"I think I have proved conclusively that the Minister of Labour (Robertson) did on a whim of his own, and against the advice of his colleagues, prolong the strike by refusing to declare in favour of collective bargaining ... I think he said himself it was in the interests of the international unions ... The negotiations leading up to the riot were carried out in a manner to prevent it (the strike) being settled."[20]

This is plain enough. Key U.S. international headquarters, and conservative union officials in Canada aligned with them, preferred a defeat for the Winnipeg strike to a victory for the movement as a whole, including their own unions. Worse still *they helped organize the defeat.*

And for this, what thanks did they get? Not long after the Winnipeg strike, the TLC and international unions asked Minister of Justice Meighen to name a trade union representative to the Board of Directors of the Canadian National Railways. Meighen replied with cold contempt:

"Through what organization? There are at the present time, I am told, 16 or 17 organizations of the railroad employees, absolutely distinct in every way. Are these ... different organizations going to make their recommendations?"[21]

In other words, if the railroad unions combined in a single, strong, industrial organization, they were socialistic; and if they retained their anarchic, craft multiplicity, they were beneath recognition. This was Meighen's logic. And the conservative trade union officials exposed themselves and their members to the lash of this logic when they persisted in their policy of class collaboration and subservience to U.S. headquarters, when they sabotaged the Winnipeg strike, and helped engineer its defeat.

* Around June 17, end-the-strike resolutions were adopted by certain locals including Brotherhood of Railway Carmen locals at the CNR and CPR shops.[19]

3. HISTORIC SIGNIFICANCE OF THE STRIKE

Objectives of the Strike:

The Winnipeg strike was defeated. But that does not cancel its major contribution to Canadian Labour's progress. It was a great struggle for great objectives and principles:

1. *Collective bargaining:* The right to organize, its achievement in direct relations with employers, its enactment in law. This was a major demand in the strike. Twenty-five years went by before it was won, and only partially won.

2. *Industrial Unionism:* Employer recognition of the Metal and Building Trades Councils was another central demand in the strike and one of its original causes implicit in this was the drive to industrial unionism—a durable of Canadian trade union evolution. In the circumstances of 1919, this meant the struggle for *combined* action by the craft locals, the building of new bodies such as councils.

3. *Labour Councils:* The Winnipeg Trades and Labour Council and its central strike committee demonstrated the potential of local councils as centres to co-ordinate Labour's struggle.

4. *Government Employees:* The right to organize for municipal, provincial and federal government employees: Their right to negotiate, strike and affiliate to a labour centre; in sum their equal rights with all other employees—no extra privileges for government as employer, no extra obligations for employees of government—this too was a basic demand in the strike, one for which Winnipeg' firemen, policemen, telephone employees and postmen fought both in legal representations and direct action.

5. *Police:* When the Winnipeg municipal police fought for their rights and sympathized with the strikers, they were not only upholding the general rights as government employees but the principle that this special group of workers should not be given orders which seemingly protect the public interest but actually foster the private interests of companies—particularly during industrial disputes.

6. *War Veterans:* The ex-servicemen's co-operation with the strikers, their refusal (for the most part) to be manipulated by private business, was patriotism at its best—the highest service they could then render their country, the working community, and themselves.

7. *Solidarity:* When Winnipeg trade unionists, acting through the Trades and Labour Council, came to the aid of the machinists and building trades workers; when Vancouver trade unionists and trade unionists in other cities as well, aided the Winnipeg trade unionists; and when, in the specific circumstances then prevailing, they raised

that aid to the level of sympathetic and general strike, they were showing what means trade union solidarity.

8. *Canadian Unionism:* The Winnipeg strike marked a new, high level in the unfolding of a decisive law of Canadian labour history—the struggle for freedom from international union domination. This was underlined by the brutal interference of U.S. headquarters which helped defeat the strike. But above all it was expressed in the constructive action of the strikers themselves, metal trades and building trades councils, their Trades and Labour Council. The Winnipeg strike showed that the solidarity between Canadian railwaymen, metal and building trades workers, between all Canadian organized workers, is greater in principle and economic potential than the thin line of per capita stretching from local unions in Canada to international headquarters in Washington, Cleveland and New York.

9. *Militant Trade Unionism:* This sums up and epitomizes the great objectives of the Winnipeg strike. It means Labour's readiness to win its demands through peaceful negotiations and representations to employers and government, but its determination at all times to depend on its own organization, strength and independence.

Social Reconstruction:

Trade unionism and social reconstruction—their long standing inter-relationship—reached a new, high point in the Winnipeg strike. This was primarily a matter of internal Canadian labour evolution. Again, it was speeded by the actual strike movement itself. Finally, it was unquestionably influenced by the revolutionary events then stirring Europe, more particularly the Russian Revolution of 1917. All this did not determine the decisive character of the strike, which was and remained a purely trade union struggle for purely trade union objectives. Still less did it justify the charges of "soviet power" wrongly attributed to the strikers and their leadership. However, by 1919, socialism—more generally the desire for social reconstruction—had a mass basis and this operated within the strike, as *one* important thread. Here are some examples:

In the *Strike Bulletin,* Rev. William Ivens looked to the day when the workers would "own and control industry". The capitalists were afraid of the workers because "they see in the slogan, abolition of production for profit, the death knell of the present system".[22] The President of the Trades and Labour Council, James Winning, a moderate trade unionist, pointed to the need for Labour "getting a more equitable share of the wealth of the world". From the strike, he concluded: "Withdraw labour power from the machine and at once profits cease."[23] The *Strike Bulletin* said that the workers' present task was to "solidify their force by gaining their right to collective bargaining. As the years go along, labour will carry on its campaign to eliminate the profit system".[24] The Secretary of the Trades and Labour Council, E. Robinson, addressing the soldiers' parliament, stated: "In days to come, strikes would not be necessary because the workers will band together and so control government and industry that every man will have a fair chance."[25]

This was in the spirit of social reconstruction. So was this poem in the *Strike Bulletin,* 9 days after the strike began—the author's initials were "R.E.H.":

> "Yet it's well that we know there are two kinds of men—
> The rich and the poor who for ages have been.
> The rich make the laws to govern the poor,
> The poor must take less while the rich must have more.
> "We read of the unemployed army of men,
> Of children in factories like birds in a pen,
> Of girls in the sweatshops on very small pay,
> While a number of suicides blight every day.
> "We hear of the thousands of babes that are lost,
> Of the trusts that hold foods at such a high cost,
> Yes, nature produces abundance for all,
> But the rich around nature have built a high wall.
> "They own all the timbers, minerals and mines,
> The railways, the steamships, the telegraph lines,
> The judges, the lawyers, the newspapers, the schools,
> The mills and the factories, machinery and tools.
> "They own all the land in a strange sort of way,
> Have most of us mortgaged to them, some men say,
> Their god it is interest, profit and rent,
> Their faith and religion is so much percent ..."[26]

What of the rank-and-file strikers? Much like Russians, Cubans, French Canadians, English Canadians, Americans, or the peoples of Africa, Asia and Latin America in our own day, *they were concerned primarily not with ideology but with their own needs.* However, so far as they found capitalism standing athwart these objectives, they turned against capitalism. One striker said: "The man who goes out to fight for his master is a brave Briton. The man who comes home to fight for his Mrs. is a bloomin 'Bolshevik'." Another said: "I am not a Bolshevik. A Bolshevik owns his own land. I own none." On Bloody Saturday, June 21, 3 strikers were arrested. The first said: "When I enlisted and fought in France, I was under the impression that I, like all other of my comrades in arms, was fighting for freedom against militarism."[27] The second, an Irish policeman, said: "It wouldn't be as tame as this in Ireland!" The third—an ex-soldier, head of family, and church member—said: "I never had much use for these Bolsheviks, those fellows in Russia, but if they were treated like this, I don't wonder. When I get out I'll be a Bolshevik myself. No more of this law and order stuff for me. We've got to fight."

This was reflected in the church too. The Revs. A. E. Smith, J. S. Woodsworth and William Ivens strongly supported the strike. Other clergymen didn't. One Sunday morning early in the strike, a striker went to church and heard a call for volunteers to join the militia and "keep order". He said: "I am through with that kind of Church!" Resentment against this misuse of the Church brought about a "Labour Church". It functioned throughout the strike, and was initiated at a gathering on Sunday, May 18 with 5,000 present. Rev. William Ivens, officiating, said the strike was the triumph of the Man of Galilee. Winnipeg Trades Council President Winning, also present, said: "Many a preacher would look with longing eyes at a congregation of this kind." Another strike leader, R. B. Russell, told the throng: "This is a new kind of church. The last time I was at church it was as solemn as a tomb."[28]

Socialism found its echo in Parliament too. On June 2, G. W. Andrews, member for Winnipeg Centre (not to be confused with Justice Department agent Andrews) spoke out in the House of Commons in defence of the strikers. He asked his fellow members how many were satisfied with the present conditions. I venture to say many of them would welcome a change of government. Some of the members then cried: "Hear, hear!" Concluding, Andrews said: "Gentlemen, if you apply the term Bolshevik to these men, you apply it to me!"[29]

Of course, as Canadians have said in more recent years, and with a grain of truth, the real "communists" were the capitalists. The day the strike leaders were arrested in Winnipeg, the newspapers reported the proceedings of an enquiry into the cost of living by a House of Commons committee. Paton was on the stand—owner of a textile mill in Sherbrooke, Quebec (to-day a branch of the Dominion Textile Company). The evidence showed that wartime profits by Paton's company were about 26% in 1915, 35% in 1916 and 46% in 1917. Paton explained: "If a man could not make money during the war there must be something wrong with him."

Committee: "Could you bring down prices by lowering your profits?"

Paton: "No doubt."

Committee: "Don't you think it's due to the public to lower your prices?"

Paton: "Our mill was not built for the glory of God or anyone else. It was built for the benefit of the shareholders."[30]

Reacting to Paton's testimony, the *Strike Bulletin* compared his earnings with those of soldiers in the trenches—$1.10 a day. It was all right to make millions, but if you fought for a living wage you were an anarchist. It was injustice of this kind, the *Strike Bulletin* went on to say, which justified the dictatorship of the proletariat—the *Bulletin* explained this was a Latin word which meant a complete turnover in the system exploiting the people of Canada.[31]

Other capitalist "communists" or "socialists" were Judge Robson and Minister of Justice Arthur Meighen. In his report on the strike, Judge Robson counterposed "craft unionism" and "radical socialism". In other words, he suggested that opposition to craft unionism was somehow identical with socialism. And yet the two were distinct: The former was a matter of progressive *trade union evolution*. The latter was one of *basic social change*. To-day (1967), this would not be disputed. But not so in 1919. Yesterday's heresy, to-day's truth! As for Meighen, he said:

"It cannot for any one moment be argued, merely because collective bargaining is acknowledged, that there shall be an unlimited heterogeneous collection of all classes of labour ... If that is to take place ... we would extend it right along until you would have every organization in the Dominion united and all asserting a united influence in every dispute that might occur. Can anyone contemplate such an event? ... Collective bargaining, unless you bring it down to some unit, is bound to reach that end ... This is the perfection of Bolshevism."[32]

Summary:

This was the Winnipeg Strike. In sum, it was a great step forward, and a great opportunity lost. It came about as part of the post-war crisis of Canadian politics. This crisis was reflected in a swift development of three durables of Canadian progress: Labour, the farm movement, Quebec. Among the workers there was a sharp upswing of union membership, economic struggles, and strikes. In the ranks of the farmers, there was a powerful turn to independent economic and political organization. In Quebec, the war and conscription crisis had generated profound discontents. And all this was connected in turn with the crisis still more acute of capitalism in Europe.

For Labour this was the moment of opportunity, and how great the opportunity is shown by what transpired in 1919-1921.

1919: Thomas Crerar's resignation as Minister of Agriculture in the Union Government, his emergence soon after as leader of the Progressives (farmers) Party; in Ontario, election of Canada's first farmer-labour government.

1920: Election of 11 candidates of the Manitoba Labour Party and 8 candidates of the United Farmers of Manitoba to the provincial legislature; election of a number of labour representatives to the Winnipeg municipal council.

1921: Defeat of the strike-breaking Borden (Union) government in the federal election; election of a bloc of 75 progressives, mostly farm candidates—the largest third party grouping ever to sit in the House of Commons.

What a difference, if there had been a strong, united trade union movement, with a strong leadership which took its orders from the membership in Canada, and welcomed solidarity from the United States, but rebuffed domination. But this factor was not present. True, the movement to united, effective trade unionism had by now become powerful, but it was not dominant. And those who identified themselves with it—as events showed—lacked not only strength, but also clarity and cohesiveness. And so, in the years that followed, trade union progress was seriously impeded. So was industrial unionism, recognition of the right to organize, social legislation. Big business was able to restore "normalcy". The third party movement disintegrated. Partial progress there was—a limited advance in farmer-labour political action; a limited extension of union recognition and social legislation; most important of all, perhaps, the standing warning to employers that they dare not push their objectives too hard, that they must provide a minimum of wage concessions, reform and social legislation. For a time could come once again when Organized Labour would fight back and unleash mighty movements on the scale of the 1919 general strike. As the *Western Labour News* put it on July 2, 1919, just a few days after the end of the Winnipeg strike:

"It can never be forgotten that over 30,000 workers struck not for themselves but for others . . . and in so doing linked themselves forever with the men who fought in Flanders Field . . . The workers are equal to the problem of the hour if they are given a chance. If they are not given a chance today, they are equal to the problem of working out a solution tomorrow."[33]

CHAPTER 12

NEW CENTRES AND MOVEMENTS
1919-1924

1. THE ONE BIG UNION

Its Rise and Decline, 1919-1921:

1919-1924 was a period of ferment. On an international scale, the new régime was consolidated in Russia. In the remainder of Europe, the fate of capitalism itself was hanging in the balance. This crisis was punctuated by events such as: a revolutionary wave in Germany; a general strike in Italy; and a deep-going radicalization in the worker's movement of France. In Britain there was a trade union upsurge involving in particular the miners and railwaymen. In the United States there was sharpening labour unrest.

So much for the international developments. In Canada, capitalism and capitalist politics had also entered a period of serious instability—though far removed from the deep-going crisis of continental Europe. This instability expressed itself in continuing industrial unrest and radicalization among the workers, in agrarian radicalism, in a partial though limited swing to labour political action.

All this reflected itself in the trade union movement of Canada. Two principal manifestations were: the emergence of a number of new movements and trends; and developments in the Trades and Labour Congress and the Canadian locals of international unions. This chapter will deal with these new movements and trends. Later chapters will outline events in the TLC and international unions, and along with them, continuing developments within the new movements.

First, the One Big Union. Its origin can be traced to a caucus of western delegates which met after the 1918 TLC convention. These delegates, embittered by the rebuff they had received at the convention, resolved to carry forward their fight for organization of the unorganized, for industrial unionism and Canadian unionism.

Then came the Western Canada Labour Conference of March 1919. That conference adopted a resolution recommending to the affiliated membership "severance of their affiliation with their international organizations ... and steps ... to form an industrial organization of all workers..." The name of the new body was to be the One Big Union. To this end, a conference decided to circularize unions across the country and hold a referendum.[1] It elected a committee of five to conduct the referendum: William Pritchard and E. R. Midgely of B.C., R.J. Johns of Winnipeg, and two others — J. B. Knight and J. Taylor.

The terms of this resolution were ambiguous. They referred to "an industrial organization of all workers". Did that mean secession from the international unions? The OBU leaders said yes; but they confused the issue by adopting a distant attitude as well to the Trades and Labour Congress—of this more later. Also, they tended to be hostile to labour political action. A resolution from the Alberta Federation of Labour to the Western Canada Labour conference called for "a united labour political party". However, Jack Kavanaugh, an outstanding B.C. trade unionist and spokesman for the Left—which was in a majority at the conference—replied that "labour representatives ... had been used ... as tools to deceive the workers". Some delegates were not sure. They said that political action in the U.S.A. and Britain had won the 8-hour day. If parliamentary labour representatives sold out their constituents, then why not a new kind of parliamentarism? "Send them (the M.P.s) there with a new platform, with new ideas, a new conception of life", elect M.P.s pledged to "destroy the capitalist system", suggested one delegate.[2] However, the negative attitude fo political action prevailed.

Meanwhile as preparations proceeded for the referendum, the Winnipeg strike began. This was not the work of the OBU. When the antagonists of the strike said it was, they were either misinformed or wanted to cast the strike in a strange, lurid light. The truth is that when the strike began, the OBU was not yet organized. For their part, the OBU leaders denied responsibility for the strike. Of course they were active in it, but only in their capacity as officers of established unions, mostly locals of international unions. It was these locals, and the Winnipeg Trades and Labour Council—a body chartered by the TLC—which made up the main force of the strike and provided its leadership. Implicitly, TLC president Moore admitted this in his letter to the Winnipeg Council on June 24, 1919, when he charged the Council with responsibility for the strike, and said it had "usurped" the function of international unions by taking over leadership of the strike.

The strike ended, OBU organization resumed. On July 8, the Winnipeg Trades and Labour Council instructed the executive to act on the Western Canada Labour Conference report. A week later, Winnipeg union members voted 8,841—705 for disaffiliation from international unions and the TLC, and for affiliation to the OBU. Soon after, the Winnipeg Council returned its charter to the TLC. In retaliation, a TLC representative, R. A. Rigg, took over the Council's seal and organized the remaining adherents of the international unions into another council.[3]

Initially, the OBU's success was striking, more particularly in Western Canada. "The whole territory (Western Canada) is a volcanic crater",[4] said R. A. Rigg that year. British Columbia was a major base. Here, the Vancouver Trades and Labour Council took action similar to that of the Winnipeg Council. It severed links with the AFL and TLC. Here too, international union representatives retaliated by setting up a rival council. Some of B.C.'s strongest labour detachments joined the OBU, the International Union of Mine, Mill and Smelter Workers, and United Mine Workers of America District 18. A referendum conducted by the B.C. Federation of Labour, with 13,769 voting out of a total membership of 20,615, showed a large majority for secession from the international unions.[5]

The OBU had now become a major force—it had 41,000 members by the end of 1919. But most were in Western Canada; in the east there were just a few scattered locals, largely in Ontario—at Carleton Place, Port Arthur, Fort William and Hamilton.[6] The second convention of the OBU, meeting at Port Arthur, Ontario, in September 1920, adopted a constitution whose aims and objects said:

"Modern industrial society is divided into two classes—those who possess and do not produce, and those who produce and do not possess . . . The One Big Union, therefore, seeks to organize the wage workers according to class . . . needs, and calls upon all workers to organize irrespective of nationality, sex or craft, to a workers' organization where they may be enabled to more successfully carry on the every-day fight over wages, hours of work and prepare ourselves for the day when production for profit shall be replaced by production for use."[7]

This was the meteoric rise of the OBU. Its decline was likewise swift. By 1921 it had only 5,300 members. Why? One reason was dual unionism. At that time, the radical trade unionists who detested business unionism and class collaboration were prone to bolt established unions, rather than stay in them and continue the fight. Sometimes it was best not to leave but to stay, because they were not being expelled, and in leaving were cutting themselves from more moderate members who also wanted a change, but did not want to break with their unions. It was not necessarily a mistake—indeed in the circumstances, and given the temper of the rank and file, it was probably right to break with the international unions. But it was almost certainly a mistake to break with the TLC—at a time when progressive trade unionists had won leadership in one body after another chartered by the TLC—particularly in Western Canada. And such was the strength of the progressives, that it would have been difficult for the TLC to expel them, even on orders from the U.S.A. Again, it was almost certainly a mistake for the OBU to insist that organization by region was primary rather than organization by industry.[8] Finally, the forces grouped around the OBU tended to bypass the existent international union locals in Canada. They sought to reorganize the membership of these locals into totally new bodies of the OBU. Probably they would have done better to conserve these locals—many of whom meanwhile had disaffiliated from their international unions—and *group* them into *cohesive Canadian industrial unions.*

One problem was that the OBU arose from the struggle for a united, militant, industrial, Canadian movement. But its leaders did not stand at the height of the fight; were too influenced by syndicalist ideas current in the U.S.A. and Great Britain; and did not base themselves enough on internal Canadian trade union experience. They operated the idea that a brand new body was needed. They gravitated too much on *structures* and not enough on the *concrete problems* and *durable issues* important to the workers—those issues which determine the adaptation of old organizations or at times the formation of new ones. Had they concentrated on these issues—for example—organization of the unorganized, better conditions, industrial unionism, an end to domination by employers, governments and U.S. international headquarters—then, such was the profound, deep, mass support, which these issues excited, and such was the height which rank and file revulsion against the old line officialdom and international union headquarters had reached by 1919—that the prospects for a success in the OBU's revolt would have been much greater.

These, then, were the OBU's mistakes and causes of its downfall. But there were other basic causes too. The OBU did reflect and uphold the progressive aspirations of Canadian trade unionists. Because of this it became the target for violent attacks by employers, governments, and international unions. Bitterly the B.C. Federation of Labour referred on one occasion to the "unholy alliance formed between the international unions and the employers to crush the new move-ment".[9] This, too, played its part in the OBU's defeat. In any case, the OBU died. What lived on was the militancy which engendered it, the struggles of coal miners, lumber workers, metal workers and other groups—in sum, the historic fight for a united, militant, Canadian trade union movement.*

2. FEDERATION OF CATHOLIC WORKERS OF CANADA** 1921

Reasons For Its Formation; Its Principal Traits:

Throughout its history (1921-1967 seq.) the Federation of Catholic Workers of Canada has operated as a general Canadian trade union centre, which accepted responsibility for Labour's progress not only in Quebec but across Canada, and which made representations to the federal government as well as the Quebec Provincial Government. In this respect, the FCWC is one of a long series of centres which have functioned alongside the largest single centre connected with the inter-national unions—in the past the Trades and Labour Congress of Cana-da, to-day (1967) the Canadian Labour Congress. Between 1902 and 1967—a period of 65 years—these centres have been the National Trades and Labour Congress of Canada, the Canadian Federation of Labour, the One Big Union, the FCWC, the All-Canadian Congress of Labour, the Workers' Unity League, and the Canadian Congress of Labour. In every case, they arose in connection with the revolt against inter-national union domination and class collaboration. However, as dis-tinct from the other centres mentioned above, the FCWC has always had this additional aspect—its connection with Quebec, the soil and workers of Quebec.

The FCWC's origins are sometimes traced back to a situation which developed in the shoe industry of Quebec City in 1900 when the Asso-ciation of Shoe Manufacturers declared a lockout against their em-ployees. The workers held out against the lockout, and then the em-ployers asked the Archbishop of Quebec, Monsignor Bégin, to arbi-trate. The workers accepted the Archbishop's decision and returned to

---

* The OBU survived until the latter 1950s, when it became a part of the Canadian Labour Congress, and most of its affiliates joined the international unions. But by that time, it was largely confined to a few local unions in Winnipeg. The OBU ceased to be a major force after 1921-1922.

** The original name was Federation of Catholic Workers of Canada. Later this was changed to the Canadian and Catholic Confederation of Labour. The present name, Confederation of National Trade Unions, was adopted in 1960.

their jobs. In his report, the Archbishop said Labour had the right to organize, but he asked the union to change the laws "to make them more into conformity with the social doctrine of the church". The union amended its constitution accordingly, and agreed to admit chaplains to its meetings.[10]

However, it is probably wrong to look on this event as the effective beginning of Catholic syndicalism. Two decades went by before there was a full-fledged Catholic labour centre in the province. Moreover, Catholic unionism did not produce a similar centre in the United States or in any other part of the British Commonwealth. Indeed, Quebec is one of the few places in the world where confessional unionism attained such proportions as to challenge "neutral" unionism.

From this, one might conclude that the hegemony of Catholic unionism is typical of Quebec, but this also is not true. Confessional unionism was a late comer in Quebec. When the FCWC was founded in 1921, trade unions had been functioning in Quebec for almost a century. The first unions in Quebec, as in Ontario, were completely Canadian (and neutral) unions. The Knights of Labour flourished in Quebec during the 1880s and 1890s—despite opposition from the clergy. It was the Knights' expulsion from the TLC which engendered the tendency to separation between organized workers in Quebec and the rest of Canada. Significantly, the FCWC historians themselves date their movement's origin to the 1902 split; and in so doing, stand on better ground than in their emphasis on the Church's intervention in the 1900 shoe lock-out. However, this latter event was an early signal that the Church could adapt itself to the trade union movement and appreciate its significance.

Let us now review developments between 1902 and 1920. The reader will recall that after 1902, a number of the locals in Quebec combined with locals in other parts of the country to form the National Trades and Labour Congress (the Canadian Federation of Labour as it was later called). But the CFL could not provide a lasting home for Quebec trade unionists. It was weak, inclined to class collaboration, ultra-imperialist in World War I, and purblind to the national question— the building of a free Quebec in a free, united, independent Canada. This created a void. In 1907, Catholic Social Action was organized in Quebec City. Much of its success seems to have been through infiltration into the national unions—those not affiliated to international unions.[11] The Catholic leaders did not do much to organize the unorganized, nor did they, for the most part, challenge the international unions directly. These national unions then had a fairly substantial membership. Their main base was in Quebec City where, after 1902, they grouped about half of the 6,000 or 7,000 union members in that city.

The infiltration work of Catholic Social Action brought results. In 1918, 2 central councils merged in Quebec City—one consisting of CFL unions, the other of unaffiliated unions.[12] This merged council then called on the church for help, and some unions asked for chaplains.

This was the chain of events so far as Catholic Social Action was concerned. What of the international unions? The minute books of the Montreal Trades and Labour Council during this period, report requests to the AFL and U.S. international headquarters for help in organizing Quebec workers.[13] It is fairly clear the response was not adequate. Small wonder that in 1920 the Quebec executive committee of the TLC complained that a "strictly French-Canadian trend" had arisen among union members in Quebec, and this it deplored for "capital is international" and "labour must be international" too.[14] And yet, this "strictly French-Canadian trend" was inevitable because the international unions were not paying enough attention to organization of the unorganized in Quebec, and the national question there; and in any case, a special problem was posed by their presence in a section of Canada sensitive to its own nationhood and to Canada's freedom from foreign control.

There was also the problem of orientation to the employers. In the statement above referred to, not only did the Quebec TLC committee complain about this "strictly French-Canadian trend", but, in so many words, it wooed the employers: "... All we have to do is build our ranks and prove to the manufacturers that we alone can secure the steadiness needed for the development of industry." In short, the Quebec TLC adherents were competing with Catholic syndicalism for the friendship of the companies. In 1921 TLC leaders at Ottawa took the same line, when in upholding international unionism as against Quebec Catholic syndicalism, they cited words of praise for the former spoken in Parliament by two enemies of Organized Labour—Arthur Meighen and Gideon Robertson.[15]

Let us pick up the thread of events after 1918. The Catholic Action leaders were now moving full speed to a new centre. In 1920-21 they issued 25 tracts to workers.[16] All this brought results. In 1921 the Inaugural Convention of the FCWC met at Hull, Quebec, with 200 delegates from 89 unions with a combined membership of 40,000.[17] Principles adopted at this convention stated: "The FCWC believes that it is wrong, an economic error, a national abdication and a political dan-

ger to have in Canada syndicates depending on a foreign centre..."[18]
They went on to say that the FCWC would have "the double character
of being national and Catholic". The class struggle was condemned:
"We must organize but this cannot signify, however, that the FCWC
is preparing troops for the class struggle". Strikes were deemed "a
dangerous weapon", and conciliation and arbitration suggested as a
preferable way to settle disputes. The right to strike for municipal
workers was rejected.[19]

Plainly, these principles had a strength and a weakness: The strength
was Canadian unionism. The weakness was class collaboration and
confessionalism.* The weakness held back the FCWC's progress. It did
not conduct an all-out fight for organization of the unorganized and
Quebec's emancipation from the trusts. Also it used the cry of neutral
union against the international unions—meaning that they were non-
confessional. But in this way it was confusing *international* and *neutral* unions, and was assailing international unions from their point
of strength, freedom from confessionalism, rather than their point of
weakness, the fact that they were unions based on the United States
and inclined at times to class collaboration.

For these mistakes the FCWC paid the price. At the end of the 1920s,
it had fewer members than when it started. How it shook off the negative, more particularly after World War II and emerged as a viable
Canadian trade union centre—a centre of national unions in Canada
which has survived to the present (1967) and strengthened—this is a
matter of more recent history.

3. TRADE UNIONISM AND SOCIAL RECONSTRUCTION

Role of the Left Wing:

The aspiration to social reconstruction is deeply Embedded in Canada's unions. This is reflected in the program of practically every union
and union centre. Previous chapters have outlined some of its expres-
sions. This section will deal with a specific expression which became
important at this time—the Left Wing, more particularly the communists. During the 1920s they became one of the decisive factors in the
Left. True that *they were only one* of several trends in the Left. There

---

* L.-L. Hardie, a labour historian friendly to the FCWC, writes about "a certain
number of employers who preferred to the neutral unions, national or international,
a CCCL prudent and moderate in its demands, for whom the strike was the ultimate
resort". (The CCCL: Canadian and Catholic Confederation of Labour—a later name
adopted by the FCWC).

was the OBU, also the Social Democrats—typified by J. S. Woodsworth and William Irvine—they made excellent contributions to the struggle for reform and progress. Concerning the specific role of communism, there is ample evidence in documents of the time—the proceedings of trade union conventions, the labour press, the Federal Government's Annual Report on Labour Organization.*

The labour press is a barometer. Consider the *Voice* (later called *Western Labour News*). Established in 1894, for years the organ of the Winnipeg Trades and Labour Council, prior to World War I its pages sparkled with socialist militancy. But after the war, enthusiasm waned. By 1921 it was a dull trades journal—no longer calling for socialization of the means of production, no longer challenging business unionism and class collaboration, but putting forward instead a vague, wishy-washy socialism of distant vistas and good wishes. In 1922 this grand old paper expired. The *Industrial Banner* suffered a like fate. Though not as radical as the *Voice,* it too was militant prior to World War I. For years it was the organ of the London Trades and Labour Council and later of the Toronto Trades and Labour Council. In 1922 it died.

This was happening just when tension was rising in the ranks of Labour, and when many workers were demanding militant leadership. In these circumstances, communist newspapers like the *Worker* began to have quite an impact. In the trade union movement itself, there was a parallel development. In day-to-day actions, in debates at union conventions, left wing advocates were identifying themselves with issues like industrial unionism, and Canadian autonomy.

At the same time, there was an important development in the world trade union movement—the founding of the Red International of Labour Unions in 1921. AFL president Gompers said it was a Kremlin tool. However, the RILU grouped about 40% of the world's trade union membership, and the evidence indicates it was a bona fide trade union body, but with an exceedingly radical policy. A Manifesto and constitution adopted at the RILU inaugural congress set forth the policy. The Manifesto said jobs and peace were the main issue. It warned that an economic crisis was coming. Goods would rot in the warehouses, wages be cut, and conditions worsened. It condemned

---

* These Reports, for 1919-1924, are a treasure house of materials on communist and other radical currents in the movement such as the One Big Union, Trade Union Educational League and Industrial Workers of the World. These Reports are the main source of the data in this section. H. A. Logan's *Trade Unions in Canada* also has valuable material on left wing activity; and there is some data in an admirable little work prepared by Margaret Mackintosh for the Federal Department of Labour— *An Outline of Trade Union History in Great Britain, the United States and Canada.*

business union-minded officials like Gompers as opportunists, bureaucrats, "a bunch of scabs", the main internal obstacle to Labour's progress. International trade union struggles showed that workers wanted leadership of a new type which could "defend and take the offensive". Militant trade unionists were told to group themselves together since the betrayed workers were going to act in any case, and better that the action be led by the Left. The Manifesto concluded:

"Workers all the world over! The first international congress of revolutionary labour unions, gathered in that bit of the globe which was wrenched by the Russian proletariat from the hands of capital, in the name of the millions of crippled and murdered in the criminal war, in the name of the sufferings of the working class, gone through under the dictatorship of capital, in the name of the victims of the bourgeois terror, in the name of the defeats suffered under the leadership of the yellow traitors, in the name of the future victories under the revolutionary banner of the Red International of Labour Unions, and lastly in the name of the Russian working class, steadfastly keeping up all alone for the fourth year the red flag over the land of the Soviets, and waiting for help from its comrades beyond the frontiers—we are calling upon you to join our ranks, we call you to the last and decisive battle. Workers of the world, unite! Long live the proletarian revolution!"[20]

The RILU constitution also said class collaboration was the main danger, and it called for industrial unionism: "The slogan of each industry should become the slogan of militant revolutionary unions." Dual unionism — the practice of precipitately quitting established unions was a mistake, for it left these unions in the hands of Gompers and similar conservative union officials. The constitution emphasized at the same time that unity was not a fetish, that trade unionists were not called upon to stay in a given organization under all circumstances: "We stand for unity but do not fear the split." If a militant trade unionist was expelled from a union he was advised not to back down, not to give up, but to carry on a last ditch fight, reject the expulsion, regroup with other members expelled, jointly conduct a struggle for readmission, and above all keep in touch with the members still in the union.[21]

After the formation of the RILU, a few union bodies in Canada and the U.S.A. showed an interest in affiliation. One state body of the AFL, the Detroit Federation of Labour, asked the AFL "to take the necessary steps to secure affiliation with the RILU".[22] In Canada, the Lumber Workers Industrial Union affiliated. The United Mine Workers of America, District 26 (Cape Breton, N.S.) told international President Lewis it would like to affiliate and asked him how he felt about it. Lewis blasted back that if the District affiliated he would lift its charter.[23]

In Britain, Canada and the United States, this new unionism expressed itself not so much in direct affiliation to the RILU as in the organization of trade unionists into bodies aimed at winning the established unions and union centres for new policies. Thus came about the National Minority Movement in Great Britain and the Trade Union Educational League in the United States and Canada. At the height of their influence in the middle 1920s, these bodies appear to have won the support, direct and indirect, of about a third of the trade union members in their respective countries.

In the United States, the Trade Union Educational League was set up at a conference in Chicago, August 26-27, 1922. The constitution stated that the TUEL was not a union or union centre, that it aimed to combine trade unionists within established organization for progressive policies. It expressly forbade the collection of anything in the nature of union dues from its members.

In Canada, the TUEL program called for Canadian autonomy, amalgamation of unions into industry-wide organizations, a labour party, and friendship with Soviet Russia. The Canadian secretary was Tim Buck, business agent for IAM Lodge 631, Toronto.* Supported by competent trade unionists like Jan Lakeman and Alex Gauld,** the TUEL's impact on the movement was considerable. In 1923, it was reported that "resolutions calling for the amalgamation of the craft unions of the type sponsored by the TUEL had been endorsed by almost every kind of union in every part of Canada".[24] At the height of its success in the middle 1920s, TUEL-sponsored policies seem to have won the support of about a quarter of the Canadian trade union membership—as measured by votes on resolutions at central union gatherings.

---

* International Association of Machinists (AFL).
** Jan Lakeman of Alberta, a member of the Brotherhood of Railroad Carmen (AFL); Alex Gauld of Montreal, a member of the United Association ... Plumbing and Pipefitting Industry ... (AFL).

CHAPTER 13

THE FIGHT FOR TRADE UNION PROGRESS
1919-1929

1. UNITY, INDUSTRIAL UNIONISM,
CANADIAN UNIONISM

Developments in the TLC:

The previous chapter has noted new trends as expressed in the OBU, FCWC and TUEL.* But the new was also manifested in the TLC. Here, too, the battle for trade union progress went on. Its 1919 convention was a stormy one. By this time, quite a number of the more radical trade unionists, particularly in the west, were out of the Congress and in the OBU, but others had stayed, come to this convention and debate was heated. Present was Matthew Woll, vice-president of the AFL, one of the most reactionary leaders ever to preside over the destinies of that body. He told the delegates: "Do you want class consciousness? Then the thing to do is to back up the Union Label Department of the AFL." At this point there was a commotion in the hall:

Woll: "I regret there are so many here who seem to view the conditions of the life of the workers in such a light manner as has been manifested here."
Voice from the Delegates: "Perhaps they come out of the workshop!"
Woll: "Brother, I came out of the workshop too."
One of the Delegates: "Since when?"[1]

Here are some major proposals submitted to the 1919 TLC convention:

1. *An all-in, effective centre.* It was proposed that the TLC constitution be altered so that the Congress could speak for Labour in "in-

---

* As distinct from the first two bodies mentioned above, the TUEL was not a centre and never aspired to be one. In its heyday, during the middle 1920s, most of its members were in TLC unions.

dustrial relations" as well as in legislation. (One organization which sponsored this motion was the Winnipeg Trades and Labour Council.) It was proposed also that the crippling amendment of 1912 be repealed—the amendment whose effect it was to exclude many national unions from the Congress. Finally, the Congress was asked to organize a "National council of labour" which would bring together the international and national unions "so that in all matters affecting Canadian labour, the full and united strength of Canadian labour would be applied".

2. *Canadian autonomy*. There should be "greater national autonomy" for the craft unions in Canada. This was linked to proposals for an "industrial form of organization", and also to protests against strike-breaking by U.S. headquarters. A stonecutter from Ottawa, a delegate at this Congress, said striking members of his union had been ordered back to work by their international. Proposals along these lines were submitted by the Winnipeg Trades and Labour Council, I.A.M.* Lodge 631, and I.L.G.W.U.** Local 113 of Montreal.

3. *Increased power for central councils:* The rank and file should have greater powers in the Trades and Labour Councils. Combined with this, the Councils should have greater powers. They should not be subject to the vetos of international headquarters, and should have the authority to conduct a general strike. Winnipeg Trades and Labour Council President Armstrong told the convention that the Winnipeg strike had demonstrated that "appealing to the internationals for the right to call a general strike meant defeat... The AFL refused to give any form of autonomy to any district to act for itself".

4. *Shorter Hours:* The Winnipeg Trades and Labour Council asked for the 30-hour week and proposed "immediate steps" by the Congress "to promulgate the same".

These were the measures proposed. The TLC leaders rejected them out of hand. They condemned the general strike policy, and said they would have nothing to do with a "strike against the public". They branded the One Big Union as secessionist. The proposal to expand the Congress' power was censured as one aimed at taking over "jurisdictional powers vested in the American Federation of Labour". Finally, the demand for a 30-hour week was rejected. The TLC leadership favoured instead a 44-hour week—to be won by legislative action. The militant delegates were angered. Winnipeg Trades Council President Armstrong warned that "if the split in the ranks of organized

---

* International Association of Machinists, AFL-TLC.
** International Ladies Garment Workers Union, AFL-TLC.

labour continues, the AFL will be responsible". A Toronto carpenter delegate advised TLC President Tom Moore—himself once a carpenters' business agent: "Advance in a continuous line and don't close doors!"[2]

In 1921, came a new blow to unity—expulsion of the Canadian Brotherhood of Railway Employees. Organized in 1909, and affiliated to the Canadian Federation of Labour, the CBRE had later affiliated to the TLC. Then it found itself under fire from another TLC affiliate, an international union, the Brotherhood of Railway and Steamship Clerks, AFL. The BRSC charged that the CBRE had invaded its jurisdiction. On the TLC's advice, the CBRE opened up negotiations for a merger with the BRSC. In a letter to the BRSC, dated November 13, 1920, CBRE president A. R. Mosher asked what assurances the Canadian membership would have to elect those officers "who will have charge of the Brotherhood in Canada". The BRSC's reply was evasive. It referred the question to the TLC executive council. A few months later, the Council took action. Instead of awaiting a regular Congress convention, it peremptorily told the CBRE its charter was cancelled herewith, for its continued recognition by the Congress "would be recognition of a dual organization, which policy the Congress had emphatically declared against at its annual convention in the City of Berlin", (1902).

The CBRE would not back down. It appealed its ouster at the TLC's 1921 convention. CBRE president A. R. Mosher told the delegates:

"We may be removed from your building but we will come back and perhaps many of you will be glad to welcome us back. The CBRE is going on in spite of you as it did before it became affiliated to the Congress."

Congress is "the mouthpiece of international trade unionism" countered TLC secretary-treasurer P. M. Draper, and TLC president Moore said:

"Congress . . . will uphold the right to restrict its membership to supporters of the international trade union movement and those in agreement with the constitution and policies of the Congress".

The vote went 394-151 against the CBRE.[3]

Then came the 1923 TLC convention at Vancouver. These key issues were debated:

1. *An effective Congress:* A resolution from Toronto IAM Lodge 235 charged that the Congress' present policy was blocking the affiliation of hundreds of local unions. The resolution called on the Congress to become "the real centre of a virile, active, powerful trade union movement". The Congress should have the power to levy assess-

ments. Affiliated unions should increase per capita payments to the Congress.

2. *Canadian autonomy:* Another resolution from Lodge 235 demanded that the Congress "establish Canadian departments" with well-defined powers of autonomy. Also Canadian sections of the international unions should have the right to strike and participate in political action. The AFL building trades department should set up a Canadian section.

3. *Industrial Unionism:* The Vancouver Trades and Labour Council proposed that the craft unions be combined into departmentalized industrial organizations to cover an entire industry, and that they be amalgamated.

These resolutions were along lines then being sponsored by the Trade Union Educational League. Still they were submitted by recognized Congress affiliates. But the Administration's reaction was hostile. John Bruce* said: "It smells like the work of that section of the organization who got a communist jag on . . . It emanated from the Workers' (Communist) Party."

The Administration's policy was set forth in a substitute resolution which became a pattern for later years. The resolution said the Congress' constitution had been drawn up for co-operation with the international unions: "Autonomy in the industrial field is vested in the said international trade unions and the American Federation of Labour." On a roll call vote this policy was adopted 120-53, with 49 abstentions.[4]

At the 1924 TLC convention, the battle blazed anew. An Edmonton BRC** Local called on the Congress to secure Canadian autonomy so that "mass action by the Canadian working class may become a reality".[5] From the Trades and Labour Councils of Vancouver and Guelph came resolutions demanding that the Congress open its ranks to "any bona fide trade unionists operating in Canada". After heated debate, these resolutions were rejected.

At the 1925 convention, a main demand was amalgamation of the craft unions. This was proposed in resolutions submitted by the Trades and Labour Councils of Halifax, Winnipeg and Vancouver.[6]

Another event was Tim Buck's bid for election as President of the Trades and Labour Congress. He was then business agent of Toronto IAM Local 235, and prominent in the Toronto Trades and Labour Council and the Trade Union Educational League. He was defeated.

* A senior trade unionist, prominent in the UA (Plumbers, AFL) and for years their Canadian international vice-president.
** Brotherhood of Railway Carmen (AFL-TLC).

Whatever the motives of the Congress leadership—the fear of communist influence, the fear that international unions would leave the Congress if the Congress did not go along with their policies; also, pressures from employers and Government, and the influence of business unionism—the situation was that the movement was splitting and the split was hardening. Action was needed. Thus came about a new formula for "national trade union unity". This was submitted to the 1926 TLC convention by the Trades and Labour Councils of Toronto and Regina. The nub of the proposal was an all-in conference of all Canadian trade union bodies. This the TLC leaders bitterly opposed. Secretary-treasurer Draper said no good would come from such a conference. Vice-president James Simpson said: "Let them (the bodies quitting or being expelled from the TLC) reap the full reward for their folly, and they will return to the fold of their accord".[7]

This policy made a new centre inevitable. In 1927 the all-Canadian Congress of Labour was established. At the 1928 TLC convention, Toronto IAM Lodge 484 revived the unity issue, but to no avail—secretary-treasurer Draper insisted "the constitution of the international trade union movement was broad enough to include workers in every calling".[8]

The TLC leaders were flying in the face of reality. By now about a third of Canada's trade unionists were in totally Canadian or "national" unions. To insist on membership in international unions as a prior condition to membership in the Congress meant—splits, blocking of organizations of the unorganized, colonization and degradation for the Congress itself. Yet that is what the TLC leaders did. The result? In 1927 a Carpenters local asked the Congress to fight for the 40-hour week. More specifically, it wanted the Congress to recommend to its affiliates that they work to enact the 40-hour week, and report to a TLC convention on the result. To this, the resolutions committee replied: "Congress was a legislative body. The resolution was not of a legislative character."[9]

●

This was the dilemma faced by trade unionists in the 1920s. They wanted unity, industrial unionism, Canadian unionism. But they were being blocked—not just by employers and government but by the very organizations they had built to win these objectives.

2.   POLITICAL ACTION

Rise and Fall of the Dominion Labour Party, 1921-1929:

Previous chapters have outlined the struggle for labour political action. The policy adopted at the 1906 TLC convention had been a turning point. It was a policy of advance and retreat: On the one hand, commitment to a labour party; on the other hand, Congress aloofness from the party once it was formed, and its emphasis rather on provincial parties. Organizationally, the result was the establishment of a few weak parties in the provinces. By 1917, the TLC executive council was admitting that the 1906 decision had not brought "the establishment of the desired political organization".[10]

In 1918-1921, political action revived. Some provincial labour parties were reorganized, and new ones set up. 1919-20 brought the provincial labour successes described in a previous page. The 1921 federal election demonstrated Labour's political strength and weakness. Of 62 socialist party candidates and farmer-labour candidates, only 2 were elected—J. S. Woodsworth in Winnipeg Lake Centre and William Irvine in Calgary East.[11] However, 65 progressives were elected—almost all farmer candidates. In 1921 there was also a flowering of municipal political action. Labour candidates were elected to city councils from Moncton, New Brunswick clear through to Victoria, British Columbia.

Out of all this, the setbacks and successes, came the decision to establish a Dominion Labour Party. This was Canada's first, and until 1961, only experiment in a federal labour party. It was inaugurated at a conference held the week the TLC convention met at Winnipeg in August 1921. That conference decided the new party would seek to unite the political power of the workers and press for a change "in the present economic and social system". Provision was made for co-operation with the farmers—the executive was instructed to confer with the Progressive (farmers) Party.

Other points in the new party's program were taken over from the TLC platform: Unemployment insurance, public ownership and nationalization of the banking system, abolition of non-elective bodies, proportional representation, direct legislation through the initiative and referendum.[12]

The first regular convention of the Canadian Labour Party met in 1922. It adopted a draft constitution which provided for annual conventions of the federal party, and also for the establishment of provincial sections of the party.*

This was progress but all too slow. At the 1923 TLC convention, some delegates demanded that more attention be given to political

---

* These provincial parties were organized somewhat later. One was established in Ontario in 1922 and functioned alongside an independent labour party already in existence. Another, established in Quebec, succeeded in electing a candidate to the provincial legislature in 1923.[13]

action: They said Congress should allot time at conventions to discuss the finances of the Dominion Labour Party. And it should rule that only candidates upholding Labour's cause would get Labour's backing. The Roadmen's and TLC leaders' reaction showed that for all their verbal support to the party, and at times their participation in its affairs, they had not given it their heart. John Bruce was against "the Congress becoming part of any political party". Gustave Francq spoke of the "difficulties of mixing trade union (matters) and political action". Congress secretary-treasurer P. M. Draper said that "labour political matters" should be left to the Labour Party. This policy was set forth in a resolution which stated "Labour political autonomy (should) be left in the hands of the established Labour Party", while Congress continued "to act as the legislative mouthpiece of organized labour in Canada, independent of any political organization".[14]

This was a step back to 1906. Ostensibly it asserted Congress' independence, actually its indifference to political action. Revealing is this evaluation by the Federal Government's *Annual Report on Labour Organization,* 1923: "The Congress maintains its attitude against political entanglements."

Then came six tragic years, 1923-1929. Undone was the hard work of decades. Craft and business unionism-minded officials based on international headquarters killed the Labour Party. Sometimes international headquarters ordered a local union to withdraw its delegates from the Labour Party on pain of having its charter lifted. Sometimes, conservative trade union officials set up a dual labour party without communist participation.* The trouble with these simon-pure parties was that they did not get off the ground; and the union members who believed that once the communists were expelled all would go well, found they had no party at all. One reason was that, contrary to the belief then widely held, the *basic* issue was not the left-right *ideological* confrontation, but the *work,* the *building* of independent labour political action, the elaboration of a program broad and advanced enough to give point, direction and impetus to that majority. Another reason for the stagnation of these reconstructed parties was that leaders who remained in them after the expulsions did not bestir themselves enough.

How far the TLC leaders had slid back from the original decision of 1921 for a Dominion Labour Party was shown by the manifesto they put out prior to the federal election of 1926. There was a crucial

* At the time, the Workers' (communist) Party was an affiliate of the Dominion Labour Party; and at various points, left wing trade unionists were active in its affairs.

election, another turning point in Canadian politics. One key issue was greater autonomy for Canada within the Commonwealth. This was a time for Labour to lead. But the TLC's manifesto did not provide the leadership. Instead it referred briefly to the need for "more representatives elected from the ranks of labour"; and even this modest advice it tended to cancel by re-stating its 1923 decision concerning independence from politics.

In the provincial labour parties, a similar process of destruction went on. At the 8th convention of the Ontario Party held at Hamilton in 1927, there were 150 delegates representing 53 organizations. It was the official convention of an official party endorsed by the official trade union movement. However, when the convention adopted decisions not palatable to the roadmen, they—and along with them, a sizeable number of other trade unionists—refused to accept these decisions and proceeded to organize a dual convention. From this sprang a dual party—the Labour Party of Ontario. In Toronto there was a similar split, when James Simpson broke away from the Toronto Council of the Canadian Labour Party. The net result of all this disruption was zero. In 1929, the federal government's *Annual Report on Labour Organization* described the Ontario labour political situation as follows: "Since Simpson's retirement, the main labour party has ceased to function." In 1929, only 2 provincial labour parties were reported —in Quebec and in Alberta. The British Columbia section had been dissolved, the Nova Scotia and Ontario sections were no longer meeting.

This is how the Dominion Labour Party was killed. The common thread in this sad sequence was the destructive action of senior Canadian trade union officials and U.S. international headquarters. But in all this there was the happier side—the constructive work done across the country and in the various constituencies; the model, however limited, of a Canada-wide progressive political movement based largely on the unions.

CHAPTER 14

TRADE UNIONISM VERSUS CLASS COLLABORATION
1919-1929

1. CLASS COLLABORATION

The Situation in Canada and the U.S.:

In the period under review, trade union progress demanded a fighting wage policy, organization of the unorganized, unity, industrial and Canadian unionism, political action. Yet the dominant trade union officialdom in Canada, and its ally, U.S. international headquarters, resisted. Why? One reason was class collaboration. Not the word or ideological trend, although it was a word and ideological trend. Not collective bargaining or legislative representations to governments. But something distinct: *Subordinating the movement's interest to reconciliation with the employers,* settling for less than it was possible realistically to get. In 1919, TLC president Tom Moore shuddered at the general strike movement sweeping Canada. He told the workers to trust in Royal Commissions. That year the Federal Government set up a Royal Commission into the causes of industrial unrest. Moore was one of its members. The Commission brought in some good proposals. But the overall result was negligible. All this was class collaboration: *not* the fact of a Royal Commission, but fostering the illusion it sufficed—in effect—deceiving the workers and disorienting them.

Again, TLC leaders would emphasize the value of government-management-labour conferences. In 1919 such a conference took place. It recommended a board consisting of government, employers and unions in order to attain uniform social legislation. Early in 1920 a federal-provincial conference considered the matter. But by September, the TLC executive committee was making its customary "no further progress" report.[1]

All this once again, was class collaboration. And this was so, not because the *forms* in themselves were necessarily wrong, but because of the *intention* with which these forms were approached, and the *use* to which they were put. Consider for example the labour-management-government conferences. Here was a form whose effectiveness varied from situation to situation, as did the skill in its use. The problem was that some of the trade union officials who participated in these conferences made harmony with employers and government their prime objective, rather than the winning of results for the workers. They spread the illusion that these conferences were a substitute for the independent struggle of the trade union movement, that a new and better way had been found. But, through the years, rebuff after rebuff, humiliation after humiliation, and defeat after defeat, had shown there was no new and better way. Of course, the labour movement did not have to turn its back on negotiations with employers, or on conferences with governments and employers. But its only sure course was the independent mobilization of the membership in struggle. This is what experience has shown. Now, the recognition and practice of this truth was militant trade unionism. Put more plainly still, it was trade unionism pure and simple—not the "pure and simple" business unionism of Samuel Gompers, but fighting bread and butter unionism. The rejection of this truth, and the practice of this rejection, was class collaboration.

By 1920, the signs were clear that the economic expansion of the war and early post war years was ending. Unemployment was increasing. The employers were opening up a wage-cutting, open shop offensive. But the conservative trade union officers did not change their course. Instead they put forward new, class collaborationist easy ways out. One was the Whitley Council.[2] Conceived in England as the latest way to advance labour-capital co-operation, it won this blessing from TLC president Moore: "The establishment of joint industrial councils ... will be of great value in promoting industrial harmony."[3]

Another mistake was excessive emphasis on the International Labour Organization—inflated hopes about what it could do. The ILO originated out of the labour provisions of the Versailles Treaty of 1919. These set forth principles like the right to organize and shorter hours. Later the ILO was established as a world body of government-management and labour, with all delegates to its conferences appointed by the member governments. Union leaders would go to ILO conferences and come back with good resolutions on wage and hour standards. But this didn't help the ordinary worker much. The reason was that the federal government would plead inability to apply the standards, and in particular it would point to its lack of jurisdiction over most industries, because of the property and civil rights clause in the BNA Act.*

Still another class collaborationist gimmick of the 1920s was co-operation in productivity and speed-up plans. This was the heyday of "Fordism" and "Mondism", named after Henry Ford of the U.S. Ford Motor Company and Alfred Mond, the British head of International Nickel. The idea was that the more the workers produced the more they got. What generally happened was that the more the workers produced, the more the employers got, and the more the workers walked the streets.*

A typical speed-up plan of the day, camouflaged as a productivity proposal, was the B & O plan, named after the Baltimore and Ohio Railroad in the United States, where it was initiated. In the 1920s, a union officer in the CNR (Canadian National Railways), F. J. Collum, described it in these mesmerized terms:

"It is absolutely essential that there be complete harmony among the members of the committee ... There should be at no time a feeling that they belong to different groups, and that either one shall seek advantage over the other."[4]

What "teamwork" meant became clear at Winnipeg when union officials presented the CNR** a list of mem to be laid off, some with 12 to 17 years service. The reason was failure to "co-operate" with the company.[5] At the TLC convention of 1927, Edmonton Lodges of the Brotherhood of Railroad Carmen, and the Blacksmiths, asked the Congress to condemn the plan. Some delegates complained "it worked to the advantage of the railway companies only." The leadership rejected this proposal because it "did not come within the jurisdiction of the Congress".[6]

Class collaboration expressed itself also in government appointments for trade union officials — not necessarily the fact of a given appointment, for that might serve a useful purpose for Canada and the labour movement—but the tendency engendered at times, leading to a separation of trade union leaders from the rank-and-file membership, and to an undesirable type of relationship between such leaders on the one hand, and employers and employer-minded circles in government, on the other. At the 1925 TLC convention, it was reported that R. A. Rigg of Winnipeg had been named director of the employment service of Canada, and that Tom Moore had been given the post of director of the Board of the CNR.[7] Speaking at that convention,

---

* Today (1967) the ILO's work has improved. In the 1920s, class collaborationist leaders cultivated the illusion the ILO was a supra-national mechanism which could get the workers what they wanted without a fight.
** Canadian National Railways.

Prime Minister Mackenzie King said that such posts meant "a real growth in the recognition of organized labour".

For a concluding example of class collaboration, we turn to the TLC conventions of 1928 and 1929. In 1928, a number of Trades and Labour Councils proposed a national conference of all organizations concerned, to work out the best way of winning federal and provincial unemployment insurance, old age pensions, and protection against ill-health. The TLC leaders rejected this. But when the Congress met in September 1929, they admitted there had been little or no success in the struggle for reform.[8] On the proceedings of this the final convention of the 1920s is the stamp of emptiness, passivity, the failure to face realities—all this scarce a few weeks before the outbreak of the economic crisis.

In order better to understand class collaboration in Canada, its counterpart in the United States deserves consideration, not only because class collaboration was so highly developed there, but also because it interacted constantly on Canada through the medium of the international unions.

Organization of the unorganized, social legislation, and political action. In the 1920s, fraternal delegates of the AFL would come to conventions in Canada and talk about the millions of organized workers in the United States. The truth was that organization there was far below that of other western industrial countries—$3\frac{1}{2}$ million union members out of a total of 20 million workers in 1927. One reason was that when the U.S. employers began their open shop campaign in 1921, the AFL leaders did not fight back effectively. There followed a series of ruinous defeats, and the AFL lost a large part of its membership. This stand-pat attitude of the AFL leaders was almost certainly a cause of the backwardness of social legislation in the United States—the lack of old age pensions, unemployment insurance and sickness insurance.[9] As for labour political action, AFL leaders tended to look on this as a sin, a red plot. This contributed to the situation of 1926, with 156 parliamentary representatives of labour in Great Britain, 90 in Czechoslovakia, 121 in France, 176 in Germany —but only 3 in the United States.

Trade union capitalism and gangsterism. Some class collaboration leaders in the United States encouraged the investment of union funds in private banking, finance and insurance projects. An official of the Brotherhood of Locomotive Engineers declared: "The engineer . . . has become a capitalist himself . . . Labour investing demonstrates labour's complete answer to the pleas of Marx and Lenin!"[10] However, at the 1927 BLE convention, the delegates of a long-suffering membership voted a $7,000,000 assessment to save their organization from the threat of bankruptcy brought on by investments in private projects.[11]

Other vices were misappropriation of funds by individual trade union officers, and gangsterism. There was O'Donald, head of the Chicago Building Trades organization, one of AFL President Samuel Gompers' favoured lieutenants. He must have been blessed with earthly wealth. Once thieves broke into his house and stole mink and sable coats valued at $3,700. When he died his coffin cost $10,000.[12] Then there was the Motion Picture Operators Union in Chicago. When it engaged in a jurisdictional dispute with the Electrical Workers Union, the rival unions sent out carloads of gunmen who shot it out.[13] At times these labour crooks used anti-communism to screen their actions. An earlier generation will recall Chicago gangster Al Capone's alert to America: "Bolshevism is knocking at our gates!"

It must be emphasized that such labour gangsterism was not typical of the U.S. trade union officialdom. However, it was a running sore reflecting the more deep-going evil of trade union capitalism and business unionism. As to employers and employer-oriented politicians, some condoned these labour gangsters, even co-operated with them and used them as a kind of gendarme to counter progressive initiative from the membership; and then they might wheel around, raise their eyes to the heavens, denounce the men they had helped corrupt, and use the corruption as a club to blackmail the movement, an excuse for anti-labour legislation.

Chauvinism and Labour imperialism — another characteristic of class collaboration in the U.S. was a foreign policy which coincided to quite a degree with the foreign policy of big business. In 1927, AFL President William Green declared: "The AFL favours a strong navy as an instrument to promote the peace of the world!"[14]

The world situation must be understood. Germany was defeated and weakened. But the victors, Britain and France, were also weakened. U.S. imperialism moved in. Into Germany it poured billions, aimed among other things at shoring up capitalism there, and averting the danger of a popular upheaval. Alone, among major western powers, the U.S. did not recognize the Soviet Union. U.S. imperialism intervened to help defeat the Chinese revolution of 1927. It spread its influence and control over Latin America. In short, it aimed to make the world safe for capitalism, more particularly U.S. capitalism, and in the pursuit of this objective, stood prepared to use all instruments —foreign investments, loans, branch plants, and on occasion, dispatch of Marines to foreign shores. Calvin Coolidge, later U.S. President, stated: "The person and property of a nation, of its citizens, are part of the general domain of the nation, even when abroad."[15] The extent to which this policy of U.S. imperialism represented the deeper, generous feelings of the American people, is much open to question. Some Americans challenged it. But meanwhile it was the policy of big business, and to quite a degree, of the U.S. Government, and that is the way its impact was felt across the world.

For rapacious, restless, egoistic, U.S. monopoly capitalism—cruel to the workers, farmers and negroes of its homeland, domineering to peoples of other lands—Canada was a key objective. In the period under review, the U.S. was supplanting Britain as the main foreign investor in Canada, and acquiring control over Canadian resources such as pulpwood, oil and water power.[16] "Canadians would do well to look to their national defence, those of an economic order, which would be more important in the coming struggle, than any military defence," said a writer in the Montreal *Standard* in 1927.[17*]

In its drive on Canada, U.S. imperialism was assisted—in the result —by international union domination from the U.S.—the material and ideological results of that domination. Again and again, those TLC leaders who were closely aligned with the AFL and international unions, would praise the international unions as being a "potent factor" in maintaining the 3,000-mile undefended frontier between Canada and the United States—undefended in fact against U.S. capital and commodities pouring into Canada.[18] By supporting the foreign policy of U.S. imperialism, by resisting the aspirations of the trade union movement in Canada to industrial unionism, unity and progress—the class collaborationist leadership of the international unions and the AFL in the United States became an important factor in holding back the emergence of a strong independent Canada, and—closely linked with this—a strong independent trade union movement. The organ of the All-Canadian Congress of Labour commented at the time the "AFL was an appendage of the government at Washington and had assumed the task of subjugating the Canadian working class ... these men have fooled many Canadian workers into accepting the belief about Canada's inevitable economic absorption by the United States".[19]

2.   MILITANT UNIONISM

The All-Canadian Congress of Labour:

In the period under review, two opposite forces were in conflict. The trade union movement was striving to live and fulfill itself. But

* The *Standard* was then issued by the publishers of the Montreal *Star*.

it was being blocked. In the first place, and primarily, it was being blocked by the employers. In the second place it was being blocked by class collaboration and U.S. interference. A positive reaction to this was the growth of militant unionism—the struggle for better conditions, for a united, effective, industrial, Canadian trade union movement. A preceding chapter has shown how this struggle expressed itself in the Trades and Labour Congress and the Canadian locals of international unions. This section will confine itself to militant unionism as manifested in the All-Canadian Congress of Labour, the struggles of the Cape Breton coal miners, and the rise of a number of Canadian industrial unions.

First, the All-Canadian Congress of Labour. Established in 1927, its principal constituent bodies were: the Canadian Brotherhood of Railroad Employees; unions affiliated to the Canadian Federation of Labour; the One Big Union; and a number of industrial, Canadian unions such as the Mine Workers Union of Canada, and the Lumber Workers Industrial Union of Canada. All ACCL unions were "national"—not connected with international unions. Some like the Canadian Federation of Bricklayers, Masons and Plasterers, or the Canadian Association of Railway Engineers, were not affiliated to either the TLC or the international unions, be it through expulsions, secessions, or simple refusal to affiliate.

The ACCL stood for Canadian unionism. Again and again, its president, A. R. Mosher, thundered against international unions and denounced them as "U.S. unions with Canadian branches".[20] Another of its leaders, M. M. MacLean, secretary-treasurer of the Canadian Brotherhood of Railroad Employees, later Deputy Minister of Labour, would complain that "Canadian workers have no power whatever to influence policies of the larger U.S. unions".[21] The ACCL also stood for industrial unionism and political action. Article 253 of the constitution stated that craft unions are either obsolete or obsolescent. The ACCL always insisted its affiliates were either industrial unions, or craft bodies aspiring to be industrial unions.[22]

It rejected red-baiting. At the second convention in 1928, Mosher said the ACCL stood for the right of Canadian workers to give free expression to their ideals, and to associate themselves "without regard to their political opinions or their attitudes towards the present economic system. We recognize others besides ourselves have valuable ideas, and we believe such ideas should be studied and analyzed irrespective of their source... An open mind should be maintained". When TLC leaders suggested the ACCL was dominated by communists and influenced by Moscow, Mosher replied the "Congress was controlled solely by its affiliated membership".[23] The ACCL also developed a certain limited leaning to socialism. A clause in its constitution stated: "Workers under the present system cannot obtain the full value of their labour."[24]

However, the ACCL did not become a central solution to the problems of the trade union movement, an instrument for its reconstruction. The ACCL leaders tended to duplicate the narrowly-sectarian attitudes adopted by earlier national trade union centres, such as the National Trades and Labour Congress of Canada, the Canadian Federation of Labour and the One Big Union with regard to the TLC and international unions. Concerning the TLC, the ACCL said that "it was not in any sense a national labour centre", that "it lost that status in 1902" that it was "essentially a lobby for the promotion of legislation on behalf of the members of branch unions of U.S. labour organizations".[25] Partly this was true. But it overlooked the other side of the TLC—its character as a historic Canadian centre, reflecting the aspirations of trade unionists. Moreover, it was unrealistic, since the TLC remained much the larger centre.[26] Again, when Mosher said international unions were U.S. unions with Canadian branches, this, too, was partly true, but also played into the hands of the international unions, who were by all means disposed to consider their Canadian affiliates as *branches* rather than Canadian entities. And once again, it was unrealistic, since most locals in Canada were international union affiliates, and despite their tendency to captive status, they were fulfilling the function of unions for Canada's workers. Instead of facing these facts, the ACCL leaders tended to regard the breaking of the U.S. bond as a pre-condition for trade union progress in general. In 1929, the ACCL executive committee told the third convention that "complete independence of the United States control" was a pre-requisite for liberation from the craft union form ... "not until the reactionary influence of the United States unions has been removed can the Canadian workers acquire a form of organization capable of curbing exploitation."[27]

This rigid, sectarian attitude to the TLC and international unions was one negative quality of the ACCL. A further one was a certain inclination to craft collaboration. In 1928 its organ, *Canadian unionist,* was approving "co-operation between capital and labour" and praising Mondism as a policy which "at least recognizes labour unions as responsible organizations".[28] In 1929, the ACCL was referring to "Canadianization of labour organizations" in a manner which looked more to government and employers for this development than to the workers.[29] That year, moreover, the resolutions committee at the third

ACCL convention was refusing concurrence to a demand for a national organization of the unemployed.[30]

These, then, were defects in the ACCL. Perhaps because of them, it remained a small body based to quite a degree on the Canadian Brotherwood of Railway Employees. However, it was a moment of the historic struggle for a united, progressive, Canadian trade union movement.

The Cape Breton Coal Miners:

Previous chapters have outlined the sequence of events leading from the establishment of the Provincial Workmen's Association—the original Canadian or "national" union of the Cape Breton coal miners—to entry of the United Mine Workers of America into the situation, and the development of a jurisdictional conflict between the two unions—in 1909-1911. Thereafter, the conflict continued. A solution had to be found. In 1917, both bodies merged in a new organization called the Amalgamated Mine Workers of Nova Scotia. Later, the AMWNS joined the UMWA.[31] One term of affiliation provided that no contract would be signed by top union officials, unless the conditions were first submitted to a referendum of the Canadian membership.

Thereafter, the Cape Breton miners fought a series of tremendous battles. Between 1918 and 1920, their wages had risen from $18.98 per week in 1918, to $21.42 per week in 1920. The Nova Scotia Steel and Coal Company decided to turn the clock back. Arbitrarily, it imposed a 37% wage cut on expiry of the contract. Thus came about the 1922 strike. It was a slow-down, and restoration of the 1921 rate was the main demand. During the 7 months it lasted, the Cape Breton coal fields blazed with militancy. From a District 26 convention of coal locals in Nova Scotia and New Brunswick, held at Truro in 1922 came this appeal to the troops:

"Over the heads of the Government, we appeal to all soldiers and minor law officers... When you are ordered to shoot the workers, don't do it. When you are asked to arrest the workers, don't do it. When you are asked to spy on the workers, don't do it."[32]

In August 1922, the slow-down became a total walk-out. The miners faced tremendous difficulties. Troops and special police were dispatched to the scene of the strike. In the United States, the UMWA's international president, John L. Lewis, denounced the miners for striking. However, they succeeded in cutting the company's production by at least a third. The strike ended when the company agreed to reduce the wage cut from 37% to 20%.

This was an uneasy truce. Soon the miners were charging the company with violation of the agreement. In June 1923, the Union declared the contract null and void. A UMW District 26 convention decided on strike. Once again, Lewis moved. He sent a telegram opposing strike action. The District 26 leadership placed the telegram before the rank and file, along with the strike ballot. A majority voted for strike. Lewis did not accept this decision. He retaliated by revoking the District's charter.

Meanwhile, steel workers employed at the Sydney plant of the British Empire Steel Company had gone into action, and this brought the situation to a head. They wanted higher wages—many of them were earning about $15.94 per week (1921 rate), and 60% were earning less than 35 cents per hour.[33] On June 28, 1923 they went on strike, demanding a 20% wage increase. Two days later, a detachment of federal troops (militia) moved in. J. B. McLachlan, the chief officer of District 26, reacted swiftly: "No miner or mine worker can remain at work while this government turns Sydney into a jungle." 8,000 coal miners, members of UMW District 26, went on strike in solidarity with the steel workers, demanding withdrawal of troops and police.

A major issue now came to the fore. Repeated use of militia in Nova Scotia coal disputes between 1920 and 1922 had become a point of bitterness. The matter had been raised in the House of Commons. An M.P. had described this incident involving a peaceful procession of unarmed strikers: "A line was drawn and a machine gun was set up before Bridgeport Catholic Church, and the men were ordered not to pass the line on peril of being fired upon."[34] On March 6, 1923, J. S. Woodsworth had charged in the House that the troops had been sent to Cape Breton "despite the protests of the towns involved", when there was no riot or threat of riot.

Against a background such as this, this latest use of troops engendered bitterness anew. Mayor Morrison of Glace Bay said: "We do not consider militia necessary . . ." On July 10, 1923, the TLC protested the use of troops in a letter to Prime Minister King. In his reply King said he had told the Premier of Nova Scotia that "we are most anxious that the military forces should be withdrawn"; and he added: "There is need for revision of the statute affecting the calling out of militia in aid of the civil power." This statement, guarded but promising, meant that prospects for a legislative victory on this issue had increased. Encouraged, on July 14 McLachlan appealed across the country for financial aid.

At this time, just when the strike had reached top effectiveness and had merged with a major issue, the use of troops in industrial disputes, there was intervention anew by international headquarters and also by the leadership of the Trades and Labour Congress in Canada. On July 6, international president Lewis sent a telegram condemning the strike as "a violation of existing agreements".[35] The District 26 executive board replied that "this is a political struggle of Canadian workers against an evil from which we have suffered for years". The jurisdiction of international headquarters did not "give it authority to prohibit workers in Canada from waging a political struggle against the use of armed forces."[36] But, Lewis persisted in his course. On July 17, he revoked the district's charter, deposed the leadership, appointed in its stead Silby Barrett, and told the miners to go back to work. Then came action through the courts. Barrett, now provisional head of the district, secured an injunction depriving the deposed officers of funds and headquarters. At Ottawa, TLC president Tom Moore said the "miners will do well to remain loyal to their international union ... (The strike was) ill advised ... had helped confuse the minds of the public as to the real issue".[37] Bitterly the Nova Scotia Steel Workers spoke, in a manifesto, about the forces arrayed against them—federal and provincial governments, corporations, press, machine guns, bayonets, provincial police: "Everyone's hand is against us in our effort to obtain enough food to sustain ourselves and our families, to have enough clothing, to allow our children to return to school!" The difficulties were too great, and the miners decided to retreat.[38] At a mass meeting held in Glace Bay, July 18, they denounced UMWA's international headquarters for having "lined up with provincial and federal governments and the British Empire Steel Corporation". Three days later, the coal strike ended; not long after, the steel strike as well. By the middle of August, the last of the troops had left. Later, legislation was enacted at Ottawa greatly restricting the use of militia in strikes. This was a major reform, and much of the credit for it belongs to the miners and steel workers of Cape Breton. After the strike, McLachlan was sentenced to 2 years in Dorchester Penitentiary. He served 4 months and was released. The *Financial Post* said:

"If any one has any doubts as to who dominated the councils of the miners, they must have been set at rest by the demonstration accorded McLachlan ... The very fact that he was free filled his followers with enthusiasm."[39]

Distress continued in the Cape Breton coal fields. In 1923, Canon Frederick George Scott visited the district, and described maximum wages prevailing of $3.25 per day. Concerning housing in the vicinity of Pit No. 11, he said:

"At the back of the house stood rows of dilapidated latrines, each family having to pay $1 to have them cleaned up. No double windows or storm windows in many of the houses, and the whole place had a squalid appearance."[39a]

In the House of Commons, J. S. Woodsworth spoke of conditions of virtual starvation in Cape Breton, "children crying from hunger, three loaves of bread for a family of seven".[40] Behind this distress were low wages and layoffs—some of the miners were getting only 6 or 7 days work a month.

From its moneyed heights the company looked on this pile of misery. It profited from the miners' work and multiplied these profits by stock market manipulations. In 1923, Canon Scott said:

"The impression was borne in on me the longer I stayed in Sydney, that the root of the trouble lay far back in the great financial manipulations of those who formed the merger."[41]

In 1925, British Empire Steel Corporation vice-president McClung was asked about the company's wage and price policy:

Question: "If the miners accept a reduction in their wages, will the company reduce the selling price of coal to the consumers?"

McClung: "No. We require the money for our bondholders and shareholders."[42]

The situation came to a head when the company cut off credit at the company stores, and proposed a 10% wage cut. The miners went on strike. They fought courageously, but faced three difficulties:

1. *Starvation.* "They cannot stand the gaff. Let them stay out for six months. It matters not, eventually they will come to us"—statement by company vice president McClung.[43]

2. *Bullets.* On June 11, at 4 a.m., a trainload of strike-breakers, protected by 60 armed company police, arrived at the New Waterford powerhouse. 19 pickets were beaten up. Seven hours later, hundreds of miners arrived and cried: "We want these men (the strike-breakers) out of the powerhouse!" The company police charged into the miners, shooting. A miner, William Davis was killed. When he was shot, he was walking along with his hands in his pockets. With him was his little son. The Toronto *Telegram* account stated: "The lad threw himself on the body, calling out "Daddy, speak to me!', then the boy turned to the police and cried: 'You killed my father, now shoot me!' " Then the miners, infuriated, turned on the company police, hurled lumps of slag at them, and pulled them from their horses.[44]

3. *Orientation of international headquarters and the TLC.* UMW international president John L. Lewis branded the strike illegal, while TLC president Tom Moore said "the days of red leadership among Nova Scotia miners are ended".[44a]

The difficulties were such that the miners decided to return to work without the settlement they wanted. In January 1926, the Duncan Commission recommended a 10% wage cut. This meant that wages were now 75% of the 1921 rate.[45]

These, then, were the Cape Breton coal miners' struggles in 1922-25. They were defeated for the most part, but had immense meaning for coal mining unionism, for trade unionism in general, and beyond that, for the historic conflict between the people of the Maritimes and big business.

Canadian Industrial Unions, 1927-1929:

A significant development of the later 1920s was the organization of Canadian or "national" industrial unions. As with the ACCL and UMWA District 26 in Cape Breton, a reason for this new departure seems to have been the tension between rank and file militancy, industrial and Canadian unionism—on the one hand; and conservative, business unionism allied with international unionism—on the other. Quite a number of trade unionists—some were left wing—had become convinced that the international unions, and a TLC leadership generally aligned with them, was blocking organization of the unorganized, and trade union progress. What was to be done? Some of these trade unionists were grouped in the Trade Union Educational League. Until now the TUEL's policy had been to transform the established unions and the Trades and Labour Congress "from within". Now the feeling was that though this policy must continue, a new move was also needed, and this was to be the building, in given industries, of industrial unions — "Canadian" unions, that is, national unions — not affiliated to international unions.

One of these new unions, the Textile Workers Industrial Union— functioned in 1928 and 1929, and was active in strikes at Toronto, Hamilton and Welland. Another, the Industrial Union of Needle Trades Workers of Canada, was organized in August 1929 at a needle trades conference held in Toronto. Its program called for organization of the unorganized, a fighting stand against the employers, and the building of a single, industrial union of Canadian needle trades workers.[46] Other unions were built in the lumbering, coal mining, steel and automobile industries. The Lumber Workers Industrial Union developed in connection with strikes in 1928-29 in the Port Arthur, Cochrane and Thunder Bay districts of Ontario; and it laid the basis for later more extensive organization among Ontario loggers. The Mine Workers Industrial Union seems to have been the product of repeated rank and file revolts against the United Mine Workers of

America, going back to the days of the One Big Union. It was active in a strike at Drumheller, Alberta, in October 1928.[47] During the strike, it denounced the UMWA as a "blackleg organization" because—so the MWIU claimed—the UMWA had tried to get an agreement with the employers behind the backs of the workers at a mine where it had little or no membership.[48]

Yet another union, the National Steel Car Industrial Union, organized in 1929, arose from a spontaneous strike by National Steel Car workers against a wage cut. This strike, fought in autumn 1929, lasted 7 weeks and resulted in a withdrawal of the wage cut.[49]

Prominent among the new, industrial unions was the Auto Workers Industrial Union of Canada. Organized in 1928, this union was originally based on Windsor and Walkerville. But it soon linked up with a movement among General Motors workers at Oshawa in 1928. Here, the General Motors Company had imposed a 40% wage cut—a climax to speed-up, declining wage levels, espionage and company unionism. Against this, the workers went on strike. Then they organized into a federal labour union, and applied to the AFL for a charter. Their organizing drive was a great success. 4,200 auto workers signed membership applications, and 2,800 paid an initiation fee of $1.00.[50] After a week the strike ended—successfully, it would seem—with no wage cut imposed.

Then came a cruel blow. AFL headquarters at Washington sent a letter to the local union, ordering it to split into crafts: "It is strictly understood that in granting a charter to your federal labour union . . . (it) shall conform to the constitution and policies and principles of the American Federation of Labour."[51] The letter aroused bitterness in the ranks of the Oshawa auto workers. Local union leaders said that when James Simpson, acting for the AFL, negotiated with them, he promised the local union could function as an industrial union, and that the AFL would organize auto workers in other parts of Canada. The outcome was that many auto workers stopped paying dues to the AFL, and joined the Auto Workers Industrial Union of Canada.[52]

Amidst this toil and trouble, something important was happening. Oshawa auto workers were laying the foundations for industrial unionism in their industry. And yet, just when support from the TLC and international unions would have helped, a recognized TLC and international union spokesman, James Simpson, was telling the Toronto *Telegram*—on November 2, 1928:

"They are all fools down there anyways, and they don't know what they want, and wouldn't know how to get it if they did. Their strike last spring was simply an expression of temperament. It should never have been held. The majority of auto workers in Oshawa are nothing but transplanted farmers, and they behave as such ... We only need about 10 members to hold an AFL charter there, and we can get those easily enough ... They will be crawling back to us within a year."[52]

3. WORLD LABOUR SOLIDARITY AND PEACE

Events in Britain, China, the United States:

While Canadian trade unionists, grouped in the TLC, ACCL, FCWC and other bodies, were conducting their struggles, major events were unfolding in Europe and Asia. In May 1926, British workers went out in a general strike. The strike lasted only 10 days and did not succeed, but it was a major demonstration of trade union power, one which moved trade unionists across Canada. On May 24, 1926, the TLC executive council pledged "full moral support" to the strike. Also it sent $1,000 to the miners, and some Congress affiliates sent funds directly. A year later, 1927, revolution broke out in China. This also moved many Canadians. At the 1927 TLC convention, the Goose Lake Local of the Brotherhood of Maintenance-of-Way employees, an international union, presented a resolution demanding withdrawal from China of imperialists and their armed forces, and the cancellation of humiliating treaties and extra-territorial rights in China for imperialist powers. The resolution was adopted.[53]

Another event moving Canadians was the Sacco-Vanzetti case in the U.S.A. Joseph Sacco and Bartolomeo Vanzetti had been active in struggles for trade union organization, better conditions and social reconstruction. On what seems to have been very thin evidence, they were charged with complicity in a bank holdup and murder. On August 17, 1927, ACCL President A. R. Mosher wired U.S. President Calvin Coolidge: "If the execution of Sacco and Vanzetti is carried out, we are convinced that the name of United States Justice will be held in disrepute by the workers of Canada forever more."[54] Despite world protests, U.S. authorities went through with the execution. At Glace Bay, Nova Scotia, 5,000 coal miners struck in protest.[55]

There was also the problem of Canada-Soviet relations. This was bound to be an issue in the movement, if only because more radical trade unionists sympathized with the socialist regime.[56] However, once again the problem surpassed the ideological confrontation of Right and Left. It was a question of reality, of those durable issues which affected all Canadians and shaped their lives, regardless of how they sometimes felt about it—issues such as peace, Canadian independence and prosperity. For instance, the continuing antagonism of western capitalists—and at times of western labour leaders—to the new Soviet regime—an antagonism which at times passed the bounds of reality and degenerated into berserk hysteria—was becoming a *new* source of the war danger, along with the original source which had operated in 1914 and was continuing to operate: the antagonism among the western powers themselves.

In this way, the problem of Canada-Soviet relations merged with the problem of peace. Again, it fused with the problem of Canada's independence and prosperity. Canada was then a young country, striving to develop its independence in the face of giants like Great Britain and the U.S. Therefore, from a strictly business-like standpoint, it was in Canada's interest, on the one hand, to maintain those institutions and values which Canadians felt best for their country; but on the other hand, to foster the kind of diplomatic and trade relations with this new powerful neighbour on the north which could offset the increasing pressures of the neighbour to the south, and the continuing pressures from Great Britain.

During the 1920s, the Trades and Labour Councils of Toronto, London, Regina and Vancouver demanded closer trade relations with the Soviet union.[57] The year 1927 was a turning point. The British Conservative Government broke relations with the Soviet Union. Canada swiftly followed suit. What had happened to the fight for autonomy within the Empire, for an independent foreign policy? The ACCL organ, *Canadian Unionist*, wrote:

"In Canada, Mackenzie King, servile servant of any foreign capitalist, whether ... British or American, is also doing some tall explaining to a public which is becoming better informed on Russia, and particularly to the workers, who are by no means out of sympathy with the one country on earth where the privileged class is the working class."[58]

In the House of Commons, J. S. Woodsworth stated:

"I hope the government will take the earliest opportunity of informing the House why it broke off relations with Russia ... Why should the Liberal government of Canada be attached to the apron strings of the Conservative party in Great Britain?"[59]

At the 1928 TLC convention, some Trades and Labour Councils and local unions submitted resolutions demanding restoration of "previously existing friendly relations" with the Soviet Union. The Congress leadership opposed these resolutions. Secretary-treasurer P. M. Draper said: "I have never yet seen anything come from the Slav psychology that was good for Canadian workers..."[60] The convention rejected the resolutions.

World Peace:

The events narrated above involved world labour solidarity. Intimately connected with this was the problem of peace. With Armistice 1918 scarce a few years away, the drive to World War II began. In 1921, the TLC protested "all preparations for war". In 1922, it supported the Canadian government's refusal to pledge automatic involvement in the war against Turkey then being planned by the British government (the Chanak incident). At the 1923 TLC convention, the Toronto Trades and Labour Council submitted a resolution proposing a dominion council of action to meet the war danger. For the administration, James Simpson said this could not be accepted because Congress was solely a legislative body. The convention adopted a substitute resolution calling for a special session of the Congress if the threat of war became imminent.[61]

The war danger combined with other factors to speed the demand for world trade union unity. A resolution submitted to the 1924 TLC convention by the Toronto Trades and Labour Council charged that international finance was rearming Germany, and proposed "one international of trade unions".[62] (The two main trade union internationals then were the International Federation of Trade Unions and the Red International of Labour Unions). In 1926, the British Trade Union Congress called for an all-in international labour conference "for the purpose of establishing a basis on which all organized workers can be rallied to one trade union international". The AFL leaders opposed the TUC's stand and threatened to leave the IFTU if that body endorsed it. The TLC leaders endorsed the AFL policy.

●

These then were the 1920s: the struggles, issues, deeper discontents.

CHAPTER 15

THE "HUNGRY THIRTIES"
1929-1939

1. THE WORLD ECONOMIC CRISIS
1929-1935

Condition of the Trade Union Movement:

In autumn 1929 the Wall Street stock exchange collapsed. History's worst economic crisis had begun. By 1932, 18 millions were unemployed in the United States, a third of the labour force. In Canada, hundreds of thousands walked the streets without work. At one point, the number of single unemployed alone was estimated at about 200,000. "Thousands of men and women are on the verge of starvation", said the Toronto Street Railway Employees Union in 1930.[1] For those so fortunate as to have jobs, conditions were bad. In Montreal, delivery boys in grocery chain stores, earned $1.50 for a 50-hour week. At the Binz Silk Mill in Montmorency, Quebec, the average weekly wage was $5.52.[2] The employers imposed drastic wage cuts—on the railroads, four in a row between 1930 and 1932.

This was a testing time for the trade union movement. The utmost combativity was needed. However, that movement—in particular the larger part of it grouped in the TLC and international unions—was now paying a bitter price for its policy of the 1920s when industrial unionism, unity, and mass organization of the unorganized had been rejected. Moreover, the policy was continuing. It was hard to shake off the dead hand of the past. In the U.S., AFL leaders said it was impossible or next to impossible to win a strike in an economic crisis. In Canada, the TLC called for unemployment insurance as early as 1930.[3] But the Canadian Government must have known that in the U.S. the parent bodies of many Congress affiliates adamantly opposed unemployment insurance.*

* At its 1932 convention, the American Federation of Labour condemned unemployment insurance as "contrary to our way of life".

How great was the resistance to change is shown by what happened at the 1930 TLC convention, when the London Trades and Labour Council called on the Congress to seek legislation guaranteeing the right to organize. Congress President Tom Moore opposed this on the ground that enactment of such legislation might jeopardize existing organization:

"It has not been found possible to grant such legislation without creating a situation which might be used to the detriment of existing organizations and to the advantage of dual organizations and the non-union workers."[4]

At the 1932 TLC convention, the leadership again drew the delegates' attention to the special status of the Congress:

"Congress is only a legislative body, while the AFL and TUC (Great Britain) dealt with economic questions of their respective unions and could also take up jurisdictional questions."[5]

There was also the problem of foreign policy, the war danger. In 1930, Prime Minister R. B. Bennett clamped an embargo on Russian goods. Sir Herbert Holt, a leading multi-millionaire of the day approved: "No truck or trade with Soviet Russia!" TLC President Tom Moore went to the Empire Club of Toronto and welcomed the Prime Minister's decision. Among many trade unionists there were misgivings. At the 1931 TLC convention, John Buckley—an outstanding figure in the Toronto Trades and Labour Council — and Jack Cuppello—a leader in the International Association of Machinists and the Montreal Trades and Labour Council — criticized president Moore's action. Some locals presented resolutions urging trade relations with the Soviet Union.[6]

Rising mass misery and resistance to TLC policy combined to give rise to a new centre, the Workers Unity League. Founded in 1930, it included unions like the Amalgamated Mine Workers of Nova Scotia, the Mine Workers Industrial Union, and a number of textile, furniture and rubber locals in Ontario.

The WUL never became a majority force in Canadian trade union life. However it was important. In 1932, its membership was reported to be 40,000. Unlike other dual centres established in Canada, such as the Canadian Federation of Labour and the One Big Union, the WUL said it would avoid a rigid, negative attitude to existing centres, principally the TLC. Instead it would complement the other centres, do what they were not doing. It called on trade unionists in these other centres to fight for their renovation, even if this meant going over the heads of their leaders.

The WUL was also active in organizing the unorganized, and in strikes. In 1934, it claimed leadership in 90% of the strikes fought that year, and said some had been won. A further WUL policy was direct action to organize the unemployed. Finally, whatever its short-comings may have been, the WUL reflected the struggle for Canadian and industrial unionism. Its constituent unions were all "national" and industrial. Its growth in membership, combined with membership in the Canadian and Catholic Confederation of Labour, and the All-Canadian Congress of Labour, thus produced an interesting situation by the middle 1930s, where about half the total trade union member-ship was grouped in "national" unions—the highest proportion to the present (1967).

Strikes and Unemployed Struggles:

Bitter strikes were fought in those early depression years. At Estevan, Saskatchewan, on September 8, 1931, 500 coal miners, members of the Mine Workers Union of Canada (WUL) went on strike when the employers refused to negotiate. They demanded the 8-hour day, a minimum of $5.40 a day for underground work, and union recogni-tion. Their leaders included Jim Sloan, Martin Forkin and Sam Scar-lett. On September 29, 400 strikers began a parade in cars and trucks on the road from Bienfait to Estevan. One banner read: "Homes, not kennel boxes!" Present in Estevan were 47 Royal Canadian Mounted Police constables armed with rifles, revolvers, steel crop sticks, and machine guns. As the strikers passed by the town hall, the RCMP and local police opened fire. Three miners were killed, between 12 and 18 wounded, and almost 50 arrested. The next day, 60 RCMP constables, transported in lorries, a machine gun mounted on each lorry, raided the union headquarters and conducted a house-to-house search through the town and district.* Across Canada, trade unionists were stirred. The Mine Workers' Union of Canada called for a national 24-hour strike. At Crow's Nest, Alberta, coal miners went out on a 24-hour strike, and at Lethbridge, Alberta, miners struck in sympathy. Not long after, the Estevan strike was settled. The terms provided for recognition of the district committee, the 8-hour day for contract work, the miners' right to appoint their own checkmen — in sum, a partial victory for the union.[6a]

The Stratford Furniture workers strike of 1933 was another major battle. The authorities sent in troops, tanks and machine guns. The strikers countered with mass picketing. The outcome seems to have been a victory for the strikers—wage increases ranging from 10% to

* Testimony given by Inspector Moorehead of the RCMP on March 12, 1932.

25%, the 44-hour week, and recognition of the shop committees. Significantly, though the strike was led by the WUL, it won aid from locals of the IAM, CBRE* and other unions. Also the TLC expressed its support.

Another major struggle was the Bloedel's** lumber strike at Vancouver Island, B.C., fought in the winter of 1934. Led by the Lumber Workers' Industrial Union (WUL) this involved about 3,500 workers. The major issues were higher wages and protection against accidents and speed-up. Again police moved in. Again there were mass arrests and evictions of strikers from their homes. And, again the WUL countered with mass marches and mass picketing. After 3½ months the strike ended with a partial victory for the union.

The militant temper of those times was reflected not only in these strikes, but still more in the tremendous struggles fought by the unemployed for unemployment insurance and jobs. Canadians of all ideologies took part in the struggle. They were moved by a very basic ideology: They were hungry, and they wanted work at decent wages. However, in the absence of effective central labour policy and leadership, the Left Wing filled part of the vacuum and provided some of the leadership. In 1931, a number of communist party leaders were organizing a national "work or wages" campaign. Eight of them, including the party general secretary Tim Buck were arrested on charges laid under section 98 of the Criminal Code, legislation dating back to the Winnipeg general strike.*** They were put on trial, found guilty, and sentenced to improoisonment at Kingston Penitentiary. This reflected the temper of the times. So did an eviction riot at Montreal in 1932 when Constable Zappa drew his pistol and later shot Nick Zynchuk dead. From Halifax to Vancouver—at Montreal, Verdun, Toronto, Winnipeg—the unemployed conducted great battles and built great movements like the Ontario Federation of Unemployed, the Quebec "Front Populaire", the Verdun Workingmen's Association.

A climax was the "On to Ottawa" trek of the single unemployed. The trek began in Vancouver, swelled in numbers, and by the time it reached Regina, had become a sizeable force. In the east, at Montreal, Toronto and other centres, thousands more waited to join. But events indicate that the Royal Canadian Mounted Police had decided to stop the trek, and that Regina would be the place. As the trekkers gathered

---

* International Association of Machinists, AFL-TLC. Canadian Brotherhood of Railway Employees, ACCL.
** Bloedel's is today (1967) part of the MacMillan-Bloedel-Powell River group which dominates the B.C. lumber industry.
*** Section 98 was subsequently repealed by the Mackenzie King Liberal Government.

at an open air meeting there, the RCMP opened fire. The trek came
to a halt, but the people's struggle did not come to a halt. Later that
year, R. B. Bennett's Conservative government was badly defeated at
the polls. Twenty-two years went by before a Conservative government
was returned to office. What is probably more important: From the
men who moved across Canada in box cars looking for work, the men
who fought their way out of R. B. Bennett's "20 cents a day slave
camps"—came much of the impetus for later union organization, democratic advance and reform—and also a good share of the personnel of
Canada's First Division in World War II; and in the despair, agony
and fighting courage of those years, many of them took a silent pledge
that they would not let these things happen again, that they would
fight and fight before they tolerated such things again.

In this situation, the demands for labour political action revived.
At the 1931 TLC convention, the Montreal Lodge III of the International Association of Machinists (AFL) submitted a resolution demanding support to the "Dominion Labour Party" which must eventually be organized. However, the Roadmen (the full-time, paid Canadian representatives of the international unions), insisted the Congress
"must confine itself to the legislative field",[7] and the resolution was
defeated. At the 1932 TLC convention, the Calgary Trades and Labour Council renewed the demand for a dominion-wide parliamentary
labour party. This was opposed by John Noble, prominent in the
affairs of the International Brotherhood of Electrical Workers, and
AFL representative in Ontario. He said: "It was not the duty of the
Congress to interfere in politics, to turn it into a political movement
would destroy it."[7a] Humphrey Mitchell—later to become Minister of
Labour in the Mackenzie King Liberal Government—also opposed the
Calgary Council's proposal. He insisted the political and industrial
movements must be kept separate.

Along with the demand for political action, radicalism grew, even
a leaning to socialism. At the TLC's 1931 convention, the Montreal
Trades and Labour Council presented a resolution proposing "a fundamental change in the present method of distributing the products of
labour". Another resolution from the Toronto Trades and Labour
Council said "surplus profits created in times of prosperity are the
private possession of the capitalist class". Most socialist of all was a
resolution from the Edmonton Local of the Operating Engineers. This
asked the Congress to bring to the attention of government and public
"the great need for socialization of all means of production, distribution and exchange". President Tom Moore objected. He said the Congress favoured some nationalization, but here was a resolution seeking

"complete nationalization".[8] However, the 1933 TLC convention endorsed a resolution from the Calgary Trades and Labour Council, seeking "co-operative ownership of the means of production, production for use and not for profit".[8a]

2. THE LATER THIRTIES
1935-1939

Industrial Unionism, the CIO, the 1937 Strike Movement:

After 1935, the pent-up desire for organization began to break through. Union membership increased from 280,648 in 1935, to 383,492 in 1937—a figure surpassing the previous high of 1919. The CIO was an important factor. In 1935, a number of large AFL affiliates, including the United Mine Workers of America, the International Typographical Union and the Amalgamated Clothing Workers of America, set up the Committee for Industrial Organization. Matters reached a boiling point at the 1935 AFL convention. There are times when a man acts, and his act epitomizes the rage of millions. The moment had come. John L. Lewis arose, walked across the convention floor and punched William Hutchison of the Carpenters in the face.*

In Canada, many workers seeking organization and industrial unionism turned to the CIO as their instrument. The first CIO office in Canada opened in Toronto, April 1937, with C. S. Jackson and Dick Steele** as voluntary organizers. A pioneer CIO organization was the Steel Workers Organizing Committee—parent body of today's United Steel Workers of America. Its Canadian leadership included Dick Steele, Harry Hunter and Harry Hamburg. Another pioneer CIO union was the United Electrical, Radio and Machine Workers of America. In 1937 this union won its first contract at Phillips Electric in Brockville, Ontario. Along with the CIO unions, other industrial unions began to be active. They included the Canadian Seamen's Union, and the United Textile Workers of Canada—national unions chartered by the TLC.

Out of the struggle for conditions, organization and industrial unionism came the strike movement of 1937. The textile industry was a pacemaker. In winter, 850 workers at Empire Cottons, (now part of the Wabasso chain owned by the Crabtree interests) struck against condi-

---

* John L. Lewis was international president of the United Mine Workers of America, and also a head of the CIO. William Hutchison was president of the United Brotherhood of Carpenters and Joiners of America—a craft union strongly opposed to industrial unionism.

** C. S. Jackson is presently (1967) Canadian President of the United Electrical, Radio and Machine Workers of America (Independent). Steel was killed in action during World War II, while serving with the Canadian Tank Corps.

tions branded by Ontario Minister of Welfare David Croll as "brutal underpayment and shameless exploitation". In July, 1,300 Canadian Cottons workers at Cornwall, Ontario walked out for a 25% increase in wages and union recognition. (Their wages were then between $6 and $14 per week.) This strike ended with a victory for the union.

The largest textile strike was in Quebec at Dominion Textiles—producer of two-thirds of the cotton goods manufactured in Canada. Hours were 60 per week on the night shift and 64 per week on the day shift. Wages were low—as low as $3.50 per week for women. The workers organized in the National Catholic Federation of Textiles (CCCL) and demanded a 40-hour week, a general wage increase in union recognition. The company refused to negotiate. Strike fever mounted. On August 2, 1937, Dominion Textile employees went on strike at Montreal, Valleyfield, Drummondville, Magog, Sherbrooke, St. Gregoire and Montmorency. Then Maurice Duplessis—just elected to his first term as premier of Quebec—proposed that Cardinal Villeneuve mediate. The union accepted and recommended a return to work. An agreement concluded later between the company and the union granted wage increases and the 50-hour week, but no effective union recognition. Within a few years organization had all but dwindled to nothing. However, the strike laid the groundwork for later developments in textile unionism, and it taught the CCCL some powerful lessons which stood that body in good stead in later years.

The automobile industry was another storm centre. Oshawa 1937—an epic. On April 8, 4,000 General Motors workers went on strike for a 40-hour week, time and a half for overtime, recognition of their shop stewards, seniority, and recognition of the union, the United Automobile Workers of America (CIO) as it was later called. Ontario Premier Mitchell Hepburn said he would break this strike. He branded the CIO communist, and sent in a special squad of provincial police, which was assisted in turn by a contingent of Royal Canadian Mounted Police. He said: "If necessary, we will raise an army too!" The strikers continued to picket—in numbers reaching 600—and set up their own strike police. Across Canada, many Trades and Labour Councils called for solidarity with the strikers. At Queen's Park in Toronto, 25,000 demonstrated in support. In protest against Hepburn's policy, 2 members of the Ontario provincial cabinet, Arthur Roebuck and David Croll—both presently, (1967) members of the Canadian Senate—submitted their resignations. Croll said he would sooner walk with the workers than ride with General Motors. The strike ended with a settlement for a 44-hour week, wage increases, recognition for the stewards, and no discrimination—a victory for the union.

3. UNITY AND CANADIAN UNIONISM

A Great Opportunity Missed:

Unity was being built. In 1935-36, the Workers' Unity League dissolved, and recommended to its unions that they join the TLC unions —which meant mostly international unions. Thus Congress ranks grew. The CIO unions were also in the Congress. So the prospect for unity had brightened. But the moment of unity was doomed to be fleeting. In its stead, more expulsions were to come, more splits and fratricidal strife. A decisive cause of this breakdown of unity was once again the international union connection—the fact of dual power in the trade union movement of Canada and the TLC. Here is the course of events.

In 1937, the TLC convention considered the dispute constantly worsening between the CIO and the AFL, and decided to maintain the status quo—in other words, to retain all affiliates within the Congress—including the CIO unions. This contrasted with the AFL policy which was one of rejecting the CIO unions and insisting that if these unions did not get out of the CIO, then they would be thrown out of the AFL. However, a closer look at the motion which was adopted shows that it was an advance but also a preparation for a retreat. The cause of unity and Canadian unionism was being taken up but half-heartedly, and with an open signal to the foe (the international unions and the AFL) that perhaps it would not be pressed too hard. A clause in the motion said any unity solution must be "on terms acceptable to the international unions"; and another clause said that the objective was "to avoid as far as possible the wholesale suspension of one section of the Congress membership", (the CIO unions) or the wholesale suspension of another section (the international craft unions)."[9]

Meanwhile events were quickening in the United States. In 1937, the AFL revoked the charters of the CIO unions. Soon it was asking the TLC to take similar action. In Canada, union after union and trades council after trades council opposed this and demanded the Congress retain the CIO unions. In 1938, just prior to the TLC convention, AFL President William Green wrote the TLC executive council: "The CIO and the organizations associated with it are dual to organizations affiliated with the AFL . . ."[10] But the convention reaffirmed the unity policy. Then the AFL and international headquarters stepped up their pressure on the TLC executive council. In the words of the Council:

"One large organization temporarily withdrew its support of the Congress, and the executive bodies of a number of others authorized their officers to take similar action if CIO unions were continuing membership in the Trades and Labour Congress of Canada."[10a]

Then came December 1938. The TLC executive council went to Washington, met with the AFL executive council, and was informed—again in the words of the TLC executive council—that "further delay in taking action respecting CIO organizations would lead to the almost complete disorganization of the Congress as it had been constituted since 1902".[10b] The TLC council then suspended the CIO unions. The unions suspended, and their membership in Canada at that time included: United Mine Workers of America, 15,000; Amalgamated Clothing Workers of America, 4,000; International Union of Fur Workers, 750; United Auto Workers of America, 200; Steel Workers Organizing Committee, 1,120; International Union of Mine, Mill and Smelter Workers, 1,100. Their total membership was not much more than 22,000. But, as with the expulsion of the Knights of Labour in 1902, the magnitude of the events much exceeded the number involved.

The suspension was fought at the London convention of the TLC in September 1939. But the roadmen (senior Canadian representatives of international unions) furiously assailed those who challenged the ouster. John Bruce of the Plumbers* said the CIO was akin to the Trade Union Educational League, the Workers Unity League and the One Big Union: "(The) CIO was equally dangerous to the success of our movement." Robert Tallon, acting TLC president, said:

"The question for you as delegates is to decide whether you are going to be inside the Congress or outside watching other organizations than your own constituting (its) membership."

In other words, Tallon was telling the delegates that if they wished to stay in the TLC, if they wanted their local unions—many of whom were affiliates of the AFL craft international unions—to remain in the TLC, then they must approve the suspension of the CIO unions, for the AFL unions insisted they would not stay in the TLC unless the CIO unions were expelled.

Soon after a majority of the delegates approved the expulsion of the CIO unions, while a substantial minority dissented. This was a grave decision—another of those crossroads decisions in Canadian trade union life. In 1902 the Congress had rejected the Knights of Labour and thus rendered inevitable a series of rival trade union centres. In the mid-1920s, the Congress had rejected national unions, yielded to the peremptory demands of international unions and the AFL, and thus rendered inevitable the All-Canadian Congress of Labour and

* United Association of Journeymen and Apprentices of the Plumbing and Pipe Fitting industry of the United States and Canada.

THE "HUNGRY THIRTIES": 1929-1939

later the Workers' Unity League. Now once again in 1939 a magnificent opportunity for unity was being scuttled. And once again, within a year, there was to be a new, rival centre—the Canadian Congress of Labour—along with the Canadian and Catholic Confederation of Labour, which was continuing to operate as a distinct centre.

This 1939 decision was the more tragic because Canada was now at war. New obligations and opportunities confronted the labour movement. These it could have more successfully met, had it been united and sovereign. In sum, once again the interests of the trade union movement of Canada were being sacrificed to the interests of the international unions.*

Was the 1939 decision a free one? On first glance—*Yes!* The delegates could have voted otherwise. Quite a number did. However had the majority voted against the executive, against the ouster of the CIO unions, then they would have been committing themselves to the building of a united, sovereign Congress—with or without the participation of key AFL international unions. They would have been defying the AFL—and their own executive council, which was siding with the AFL. For this they were not ready. They were oppressed by the burden of the international unions' threats to withdraw from the Trades and Labour Congress, to break it up and perhaps set up a new centre. And behind this threat was the reality of the power of the international unions, reaching into almost every union local in the country, and into the various union structures—from local trades councils to the executive council of the Congress itself. Despite all this, conceiva-

---

* The CIO unions suspended from the TLC in 1939, were also international unions. This would seem to suggest that international unionism was not the issue, that the problem was rather the international craft unions *of the AFL*. However, in the concrete circumstances of 1939, this was not so. The CIO unions both in the United States and Canada were not yet consolidated. Moreover they were still young, flexible, and generally under progressive leadership. Had the Congress taken a stand, had it retained the CIO unions in its ranks, then such was its authority, stability and strength—as compared to the young CIO unions, that almost certainly the parent bodies of the CIO unions of the United States would have accorded at least home rule to their organizations in Canada. Moreover, had the Congress challenged the AFL in 1939 and kept the CIO unions in its fold, it would have been shaking off its character as a "mouthpiece" or centre for AFL international unionism in Canada. It would have been taking a long step back to its original status in the 19th century as an *all-in trade union centre*. In turn, a TLC, thus exercising the function of an all-in trade union centre, would have greatly elevated its prestige. It would have been a centre for organization of the unorganized, a sovereign centre working *in co-operation with the international unions of the CIO and all those international unions of the AFL who wished to enjoy the benefits of membership in the Congress*. Is this line of argument far-fetched? The facts are that within less than ten years, the leadership of the TLC was saying just about the same thing itself!

bly the AFL could have been challenged successfully in 1939. Certainly the minority who voted against the Executive Council must have inclined to this view. But this compels a closer look at the question: Was it a free decision? Was the TLC ouster of the CIO unions in 1939 a free, Canadian decision? The answer generally would be—*No!*

4. THE FIGHT TO PREVENT WORLD WAR II

Problem of Trade Union Policy:

The complex trade union events outlined above were part of the Canadian and world situation. The crux was the fight *for* prosperity, peace and progress, *against* economic crisis, war and fascism. In Canada, the worst of the economic crisis had passed, but hundreds of thousands still walked the streets. "Thousands have died as a result of exposure, illness, actual starvation or lack of care", stated Denton Massey, a Conservative Member of Parliament in 1939.[11]

A situation of this kind generated labour political action. Various trade union bodies endorsed candidates in the municipal, provincial and federal fields. At Toronto the Trades and Labour Council organized a Labour Representation Association to further its activity in the municipal field. Radicalism increased too. This was reflected in the growth of the CCF (Co-operative Commonwealth Federation), and in the size of the vote received by some communist candidates—in 1937 the communist leader, Tim Buck, ran for Controller in Toronto, won a third of the votes and just missed election.

Peace was the prime issue. Defeat of peoples' Spain was a turning point—the failure of the western democratic governments, Britain, France, the United States and Canada, to support Spain in its stand against fascist German and Italian aggression. Munich, September 1938 was a decisive turning point—refusal of the western democratic governments to honour their pledges to Czechoslovakia and uphold that little country against the aggression of fascist Germany. At the height of the Munich crisis, the Montreal *Star's* editorial caption read: "Chamberlain Brings Back Peace . . . He Set Out to Prevent War and he has Succeeded . . ." The Montreal *Gazette* hailed Munich as "the greatest diplomatic victory in modern times!"[11a] On September 21, 1938, the Montreal *Star* stated in an editorial:

"What will he (Hitler) do? Where will he launch the 'large-scale' war? Will he send his millions to die in front of the Maginot Line? Will he go overseas to take our colonies? With what? In fact he has said that he will never attack either France or Britain, wise boy! And he commonly means what he says. Of course he will be very apt to seek the opportunity to show the Russians, as he has boasted, how to exploit the wheatfields of the Ukraine ... This is, we imagine, the 'certain' war that is coming 'tomorrow' ... Isn't it a good gamble?"

What of the trade union movement? In its annual presentation to the federal government in January 1938, the TLC demanded that Canada not be involved in any war unless this had "first (been) approved by the people in a referendum vote". In September 1938, the TLC convention condemned the appeasement policy and proposed that the Canadian government "co-operate with other peace-loving countries of the world in whatever steps are deemed essential to destroy the reign of terror being imposed by Nazi and Fascist dictators". But the Congress did not set into motion the mass action which might have given power to the resolution. The problem of trade union policy in the western democracies is epitomized by what happened at the AFL convention of 1938. That convention met just a few weeks after the Munich crisis. Before it was a resolution from the Hotel and Restaurant Workers' International Union. The resolution endorsed President Roosevelt's call to "quarantine the aggressor". Here was an appeal which might have saved the peace had the U.S., Canadian, British and French governments wholeheartedly accepted it. Certain that it deserved the endorsation of the trade union movement. But the AFL resolutions committee moved non-concurrence instead:

". . . United action . . . would seem to imply military action as well as political and economic action. It is the opinion of your committee that we cannot form a judgment that would apply to all cases. In the recent crisis in Europe, united action went almost to the point of war and we would have gone into actual war had not a last minute compromise averted the onrush of arms. Would the United States have joined other democracies in such a war? Your committee cannot feel sure. And if we cannot feel sure about a past incident, how much more doubtful must we be about a future incident, the facts of which are as yet unformed. Therefore we recommend non-concurrence."[12]

●

These, then, were the 1930s: In the earlier stage 1929-1935: Economic crisis and the employer drive on conditions; but also unemployed struggles and militant strikes. In the later phase 1935-1939: Growth of industrial unionism and organization of the unorganized in the mass production industries; the fight for unemployment insurance and uniform social legislation; for unity and Canadian unionism; the struggle against fascism and war; and finally the outbreak of World War II.

PART 4
1939-1959

CHAPTER 16

EMERGENCE OF A MASS TRADE UNION MOVEMENT 1939-1948

1. WORLD WAR II

Labour and the War:

During the wartime years, the trade union movement made great advances. This was connected with the war effort—the expansion of production, the relative scarcity of labour, the need for concessions to win working class support for the war. It was part of Canada's contribution to the cause of victory over fascism. That contribution was important, both in the theatre of operations and in production. Production expanded enormously—between 1939 and 1944 the value of manufactured goods annually produced increased from 3 billion to 9 billion dollars. Over a million men and women were engaged directly in war industry.

In this situation, it was necessary for the trade union movement to conduct the kind of fight for conditions and organization which would consolidate the workers and combine their elemental economic needs with the general cause of victory over fascism. The strengthening of the movement became decisive. That is what happened: for the unions these were years of progress unprecedented, with giant strides in membership, unity and consciousness.

1941 was a turning point. At the beginning of 1941, membership still lagged behind that of 1919—22 years earlier. By the end of 1941, it surpassed 1919. Thereafter it grew rapidly until by 1945, it was twice that of 1940—362,223 in 1940, 711,117 in 1945.[1]

A big fact behind these statistics was organization of the unorganized in the mass production industries, and growth of industrial unionism. The fledgling unions of the latter 1930s—organizations such as the

United Steel Workers of America, the United Auto Workers of America, the United Electrical, Radio and Machine Workers of America, the International Union of Mine, Mill and Smelter Workers—were coming into their own. The union was becoming a power in major industrial units like the Steel Company of Canada at Hamilton, and International Nickel at Sudbury. Progress in Quebec was outstanding —about 100,000 new members in 1942-1944.

Canadian unionism advanced too. Many federal locals were organized—locals directly chartered by centres in Canada. Also, the new industrial unions grouped the workers more cohesively as compared with the craft unions, and in that respect increased the potential for resisting pressure from the United States. This did not cancel the problem inherent in an international union structure based on the U.S. But during these wartime years, with a mass influx of members, and frequently a forward-looking leadership in Canada and in the United States (more particularly in the CIO wing of the U.S. movement), the problem of connections with U.S. unions did not pose itself so sharply.

The founding of the Canadian Congress of Labour in 1940 was a major forward step. The CCL was a merger of the All Canadian Congress of Labour and the CIO unions expelled from the TLC. Thus was engendered a situation for Canada comparatively simple, with most union members grouped in 3 centres, the TLC, CCL and CCCL.

We turn now to the wages problem. At this time, while many hundreds of thousands served in the armed forces, and millions in industry, big business pursued a program of keeping wages down, keeping profits up. Capital accumulation mounted. Excess profits taxation in World War II was much higher than in World War I. Yet many millionaires were made in World War II, and some blessed with millions multiplied them. Ottawa became a centre of big business executives. They filled key posts in the administration, more particularly in the Department of Munitions and Supply. They were the dollar-a-year men. They were there on legitimate war business, but many Canadians complained that they took too much power to themselves.* In contrast to big business profits was the depressed conditions of wages. In 1941, 32.9% of the wage earners were earning less than $450 per year, and only 6.8% were earning over $1,949 per year.[2]

* On April 29, 1942, CCF leader, M.J. Coldwell, charged in the House of Commons that C. D. Howe's Department of Munitions and Supply was a concentration point for the Canadian Manufacturers' Association and its friends. On May 14, 1941, another M.P. told the House: "We are in a large degree losing responsible government. Responsible-government by the elected representatives of the people has been largely superseded by control handed over to dollar-a-year men who are big businessmen in this country . . ."[14]

The trade union movement's new organizational strength, combined with the scarcity of labour, made possible an improvement in these pitiful conditions. But there was constant resistance from the companies, and blocks imposed by the government. Federal Government order-in-council 7440 issued in December 1940, provided that the 1926-1929 level of wages would be the norm for a fair and reasonable wage. When wages went below this level, they could be increased, but the increase was restricted to 5% and under for any one year. It also provided for payment of a cost-of-living bonus.

In November 1941, came order-in-council P.C. 8253. It provided for a National War Labour Board with powers of investigation and recommendation on wages and conditions. Increases in basic wages were prohibited, save by permission of the Board. The Board was empowered to block payment of the cost-of-living bonus where it found wages too high. P.C. 9384 enacted in 1943, stipulated that a wage adjustment could be granted only where it was necessary to correct "a gross inequality or gross injustice"—and this consistent with the employer's ability to pay. Any other monetary compensations to employees were forbidden, save for a Christmas gift, and this was confined to $25.

Given the attitude of the companies and federal government, strikes would have been widespread had it not been for the no-strike policy generally followed by the trade union movement. Probably the policy was correct, though at some points, as in Quebec, it was applied too rigidly. In 1942 and 1943 many workers were on strike, but the duration of these strikes was not very great—4.77 days lost per worker on strike in 1943. In such strikes as did occur, a prime issue, along with wages, was union recognition—as in the famed Kirkland Lake strike of 1942, led by the International Union of Mine, Mill and Smelter Workers (CCL).

Along with better wages and union recognition, the movement sought social legislation. Enactment of the Unemployment Insurance Act in 1940 was a major break-through. During the 1930s the Federal Government had refused this legislation—pleading the constitutional barrier—clash of jurisdiction between Ottawa and the provinces. But in wartime, the door of the constitution opened wide. P.C. 1003 in 1944, was another forward step. It provided for a Labour Board with powers to certify a union which had a majority in a bargaining unit. The employer had to negotiate with the union thus certified. If the negotiations did not result in an agreement, either party could apply for conciliation. If there was still no agreement, a Conciliation Board could be set up. Strikes were banned until these procedures were completed.

In contrast with progress in the economic and legislative field, was the movement's halting performance in political action. A reason was the "neutrality" policy of the AFL international unions – no interference in politics. In particular this affected the TLC. In 1943 the Congress set up a political action committee, and recommended to its affiliates that they set up similar committees, so that they could "play a more direct role in influencing and shaping the great movement for independent political action".[3] In practice, this did not yield much. In 1942 the CCL endorsed the CCF as the "political arm of labour". CCL ranks were not unanimous. Canadian UE president C. S. Jackson, then influential in the CCL, said the solution was a federated labour party—a new party, or conversion of the CCF into such a party. Another political action problem was Quebec. The central trade union movement did not pay enough attention to fusing Labour's strivings with Quebec's. In all, whatever the cause, there was the result: In Canada's first post-war federal election in 1945, most seats were won by Liberals and Conservatives—a result far below the movement's progress in the industrial field.

Still, as a whole, the war-time period was one of creative advance. The struggle against fascism—the most concentrated anti-labour force the world has ever known; the building of the grand coalition of nations, including Canada, which later became the foundation of the United Nations; the contributions of Canada's soldiers, sailors, airmen, merchant marine, including the many thousands who gave their lives: the work of the people on the home production front; the expansion of the economy; the immense growth in the organizational strength of Labour; the major breakthrough of trade unionism in Quebec and the emerging, national renaissance there—all this made the war-time period a great one for Organized Labour.

2. BREAKTHROUGH   1945-1948

Ford Strike, 1945; Strike Movement of 1946; Progress in 1947-48:

War is the time of bloodshed and promises, and peace is the time for breaking promises and preparing new wars. So it was after the Napoleonic Wars, and after World War I. So big business in Canada fully intended it would be after World War II. But a new world situation now prevailed, and also a new Canadian situation. The trade union movement had emerged from the war with increased strength and stature—gains in membership, living standards and legislation. Could it hold these gains? The dangers were many. In most major industrial units, the movement had not yet won its first contracts. There was also the problem of government policy, of wage and price controls. Should they be retained? Management wanted wage controls but no price controls. Labour wanted price controls but no wage controls. The Government dropped both—seeming a compromise, in fact a boon to management which dominated the economy and now had more freedom of action.

In this way, direct management-labour relations, as distinct from relations to government, became the main arena of struggle. The Ford strike was the first big test. In September 1945, 11,000 members of United Auto Workers of America Local 200 went on strike, demanding a union shop, seniority for returned men, lay-off or reconversion pay, and 2 weeks' vacation with pay. Militancy was high. Federal Minister of Labour Humphrey Mitchell looked at the mass picket lines and saw the phantom of revolution: "I saw it happen in Canada in 1919!"[4] Operation of the Ford power house at Windsor became a central issue. Here the union had withdrawn the maintenance men. Mitchell was bitter about this and said it made conciliation practically impossible. Probably the opposite was the truth — the more paralyzed the company's production, the more possible conciliation became.

This issue, operation of the powerhouse, brought the strike to a head—on November 1 and 2. On November 1, the Association of Insurance Underwriters of Ontario wrote the Attorney-General of Ontario and said Ford property was endangered by absence of maintenance men. Ontario Premier Drew then rushed to Ottawa and asked Prime Minister King for help. The Prime Minister responded by authorizing dispatch of RCMP reinforcements to Windsor.* The next day, Windsor was jammed with police—Royal Canadian Mounted Police, provincial police, civic police. Over the protests of the mayor, the Windsor Police Commission instructed police to force open the picket lines, so that company security police could enter the power house. In response, the strikers set up a blockade of thousands of cars around the plant, a blockade in depth, stretching back 20 blocks. This helped defeat the attempt to break the strike.

By now, the strike had become a national issue. The UAW's major demand, the union shop, was something every worker could understand. Large sections of the public were becoming disgusted at the way Ford President Wallace Campbell and Minister of Labour Humphrey Mitchell tossed the responsibility to each other. There were sugges-

---

* It has been reported that tanks and troops at Camp Borden were being readied to intervene in the strike.

tions the government take over the company and appoint a controller to negotiate with the union. At Windsor, Chrysler Local 195 joined the strike, and across the country union locals set up Ford committees. Such was the pressure that the company and government decided to retreat. A settlement was arranged. It provided for return to work without discrimination, and for appointment of an arbitrator (Mr. Justice Ivan Rand) to bring the parties together in negotiations. In the final agreement, one term provided for compulsory payment of union dues by all employees while union membership remained voluntary. This was the "Rand" formula—named after Justice Rand. It fell short of the union shop, but was an advance in union security.

The Ford strike was the prelude to 1946, a great year for Labour—with membership increased by 120,000, a strike movement involving 139,474 workers, and 4,561,393 man-working days lost. There were strikes clear through from Cape Breton to Vancouver Island, affecting one major industry after another, mostly in manufacturing but also in mining, logging and transport. The strike movement began in May, when British Columbia loggers, members of International Woodworkers of America (CCL) walked out. Then came strikes of seamen, textile workers, rubber workers; later, electrical and steel workers at Hamilton; in the autumn, lumber workers in northern Ontario.

Among the more important was the seamen's strike. It involved 5,000 seamen on the Great Lakes, members of the Canadian Seamen's Union (TLC). Their grievances were serious — a working day of 12 hours, a monthly average pay of about $112, the constant threat of onerous clauses in the Canada Shipping Act—a seaman going on strike could be arrested for desertion. The union's main demand was the 3-watch system (8-hour day).

Again, as in the Ford strike, the federal government swung its weight to the employers. It sent in RCMP, declared the docks public property, and forbade seamen to enter on pain of being declared trespassers. Minister of Labour Mitchell blamed the strike on the union, and showed more of his dubious neutrality. On one occasion, he received a report that 600 strike-breakers recruited by the companies were moving in on Cornwall to man the boats, whereupon with equal abandon he condemned the union and company. He suggested communists had a hand in the strike. On June 22, 1946, the UAW Canadian District sent him this telegram: "None of the existing strikes ... will be brought any closer to settlement by red-baiting statements."

Meanwhile, the strike was getting much public support. At Cornwall and Thorold, the mayors protested Ontario provincial police activities. At Cornwall, 5,000 union members gathered to protest "scab-herding" by the Ontario provincial police and the RCMP. At the Stormont Cotton mill facing the canal at Cornwall, girls in the weave room hurled bobbins at strike-breakers passing in the boats below. At Collingwood, Ontario, townspeople gathered and convinced strike-breakers to get on the train and leave town. Finally, the federal government acted to impose a settlement. Using its war-time powers, it took over 29 shipping companies and appointed a controller and commissioner to adjudicate on wages and conditions. The outcome was a victory for the union, the 3-watch system—a great reform.

The Dominion Textile strike was another important battle. It involved 6,000 employees at Montreal and Valleyfield, organized in the United Textile Workers of America, Canadian District (AFL-TLC). The demands were a 25 cents hourly increase, 40-hour week, union recognition. Victory or defeat could have important results. The Dominion Textile Company was the giant producer in the cotton sector of the textile industry. If textile unionism was to be consolidated, it was important to win a contract with this Company. Moreover, located as it was in Quebec, its ownership mainly English-Canadian, its work force mainly French-Canadian, Dominion Textile epitomized the domination of Quebec's economy by Anglo-Canadian and U.S. corporations. In this way, the strike, though essentially economic—aimed at improving conditions—also reflected the national issue. Dominion Textile President Blair Gordon fought the union furiously. He issued large newspaper advertisements pledging "never, never" to sign a contract with the Canadian leaders of the union, R. K. Rowley and Madeleine Parent. He was supported by Quebec Premier Maurice Duplessis. Duplessis and Minister of Labour Antonio Barrette turned a cold shoulder on a settlement at Montreal, and they said the Valleyfield strike was illegal; a "communist" conspiracy. They charged that the union at Valleyfield had gone on strike without having recourse to arbitration; and yet, at Montreal, in earlier years the union had accepted arbitration, and judicial tribunals had handed down decisions recommending to the company and union that they begin negotiations, but the company had refused.

Despite the opposition of Mr. Gordon and Premier Duplessis, cotton production remained almost totally paralyzed. The trade union movement and broad circles of public opinion were demanding that the provincial government act to settle the strike. On July 26, the company and the union concluded an agreement which provided for union recognition, the check-off of union dues, a wage increase of 7 to 11 cents per hour, and most important of all—the 8-hour day with time and a half after 40 hours. For Dominion Textile workers, this was a historic advance, a break with slavery.

But the company would not settle for Valleyfield and went on trying to break the strike there. It secured the arrest of local union president Trefflé Leduc, an employee who had 48 years service with the company. Also, it tried to convince the Valleyfield municipal police to take action against the strikers. Such was the indignation of the population, that Valleyfield Mayor Cauchon said: "The attitude and action of the company lead me to conclude that the interests of the union are the interests of the people of Valleyfield".

Matters came to a head on August 13. That morning a task force of Dominion Textile private police, provincial police and "strong-arm-men" from Montreal entered Valleyfield. With their support, a few hundred strike-breakers got into the mill. Things began to look dark for the union. But as the day went on, thousands of strikers and townspeople gathered before the giant mill which architecturally resembled a medieval fortress, and not just architecturally. The time came for those inside the mill to leave. As the motley group of strike-breakers, strong-arm-men and police moved out, some in automobiles, the enraged crowd outside tore up blocks of cement from the street and dropped them through the windshields of the cars. The windows of the plant were smashed along the entire length of the first floor. Against the crowd, the provincial police used tear gas. The outcome was that this attempt at strike-breaking was defeated. The plant stayed shut.

Duplessis then made another strike-breaking move. He ordered the arrest of union leader, R. Kent Rowley for sedition and conspiracy,— charges arising from the events of August 13,—and he demanded Rowley be held without bail. The Court so ordered. The Premier's move to behead the leadership failed. The co-organizer, Madeleine Parent, took over to assist the local strike committee. Meanwhile, public opinion was turning against the company. On August 9, CCF M.P. Angus MacInnis, speaking in the House of Commons, had recalled the testimony of E.E. McRuer—counsel to Justice W.F.A. Turgeon who headed the 1936 Royal Commission into the textile industry. McRuer had described the record of the textile millionaires in these words:

"A shameful, sickening story of heartless exploitation and wholesale robbery by men prominent in the public life of Canada. Inordinate barefaced lying, general fraud, characterized the careers of this gang of high-placed crooks. These were the leaders in the cotton manufacturing industry."[5]

On September 12, the 98th day of the strike, the company settled. The terms provided for return to work without discrimination; a vote between the union and a company association set up during the strike; negotiations with whatever union won the vote; and signature of a contract on a basis similar to the Montreal strike settlement. On September 21, 1946, one day before the vote, Premier Duplessis ordered the arrest of organizer Madeleine Parent. The next day at Valleyfield, 4,000 marched in protest and at Windsor where the TLC convention was in session, the delegates arose and demanded unanimously the release of Madeleine Parent. The next day the vote was held. The large majority voted for the union. Later came negotiations with the company, and signature of a union contract. However, Dupplessis did not withdraw charges against R. K. Rowley in connection with the events of August 13 (see page 273). The union leader's trial took place at Montreal towards the end of 1946. He was found guilty. Before pronouncing the sentence, Judge Wilfrid Lazure asked whether he had anything to say. Rowley replied: "Your Honour, I am here because of a conspiracy between Blair Gordon and Maurice Duplessis!" The Judge sentenced him to 6 months in Bordeaux Jail, and he served his time in 1947. Meanwhile the Dominion Textile workers whose struggles went back to the 19th century and the early years of the 20th century, had achieved a union contract, a stable union and a base for textile unionism at the Company's Montreal and Valleyfield plants.

The textile and seamen's strikes, along with other strikes in 1946—steel workers* at Stelco in Hamilton; rubber workers** at a number of centres in Ontario; electrical workers*** at Hamilton, Welland, Leaside and Toronto; lumber workers**** in Northern Ontario,—had a common characteristic: they were won. That is one way 1946 differed from other major strike years like 1919 and 1937. It was an earnest of the new, favourable situation created for labour by victory over fascism in World War II. Such victories were giving a progressive stamp to the early post-war years. Canadian Labour was deciding in action not to go back to pre-war conditions. The mass production industries were being organized, and largely on the basis of industrial unionism. The workers had never been so strong, united, militant, victorious.

1947-1948 completed the work of 1946—with continued advance in membership, conditions and social legislation.[6] 1947 was a big year for strikes—104,120 on strike with a time loss of 2,397,340 man-working days. Strikes were less numerous in 1948, but that year brought the

    * United Steel Workers of America (CCL).
   ** United Rubber Workers of America (CCL).
  *** United Electrical, Radio and Machine Workers of America (CCL).
 **** Lumber and Sawmill Workers Union (United Brotherhood of Carpenters and Joiners of America—AFL-TLC).

fruit of the previous 2 years' struggle, with many a good settlement
won in negotiations. Growth of membership is shown in this table:[6a]

Year	Number of Members	Percent increase over previous year
1946	831,697	17.0
1947	912,124	9.7
1948	977,594	7.2

Progress in workers' conditions,—and in this the movement was a
pacemaker—is shown in this table:[7]

Year	Average Hourly Earnings, Cents Per Hour	Average Hours Per Week
1945	69.4	44.3
1946	70.0	42.7
1947	80.3	42.5
1948	91.3	42.2

These figures show a major break with previous years. During the
war, the freeze of wages had prevented substantial advance from depression conditions. In turn these conditions connect with earlier
years of the century, and even to a degree with the 19th century—at
the end of World War II, the work day was shorter than at the end
of the 19th century, but hours were still excessive. This shows how
much 1945-48 was a break with the past. But it also shows how much
Canada's progress has been held back by the domination of big business: 1900-1948—almost 50 years of wage struggles, strikes, prosecutions in courts, jailing dismissals, victimizations, in the 20th century,
before Canada broke with conditions carried forward from the 19th
century!

In sum, 1945-48 were years of unity, action, advance. The workers
were organizing, and coming to recognize their unions as vital instruments for their progress. The way they fought—the day to day struggle
of the millions in the mines, mills and factories; the tens of thousands
of activists in organizing wage and strike movements; the work of shop
stewards, local officers, organizers; the diversity of trade union trends
—conservative, middle-of-the-road, progressive, left—united better than
ever before and compensating each other's limitations; above all united
in action on the basis of working class needs—all this stands as a model
for the future.

3. "CO-OPERATION YES, DOMINATION NO !"

The Seamen's Issue; The Victoria Convention, 1948:

In 1946-1948, unity strengthened. There were then three trade union centres—the Trades and Labour Congress of Canada, the Canadian Congress of Labour, the Canadian and Catholic Confederation of Labour. Their amalgamation, integration or united action remained a matter for the future. But within each centre there was more unity than in the past.

Canadian unionism also strengthened — the historic movement to an autonomous sovereign movement. An increasing proportion of the TLC and CCL members were in "national" unions — unions not affiliated to international unions — and in federal locals — local unions directly chartered by a centre. Moreover, the Canadian Districts of quite a number of international unions had a vigorous, forward-looking core of active members, local officers and senior leaders, disposed to run their own affairs with or without help from international headquarters U.S. international headquarters did not find trade union centres in Canada at their beck and call to the same degree as in the past. When the AFL expelled the International Association of Machinists, and called on the TLC to do likewise in 1946, the TLC refused.

This struggle for Canadian unionism reached a high point with the Seamen's issue. The Canadian Seamen's Union had been founded in 1936 and chartered by the TLC. In 1944, the AFL decided to give Canadian seamen another union, the Seafarers' International Union of North America. That year, the AFL convention ruled: "The SIU had been granted jurisdiction over seamen and fishermen in all waters of North America and Canada."[7a] TLC president Percy Bengough was horrified. On July 18, 1945, he told AFL president William Green the SIU was dual—meaning that its jurisdiction in Canada clashed with that of a Congress affiliate. He asked how the Congress could be expected to expel the CSU's 7,000 members in return for the "corporal's guard" of the SIU. Was this the fate awaiting other Canadian unions in the shipping industry, like the Marine Engineers—absorption by U.S. organizations? "Members of unions cannot just be taken out of one union and put into another like cattle taken out of one stall and moved into the next."[7b]

Then came 1948. Pat Sullivan, CSU president and TLC secretary-treasurer, suddenly resigned from both posts and organized a rival union, the Canadian Lake Seamen's Union. Although the CSU was the legal bargaining agent, the shipping companies signed a contract with Sullivan's union. In April 1948, the Brockington-McNish Commission appointed by the federal government reaffirmed the legal status of the CSU. A government-supervised strike vote followed. 93% of the seamen voted for strike action. In June 1948 the CSU went on strike on the Great Lakes. Again, the pattern of dubious impartiality by Minister of Labour Humphrey Mitchell. He stated the situation was confusing. There was Sullivan, the companies, the AFL, the CSU. Implicitly, he supported the shipping companies by suggesting they were moved by the desire not to deal with an organization led by the Communist Party. It must be emphasized that Mitchell was referring here to a union certified under the law of Canada, and that he was personally sworn to uphold that law. His orientation prompted this comment from CCF M.P. Angus MacInnis: "I gather from what the Minister of Labour says this morning, that certain employers' organizations can ignore and defy his laws if they would, on the basis of the political affiliation of a labour organization."[8]

During the strike, the shipping companies let loose violence on the CSU. Strike-breakers and gangsters were hired and armed with shot guns. At one ship, the S.S. Glenelg, live steam was turned on the strikers.[9] More serious than the shipowners' violence was the SIU's role. Such was the opposition of trade unionists to this organization, that normally its entry into the situation would have been impossible. But its way was paved by the "Roadmen"—full-time Canadian vice-presidents of international unions. When the TLC called a mass trade union conference at Ottawa in support of the CSU, many Roadmen opposed the conference, and set up a "picket line" at the entrance to the hall, to scrutinize delegates as they came in. Later, the Roadmen told the press that this conference—with delegates carrying credentials from trade union locals grouping half a million members—was "composed of 98% communists and 2% fellow travellers".

The patience of the TLC executive council was exhausted. On September 10, 1949, it condemned the actions of Frank Hall and other Roadmen as "a direct and flagrant violation of the Congress constitution". It suspended Hall's union, the Brotherhood of Railway and Steamship Clerks,* and charged that communism was being used as a smoke-screen to cover up the real issues. The Council stated: "We must always condemn the actions of the Sullivans and Halls in siding with the employers where workers are out on strike."[10]

This was the chain of events leading to the Victoria convention of the TLC in September 1948. The U.S. headquarters of international

---

* The full name is Brotherhood of Railway and Steamship Clerks, Freight Handlers, Express and Station Employees (AFL-TLC).

unions approached this convention as if it were an enemy target to be demolished, rather than a fraternal body. In the words of the TLC executive council, they "issued specific instructions through their paid representatives to fight the elected officers of the Congress."[11]

The issue was: to endorse or not to endorse the BRSC's suspension. For the council, TLC president Bengough explained that the Congress constitution provided not only for international but for national affiliates. The BRSC had sponsored the SIU, an organization dual to the Congress. Hence its suspension was in order.[12] The Roadmen challenged this. Archie Johnstone, international vice-president of the Hotel and Restaurant Workers* said any union chartered by the AFL automatically had the right of affiliation to the TLC. Russell Harvey, AFL organizer in Ontario, invoked the TLC's semi-colonial past as his authority: Was the TLC to be the "legislative channel through which members of the AFL unions bring pressure to bear on various governments of the country", or did it intend to go beyond that and take up other functions?

The chief spokesman for the Roadmen was Frank Hall. He cited the precedent of the CBRE's expulsion from the TLC in 1921, and said the international unions' right to Congress affiliation was unqualified and prior to that of national unions. He argued that the clause in the TLC constitution prohibiting affiliation of unions whose jurisdiction clashed with present affiliates "was never in our position, intended to apply to American Federation of Labour organizations". Anti-labour employers did not present a large problem: "If we have a strong trade union movement, we don't need to worry about employers." The real issue was "revolutionary trade unionism". He assured the delegates that "two-fisted Harry Lundberg" (U.S. leader of the SIU) was "absolutely opposed to communism in the trade union movement".[12a]

This was the Roadmen's policy. It disturbed many rank-and-file delegates. One, from Toronto said:

"I am a delegate here today. Last week I was pushing a truck along the street. I am a worker ... Hall by his actions not only stabbed the seamen in the back ... but he is stabbing the entire labour movement in the back."[13]

Then came the vote on the motion endorsing the council's action. The council won a smashing victory, 545-198. The result showed that, in many cases, the Roadmen were not supported by their own dele-

* Hotel and Restaurant Employees' and Bartenders International Union (AFL-TLC).

gates from international union locals in Canada. One international union had 67 delegates, of whom only 5 voted against the council, and most of the 5 were paid organizers.[14]

After the convention, the council went to Miami, Florida, and met the AFL executive council. The latter's policy was, in effect, an attempt to force back the Congress to the semi-colonial degradation of the 1920s. In the words of the TLC executive council, the AFL proposed the Congress' constitution should be altered so as to permit "each international union to deliver a block vote at the convention through its Roadmen". This, said the TLC council, was "nothing less than an audacious attempt to disfranchise the Canadian members and to make the Trades and Labour Congress of Canada a special appendage of the American Federation of Labour".[15]

On its return, the council issued the celebrated statement, *"Co-operation, Yes. Domination, No!"* This affirmed, in flaming words, the historic character of the TLC as a sovereign labour centre. It cited cases of interference in its affairs going back to 1910. It told the truth about the Roadmen, not all the truth, but enough to hurt. The men gathered around Frank Hall were "in the main international representatives discredited by the convention delegates from their own organizations" ... They were men who had "drifted away from their membership in their anxiety to follow instruction from pay headquarters". *Co-operation, Yes. Domination, No!* lashed back at insults the TLC was financed by international headquarters, It pointed out that international headquarters' per capita payments to the Congress were more than compensated by Canadian members' per capita payments to international headquarters.* Then it rose to a roaring climax by doing the one thing many trade unionists had fought, hoped and prayed for through 5 decades: It told the AFL leaders that Canadians had had enough of their blackmail. If the international unions carried through their secession threat, it was they who would find themselves seceded from their members in Canada:

"If any international union decided ... to sever their affiliation, then we will have no other choice than to take over jurisdiction of that international union and to issue national or federal charters to cover those that remain loyal to our cause."[16]

Co-signatories of this historic statement were TLC President Percy Bengough and Secretary-treasurer John W. Buckley.

---

* The reference above involves 2 types of per capita: Firstly, the part of the member's dues remitted by his local union to international headquarters; secondly, the block payment of affiliation dues by an international union to the Congress, based on a given amount per member, and the number of members in Canada.

CHAPTER 17

DOUBLE, DOUBLE, TOIL AND TROUBLE
1947-1953

1. DEVELOPMENTS IN THE TLC

Deep-Sea Shipping Strike;
"Co-operation, Yes — Domination, No!" abandoned; 1949:

When the delegates to the convention of the Trades and Labour Congress, meeting at Victoria in 1948, had defied the intimidation of the international unions, and taken a stand for a Canadian trade union movement—this had reflected the high point reached by the trade union movement of Canada that year. But the sheer fact and extent of this intimidation by the international unions had also laid bare the deeper discontents of the Canadian movement—its persisting problems of policy and structure. Now these persisting problems merged with a sharp turn in the world situation—a deterioration of friendly relations among the powers. This began around 1947. Crucial was the breakdown of the alliance and even of peaceful co-existence among the victors in World War II—the socialist countries, principally the Soviet Union, and the Western powers, principally the United States. An armaments race began—defence budgets of 40 billions per year in the U.S.A., and more than 1½ billions in Canada. The danger of nuclear World War III had opened up.

The complex developments in the movement must be seen in this light. The Seamen's strike of 1949 was a signal. Late in 1948, the deep sea shipping companies decided to impose a $20 to $50 a month wage cut, and abolish the hiring hall. The Canadian Seamen's Union (TLC) voted for strike action. The companies then terminated their recognition of the CSU, though it was the certified bargaining agent, and signed contracts with the SIU—though it had practically no membership. The SIU then accepted the wage cuts.

On March 31, 1949, 6,500 CSU members went on strike. The employers and various agencies of government took strong measures. By

May 1949, 400 seamen had been arrested at ports in Britain, the West Indies, and elsewhere. Late in April, "strong arm men"—sometimes termed "goons"—were hired in Montreal, armed with sawed-off shotguns and despatched to Halifax aboard a special Canadian National Railways train. There they obtained additional protection from 200 Royal Canadian Mounted Police and armed Canadian National Steamships police. Emboldened by their arms and what seemed to be the support of the government, this band broke through the CSU picket lines, boarded a vessel of the Canadian National Steamship Lines, and from the deck they fired at pickets on the dock. Eight seamen were shot.[1]

The Halifax incident disclosed collaboration between shipowners, government and SIU—or at least a coincidence of action against the strike. On April 27, CCF* member, Claire Gillis asked in the House of Commons if "the men who boarded the vessel (were) Canadians". Transport Minister Lionel Chevrier said he was "not able to say".[2] During the strike, another Cabinet Minister, C. D. Howe, complained that nowadays ship's officers could not get "a fair day's work out of the crew".[3] As for federal Minister of Labour Humphrey Mitchell, he said the strike was a "jurisdictional dispute". In other words, he seized on a *secondary* effect in this situation and overlooked a primary cause: an invasion by a U.S. union with practically no membership among Canadian seamen, against an established Canadian union which was their bargaining agent and was certified as such by the Canada Labour Board. In so doing, in shutting his eyes to the main point—a SIU raid condoned and encouraged by the shipowners and the government-owned Canadian National Steamship Lines—Mitchell was implicitly encouraging the violation of those very laws and rights which as Minister of Labour he was sworn to uphold. But if this troubled him very much, he did not admit it at the time. Those who sow the wind will reap the whirlwind. The pattern of violence and chaos on the waterfront which made necessary the Norris enquiry and government trusteeship of the 1960s, was created in 1949 by this unhappy coincidence of actions involving shipowners, cabinet ministers, senior trade union officials, the SIU, and goons.

Meanwhile the CSU members were making the strike effective and were getting a fair measure of support in Canada and across the world. By May 1949, they had tied up Canadian shipping at ports in Great Britain, Western Europe, Latin America, Africa and New Zealand. Trades and Labour Councils at Regina, Hamilton, Edmonton and

* Co-operative Commonwealth Federation.

Vancouver were protesting the alleged violence against the CSU in the Halifax incident. At Saint John, N.B., rank-and-file ILA* longshoremen defied the order of the international president, P. J. Ryan,** and backed the CSU.

World support to the CSU reached a high point on the docks at London, England when longshoremen refused to work a Canadian ship, the S.S. Beaverbrae, and declared it "black"—a ship manned by strike-breakers. The shipping companies retaliated by locking the dockers out. Then 50,000 dockers ceased work—most of them at London but also at Southampton and elsewhere. At London, 127 ships were tied up. This work stoppage lasted 74 days into July.

In Canada, the strike had become a major test between Management and Labour. The U.S. headquarters of international unions now stepped up their pressure on the TLC executive council. International headquarters warned the Council they would leave the Congress if it did not expel the CSU. Under this pressure, the Council then decided to reverse the decisions of the 1948 Victoria convention — decisions which had endorsed the CSU, censured the BRSC, and condemned the violation of Canadian trade union autonomy by international union headquarters. On July 3, 1949, the TLC Council suspended the CSU. The Council charged that CSU strikers were keeping "members of other affiliated unions from the performance of their usual work" and thus violating "the sanctity of contracts". The Council also said that this was connected with a world communist conspiracy. In proof of this it pointed to the dockers strike in Britain.

Unquestionably many trade unionists supported the executive council's decision. But many others wondered bitterly what had happened to "Co-operation, Yes! Domination, No!".

The plain facts are that regardless of troubled and mitigating circumstances—there are always troubled circumstances and sometimes they seem mitigating—once again, as in 1902 when the Congress had expelled the Knights of Labour, in 1917 when it had failed to take an effective stand against conscription, in 1921 when it had expelled the CBRE, in 1939 when it had pitched out the CIO unions—so now in 1949, the Trades and Labour Congress was lowering its banners, surrendering to the international unions.

"What did we have to sell to the AFL to get this harmony?" asked a delegate at the Calgary TLC convention which met soon after—in Sep-

---

* International Longshoremen's Association (AFL-TLC).
** Ryan was later implicated in various charges, as a result of enquiries conducted by U.S. government agencies, and resigned as ILA president.

tember 1949. Another delegate said: "I think it is just about time we Canadians told these people ... we are going to be masters in our own house." TLC president Bengough denied there had been pressure from the United States.* In the vote which followed, a majority sustained the Council but several hundred abstained from voting.[4]

A delegate who voted with the Council told the convention why: "I have been threatened with expulsion, Mr. Chairman. This would involve my job, my livelihood ... I am convinced there would probably have to be revocation of charters, general disruption, and I think we've had enough. I am not in agreement with this motion, Mr. Chairman. My members in Vancouver are not in agreement with it. They expect me to vote against it, and I am going to have a difficult problem when I return to convince them that I was correct ... Is there no democracy or freedom in this great trade union movement of ours? ... I have been proud always to call myself a Canadian ... My father supported all the campaigns for Candian autonomy through the years..."[5]

Another decision of this 1949 convention was to reject a resolution aimed at ending the practice under which per capita payments to the Congress, for international union members in Canada, were made by international union headquarters in the United States. The resolution proposed that these payments be made direct to the Congress by local unions in Canada. Presumably the objective was to liberate the Congress from financial dependence on international union headquarters and bind it exclusively, at least in matters financial, to the local unions in Canada. The defeat of this resolution meant that the TLC was moving away from the Canadian autonomy policy decided at the Victoria convention of the preceding year.

The convention also took a sharp turn to the right in foreign policy. It rejected a resolution which demanded that Canada's trade not be restricted by ideological considerations, that Canada be free to trade with all countries. In moving non-concurrence with this resolution, the convention resolutions committee charged that it was "an attempt to poison the minds of the delegates ... against those who are charged with the responsibility of conducting international relations".[6] Another foreign policy decision was endorsation of the Marshall Plan. As carried through by the U.S. government in the late 1940s, the Marshall Plan's effect was to make U.S. credits available to various countries. Many Canadian trade unionists supported the Plan as a token of U.S. generosity to countries whose economy had been weakened by the war.

* The report of the committee on officers reports at the 1949 TLC convention, in upholding the executive council's suspension of the CSU, stated: "... Fourteen affiliated international unions have taken the stand they would not continue affiliation as long as the Canadian Seamen's Union remained affiliated."

Others opposed it and charged that in return for these credits, the U.S. was implanting its power in various countries, interfering in their internal affairs, and securing changes in their governments. This issue — the Marshall Plan — had now become a highly divisive one in the trade union movements of Western Europe, Britain and North America. There is this distinction however: Whereas in a country like Britain, the Trade Union Congress though endorsing the Marshall Plan, did not become involved in extensive expulsions of unions on this matter—in the United States and Canada, the opposite was the case.

Still another motion adopted at the 1949 TLC convention provided that "no known communist shall be permitted to hold office in the TLC, provincial federations and central bodies, nor be permitted to sit on any committee of the convention."[7]

Here again, many trade unionists supported this because they believed it was aimed at communists. They felt the communists had become a disturbing element in the movement. Even if these communists were good trade unionists, perhaps their exclusion would remove a bone of contention. As against this, other trade unionists argued that the policy of excluding communists was one striking at the vitals of trade union unity and democracy. They said that a local or general union had the right to elect delegates of its own choice to central union bodies. Again, if the Communist Party was a legal party and Canadians were free to vote it in elections, why should a union member be disqualified from voting for another union member because the latter was a communist?

National Railway Strike, August 1950:

At the 1949 TLC convention, a delegate said it was better to trade with the Chinese people "than to send Mosquito Bombers to kill these people".[8] Nine months later, the United States, Great Britain and Canada were at war in Korea. The danger of World War III had sharpened. Meanwhile the two giant railway companies in Canada, the Canadian Pacific Railway and the Canadian National Railways, organized their own private war on their employees. The non-operating railroad workers were then demanding a 40-hour week with no reduction in take-home pay, and a general wage increase of 10 cents per hour. When these demands were refused, they went on strike, 130,000 of them—the largest strike in Canadian history.

A key company argument against the strike was the critical world situation—NATO, Korea. On August 11, 1950, CNR President Donald Gordon said: "The strike was being imposed at a time when we badly

need to devote our energies and thoughts to the grave threat of war."⁹
But, amidst the hurtling of shot and shell, Gordon and Crump* kept
their heads. They did not surrender the increase in their Company's
profits resulting from the war tensions.**

Soon from big business came the call for coercion. On August 19, the
Ottawa correspondent of the Montreal *Gazette,* Arthur Blakeley, wrote
about a "massive reserve of dictatorial authority" in the hands of
government, the War Measures Act.¹⁰ A few days later the *Gazette*
demanded legislation to outlaw the strike. The *Gazette* had to face
the fact that the Prime Minister himself affirmed the railway unions
had broken no law. So, it suggested that "this fact (that the unions had
broken no law) is the most important reason why the passing of such a
law should be Parliament's first consideration",—a policy whose logic
was that a general rail strike must be illegal, and if it is not illegal,
then enact legislation to make it illegal!

On August 28, Parliament convened in special session. The Prime
Minister said the strike was harming the United States — a country
which depended on "effective co-operation from Canada". Moreover
it would be hard for the Government to get taxes for defence if the
economy was tied up by the railroad workers. He was bringing in "An
Act to Provide for the Resumption of Operations of the Railways and
for the Settlement of the Existing Dispute". Under its terms the railroad strikers had to return to work within 48 hours. It took the M.P.s
decades before they adopted old age pensions and unemployment insurance, but in 72 hours they jammed through this legislation which
was just plain statutory strike-breaking. That was a serious thing to do.
It meant that a precedent had been created for compulsory arbitration
and banning of strikes by Parliament—a precedent to hover over railroad negotiations for years to come. Prime Minister Louis St. Laurent
denied it was a precedent. But the result was there. The eminent Canadian journalist B. K. Sandwell stated:

"Parliament's actions served notice . . . that the nation's economic machinery must be kept going by the use of the sovereign power to prevent strikes and lockouts, whenever no other means is effective."¹¹

Sandwell was not entirely right. The idea that brutal coercion
against labour was necessarily successful or most effective, even from
an employer standpoint, was an illusion. Mackenzie King, a wise man,
knew this well. And indeed, the debate in the House of Commons in
this crisis period, August 29-31, revealed a delicate balance of indeci-
sion. The government was not that sure, nor were the members. From

* Donald Gordon, CNR president; N. R. Crump, CPR president.
** In May 1950 CPR profits were 130% higher than in May 1949.

across the country, resolutions were pouring in protesting the proposed legislation. What would Government and Parliament have done, if they had now been confronted with the threat of a general strike? However, the dominant section of the labour leadership was not countenancing such a move, and what is more, it seems the government knew it. On August 29, Frank Hall, who headed the negotiations for the non-operating employees, declared: "If a law is passed ordering the men to go back, they will obey it, but they won't like it."[12] That same day Canadian Congress of Labour President A. R. Mosher stated: "If the law requires resumption of negotiations, unions will no doubt comply."[13] It must be emphasized these declarations were made while the legislation was still before the House of Commons, before it was adopted. On August 30, the following interchange took place between Prime Minister St. Laurent and Conservative Opposition leader George Drew:

St. Laurent: "I have been informed from what I take to be reliable sources, that as soon as the legislation is in force, no time will be lost either by the railway companies or by the operators in getting things moving again."

Drew: "Are we to take it from this that this Bill perhaps interprets an agreement that has already been reached?"

St. Laurent: "No. No agreement has been reached. Of course no man can make a commitment as to what 125,000 other men will do, but I was told it was believed that when parliament had spoken, law-abiding Canadians everywhere, whether in management or operations, would heed the directions coming from parliament."[14]

It would seem therefore that before the legislation was adopted, while it was still being considered by the House, persons unnamed but presumably in a position of authority so far as the strikers were concerned, had provided the government with assurances; and the government, in effect, was using these assurances to encourage adoption of the legislation. What is definite is that prior to adoption of the legislation—the dominant section of the rail union leadership pledged their co-operation in the mechanism of terminating the strike. On August 30, A. R. Mosher declared: "The men will be back as fast as we can get them back ... If the Bill should pass at midnight and we can go on the air, the first shift will be back at 8 a.m. tomorrow."[15] The leaders also said they were cancelling a scheduled mass demonstration before the parliament buildings because "such a step would associate the railroad leaders with communist tactics in the minds of the public".[16] Then they announced through the radio that the strike was being called off —a step taken without a vote of the membership, though presumably authorized under the powers given to negotiating committees in railway negotiations as conducted at that time.

Thus ended this great railroad strike, after weeks and months of negotiation, conciliation, arbitration and strike balloting. Several days later, A. R. Mosher issued another statement regretting "any inconvenience to which the Canadian public has been put ... but we regret (still more) the comfort given to the subversive elements ... the slowing down of the war effort directed against the communists in North Korea".[17]

The outcome was that the strike was not won, although, probably, the possibility for winning it was reflected (inversely) by the Prime Minister when he said: "The country cannot afford a railroad strike." However, the strike was by no means a total loss. Later, an arbitration decision granted the 40-hour week and a 4 cents per hour pay increase. The period that followed did not bring stability to railroad industrial relations. Instead there was year after year of protracted negotiations, of strike votes conducted under the standing threat of compulsory arbitration and illegalizing of strikes, of wages declining below those in the durable goods industries.

1950 TLC Convention; Developments in Foreign Policy, 1950-1953:

Two weeks after the rail strike ended, the TLC convention opened. The atmosphere was tense. One reason was the "screening" policy. Under its terms, on recommendation of the executive council, the credentials of some delegates allegedly connected with communism, were not accepted, and they were not seated. On the floor of the convention there were doubts. A delegate stated: "It was a pity when a labour organization was aiming to tell a local union whom they can and whom they cannot send as delegates."[18] Another said: "If this convention will not permit delegates elected by their local unions to sit in convention, then this convention is no longer a free convention!"[19] For the executive council, President Bengough said the policy had been decided "by the convention of last year"[20] — a statement probably true in its broad lines, although this writer did not locate the record of any such specific decision in the proceedings of the 1949 TLC convention. President Bengough also said the screening policy was justified by the need of "arming for defence" and the situation in Korea.[21]

He was supported by the international vice presidents. Hugh Schollie, IAM* national vice president, charged there had been left wing activities in his union—these were facts, he said, and "no commie or fellow traveller can come around and deny them".[22] Bernard Shane, ILGWU** international vice president, was "sorry that we still have

* International Association of Machinists (AFL-TLC).
** International Ladies' Garment Workers Union (AFL).

so many (left wingers) in this hall", and he hoped that at the next convention "we shall see to it that not one of them shall pose as a representative of labour".[23]

Other influential delegates opposed the screening policy. Alex Gordon, B.C. vice-president of the TLC in 1948, said the convention had become an instrument "for certain people who would like to use it for their own purposes".[24] Another, J. Hines, a delegate from a local of the Brotherhood of Painters, Decorators and Paperhangers of America (AFL) declared:

"I say that the fear that has been planted in this convention this week, is fear from a foreign country, and that foreign country is the United States, and the agents of the United States are on the floor of this convention, and in all possibility are directing the policy of this convention at this time."[25]

Later, by a large majority the screening policy was endorsed. Also, the convention adopted an amendment to the constitution which provided that "no organization officered or controlled by the communists or members of the LPP* . . . shall be allowed representation or admission to this congress or any organization chartered by it".[26]

These then were decisions taken at the 1950 convention. At the time an appreciable number of trade unionists believed that such decisions were reactionary, that their effect would be to silence those who opposed the foreign and domestic policies of big business and of the U.S. and Canadian governments. As against this, many other trade unionists felt they were wise decisions. But even among this latter group, there were misgivings. Significant was the reaction of one trade union official who endorsed the decisions—Russell Harvey, then Ontario organizer for the American Federation of Labour—an astute, conservative trade unionist. He told the delegates to the 1950 convention that their gathering "would be branded as the most reactionary convention in the history of the Trades and Labour Congress in Canada in certain quarters". He felt that such departures "from the process of enlarging democratic principles" were justified by the fact that "we are at war with communism". However, he hoped "that the time will come when we can again return to normal procedures".[27]

A few words now on foreign policy. When the Korean War began in 1950, the TLC and CCL executive councils supported it and condemned the "phoney Stockholm peace pledge" and "ban the A-bomb resolutions". At the 1950 TLC convention, some delegates protested. A French-Canadian carpenter from Timmins said it "would drag Canada into a third world war".[28] The majority voted for the leader-

* Labour Progressive Party, presently (1967) called the Communist Party of Canada.

ship's policy. One of the delegates who supported this policy was Annette Langevin, a staff representative of the International Ladies Garment Workers Union. She stated: "We will let them come and throw bombs at us over here... No, I say we won't. We will stop them over there, not over here... Those who do not like it are welcome to go back to their countries."[29]

In 1951, the Trades and Labour Congress, Canadian Congress of Labour, the Canadian and Catholic Confederation of Labour* and the Railway Brotherhoods presented a joint brief to the Federal Government. It stated: "We are and have been for some time at war." The free world was facing "the most ruthless and powerful agressor in history". The best that could be hoped for was "long years of heavy defence expenditures." Canada's allies and "particularly our most powerful ally, the United States" would not "tolerate a Canadian defence on scale notably smaller than her own". The brief referred to "single-mindedness of purpose" during World War II and asked: "Have we no such singleness of purpose about winning the war against communism?" It concluded with a reference to Labour's readiness to consider wage controls under certain conditions:

"Whether some form of wage control or wage stabilization will be necessary is a question for investigation... The labour movement recognizes that wages could go up fast enough and far enough to break the price ceiling... It believes that the proper way to deal with this question is a government-labour-management conference to work out ways of wage stabilization... If our government should introduce a general policy of wage and price controls, labour is ready to take part in a joint government-labour-management conference to consider wage stabilization."[30]

The 1952 TLC convention considered a further development in policy: the demand for the outlawing of the Communist Party. This was pressed in a resolution which was concurred in by the convention resolutions committee. A Toronto delegate protested: "You can't destroy communism or its party by this type of legislation." The resolution was defeated.[31]

Lumber Workers, Chemical Workers, B.C. Fishermen, Textile Workers:

This sharp turn in TLC policy coincided — at least in time — with operations by U.S. international headquarters in relation to a number of their Canadian districts: dismissals of Canadian staff, seizure of funds, lifting of charters. In Canada, many trade union officers and members supported these measures on the grounds that the interna-

* The writer does not know what circumstances led the CCCL to endorse the brief. Its foreign policy, as distinct from that of the other bodies named above, tended to be more reserved and non-commital.

tional unions were entitled to "clean house" of communist influences in Canada. They said this disciplinary action was necessary because there was a danger of world communism, of military aggression from the Soviet Union and other socialist countries. As against this, some union members and officers vigorously opposed the international unions' sanctions. They argued that these measures violated Canadian autonomy and trade union democracy; that they were supported by companies, governments and the big business press; that they blocked united action for wages and conditions; and finally, that they were a smokescreen under which the U.S. take-over of Canada was being carried through—while the force which could best resist this—the trade union movement—was being divided, and some of its most militant elements were being silenced or expelled.

We will consider first the case of the Lumber and Sawmill Workers' Union. This body, located largely in Ontario, had about 10,000 members at the time and was affiliated to the United Brotherhood of Carpenters and Joiners of America (AFL). In 1951, the UBCJ's international representative in Canada, Andy Cooper—acting under powers conferred by his union's international constitution, and on directions by international headquarters—took legal measures to sequester the funds of LSWU locals. It would appear that most members in the local unions objected, voted confidence in their elected Canadian officers and denounced "inquisition by aliens".

Another union likewise affected was the Canadian District of the International Chemical Workers' Union, AFL-TLC. Here an intense struggle developed at the large Consumers Gas local of the ICWU in Toronto. This was resolved after International President Bradley came to Toronto and held a constitutional trial of a number of the local union's elected officers. The officers were then expelled from the union and later dismissed from their jobs with the company.

Then there was the United Fishermen and Allied Workers' Union, of British Columbia—a "national" union—chartered by the TLC. In November 1953, the TLC executive council suspended the UFAWU because its newspaper had protested Congress' sponsorship of a union dual to the Vancouver Civic Employees' Union, Outside Workers. The council also pointed out that the UFAWU would stand suspended until it gave "proof of taking all reasonable and necessary measures to rid itself of communist leadership and leanings".[32] In opposing this step, the UFAWU contended that its only "leanings" were to the decisions of its membership. It also declared that its suspension was unconstitutional: "We have not violated the Congress' constitution —

unless the act of electing our own officers by secret ballot without political barriers can be termed a violation ... To refuse to a member the right to stand for office in the union because of his political opinions means to refuse members the right to vote for that particular member."[33] In 1954 the UFAWU appealed its suspension to the TLC convention and that appeal received the support of some local unions represented at the convention. TLC president Percy Bengough, though supporting the UFAWU's suspension, declared that "the union had done a good job and the officers of the union had done a good job for the members in the fishing industry". In the vote which followed, a majority rejected the UFAWU's appeal.[34]

Finally, there were the textile workers. In 1952, the Canadian District of the United Textile Workers of America (TLC-AFL) entered into a grave dispute with the Dominion Textile Company. The company had introduced a bonus incentive plan which provided small increases in pay in return for large increases in workload. Through 8 months of negotiation and arbitration, the company did not abandon the plan or modify it significantly. On April 1, 1952, 5,500 cotton workers went on strike at Montreal and Valleyfield—a legal strike. The company continued to refuse any further concessions. Also it refused to meet with the union's Canadian leadership and in this, in effect, it was supported by the Premier of Quebec, Maurice Duplessis. The situation became more complex still when Claude Jodoin, President of the Montreal Trades and Labour Council (TLC), and the late Roger Provost, President of the Quebec Provincial Federation of Labour (TLC), issued statements criticizing the UTWA's Canadian leadership. However, after 7 weeks, the mills were closed tight.

Then came a series of events involving Washington headquarters of the union. On Sunday, May 25, Lloyd Klenert, the UTWA's international secretary-treasurer, arrived from Washington, and appeared before the Montreal-Valleyfield joint strike committee at a meeting held in the St. Thomas Acquinas Hall on St. Antoine Street, in the St. Henri district of Montreal. When members of the strike committee asked him what financial assistance could be expected from Washington headquarters, he gave a non-committal reply. When they asked him whether it was true that Sam Baron was being considered for a leading post in the union, he answered, "when need be we must deal with the devil"* and "always keep your eye on the ball!"

In the early hours of the next morning, Monday, May 26, persons

---

* Baron had been the Canadian head of the rival Textile Workers of America (CCL-CIO)—a body which had sought to supplant the UTWA as bargaining agent at the Montreal and Valleyfield Mills in 1950 and he was therefore repugnant to many of the UTWA members.

unknown burst into the Canadian headquarters of the union at Montreal and stole its records. Later that day came a statement from Washington headquarters that it had dismissed the entire Canadian staff of 12 organizers headed by R. Kent Rowley and Madeleine Parent, and was now giving Canadian textile workers a "safe, clean" leadership headed by Sam Baron and Roger Provost.[35] A day or two later, the president of the Dominion Textile Company, Blair Gordon, expressed his satisfaction that the textile workers had leaders like Sam Baron and Roger Provost who "understand that the well-being of the workers depends largely on the well-being of the industry".[36] Others re-acting positively to this development were Premier Duplessis, Quebec Minister of Labour Antonio Barrette, and H. C. Banks of the SIU. Duplessis told Roger Provost: "This is excellent news!"[37] Barrette said: "I am pleased!"[38] H. C. Banks said: "This news is indeed welcome to myself and the organization I represent."[39]

Then negotiations opened with the company—negotiations not authorized by the majority of the members at Montreal and Valleyfield, who had elected their own bargaining committee some months earlier. The negotiators included Frank Hall, Bernard Shane, Sam Baron, and H. C. Banks.* However, the textile workers did not go back to work, and the mills remained closed 7 weeks longer. Early in July, after being on strike 3 months, the workers decided to return to their jobs. Later the company imposed the speed-up plan. Some employees lost their jobs, while others left sooner than accept the new workloads.

These events had a curious aftermath. The reason given for dismissing the officers had been that the workers needed a "clean leadership". TLC President Percy Bengough had said: "I am pleased to see

---

* Frank Hall—International vice-president of the Brotherhood of Railroad and Steamship Clerks, (AFL-TLC); Bernard Shane, international vice-president of the International Ladies' Garment Workers' Union (AFL-TLC); Sam Baron, newly-named Canadian director of the UTWA (AFL-TLC); H. C. Banks, Canadian Director of the Seafarers' International Union of North America (AFL-TLC).

** President Bengough's orientation throws light on the tragedy of these times. In 1947 Bengough in addressing the Canadian Conference of the UTWA at Ottawa, expressed his appreciation for the performance of the Canadian district and its leaders R. Kent Rowley and Madeleine Parent. In 1948, at the Victoria TLC convention—with just one exception—Rowley was the only international vice-president who supported Bengough in his hour of trial when he was being assailed by the AFL and international unions. The truth is that Bengough—a veteran, experienced trade unionist—had a warm spot in his heart for the textile workers. This underlines the importance of lifting the textile situation of 1952—and similar situations—above the level of personalities and ideological differences—their weight was exaggerated at the time—and gripping the decisive question: "What was best for the textile workers, the seamen and lumber workers, the Canadian workers as a whole?"

the textile union cleaning house!"** The Montreal *Star* had stated: "A cleaner, saner chapter of the organization's record is now opened." UTWA international secretary-treasurer Lloyd Klenert had declared:

"We are now providing a clean trade union leadership for the textile workers of Quebec."[39a] The combined opinions of all these authorities must be given the weight and consideration they merit. However, there is also the report of the Ethical Practices Committee of the American Federation of Labour—Congress of Industrial Organizations, dated September 16, 1957. Here are some extracts:

"In April 1952, Klenert and Valente* each contracted to purchase new homes. The total purchase price for the two homes was $95,000. During May 1952, Klenert and Valente brought in $95,000 in union funds to the title company, and told them to go ahead and close the home purchases. At one point, cheques were written for the entire $95,000 to close the home deals, but these cheques were subsequently voided, and only $57,000 out of the $95,000 deposit was used for the home purchases, leaving $38,000 on deposit with the title companies . . .

"As it stood, on May 15, 1952, Klenert and Valente had taken $95,000 of union funds, deposited it with the title company, and used $57,000 of this money to buy homes for themselves. They then took $57,000 more of union funds and sent it to the title company, in order to get the cheque back for $95,000. In other words, Klenert and Valente 'took union funds to replace union funds which had been used to purchase their homes'."[40]

If this AFL-CIO report is to be accepted, the implication is clear. At the very time Canadian textile workers walked the picket lines of Montreal and Valleyfield, their international officers at Washington used union funds to purchase mansions. It would also appear that also, just 11 days before Dominion Textile Company president Blair Gordon, the Montreal *Star*, Quebec Premier Maurice Duplessis, and TLC President Percy Bengough welcomed these international officers as "clean" leaders, persons well-qualified to deliver textile workers from their allegedly "red" Canadian leaders, these officers at Washington were misappropriating the funds of their organization.

Again, there is testimony given to the U.S. Senate Select Committee on Improper Activities. This testimony suggested that between 1954 and 1956 Lloyd Klenert spent $65,000 of union funds for personal purposes, including these items: cash advances from hotels; merchandise paid for by hotels; personal goods purchased and charged to the union; hotel charges in Miami Beach, Bermuda and Maine for Klenert, his wife, family and relatives; air travel for family and relatives of Klenert —not connected with union business.[41]

---

* Lloyd Klenert, international secretary-treasurer of the United Textile Workers of America (AFL-TLC); Antone Valente, international president of the same union.

Following on these Senate hearings in 1957, AFL-CIO President George Meany met with the UTWA executive council. Klenert had already resigned. This conversation took place:

Meany: "Has there been any financial arrangement made with him?" (Klenert)
UTW Officers: "Oh yes, we are to pay him $100 per week."
Meany: "For how long?"
UTW Officers: "Oh, for twenty years!"

Meany summed up the situation this way: "They made a very simple arrangement when he (Klenert) resigned, to pay him $100 a week for twenty years, as a reward for stealing the union's money to the extent of well over a quarter of a million dollars."[42]

2. DEVELOPMENTS IN THE CCL, 1947-1953

Problems of Expulsions and Foreign Policy:

Parallelling developments in the TLC were events in the Canadian Congress of Labour, Canada's second largest trade union centre. At the 1947 convention, the leadership welcomed the Marshall Plan as "a symbol of the generosity of the people of the United States and Canada", and praised military co-operation between the two countries as "geographically logical".[43] Canadian UE* President C. S. Jackson objected that if war came, Canada would be a fighting ground for the U.S.A.[44] The convention adopted the administration's policy.

In 1948, the CCL convention debated NATO.** C. S. Jackson opposed endorsation: "Everyone knows that military co-operation is never for peace but always for war."[45] CCL secretary-treasurer Pat Conroy supported endorsation and exclaimed: "I would like to know if the Delegates to this convention are Canadians or Russians!"[46] The convention endorsed NATO. In 1949, the CCL withdrew from the World Federation of Trade Unions. In 1950 the CCL convention endorsed the joint TLC-CCL statement supporting the war in Korea. Some delegates had misgivings. One wanted to know how the government could be trusted in foreign policies when it acted contrary to Labour in domestic policy.[47] Again, in 1952, the CCL leadership pointed to the necessity of heavy military expenditures in these terms: "The defence of the free world now makes necessary the expenditure of large sums for the government."

This turn in the CCL's foreign policy was accompanied by the ex-

* United Electrical, Radio and Machine Workers of America.
** North Atlantic Treaty Organization.

pulsion of a number of its affiliate unions, in particular the United Electrical, Radio and Machine Workers of America, the International Union of Mine, Mill and Smelter Workers, and the International Fur and Leather Workers Union. This was a major development in the life of the CCL. Two of these unions—IUMMS and UE—then had substantial membership in Canada: the UE about 18,000 members, the IUMMS about 30,000 members. Both had been founding bodies of the CCL. Their expulsion was related to developments in the United States. Here the UE, IUMMS and IFLWU had been expelled from the CIO (Congress of Industrial Organizations). In the case of UE, the CIO sponsored a rival union—the International Union of Electrical, Radio and Machine Workers (IUE); and there followed a condition of chaos and conflicting jurisdiction in the U.S. electrical industry which has persisted down to the present (1967). Another U.S. development was election of Walter Reuther as president of the UAW.* Reuther was a strong supporter of U.S. foreign policy in its general lines, and of CIO sanction against UE and the IUMMS. One result was a change in the relation of forces within the U.S. CIO. In turn this had an important bearing on the situation in Canada. Here the situation was that the UE, IUMMS and IFLWU, though expelled from the CIO, were still members of the Canadian Congress of Labour. And yet the CCL's main affiliates were international unions like the USWA and UAW, who formed the main body of the CIO in the U.S.A. Something had to "give". In 1948 the CCL suspended the IUMMS on the grounds that an article in the latter union's newspaper had charged CCL President A. R. Mosher and C. H. Millard (Canadian director of the United Steel Workers of America) with settling "for less than agreed upon" by their union.[48] This suspension was ratified at the 1948 CCL convention.

In December 1949, the CCL suspended UE. This was debated at the 1950 CCL convention. The UE representatives said: *First.* Their union was being singled out because it opposed the policy of the CCL leaders. *Second.* The CCL leaders were not being militant in the fight for higher wages. *Third.* "Splitting, raiding and expulsions" had become the dominant policy of the Congress leaders, and if this went on, "big business will succeed in loading the cost of the war program on the backs of the people".[49] For the administration, CCL president A. R. Mosher replied bluntly that "we shall refuse to permit any communist-dominated union to remain in the Congress";[50] and CCL secretary-treasurer Pat Conroy charged that "every staff officer in the UE, every leader, is a prisoner or political slave of the communist party in

* United Automobile, Aircraft and Agricultural Implement Workers of America (CIO).

Canada or the United States, is a complete vassal of uncle Joe Stalin. The leaders of the UE were people crawling on their bellies to uncle Joe Stalin".[11] The convention ratified UE's suspension.

In 1951 the CCL expelled the International Fur and Leather Workers' Union. The CCL executive council pointed out that a IFLWU local meeting at Winnipeg had criticized the joint TLC-CCL statement supporting the Korean War. Moreover, the Winnipeg meeting had accused the CCL leaders of supporting government plans for a freeze on wages. Finally, Robert Haddow, Canadian IFLWU president, had attended the Winnipeg meeting. All this, said the executive council, proved that the IFLWU was "following the principles and policies of the communist party". Therefore, the CCL was now expelling the IFLWU, in accordance with section 9, article 3 of the constitution, under which the executive council was empowered to "expel any union which in its opinion was following the principles or policies of any communistic or fascist organization".[12] The 1952 CCL convention ratified this decision.

Having expelled these unions, the CCL executive council, along with two of its affiliate unions—the USWA and the IUE now made a determined effort to dislodge them from bargaining units where they held Labour Board certificates and contracts. Between 1947 and 1953, the CCL assisted the USWA and IUE in 37 such efforts against UE alone. At General Electric in Peterborough, Ontario—one of Canada's largest plants—IUE* tried on three separate occasions to replace UE as bargaining agent. The IUMMS was likewise affected. In the early 1950s, the USWA tried to win bargaining rights at Cominco, in Trail, B.C. — another of Canada's giant plants. Most of these efforts — denounced as "raids" by the incumbent unions — were unsuccessful, save in Quebec. The outcome was that the expelled unions went on functioning as independents.

3. THE PROBLEM OF UNITY

Astonishing and Tragic Events:

Events in the TLC and CCL have been noted above. They were part of the general problem of unity—as witness this astonishing incident in the closing days of the 1951 CCL convention. Pat Conroy had just been re-elected secretary-treasurer, but Sam Baron, closely associated with him, had been defeated in a bid for re-election to the

* International Union of Electrical, Radio and Machine Workers.

executive council. Conroy then told the convention: "I formally tender my resignation effective at once!" and later left the hall.[53] President Mosher declared: "I would hope that he (Conroy) would accept the unanimous decision of this convention but he has left the hall."[54] Thus ended the career of Conroy in one of the highest posts the labour movement could bestow on a member. Subsequently, the Canadian government appointed Conroy labour attache at Washington.

At the 1952 CCL convention there was another astonishing incident. J. R. W. Whitehouse, an official of the Textile Workers' Union of America (CIO) arose and said his organization had been the victim of "the worst attempt at mass raiding in the annals of Canadian labour", and that the man responsible was Sam Baron.[55] Now, between 1946 and 1951, Baron had been Canadian director of Whitehouse's union, the TWUA and had led it in 6 years of "raiding" the Canadian district of the United Textile Workers of America (AFL-TLC). Moreover, Baron had been a member of the CCL executive council and a strong supporter of administration policy in international relations, and in sanctions against UE, IUMMS and IFLWU. What had happened? As noted in a previous page, by decision of UTWA international headquarters, Baron was now Canadian director of the UTWA, and in this new capacity, he was "raiding" the union he had once led, (TWUA) in six years of raiding the union he now led (the UTWA). And if this seems complicated, perhaps the complication is more in the event, and those who made and tolerated them, than in our narration. Behind such incidents — in themselves just incidents — was the deeper reality, the deterioration of textile workers' conditions, the gaping wound in the body of Labour.

In the TLC, there were also astonishing and tragic developments. There was this resolution adopted at the 1949 convention (author's italics):

"Therefore be it resolved, that while this 64th convention is of the most definite opinion that unity in action in one body is of paramount importance to the workers of this country, this Congress finds itself in the position that our objectives of united action *must be held in abeyance, until a clear, concise policy of unity has been worked out between the executive of this Congress and other trade union bodies;* "And be it further resolved that all efforts of united action by the various provincial executives, federations of labour and affiliated organizations of this Congress *shall not be entertained* until this unified policy has been accomplished."[*56]

The 1952 TLC convention brought a further development. During the period following on the Korean War, the TLC and CCL executive

* Writer's italics.

councils had agreed on a policy of joint presentations to the government—for example their joint presentations on various points of economic policy, and in support of the Korean War. At the 1952 TLC convention, the executive council recommended that this policy of joint presentations be annulled. It was explained that these joint presentations had led to a situation where "others (a reference, we presume, to the CCL) have gained ... and we have gained little".[57] This standpoint was supported among other by Edouard Larose, a senior Canadian officer of the United Brotherhood of Carpenters and Joiners of America, (AFL-TLC). He declared: The further away the executive keeps from these people (again we presume a reference to the CCL) the better off they will be."[58] Some delegates protested. One, from Toronto, said a union man was a union man whether he was in the CIO, the Catholic Syndicates or any other body.[59] Another ventured the opinion that "the brother who was in the Catholic Syndicates or the CCL was at least a Canadian citizen".[60] The convention ratified the executive council's policy.

At the 1953 TLC convention a resolution was presented, calling for "an all-inclusive labour council" to include the TLC, CCL and CCCL (Canadian and Catholic Confederation of Labour).[61] In a hot debate which followed, other delegates opposed this. Harry Colnett of Toronto charged that UAW* strikers at Windsor had refused "to let our men go in to work".[62] Another delegate, John Bruce,** claimed that the resolution endangered the union shop: "I doubt if any organization represented on this floor that has a union shop agreement could support the resolution." He also charged that the CCL-CIO unions were "breakaway unions", and exclaimed: "You can't live with snakes, and I say they are traitors."[63] The view of those who supported the unity resolution was reflected in what R. C. McCutchan*** said:

"Have you got to wait for the boss to drive you together? ... Let's control our Canadian policies to the extent of saying: 'Well, if you Yankees can't get together, we in Canada have brains enough to do it'."[64]

By a majority, the convention rejected the resolution.

Disunity was intensified by competititon among unions, with some seeking to replace others as bargaining agent. Sometimes a union told its members to cross the picket lines of another union on strike. TLC unions "raided" CCL unions, and vice versa. TLC and CCL unions

* International Union, United Automobile, Aircraft and Agricultural Implement Workers of America (CCL-CIO).
** Canadian International vice-president of the United Association of Journeymen and Apprentices of the Plumbing and Pipefitting Industry of the United States and Canada (AFL-TLC).
*** An officer in the Winnipeg organization of the Retail Clerks International Protective Association(AFL-TLC).

"raided" independent unions and CCCL unions. TLC unions "raided" each other.[65] In 1952 when the IBEW was on strike at Windsor, Ontario, a CCL affiliate respected the picket lines but some building trades unions who were brother affiliates of the IBEW in both the AFL and TLC told their members to cross the picket lines.[66] In 1954, at Vancouver, a TLC affiliate raided the Bakery Workers*—also a TLC affiliate. That year, a delegate to the TLC convention charged that "the international unions in the building trades are raiding each other every day of the week".[67]

These then were developments in the TLC and CCL during 1947-1953, a time of "double, double, toil and trouble". Powerful forces were at work. They included:

1. The gathering war danger.

2. Big business pressures on organized workers seeking better conditions.

3. Increasing U.S. economic, political and military penetration of Canada.

4. The internal strength and weakness of the labour movement—the element of surprise and perturbation in a movement partly long existent and burdened by its past, partly newly-organized and lacking in experience.

5. The specific circumstance of a movement made up mainly of international union locals whose U.S. headquarters were almost all endorsing the foreign policy of the U.S. government.

There were other factors:

1. The call of patriotism—many union members felt they should not thwart their government's policy in a time of crisis.

2. The confusion between national and social upheavals in Eastern Europe, Asia, Africa and Latin America, *and* the problem of world communism: too quick consent to the idea then being pressed by the U.S. government and Secretary of State John Foster Dulles, that the struggles of hundreds of millions were somehow the product of a "world communist plot".

3. The sincere conviction of many union members that the change-over to communist regimes in Eastern Europe and China represented a danger of communist military expansionism, constituted a threat to Canada's security, and that all this demanded close co-operation with other western countries, in particular the United States.

This much is clear, the trade union movement of those years must be seen as a whole. Decisive factors in this whole are: *First.* The total

* International Union of Bakery and Confectionery Workers of America, AFL-TLC.

of world and Canadian realities. *Second.* The movement's power to react wisely to these realities—its material and moral strength and weakness. *Third.* The movement's day-to-day work. *Fourth*—and not least. The standpoint and struggles of the basic membership—their needs, feelings, interests.

CHAPTER 18

WAGE AND STRIKE STRUGGLES
1950-1959

1. CONDITION OF THE WORKING CLASS

The 1950s were a troubled decade, marked by: wars, rumours of wars, the brooding danger of thermonuclear war; billion-dollar defence budgets; increasing U.S. economic, political and military penetration of Canada; a slow-down in the rate of economic growth as compared to the 1940s; rising productivity *but* also rising prices and living costs.

Progress in wages there was—the accumulated result of post World War II economic developments and trade union struggles. This is indicated in the following table:

Industry	Average Hourly Earnings, in Dollars	
	1945	1959
Mining	0.85	2.04
Manufacturing	0.69	1.72
Construction, building and structures	0.81	2.01
Construction, highways, bridges and streets	0.63	1.56
Service	0.43	1.00

The picture was not so bright when put in terms of real wages—money wages as modified by price changes. For example in July 1959, the Dominion Bureau of Statistics index of real earnings of manufacturing was only 133.2—scarce an increase of 33% over the base year, 1949. And wages in this base year were not so far removed from the 1930s and early 1940s, when a depressed condition of wages prevailed. Moreover the Dominion Bureau of Statistics real wage index based itself on the *gross* real wages of the workers, not on their *net* average return—after government deductions for taxes and unemployment insurance. Nor did the DBS index take into account periods of layoff and unemployment — which in certain industries like the building trades, might tend to reduce real hourly earnings taken on a whole year's basis. In 1957 it was estimated that the income of almost 60% of the working force was less than $3,000 per year—$1,000 per annum below the income considered necessary to sustain a family of 3 in minimum decent conditions.

In hours, as in wages, there was also progress. This is indicated in the following table:[2]

Industry	Average Hours Worked	
	1945	1959
Mining	43.9	41.5
Manufacturing	44.1	40.7
Construction, building and structures	40.2	39.6
Construction, highways, bridges and streets	36.7	41.2
Service	43.8	39.4

By the end of the 1950s, the 40-hour week was prevailing in many plants. As against this however, the hours worked might exceed this because of overtime and "moonlighting"—workers holding more than one job.

Industrial accidents were a serious problem. "There is blood on the bricks of our skyscrapers and the ghosts of the sacrificed wage earners can be visioned in every room." So said *Canadian Unionist,* organ of the All-Canadian Congress of Labour in the late 1920s.[3] To a degree, this applied to the 1950s. The labour history of this period must include the coal miners of Springhill, Nova Scotia who perished in 1959; the 12 uranium miners who were killed at Elliott Lake, Ontario in 1959; the 19 structural steel workers who lost their lives while building the Second Narrows Bridge in British Columbia in 1958; the many other workers who lost their lives in industries such as logging, mining and manufacturing. Between 1945 and 1959 there were close to 4,993,696 accidents in industry, of which 12,634 were fatal.

Yet another problem was the gap between productivity and jobs— lagging job opportunities as compared to increasing output. Between 1949 and 1959, total manufacturing output increased 48%, but employment only 11%. Between 1952 and 1959, the number of electric ranges produced increased 82%, with no change in the number of workers. The gap between productivity and labour expressed itself also in lagging real wages as compared to rising productivity. Between 1949 and 1959, manufacturing productivity per man hour increased 48%, but real wages only 37%.

This rising productivity was caused by technological innovation. But it was also caused by intensification of labour—the increase in the workload. In the 1950s, there was much job evaluation, much time study, many bonus incentive plans. Conflicts over the workload became an issue in a multitude of grievances and strikes.*

How did these conflicts develop? Companies would increase the workload.** They would insist changes were routine, a matter of more efficiency or technological improvement, something strictly in their jurisdiction and not subject to negotiation. At Sherbrooke, Quebec, in 1957, the National Catholic Federation of Textiles, CCCL, charged that the Dominion Textile Company had increased the workload by 25% without any increase in pay. The company insisted it was a "routine" change. At Magog, Quebec, in 1959, the NCFT charged that Dominion Textiles had increased the weight of bobbins and this was increasing the fatigue and monotony of work, and reducing the bonus earnings of employees.[3] This problem—how to make workloads and technological innovation as much a matter for negotiations as wages and hours—was also an issue in the CPR Firemen's strikes of 1957-1958.

Disputes arose also in connection with the way time study plans were imposed. Unions said the tests were often not typical, and that short trial periods selected did not register the true average of stress and strain on the worker.

Finally, there were many disputes springing from the reclassification of jobs, the fusing of different jobs into a single job; the transfer of women to do men's work but allegedly at "women's" wages;*** the change from hourly to piecework rates or vice versa with perhaps an

---

* Examples are disputes at: the Chrysler auto plant in Windsor, Ontario (UAW); Massey-Harris-Ferguson at Toronto, Ontario (UAW); Dominion Textiles in Quebec (National Catholic Federation of Textiles, Inc., CCCL); the Canadian Textile Council, UTWA; Canadian Cottons at Cornwall, Ontario (Textile Workers Union of America, CCL-CIO—later AFL-CIO-CLC); Shawinigan Chemicals at Shawinigan, Quebec (National Metal Trades Federation, CCCL); H. A. MacKinnon Industries at St. Catharines, Ontario, (UAW); Firestone Tire at Hamilton, Ontario (United Rubber, Cork, Linoleum and Plastic Workers of America, CCL-CIO—later AFL-CIO-CLC); Conflicts over the workload were an issue also in two major cotton strikes in Quebec in 1950s—the Montreal-Valleyfield strike of 1952 (CTC-UTW) and the Magog strike of 1959-1960 (National Catholic Federation of Textiles, Inc., CCCL).

** In 1959, the Aluminum Company of Canada at Shawinigan Falls increased the workload in the potroom from 85% of standard to as much as 130% of standard.[4] This increase was fought by the National Metal Trades Federation, CCCL.

*** At Dominion Oilcloth in Montreal, 1959, 5 women replaced 5 men on certain jobs, did the same work, but were paid 25 cents per hour below the men's rate.[5]

attendant drop in earnings for the workers.**** During the 1950s, such problems became the issue in a multitude of grievances, arbitration boards, unofficial work stoppages and at times full scale strikes.

This was the workload. Then there was technological innovation—something distinct from the workload, but in real life meshed in with it. An example is dieselization on the railroad. Between 1950 and 1957 the proportion of diesel locomotives increased from 25% to 80%. In the railroad shops, the total of machinists, machinists apprentices and helpers decreased from 8,000 to 5,600, and the total of boiler-makers and blacksmiths decreased by 70%. Then there was a new type of technological innovation—automation. This was spreading rapidly in offices and also in industries like railroad (the freight yards), communications, and the larger postal depots.

Finally, there was economic recession and unemployment. "It's a crying shame that in a country with all the natural resources we have, we have to see people on the street", said an auto worker in 1958.* Incidence of unemployment is indicated in the table below.[7]

Year	Percentage of Labour Force Not Employed
1950	4.63
1951	2.83
1952	3.30
1953	3.43
1954	5.87
1955	5.44
1956	4.05
1957	5.45
1958	9.36

This unemployment was partly connected with the cyclical movement of prosperity and recession. But it was also related to: *First*. The burden of defence expenditures—the resultant dislocation in the economy and decrease in consumer income through higher taxes. *Second*. The growing inbalance of payments between Canada and the United States—to put it more plainly—increasing economic dependence on the United States. This is suggested by the industries most hard hit. They included mining (coal, base metal, uranium); merchant marine and shipbuilding, farm equipment; electrical and textiles.

**** This seems to have been the case in an unofficial work stoppage conducted by 50 women at a department of Firestone Rubber at Hamilton in 1956. The women claimed they had been but $3 to $4 per day.[6]

* Statement by a UAW delegate at the 1958 convention of the Ontario Federation of Labour, CLC.

Two further peculiarities of the recessions were that prices did not decline, but maintained their level and at times even increased; and, secondly, in the recovery phase, production tended to expand without a corresponding expansion of employment.

How many unemployed? Government and Labour did not agree. During the 1958 recession, Federal Government statistics indicated half a million unemployed, while trade union statistics showed 3/4 of a million.[8] A special factor was part time unemployment—short term layoffs, short time.

2.　WAGE AND STRIKE STRUGGLES.　1950-1959.

The Problem Outlined; Strike Statistics:

The economic and political conditions of the 1950s—described in the previous section—generated much action on the collective bargaining front. Most contracts were signed without a strike, but negotiations were often hard-fought and prolonged.　There were many strikes — between 1950 and 1959, 2,022 strikes and lockouts involving 976,671 workers with total time lost of 17,865,248 man work days. The strikes took place in every province from Newfoundland to British Columbia. They affected practically every industry: primary industries like mining, logging and fishing; building trades and transport; manufacturing; office, professional and government employees. The strike issues varied: first and foremost wages, hours and speed-up, then seniority, union recognition and union security; finally, sympathetic actions with other workers on strike and resistance to employer and government attempts to curb or destroy unions.

The significance of the strikes should not be exaggerated. At no time did they affect more than a small percentage of the total working force; and time lost through unemployment and sickness far exceeded time lost in strikes. Moreover, the strikes must be seen in the context of the *total* economic struggle: the thousands of negotiations concluded with with or without a strike; the hundreds of thousands of grievances fought; the day-to-day, month-to-month and year-to-year continuous activity of the movement. However, within these limits, the strikes did serve as indicators of trade union life. They reflected decisive issues such as conditions and the right to organize; and to a degree, they became tests of strength as to how these issues were resolved, whether in favour of Labour or Business, and to what degree—in short the balance of forces in industrial relations.

The three tables that follow provide data on the strike situation of the 1950s:

TABLE I

TOTAL STRIKES AND LOCKOUTS IN CANADA. 1950-1959.[9]

Year	Total Number of Strikes	Total No. Workers Involved	Total No. Man Working Days Lost
1950	161	192,153	1,389,039
1951	259	102,870	901,739
1952	222	120,818	2,879,955
1953	174	55,988	1,324,715
1954	174	62,250	1,475,200
1955	159	60,090	1,875,400
1956	229	88,680	1,246,000
1957	243	86,198	1,607,180
1958	260	107,497	2,879,120
1959	218	100,127	2,286,900

TABLE 2

STRIKES INVOLVING OVER 500 WORKERS[10]
1950 - 1959

Year	Total No. Strikes	Workers Involved	Average Duration (Days)
1950	21	172,454	16.2
1951	43	78,601	13.8
1952	36	98,862	49.3
1953	29	37,735	31.2
1954	20	32,414	44.6
1955	19	34,111	30.6
1956	38	48,716	16.4
1957	42	65,930	32.7
1958	32	69,506	31.0
1959	29	80,176	30.1

TABLE 3

SELECTED MAJOR STRIKES OF LONG DURATION
1950-1958[11]

Strike	Place	Year	Duration (Days)
Associated Textiles	Louiseville	1952	321
Clothing	Sherbrooke	1952	169
Simmons Bed	Montreal	1952	119
Dominion Textile	Montreal & Valleyfield	1952	95
Rubber	Hamilton	1952	114
Building trades	Vancouver	1952	102
Canadian Copper Refineries	Montreal	1952	166
Gold, silver, copper	Ontario & Quebec	1953	216
Loggers	B.C.	1953	98
Gold and copper	Ontario & Quebec	1953	173
Loggers	B.C.	1953	104
Ford	Windsor	1954	111
Building trades	Toronto	1954	110
Aircraft	Downsview	1955	123
General Motors	Ontario	1955	151
Canada Wire & Cable	Toronto	1955	106
Dominion Textile	Drummondville, Magog, etc.	1956	184
Gaspé Copper	Murdochville	1957	215
Lever Brothers	Toronto	1957	146
Alcan	Arvida	1957	122
Fishermen	B.C.	1957	143
Windsor Quarry	N.S.	1957	379
Hyde Park	Montreal	1958	167
Plumbers	Vancouver	1958	130
Inco	Sudbury	1958	92
Loggers	Newfoundland	1958	90

The situation, 1950-1957;
Founding of the CLC:

1950 was a stormy year if only because of the railroad strike. 1951 was quiet. 1952 was a peak year for strikes—a strike movement sweeping from coast to coast: in *Nova Scotia*, building trades workers at Halifax; in *Quebec,* a far-reaching strike movement; in *Ontario*—a major strike of street transport workers at Toronto and also of rubber workers; in *British Columbia,* disputes affecting building trades workers and fishermen.

In 1953 the impact of strikes declined. That year the gold miners of Northern Ontario and Quebec fought a prolonged strike led by the United Steel Workers of America (CCL-CIO).

1954 brought a favourable turn in international relations—settlement of the war in Indo-China, the first summit meeting bringing together the United States, Soviet Union, Britain and other powers at Geneva. The war danger had thus diminished, but it persisted through the decade. In Canada this year was marked by a recession. The Canadian Manufacturers' Association put out the call—"No wage increases". Serious strikes developed. The most important was the Ford strike in Ontario. Led by the UAW, it involved 5,700 workers at the company's main plant in Windsor, Ontario. Then it spread to Ford workers in other centres. Eventually over 10,000 were on strike. After 108 days, this dispute terminated with a settlement providing for wage increases, improvements in the seniority and welfare clauses of the contract and a province-wide agreement with the company—in all a victory for the union.

Less favourable was the outcome of a dispute involving the non-operating railway employees. The cause of this dispute was the refusal of the Canadian Pacific Railway Company and the Canadian National Railway Company to grant a number of union demands including three weeks vacation with pay and an extra statutory holiday. The unions took a strike vote of their 145,000 members grouped in 16 international and "national" unions, and 90% of the membership voted for strike.

Then the federal government coolly announced there would be no railway strike. Parliament would be convened, and if necessary, legislation would be adopted to ban a strike and impose compulsory arbitration. The rail union leadership then cancelled the decision to strike, and accepted settlement by compulsory arbitration. Frank Hall, heading negotiations for the unions, said "We agreed to compulsory arbitration. We call it compulsory arbitration, although we voluntarily agreed to it." Later an arbitration award granted some concessions to the unions but through the 1950s the ghost of federal government intervention stalked the bargaining tables of the industry. In 1959, the overall average wage of rail non-operating employees was $1.76 per hour—well below the average prevailing in the durable goods industries—this in an industry organized decades before the durable goods industries, where employees were predominantly male and where the percentage of union organization was much higher than in the durable goods industries.

In 1955, 1956 and the first part of 1957, there was an upswing in the economy but employers continued to resist wage increases; negotiations were difficult, and strikes developed.* The GM strike demonstrated labour's new economic power, its ability to conduct a sustained operation on a wide front and win. For 148 days, in 1955-56, the plants of General Motors—one of the largest corporations in the world and the epitome of the U.S. branch-plant system in Canada—were shut tight at Oshawa, St. Catharines, Windsor, London and other centres. The union, the UAW, fought hard. The strike ended with a settlement favourable to the workers: a 25 cents per hour wage package and a supplementary unemployment insurance benefit.**

We turn now to a major development in union structures — the founding of the Canadian Labour Congress in 1956. A major link leading to this event was the merger, in the United States, of the American Federation of Labour and the Congress of Industrial Organizations. Thus came about the AFL-CIO, in 1955. Another link was the co-ordinating committee set up in Canada by the two largest trade union centres, the Trades and Labour Congress of Canada and the Canadian Congress of Labour. The task of this committee was to work out the principles for a merger of the two bodies. These principles were endorsed by conventions of the two centres, in 1955.

The inaugural convention of the Canadian Labour Congress met in Toronto in April 1956. Assembled were delegates from 640,000 members of TLC affiliates and 330,000 members of CCL affiliates. The Convention adopted a constitution which provided for assistance to "affiliated and chartered organizations" and the "organization of the unorganized into unions . . . giving recognition to the principle that both craft industrial unions are appropriate, equal and necessary as methods of union organization".*** Another clause provided for bi-annual conventions.

The chief officers of the CLC were to be the President, Secretary-Treasurer, two executive vice-presidents and four general vice-presi-

---

* Examples are the Massey-Harris strike at Toronto led by the UAW; the plumbers strike at Montreal led by local 144 of the UA; the Canada Wire and Cable strike and the Ferranti Electric stike, both in Toronto, led by the UE; the Dominion Textile strike in the Eastern Townships and other centres, led by the National Catholic Federation of Textile Workers, CCCL.

** A supplementary unemployment insurance benefit (SUB) is a company contractual obligation to pay benefits to a worker laid off, under certain conditions. In the GM settlement, the benefit was between 60% and 65% of normal take-home pay for first 26 weeks of layoff.

*** The source for details and extracts from the constitution is the text as revised, Apr. 1958.

dents. Also there were to be thirteen vice-presidents elected on a geographical basis. All these officers were to constitute the Congress executive council — "the governing body of this Congress between conventions". This council was to meet "at least four times each year".

The constitution also provided for "trade departments in industries such as building trades, metal trades and railway trades. A system of "Congress departments" was set up covering fields such as Organization, Legislation, Education, Research, International Affairs, Government Employees, Provincial Federations of Labour and local Labour Councils, Political Education and Public Relations.

The main source of Congress revenues was to be the "per capita tax" of seven cents per member per month, to be paid by each national and international union affiliate.

The 1956 convention elected Claude Jodoin to the leading post-President. Prior to this, Mr. Jodoin had been an organizer on the Montreal staff of the International Ladies' Garment Workers' Union (AFL-TLC), a President of the Montreal Trades and Labour Council (TLC), and President of the Trades and Labour Congress of Canada.

The founding of the Congress brought together 111 general unions and 322 federal locals, almost all of whom had been members of the TLC or CCL. During the years 1956-1958, the provincial federations and local labour councils, formerly chartered by the TLC and CCL, also merged. The outcome was ten provincial federations and about 100 local labour councils — all chartered by the CLC. The largest labour councils were at Toronto, Montreal, Winnipeg and Vancouver.

With the founding of the CLC, this was the condition of trade union structures by the end of the 1950s:* Somewhat over a million were members of unions affiliated to the CLC. About 100,000 were members of the Canadian and Catholic Confederation of Labour. Finally, about 200,000 were in independent unions, that is, international, national, regional and local unions not affiliated to either the CLC or CCCL.**

1958 — CPR Firemen and Inco:

We return now to the main theme of this Chapter — the wage and strike movements of the 1950s.

1958 was a decisive year: tensions abroad and at home, war crises in the Middle East and Far East; in Canada—recession, wage increases hard

** The source for data on union membership is the 1960 edition of Labour Organization in Canada.
** There was also a small number, about 30,000, who were members of unions affiliated to the AFL-CIO only.

to get.* The large companies were bent on their "wage restraint" policy. They pointed to the demands of the large defence budget, high taxes, the need for management-labour co-operation in the free world struggle against "communism"—a term then much used to describe the struggle for national and social liberty then going on in Africa, Asia, Latin America, Europe and to a degree also in North America too. Meanwhile quite a number of these companies were making large profits. Some were provocative—as at Vancouver, when building trades employers locked out the plumbers.**

Assailed by this employer offensive, the unions had to fight back or sustain a serious defeat. The 1958 Canadian Labour Congress convention rejected the "wage restraint" policy. The Canadian and Catholic Confederation of Labour, and most important independent unions rejected it too. A major wage and strike movement followed. The outcome was no sweeping victory for Labour but a defeat to the employers' "wage restraint" policy.

The strike movement began in the spring in British Columbia, when the Teamsters and Plumbers walked out.*** By midsummer and early autumn, the movement spread to Quebec and Ontario. At Hamilton, Ontario, 8,077 members of the United Steel Workers of America Local 1005 were on strike at the Steel Company of Canada for 84 days with a $50,000,000 production loss to the company. This strike ended with a union victory—a wage increase of 27.8 cents per hour spread over three years.

The CPR firemen's strike was led by the Brotherhood of Locomotive Firemen and Enginemen (AFL-CIO-CLC). The issue was the Canadian Pacific Railway's decision to remove firemen from the yard diesel locomotives. The company defended this on grounds of technological improvement, while the union assailed it as speed-up and unsafe. The CPR's operations were tied up, particularly in western Canada. However the strike did not attain top effectiveness. One reason was—again —not enough unity in Labour's ranks. A month prior to the strike, the CLC convention voted support to the BLF—one of its affiliates. However during the strike, Louis Laberge, a Quebec CLC vice-president declared the strike concerned only the firemen and was not endorsed by other unions. Also, a senior official of the Brotherhood of Loco-

---

* Between October 1957 and March 1958, at 265 selected establishments, 44% of the agreements signed provided increases of 5 cents per hour and less.
** United Association of Journeymen and Apprentices of the Plumbing and Pipe-fitting Industry of the United States and Canada, CLC.
*** International Brotherhood of Chauffeurs, Warehousemen and Helpers of America (CLC); United Association of Journeymen and Apprentices of the Plumbing and Pipefitting Industry of the United States and Canada (CLC).

motive Engineers (Independent) sent a letter to his members telling them that it was illegal to refrain from going to work. The strike ended with a settlement which provided that 500 firemen keep their jobs in the yards and not be transported to other jobs as originally proposed by the CPR. This was a partial victory for the BLF. Also the union reserved the right to bring the spare firemen issue up again in negotiations since every contract is a new contract.

In magnitude and duration the Mine-Mill strike at Sudbury and Port Colborne was one of Canada's greatest in the 1950s. Ranged against each other were the International Nickel Company—owner of the largest nickel mines in the world, and local 598 of the International union of Mine, Mill and Smelter Workers—with 16,000 members, the largest union local in Canada.

The cause of this strike was company policy. The company had accumulated a large stock-pile of nickel and cut the work week. In negotiations it refused an increase point blank. The union would not go along with this. That is how the strike came about. It became a prolonged strike. One reason was the chilly attitude of the Ontario Provincial Government. Despite union demands and the requests of a large section of the Sudbury population, the government would not intervene to settle the dispute. Another reason was the same difficulty which had darkened prospects in the CPR Firemen's strike—disunity in the ranks of Labour. Even before the strike began the Sudbury *Star*, in a front page statement raised the prospect that if the IUMMS went on strike, this would open the door for a move by the United Steel Workers of America (CLC) to supplant the IUMMS as bargaining agent. Also, in the early days of the strike, the *Financial Post* speculated about the possible entry of the USWA into the situation.

Despite all these difficulties the union held its ground, received financial support from its brother IUMMS locals across the country and also from other unions, including quite a number of CLC affiliates. In December 1958, the strike ended—92 days after it had begun. The settlement provided a 15 cents hourly increase to be paid in three installments between 1959 and 1961.

1959 — Newfoundland Lumber Strike:

In 1959 the recession lifted but employers continued to take a "tough" line in negotiations. Wage settlements signed ranged from 5 to 7 cents per hour. Once again strikes broke out. The most important was the Newfoundland loggers strike.

In 1959, Newfoundland—Canada's newest province—epitomized the big business domination which has blocked Canada's progress. Here the misery of the past joined the misery of the present. For if in its poverty, lack of industrial development and dependence on primary extractive industries like fishing and mining; and if in its comparatively recent emergence from subordinate political status in the Commonwealth, Newfoundland was a portion of Canada's past, it is also true that in its near total domination by foreign capital, it stood but as the extremity of Canada's present. Among the main foreign companies exploiting the province were the Anglo-Newfoundland Development Company and the Bowater Company. They owned great tracts of land mostly tax free. In 1959 Bowater was exempt from provincial taxation, and AND was not paying very much. The scale on which these companies enriched themselves is indicated by AND profits between 1947 and 1959—$90,000,000 before taxation. These companies' colonizing attitude to Newfoundland is reflected by their haughty statement during the strike:

"The paper companies do not intend to allow the International Woodworkers Association to further endanger the economy of Newfoundland by perpetuating its presence in the province through collective agreements."

What of conditions? In 1935, a government commission, reporting on conditions in the woods, found "wages were low, camp conditions were bad, food was bad and the living standards of the loggers abysmally low." Twenty-three years later, in 1958, at a main lumbering centre, average annual earnings were $1,500 per year, the 10-hour day and 6-day week prevailed, 50 men were lodged in a bunkhouse designed for 35, a ditch was used for toilet facilities, and few loggers or their children had tasted eggs, ham, bacon or fresh milk. At Grand Falls—dominated largely by British capital—lumber wages were $1.05 per hour, milk sold at 50 cents a quart, fresh meat at a dollar a pound and up, and vegetables were being imported.

After 1956, the loggers began to join the International Woodworkers of America (CLC). By January 1957, 87% of the AND employees had joined and paid initiations. Early in 1959 86.4% of the loggers voted for the union. The Newfoundland Labour Relations Board granted certification. Negotiations followed, and a conciliation board report recommending a 5 cents hourly increase spread over 2 years and a 54-hour work week. The company rejected these proposals. The loggers voted 98.8% for strike.

The strike began December 31, 1958. Originally it involved about 1,200 AND workers, but it seems to have become in part a regional general strike because for a time it was joined by 1,400 loggers of the Bowater Company and by members of the International Brotherhood of Pulp, Sulphite and Paper Mill Workers (CLC).

This meant a powerful movement—one which could be defeated only by draconic measures. But Newfoundland had a premier who, as he understood matters then, was prepared to adopt such measures. On February 16 Premier Smallwood called for a company union to replace the IWA. On February 17 he said he would organize one himself, expressed confidence the companies would deal with it, and predicted the strike would be over in 2 weeks. He also brought in legislation decertifying the IWA. This was adopted by the Newfoundland provincial legislature on March 7.

Then came the tragic events of March 7. Several busloads of strikebreakers were moving along the road to Badger, escorted by between 100 and 125 police, mostly Royal Canadian Mounted Police. Encountering picketers on the road, the police ordered them to the side. The picketers obeyed, whereupon the police assaulted some of the picketers. IWA organizer Landon Ladd reported: "The police then marched between them (the picketers), turned and bore down on the men, swinging clubs in brutal fashion..."

The strike had come to a crisis—a test for Labour across Canada. The Montreal Labour Council, CLC and Hamilton Stelco Local 1005 of the USWA proposed the CLC call an emergency national conference of the trade union movement. The CLC executive council did not act on these proposals. What it did was to dispatch a strong protest to the International Labour Organization against Premier Smallwood's decertification bill, and to ask Minister of Justice Davie Fulton to ensure that Royal Assent be denied to the bill once adopted. Also it sponsored a strike fund which raised about three-quarters of a million dollars for the loggers.

This strike was lost. However, the IWA continued its efforts to reorganize, while Newfoundland trade unionists, led by the Newfoundland Federation of Labour (CLC), fought Smallwood's legislation. Tragically, horizons were clouded by the "raiding" activities of the United Brotherhood of Carpenters and Joiners of America (AFL-CIO-CLC).

B.C. Strike Movement, 1959:

Just as this strike in Canada's easternmost province passed its high point, a new round of struggles began in the west, in British Columbia. It involved provincial government employees, hard rock miners,

marine engineers, longshoremen, bridge workers, fishermen, loggers—
a sizeable portion of organized labour in that province. The struggle
was fought in the setting of a province whose economy was largely
dominated by powerful corporations, some U.S.-controlled, and whose
government, headed by Social Credit Premier Bennett was unfriendly
to Labour.

The movement began in the spring—a peaceful settlement won by
the International Union of Mine, Mill and Smelter Workers in negotiations with one of B.C.'s major companies, the Consolidated Mining
and Smelting Company at Trail. One term provided for pension
vesting—an advance notable for the times.

Then came the strike of the B.C. government employees—described
in a later page. Meanwhile, the provincial government had brought in
Bill 43. This was anti-labour legislation which facilitated injunctions
against picketing.

By the summer of 1959, the B.C. strike wave was at its height. Two
major disputes involved the National Association of Marine Engineers
of Canada, Inc. (CLC) and the International Association of Bridge,
Structural and Ornamental Iron Workers (CLC). The NAME strike
was short—from June 26 to July 16, but packed with action. The employers—Northland Navigation Company—secured an injunction for-
bidding picketing by the union and curbing sympathetic picketing by
members of other unions. The picket lines were then replaced by
columns of "observers"—mostly members of other unions in Vancouver.
They said they were not picketers—this was banned by the injunction
—but a 24-hour "presence" of Labour. They carried no signs, just
walked up and down, like the Greeks of old, and meditated. This came
to be called the "Northland Formula". The strike ended with a victory
for the union.

During the Bridge strike this same problem—injunctions—was encountered. This strike was conducted by Vancouver Local 197 of the
BSIW. After the strike began, in June 1959, Supreme Court Justice
Manson issued an injunction. Under its terms the judge, basing himself on the 1959 B.C. Trade Union Act (Bill 43)—ordered the strikers
to return to their jobs on the Second Narrows Bridge. However the
union continued to strike and subsequently it won. It also won some
important court battles.

The 1959 B.C. strike movement was rounded out by the loggers and
fishermen's strikes. In terms of time lost, the former strike, conducted
by the International Woodworkers of America (CLC) was one of the
major strikes of the postwar years. It lasted from July to September,

involved 30,000 loggers working for 134 companies, and ended after 66 days with a settlement providing for a 10 cents wage increase in 1959 and a further 10 cents increase in 1960.

The Fishermen's strike began in the latter part of July, while the loggers were still on strike. Led by the United Fishermen and Allied Workers Union, it was a short, swift and effective strike and was marked by united action between the UFAWU and other unions in the B.C. fishing industry.

So much for the B.C. strike movement. It was a struggle on two fronts: economic conditions and trade union rights (the struggle against injunctions). The struggle reflected rising militancy among B.C. trade unionists. So did the demand for the 7-hour day adopted that year by the annual convention of the B.C. Federation of Labour (CLC). Also there was a widespread feeling that the labour movement should conduct a general strike against Bill 43. A special convention of the B.C. Federation of Labour met to consider action. The convention decided to fight injunctions and Bill 43. But the leadership of the B.C. Federation of Labour did not recommend a general strike and the convention did not adopt this measure.

In all, the result of the B.C. strike movement was partial victory—victory in specific strikes, but no victory down the line.

Government Employees, 1959:

We turn now to major struggles of government employees in 1959. That year 12,000 B.C. provincial government employees went on strike. To begin with, their union, the British Columbia Employee's Association (CLC) demanded higher wages. However, the B.C. provincial government's opposition to bargaining rights for provincial public servants brought to the fore a further issue—the civil servants' rights to organize and strike. When the union set up its picket lines at the government buildings, the government demanded and secured an injunction. When he granted the injunction, Justice J. A. Ratten said:

"Picketing of government buildings would amount to a virtual blockade. The overall purpose was nothing less than the complete control of the movement of persons and supplies to and from the government buildings."

The union replied:

"There is a point here as to whether the law of the land is to apply equally to government employees. Either we have the legal right to strike and to picket like any other union organization in Canada or we haven't."

In these circumstances, confronted by these obstacles, the union decided to end the strike.

Then came the dispute between Dominion civil servants and the federal government. The issue was the government's refusal to grant the wage increases demanded. The civil servants set up a national joint action committee representing a combined membership of 150,000. Some postal workers' organizations—they were among the most active in the situation—proposed a strike vote. A Vancouver branch of the postal workers even suggested a 1-day stoppage during Christmas. However the general committee rejected these proposals. Also, one of the civil service organizations representing higher paid technicians and scientists withdrew from the general committee. The following year (1960) the government granted an increase but much less than the original demand.

CHAPTER 19

LABOUR AND QUEBEC
1947-1959

1. STATISTICS. A SERIES OF INTENSIVE STRUGGLES:

Organized Labour's battle in Quebec in the period under review was part of its battle across Canada, but was also fused with the struggle for the economic, social and political liberty of Quebec — a free Quebec in a free, united Canada. In turn, given that identity with this latter cause is a vital part of Canadian Labour's total struggle, it follows that close attention should be given to the general progress of the trade union movement in Quebec in the sphere of organization, collective bargaining and social legislation—and in that context, to momentous struggles at Lachute, Asbestos, Louiseville, Arvida and Murdochville. Here again, strike statistics can serve as an indicator.

TABLE 1
QUEBEC, TOTAL STRIKES; 1946-1959[1]

Year	Total Strikes	Number Involved	Man Days Lost
1946	42	15,913	430,267
1947	51	20,070	236,733
1948	31	8,652	233,316
1949	23	8,306	531,857
1950	32	8,185	97,309
1951	39	7,806	196,686
1952	40	17,514	853,936
1953	20	10,482	377,385
1954	34	14,275	383,599
1955	30	7,483	186,225
1956	46	19,190	334,365
1957	40	14,047	725,401
1958	28	8,834	200,170
1959	38	8,191	210,080

TABLE 2

72 SELECTED STRIKES, QUEBEC, 1946-1959[2]

Year	Strike	Industry	Place	No. Involved	Duration In Days
1946	Brewery	Beverage	Montreal	700	54
	Asbestos	Mining	Thetford	625	7
	Dominion Textile	Textile	Montreal Valleyfield	5,253	99
	Canadian Tube	Metal products	Montreal	850	24
	Gold and Copper	Mining	Noranda	913	38
1947	Gold and Copper	Mining	Noranda	650	40
	Ladies' handbag, etc.	Leather	Montreal	1,800	69
	Ayers	Textile	Lachute	683	152
	Dominion Textile	Textile	Montmorency, Drummondville, etc.	6,020	8
	Dominion Shuttle	Textile	Lachute	530	132*
	Plumbers	Construction	Montreal	1,200	9
	Public Works	Construction	Montreal	2,400	1
1948	Hosiery	Textile	Drummondville	400	45
	Clothing	Clothing	Granby, Roxton Pond	290	63
	Hosiery	Textile	Sherbrooke	97	
	Textile	Textile	St. Johns	400	168
	Woollen	Textile	Sherbrooke	454	77
	Furniture	Woodwork.	Arthabaska, Beauharnois, etc.	1,150	116
1949	Asbestos	Mining	Black Lake, Thetford Mines	4,650	140
	Seamen	Maritime	Canada	1,500	208
1950	Regent Knit	Knitting	St. Jérôme	• 504	59
	Dom. Wire & Cable	Metal prod.	Lachine	164	90
	Steel	Metal prod.	Montreal	1,000	36
	Municipal Transport	Transportation	Montreal	2,900	1
1951	Singer Sewing	Machine	St. John	2,400	88
	Aluminum	Metal prod.	Shawinigan	950	44
	Imperial Tobacco	Tobacco	Granby, Montreal		41

Year	Strike	Industry	Place	No. Involved	Duration In Days
1952	Can. Copper Refinery	Metal refining	Montreal	500	166
	Associated Textile	Textile	Louiseville	702	321
	Rubin Bros.	Clothing	Sherbrooke	210	169
	Dominion Textile	Textile	Montreal, Valleyfield	5,868	95
	Grover Knit	Clothing	Montreal	490	230
	Ilmenite	Smelting	Sorel	374	58
	Warden-King	Metal prod.	Montreal	600	66
	Davie Bros.	Shipbuilding	Lauzon	1,850	57
	Vickers	Shipbuilding	Montreal	1,537	70
	Simmons Bed	Furniture	Montreal	380	119
	Dupuis Fr.	Retail	Montreal	1,035	88
1953	Gold and Copper	Mining	Noranda	1,600	171
	Gold and Copper	Mining	Noranda	572	135
	Copper	Mining	Noranda	425	121
	Copper	Mining	Noranda	347	114
	Hosiery	Textile	Montreal	490	195
	Municipal Transport	Transportation	Montreal	5,000	1
1954	Dominion Engineering	Machine	Lachine	950	22
	Dominion Bridge	Steel	Lachine, etc.	1,132	47
	Dominion Oilcloth	Linoleum	Farnham, Montreal	1,358	84
	Plumbers	Construction	Montreal	4,000	55
1955	Knitted goods	Textile	St. Hyacinthe	417	125
	Pulp and Paper	Pulp and paper	Shawinigan	799	101
	Teamsters	Transport	Montreal	1,500	20
1956	Dominion Textile	Textile	Sherbrooke	888	17
	Dominion Textile	Textile	Drummondville, etc.	1,320	44
	Cotton	Textile	Montmagny	453	97
	Grover Knitting	Textile	St. Jérôme	642	103
	Pulp and Paper	Pulp and paper	Jonquière, etc.	1,600	7

Year	Strike	Industry	Place	No. Involved	Duration In Days
	Shipyard Electricians	Shipbuilding	Sorel	1,500	2
	& Helpers Stevedores	Construction	Montreal	1,650	1
	Office clerks	Longshore	Port Alfred	866	34
1957	Plumbers	Construction	Montreal	1,200	7
	Atlas Construction Co.	Construction	Baie Comeau	850	34
	Perini, McNamara & Quemont	Construction	Chutes des Passes	1,200	2
	Gaspé Copper	Mining	Murdochville	964	215
	Aluminium	Metal prod.	Arvida	6,199	122
	Fur Dressers	Fur	Montreal	750	4
1958	Millinery	—	Montreal	2,000	10
	Hyde Park Clothes	Clothing	Montreal	278	167
	Davie Bros.	Shipbuilding	Lauzon	2,135	62
1959	C.B.C.	Broadcasting Television	Montreal	2,150	69
	Catelli	Food Process	Montreal	455	32
	Fry-Cadbury	Food Process	Montreal	605	62
	Dominion Textile	Textile	Magog, etc.	1,825	140

2. LACHUTE AND ASBESTOS. 1947, 1949.

Lachute, 1947:

In 1947, there were many strikes in Quebec — rubber workers at Chambly*, Dominion Textile workers in the Eastern Townships, wood workers at Montreal, woollen workers at Lachute.

The Lachute strike involved only 700 workers, but was important. The Ayers woollen mills at Lachute was then owned by the Ayers family which had traditionally been a dominating force in the economy of that district. The medieval character of conditions in the mill was indicated by the pay envelope of one woman worker—108 hours for $11.17. The woollen workers organized in the Canadian District of the United Textile Workers of America (AFL-TLC), and opened negotiations with the company. When the company offered only

* United Rubber, Cork, Linoleum and Plastic Workers of America (CCCL).

trifling wage increases, the union went on strike. At once Premier Duplessis said the strike was illegal since there had been no arbitration. Union leader R. K. Rowley replied: "The right to strike is a fundamental right. Slavery does not exist in the province of Quebec." The union's lawyer, the late Jacques Perrault—a pioneer precursor of the "Quiet Revolution"—argued in the courts that the clause in the Quebec Labour Relations Act which banned strikes until conciliation was completed was unconstitutional, since to work or abstain from work is a natural right. Meanwhile the Quebec Labour Relations Board decertified the union. This was the train of events leading to Friday, May 2. Early that morning, 150 provincial police burst into the little town whose population numbered scarce a few thousand. A column of strike breakers formed and marched to the mill. In its ranks were provincial police clad in civilian clothes, and company officials. Awaiting them at the mill gates were more provincial police. The police descended on the picketers who numbered about 100, struck out savagely with their clubs, and arrested about 40 union members including the strike organizer, Madeleine Parent. In police hands, the arrested union members were treated like prisoners of war—some were offered liberty if they would sign statements implicating the union leadership in "seditious conspiracy". Lachute took on the air of an occupied town, with provincial police patrolling the streets, intimidating women and children, visiting workers' homes and telling them they must return to work. The strikers did not submit. "The strike goes on!" they said. The strike did go on, though Duplessis intensified the terror, ordered the repeated arrest of strikers, and the strike leaders, R. Kent Rowley and Madeleine Parent. John L. Lewis once said: "Troops don't mine coal!" In Lachute provincial police clubs did not weave woollen blankets. The strike went on to become one of Canada's longest—five months. It spread to the nearby Dominion Shuttle Plant, also owned by the Ayers family.*

The Lachute strikers were defeated. The Union terminated the struggle with no contract won. But, meanwhile, at Ayers, the company which had refused more than 4 cents per hour increase during negotiations had increased rates by 20 − 30 cents per hour — thus doing against the union what it would not do with the union. Later, 2 union organizers, Madeleine Parent and Azélus Beaucage were put on trial for "seditious conspiracy". They were defended by a team of lawyers—the late Jacques Perrault, Roger Ouimet—today (1967) Judge Ouimet—and Bernard Mergler. The organizers were found guilty and

* Dominion Shuttle employees sometimes called their plant "the cripples' hospital" because some had lost their fingers tending the machines.

sentenced to two years in jail. Then bad luck struck Duplessis. The court clerk died. For technical reasons a new trial became necessary, but Duplessis never ordered it—fearing perhaps a new upsurge of public opinion. So Madeleine Parent did not go to jail; yet for years later, workers in Quebec and across Canada were surprised when they saw her free—such was the shock and dismay engendered by the Duplessis terror then visited on the organized workers' movement in Quebec.

All in all, this strike was a milestone on the Quebec workers' road to higher wages and union recognition. It exposed the growing gap between the people of Quebec and the Duplessis provincial government.

Asbestos, 1949:

On Sunday, February 13, 1949, asbestos miners gathered at a union meeting at the town of Asbestos, were informed that the companies, principal among which was the giant U.S. corporation Johns-Manville, had rejected their demands for higher wages and improved safety and sanitary conditions in the mines. The CCCL leaders also informed them they could have recourse to arbitration; but their mood brooked no delay and from their ranks came the cry: "Strike, strike!" At 12:01 a.m., Monday, February 14, the strike began. Duplessis reacted at once. He sent in 100 provincial police. For its part the company secured an injunction against the union* and sued it in the courts for half a million dollars. The strikers refused to yield. Their strike became a siege lasting through February, March and April of 1949.

Then came May 5. The time had come to break the strike, so the companies believed. Early that morning, automobiles filled with strike-breakers were approaching the town of Asbestos from several points, but as these automobiles arrived at key intersections they were halted by union picketers. In the town of Asbestos, pickets took up their posts at the entrance to Johns-Manville. At 7:50 a.m. a procession of several hundred union supporters, mostly women, marched by the company gates reciting the Rosary. About 5 minutes later, as several strikers were slowly approaching the company gates, provincial police —who had gathered meanwhile on the roof of the company premises and were armed with machine guns, revolvers and tear gas bombs— let loose some of their tear gas bombs. Later that day there was another incident on the highway leading to Asbestos. A carload of police was blocked, and then a shot was fired. The police got out of their car, and the car was sent to the bottom of a 10-foot ravine.

* National Federation of Mining Industry Employees, Inc. (CCCL).

Meanwhile, the provincial police authorities were bringing considerable pressure to bear on the union leadership. The strike leaders were informed that 500 provincial police had massed at Sherbrooke. Provincial Police director Hilaire Beauregard stated that the Riot Act would be read the next day. Despite all this, the picketers refused to abandon their posts on the highway. Finally they were convened to the union hall and after much shaking of heads, they agreed to stop their picketing and go home*.

The union's intention in withdrawing the picketers had been to avert bloodshed and violence. However, the provincial police chose to use that decision for their own ends. Soon after, provincial police burst into the town of Asbestos, visited reprisals on such union members as they could lay their hands on, crashed into the premises of a church and, encountering there some young union members from Thetford Mines, they beat them savagely. Then came the reading of the Riot Act and the arrest of 125 strikers and townspeople. Some of those arrested were taken to company quarters and there interrogated, Duplessis-style—they were given savage beatings.

The heroic struggle being conducted by the Asbestos miners, and along with this, the vicious reprisals being visited on them by the provincial government, combined to stir up public opinion in the province. At a joint conference of the three union centres in the province there were suggestions for a general strike. Also, important leaders in the Roman Catholic church took a stand. On Sunday May 2, within the venerable stone walls of Notre Dame Cathedral of Montreal, the Archbishop of Montreal, Monsignor Joseph Charbonneau preached a historic sermon in which he said:

"The working class is the victim of a conspiracy which seeks its destruction and when there is a conspiracy to crush the working class it is the duty of the Church to intervene... We want social peace but we don't want the crushing of the working class. We are attached to man more than to capital. That's why the clergy has decided to intervene. It wants to have justice and charity respected and desires that there shall cease to be a situation where more attention is paid to money interests than to the human element."[3]

Two weeks later Philippe Desranleau, beloved Archbishop of Sherbrooke sent a letter to his parishioners appealing that they support the strikers: "Like Jesus my pity is with the throng and with all my soul as a Bishop I support the Asbestos workers in their just demands."[4]

* It is said that the union's chaplain (aumonier) Abbé Camirand, was the man who convinced the picketers to go home. Ironically during those crisis days, it was reported that Camirand was in danger of arrest.

Then the Bishops sponsored their famed "quête" or collection at the Church doors on behalf of the strikers' children.

Archbishop Charbonneau's action was historic. Given that the Church sprang from working people in the first place, from slaves and oppressed, its positive attitude could have been taken for granted. But, in fact, it excited widespread comment as something unusual. Duplessis was furious, and initiated measures to get Charbonneau dismissed, including the despatch of Minister of Labour, Antonio Barrette to Rome. "No one ever denied," said Abbé Gérard Dion some years later, "that Duplessis sent an emissary to Rome to obtain withdrawal of support from the strikers by the ecclesiastical authorities." Not long after the strike, it was announced that Charbonneau had submitted his resignation. He was sent to a retreat in B.C., and there died some years later.

Meanwhile, after much hardship, the asbestos miners emerged victorious from their strike. That meant consolidation of a strong union base in the Thetford Mines - Asbestos district; a victory for the trade union movement of Quebec in general, and more particularly for the Canadian and Catholic Confederation of Labour, also a strengthening of the militant trend within this organization. The victory also influenced other social strata such as the middle classes in the province. This was the period when French Canadian newspapers such as Montreal's *Le Devoir* and *La Presse* heightened their recognition of the aspirations of Labour. Some years later, Professor Jean-Charles Falardeau of Laval University, Quebec City, was to state that this strike "exploded social structures". The Asbestos strike was a major moment in the progessive evolution of the workers of Quebec and their trade union movement.

3. TRAGIC YEARS, 1952-1954.

1952 Strike Movement; The Problem of Unity; Bills 19 and 20:

After the Asbestos strike of 1949, the next high point was 1952; a sweeping strike movement of 17,524 workers—in CCCL, CCL and TLC and Independent unions. Major strikes were fought at Dominion Textiles, Montreal and Valleyfield, Associated Textiles, Louiseville (this extended into 1953); at Dupuis Frères' Department Store, Warden-King, Vickers, Simmons Bed, Canadian Copper Refineries, Grover Knit—all companies located in Montreal.

The movement began with the Montreal-Valleyfield textile strike (See page 291). It ended with the textile strike at Louiseville. The

Louiseville strike was a marathon battle—another unquiet prelude to the "quiet revolution" of the 1960s. On March 2, the workers at Associated Textiles in Louiseville, angered by their company's duplicity in negotiations, went on strike. Once again Premier Duplessis intervened with hostile intent, sent in provincial police, and ordered the arrest of strikers. Through the weary months of spring, summer and autumn, 1952, the textile workers—organized in the National Federation of Textiles, CCCL—faced the picket line. Then came November 11. The strikers had organized a parade. But on the roof of the Company's premises were provincial police, armed with clubs, fire arms and tear gas bombs. They injured some strikers, then rushed to the union office, and one or more of them fired their revolvers at the strikers and wounded one striker. Indignant, CCCL members at Shawinigan and other centres called for a general strike. In December 1952, a CCCL emergency conference at Quebec City decided on "the principle of a general strike which shall take place with the least possible delay"—the first general strike threat confronting Canada since 1919. Duplessis stepped up his intimidation and said he would destroy the CCCL. Given the general situation in Quebec, and more particularly in the labour movement, the CCCL cancelled the strike decision.

This was the 1952 strike movement. Average duration of major strikes fought was about 130 days. In practically every strike the right to organize was a major issue, because of company refusal to negotiate, unfair decisions of the Quebec Labour Relations Board, or mass arrests. In practically every strike the workers fought courageously. Yet most strikes were defeated. Why? Plainly there was the basic obstacle of hostile companies, and hostile provincial government aligned with these companies. But connected with this there was a further decisive obstacle—the lack of solidarity and co-ordination. For instance, when the CCCL decided on a general strike many TLC and CCL members sympathized and wanted common action. But the larger part of Quebec's organized workers were members of the Quebec Federation of Labour (TLC) and the Canadian Congress of Labour, and neither of these centres assured the CCCL of effective support if it went through with the strike. Again, there was the situation prevailing in the spring-time of 1952 at Dominion Textiles. The employees were grouped in 2 unions—about 6,000 in the National Federation of Textile Workers (CCCL), about 6,000 in the Canadian Textile Council (TLC, later Independent). Had the company been confronted by a united front of its 12,000 employees, it might have cancelled its "bonus incentive" (speed-up) plan, a strike might have been averted; or, alternatively, had the company refused to back down then a strike could have been fought with greater prospect of success. However, serious efforts made to implement united action prior to the strike did not succeed. Again, in the east end of Montreal, practically within walking distance of each other, were 3 strike-bound plants, Vickers (National Metal Trades Federation, CCCL); Canadian Copper Refineries (Oil Workers International Union, CCL); and Warden-King (United Electrical, Radio and Machine Workers of America, Ind.). Here too united action would have helped. But efforts to implement it met only with partial, inadequate success. The UE and Oil Workers' strikes were lost. The NMTF strike at Vickers was partly won, but was followed by several years of running battles with the company, with another strike in 1958, and the union's position consolidated only by the end of the decade.

Then the tragic climax at Louiseville. With one strike after another defeated, with the trade union movement not united in action, was it surprising that Premier Duplessis felt emboldened now to turn his wrath on the Louiseville strikers, to slander CCCL textile leaders as "anarchists and revolutionaries", and brand the Montreal *Le Devoir* as a "Bolshevik organ"?

Worse still, confusion was piled on confusion, and disunity on disunity. Just at this time, — while strikers were being shot and jailed, and their families going hungry — the mass expulsions and dismissals of staff — described in a preceding chapter — were going on in the Trades and Labour Congress and Canadian Congress of Labour. The merit of these actions is not under consideration here. However, they affected Quebec much more than any other province. For example, in the electrical industry, the UE with more than 10,000 members in Quebec was all but eliminated. At the large RCA Victor plant in the St-Henri district of Montreal, the company dismissed a dozen UE chief stewards, the Quebec Labour Relations Board cancelled the union's certificate, and later the company signed a contract with the International United Electrical Workers of America, (CCL). At the Warden-King plant, when UE went on strike, first the International Brotherhood of Electrical Workers (AFL-TLC), then the United Steel Workers of America (CCL-CIO) tried to organize the workers into their own ranks. UE's strike was broken. Later the company signed a contract with the United Steel Workers of America.

Bitterly, UE and other unions likewise affected charged that all these actions were being conducted in collusion with companies, provincial police and the provincial government; that in no major case had the workers affected been given the chance to vote on what union they wanted for their bargaining agent. For their part, the TLC and CCL leaders explained that these actions were a necessary part of their program of providing responsible leadership for the workers of Quebec along the lines decided by the parent centres at Ottawa and the United States. They said that in the long run the changes would prove beneficial to Labour.

This then is how the problem of labour solidarity posed itself in 1952. Combined with other adverse circumstances—hostile companies and a hostile government, it produced the defeats engendered that year. And that was the tragedy of 1952, heroic working class struggle —and defeats.

Then came the next inevitable step,—Bills 19 and 20,—late in 1953. They were a Quebec variant of the U.S. Taft-Hartley laws. Minister of Labour Antonio Barrette called them "the logical follow-up of the Padlock Law". Bill 19 banned certification of a local union whose officers were communist. Bill 20 said that if a union in public utilities or the public service went on strike, threatened to strike or talked about strike, it would be decertified.

In a move to defeat the legislation, the CCL and CCCL decided on a "march" to Quebec City. But once again labour disunity queered the pitch. In the Quebec Provincial Federation of Labour (TLC) some supported the march and took part in it, but the leadership said it would not join the "cartel" against Bills 19 and 20, or join the "march". When Claude Jodoin, president of the Montreal Trades and Labour Council (TLC) was asked for his views on Bills 19 and 20, he replied: "No comment!" On January 19, 1954, so the Montreal *Star* reported, there was a closed meeting between QPLF—TLC* officials and the Cabinet—represented by Premier Duplessis and Minister of Labour, Antonio Barrette. At this meeting, the union officers advanced a compromise proposal that proceedings under Bills 19 and 20 be taken through the Quebec Labour Relations Board and carried through by that body rather than by the Attorney-General (Duplessis)**. On the eve of the "march on Quebec",— Feb. 2, 1954 — QPFL president Roger Provost told the *Star* the QPFL "would not take part in any joint labour protest to which the CCCL was a party." A few days later the bills were adopted; and Duplessis publicly thanked Provost and his fellow-officers for what, so the Premier felt, was their co-operative attitude.

---

* Quebec Provincial Federation of Labour (TLC); Montreal Trades and Labour Council (TLC).
**The CCCL-CCL were demanding total withdrawal of bills 19 and 20.

In sum then, 1952-1954 were tragic years for Organized Labour. However, good work was being done: In the Quebec Federation of Labour (TLC) wing of the movement, for instance, there was the success of the Tobacco Workers' International Union in winning wage gains and other concessions, in its important strike against the Imperial Tobacco Company in 1951. In the Canadian and Catholic Confederation of Labour wing of the movement, there were struggles at Louiseville and other centres. And even when trade unionists were defeated, as often happened, still their fighting stand was helping lay the groundwork for a happier phase to come in the life of the province, in the 1960s.

4.   1955-1959: A NEW ROUND OF STRUGGLES.

Arvida, Murdochville, Catholic School Teachers, CBC:

The struggles of 1947-1954 had exposed the gulf between Quebec workers seeking better conditions and English-Canadian-U.S. corporations — corporations dominating Quebec's economy, and supported by the provincial government, and usually by newspapers like the *Montreal Star* and *The Gazette*. This deep-going conflict was reflected in the Arvida strike of aluminum workers and the Murdochville strike of copper miners of 1957. The Arvida strike, like the GM strike of 1955 (see page 309) demonstrated Organized Labour's rising economic strenghth. It involved 6,500 employees of the Aluminum Company of Canada at Arvida and other centres, and was led by the National Metal Trades Federation (CCCL). After 122 days, it ended with a settlement providing a wage increase spread over three years not far removed from the union's original 47 cents per hour demand. Also there was now to be what was virtually a master agreement for all Alcan plants in Quebec.

The Murdochville strike, led by the United Steel Workers of America (CCCL) was another battle which moved events forward. The struggle began when employees at Gaspé Copper Mines, a Noranda subsidiary, organized in the United Steel Workers of America (CLC) and applied to the Quebec Labour Relations Board for certification. The company then petitioned the Superior Court for a writ of prohibition to halt Board proceedings in this case. The company's grounds was that it was the victim of a "secret and intangible conspiracy". With this matter before the courts, but without any court decision, the Labour Relations Board now halted its proceedings on the USWA's application. That meant the union could not call a "legal" strike. The next move came from the company, It dismissed the local union president Théo Gagné. Sooner than see their union smashed, the 1,100 copper miners went on strike. Then the provincial government moved in — provincial police were sent to Murdochville. In the courts the company initiated actions against the union.

A turning point was the incident of August 19. 400 Canadian Labour Congress and Canadian and Catholic Confederation of Labour delegates, including Claude Jodoin, had come to Murdochville to picket in solidarity with the strikers. They were beset and stoned by a gang of thugs and strike-breakers including German immigrants brought in by the company to replace the French-Canadian strikers. From a ridge above the scene of picketing, this gang hurled stones and other missiles on the picketers. Meanwhile the Quebec Provincial Police stood by doing little or nothing; but not long after they went to the USWA organizers — not to offer protection, but to suggest they leave town!

Then came a further development. The courts rejected the company's petition for a halt to board proceedings. Somewhat later the union terminated the strike—without a contract. The Labour Board now acted on the USWA's application for certification; its decision—certification denied; somewhat later another decision—certification of a company association. Thus the circle of bafflement was completed—for the time being.

During the period under review, professional workers were beginning to conduct important struggles. In 1949 the *Alliance des Instituteurs Catholiques* (Catholic Teachers Alliance) went on strike at Montreal. Wages was the main issue. In some working class districts, the students helped teachers picket the schools. The fourth day of the strike, the Labour Board decertified the union. The unio then ended the strike.

Then began a protracted struggle by the AIC. It defended its merbership's economic conditions and went on functioning as a solid organization in a situation where it had no certificate, no contract, and where a company association had been recognized by the Montreal Catholic School Commission. Also, the AIC instituted court proceedings aimed at cancelling the Labour Board's decertification.

Forward and backward went the cycle of victory and defeat as one court reversed the decision of the other. Finally, in 1953, the Supreme Court of Canada quashed the Labour Board's decertification; and in 1957 the Quebec Superior Court nullified the Board's certification of the company association. Thereafter the company association merged with the AIC — a constructive development. Tragically, in the merger, AIC president Léon Guindon was removed from leadership — he had been the brilliant, modest general of the AIC's 10-year battle. Still, there was the result: a contract at last between the AIC and the Catholic School Commission.

We turn now to the CBC strike. In its variety of aspects: a government-owned corporation; a major public service; a combination of "mental" and "manual" workers; a complex internal union situation; a militant struggle with new developments in tactics; a labour force predominantly French-Canadian and a management predominantly English-Canadian; a management which combined employer arrogance with bureaucracy but had the saving grace of downright confusion — in all these ways, the Montreal CBC strike of 1959 was higly significant.

The beginning was simple. At 4:40 p.m., December 29, 1959, 74 producers* went on strike after the management refused to recognize their organization, the Producers' Union. The next day, most of the Montreal CBC workers joined the strike. They were members of the host of unions there, including ARTEC, NABET and IATSE.** Management ordered the employees back to work, but largely to no avail. The government refused to interfere on the grounds that the CBC was a Crown corporation which set its own policy. The battle was now joined. The situation was complicated when Hugh Sedgewick, senior Canadian official of IATSE told the Montreal membership to return to work. He said this was on instructions from New York headquarters. For the most part, the IATSE members did not comply with this order. The situation was complicated further by Montreal police action. This was still the pre-quiet revolution Quebec, when police often clamped down on labour actions. During one demonstration before the CBC building on Dorchester Street West the police arrested 29 strikers and strike sympathizers. Then Montreal police chief Langlois told the press "machine guns" might have been necessary if the dancers, actors and artists who participated in this demonstration had entered the CBC building. Langlois' statement excited from Montreal *Le Devoir* the comment: "This is a case for the clinic."

December 1959 had passed into January 1960, January into February, and February into March. Still no settlement. Then came 6

---

* Producers are TV workers whose task is to co-ordinate a production or section of a production.
** The Association of Radio and Television Employees of Canada (Ind.); National Assoication of Broadcast Employees and Technicians (AFL-CIO-CLC); International Alliance of Theatrical Stage Employees and Moving Picture Machine Operators of the United States and Canada (AFL-CIO-CLC).

climactic days: March 2-7. On March 2 the strikers held a large demonstration in front of the CBC building. On March 6 there was a mass picket of over a thousand. Also, Montreal CBC executives* said they would resign if the strike continued. Finally, after 68 days, the strike ended. The key point in the settlement was a management pledge to recognize the Producers' Union.

Here was a strike reflecting the rising struggle of Quebec professional workers, and the fusion of this struggle with Labour and Quebec. From the ranks of the strikers came talented leaders like Jean Duceppe of the Actors' Union, and René Lévesque, later Minister of Natural Resources in the Liberal provincial government. The strike was well conducted, with rousing meetings, sometimes daily, at the Canadian Legion Hall on Mountain Street and the Orpheum Theatre on Ste. Catherine Street West where strikers gathered and listened intently as leaders boomed forth labour aspirations. From the public there was much support. Once again, as at Lachute, Asbestos, Louiseville, Arvida, Murdochville — Labour's unquiet struggle was helping la ythe foundation for a better Quebec to be. In much the same way, through 133 years of its history, 1827-1959, Canadian Labour's unquiet struggle had helped lay the foundation for a better Canada to be.

---

* Executives are senior CBC staff members in charge of production.

CHAPTER 20

CANADIAN UNIONISM

CANADA'S labour history has been marked by a continuing fight for a sovereign trade union movement. How stands that fight today? The answer of the Canadian Labour Congress leadership is simple. They say the fight is just about won. In support of this contention they point to the Congress itself, which, they insist, is a sovereign centre. But against this cherubic outlook stand two massive facts. First, Canada's unions are mostly international unions, and it is they who are the main components of the Congress. Second, the Congress was founded during the Cold War when the bases of Canadian unionism in the chemical, textile, lumber, and other industries had been destroyed. It was founded, not as the product of the fight for Canadian autonomy, which reached a high point in the TLC Victoria convention of 1948, but as a sequel to the defeat and betrayal of that cause. Moreover, not content with the practical domination they had established, the international unions wrote that domination into the Congress constitution: a clause provides that, where jurisdiction is affected, present affiliates to the Congress, which means mainly the international unions, can vote the affiliation of new bodies. This is a clause which gives US headquarters virtual power of decision on the admission of the CNTU and independent unions like Mine-Mill and United Electrical Workers. Of course, a Congress convention could decide on their admission; yet weighing constantly on the Congress is the threat of dismemberment, the threat that international unions will 'pull out' and organize perhaps a dual centre.[1]

The degree of sovereignty held by the CLC may be debatable, but there are objective standards by which the freedom of Canadian members of international unions can be measured:

1 Constitutional powers: the powers of the Canadian membership under the constitution as compared with powers of international headquarters.

2 Operative powers: the power to strike, control over funds, appointment of

staff in Canada.

3 Canadian organs of control: their efficacy and effectiveness.

4 Violations of Canadian rights: their number and quality.

5 Freedom of action of the Canadian membership: in politics and foreign policy.

We shall deal with each of these in turn.

CONSTITUTIONAL POWERS

The constitutions of international unions grant considerable powers to general officers. These include: approval of collective agreements; discipline of locals; granting or rejection of requests for financial aid; revocation of charters; putting of locals into receivership and seizure of their funds; installing of an international officer to run the local. Given such powers, given that the bulk of the membership is located in the United States, given that Canadians seldom constitute more than 10 per cent of total international membership, it follows that Canadians stand in a relationship of subordination to parent bodies in the US. The point is not that international officers possess powers, for that is inherent in the constitution of any organization; nor is it the type of powers they possess. The point is that these international officers are not subject to membership in Canada, but are subject primarily to membership in the United States. That is to say, the presence of international unions in Canada is in its very nature a denial of Canadian sovereignty, and beyond that it is a denial of something even more precious – sovereignty of the Canadian working class.

It has been suggested that amends can be made for such a situation by inserting in the international constitutions clauses under which certain powers are non-operative in Canada. But for such clauses to have their maximum effect, they would have to provide for the complete right of self-government by the Canadian membership, including the right of seceding from the international union; and in turn, for such rights to be effective, the Canadian membership must have its own organization, its own elected officers, and its own finances. But even in such a situation – the most ideal possible under an international union – and even where there was a dedicated progressive leadership in the United States prepared to do its utmost to uphold the right of the Canadian membership, the element of servitude would remain, for all these Canadian powers would still be subject to the will of people in another country. Therefore, the only sure basis for Canadian self-government in union matters is the sovereign Canadian union, as distinct from the international union. Of course, it is inherent in the very fact of a sovereign Canadian union that it could decide to enter into a relationship with a union in the United States and that it could decide also to terminate that relationship.

So much for the formal rights of the Canadian membership in international unions. In practice, the situation varies from local to local and from union to union. It is determined by such factors as the general level of development of the membership in given situations, their degree of mass participation, the relative weight of progressive and reactionary trends among them. It is determined also by the policies which prevail in the international union. A change takes place in the situation in the United States – a change in leadership, new pressure from courts, Congress, the National Labour Board, the Department of Labour, the President – and the results may soon be felt in Canada. The winds shift in the US, and all too often the House of Labour in Canada gets blown down.

OPERATIVE POWERS

A typical operative power is the power to strike. As of 1958, most Canadian locals of international unions did not have that power, not completely.[2]

Against this, the argument has been advanced – as in the Report of the Royal Commission on Canada's Economic Prospects, 1956 – that 'approval by International Headquarters is typically formal and granted as a matter of course.' That is not true, for there are many cases where approval is not granted – for example, the Halifax building trades strike of 1952. But it is not just that the contention is factually false. It is also intrinsically false. For, if the strike fund is located in the United States, if the power to ratify or vote a strike decision is located in the United States, then approval can scarce be merely 'formal.' The day will never come when the man who has the cash stands in a merely formal relation to the man who needs the cash.

So much for the power to strike. There are other operative powers. They include control over money and appointment of staff. As far as money is concerned, a good part of the union dues goes as per capita to US headquarters and Canadians cannot decide how it will be spent. As far as staff – always a prime lever of US domination – is concerned, the top officials in Canada are appointed and their salaries decided by the American officers. Of course, a chief appointee in Canada may be, and usually is, a Canadian, though sometimes he is an American who has taken up residence in Canada, as in the case of Harold Daoust of the Textile Workers Union of America and H.C. Banks of the Seafarers International Union. But the nationality of the leading union officer in Canada is not the main thing, any more than the nationality of a company executive is the main thing. Decisive is ownership and control. In 1948, at the Victoria Convention of the Trades and Labor Congress, Frank Hall, Canadian representative of the Brotherhood of Railway and Steamship Clerks said, 'I am not responsible to this Congress ... When you leave this Convention, Brothers and delegates, regardless of what disposition is made of this question, I shall still be Vice-President of the Brotherhood of Railroad and

Steamship Clerks.' Hall did not say, but he could have said, that he was also not responsible to his own membership in Canada, for he owed his appointment to international headquarters.

CANADIAN ORGANIZATION:
ITS EXTENT AND CHARACTER

A basic unit of Canadian organization in the international union is the local. It has two sides. It is a Canadian body, but it is a Canadian body connected with a union, most of whose locals are in the United States. Now, for the US locals, an international union can fulfil the function of a general union. Constitutionally, at least, the US locals can determine the policy and leadership of their organization. But that is not the case for the Canadian locals. They are often isolated from each other and so the more dependent on their links with international headquarters. And even when they are grouped in a province-wide or Canada-wide organization, they cannot determine the policies of the international union. So Canadians pay for a general union but don't get it. They are told that through the international unions they get 'big organization,' when in fact they get the opposite – the reinforced tendency to local isolation. A Canadian Auto Workers Union of 60,000 members, a sovereign Canadian Steel Workers Union of 80,000 members, a Canadian Railway Workers Union of 150,000 members, a sovereign Canadian Teamsters Union of 40,000 members – such bodies for Canadian purposes would be so much more powerful than their present international union counterparts, that their sheer coming into being would entail a substantial change in the relation of forces of organized labour and capital in Canada.

With Canadian union feeling rising in recent years, a tendency has developed for a closer knitting of international union locals in Canada. Provincial districts and Canadian districts have been set up. But even where there are such districts, though they serve as levers for expansion of Canadian autonomy, they may also serve as a lever for tightening the grip on Canadian locals, for centralizing US control of Canadian locals behind the facade of Canadian district organization; and in any case, the predominant tendency remains of comparatively isolated locals confronted by the power of the international union. This is particularly true for craft unions like the Plumbers, Carpenters, Electricians, Machinists, and Printing Trades. The problem is illustrated by three events which occurred in the period 1954-1958.

In 1954, when the Bookbinders asked for an elected vice-president, they were told that this would be tantamount to a state body in the United States asking for such a privilege.[3]

In 1955, many United Auto Workers members in Canada were demanding that a Canadian director be elected in Canada instead of at the international convention, where, it was said, Canadian delegates were subject to the pressure of the organization in the United States. That demand was rejected.

In 1956, the BC Provincial Council of the United Brotherhood of Carpenters and Joiners (UBCJ) demanded that a Canada-wide section of the union be established. As of 1964, there was no Canada-wide organization of the Carpenters.

What about the Canadian district? In 1957, of ninety-three international unions, only six had a Canadian district and a Canadian director. That covered about a fifth of the total Canadian membership of international unions. Moreover, where there is a Canadian district, that does not necessarily mean real autonomy. Is that district truly free? Does it have its own national convention of local delegates to decide policy and also leadership? Does it have its own treasury and strike fund? Does it get the bulk of the union dues spent from what stays in the locals? As of 1964, there were scarcely any international unions in Canada which could pass such a test, save a few progressively led international unions – a special and exceptional case to be considered below.

VIOLATIONS OF CANADIAN RIGHTS

What is the record of violations? Between 1950 and 1962, receiverships were clamped on locals, local elections voided, strikes broken or denied assistance, whole unions destroyed – the period is full of these events, involving Carpenters, Teamsters, Plumbers, Bridge and Iron Workers, Textile Workers, and many other unions – all in all, a considerable proportion of trade union membership in Canada.

Here are a few examples:

1950, Chemical Workers. International ICWU headquarters dismisses its Canadian staff and violates the right of its Toronto local at Consumers Gas to appoint its own business agent.

1950, Rubber Workers. International headquarters of URWA dismisses entire Canadian staff.

1951, Lumber and Sawmill Workers, Ontario. International headquarters of UBCJ seizes the treasury of certain locals of this body – one of its affiliates in Canada – and lifts their powers.

1952, Canadian Textile Council. International headquarters of UTWA dismisses the entire Canadian staff of this body, its affiliate in Canada.

1953, Teamsters. International headquarters dismisses the Canadian director, MacArthur, and also Neil MacDonald, business agent-elect of Montreal local 106. It clamps a trusteeship on that local, and somewhat later it imposes trusteeships also on other locals, such as local 938 at Toronto.

1954, Plumbers, Montreal. International officers of the United Association of Plumbers and Steam Fitters negotiate an agreement with certain oil companies against which the members of Montreal local 144 are on strike. They do this behind the backs of the membership, and when the membership wishes to continue the strike, international headquarters denies it strike benefits. All this is a stab in the back, not just to the Montreal local, but to Quebec labour unity, for involved in that strike as well is the Plumbers union of the CNTU.

1956, International Brotherhood of Electrical Workers, BC. International headquarters of IBEW dismiss the business agent of their Vancouver local. They despatch to Canada a phoney board of enquiry into communist tendencies among Canadian members.

1957, International Alliance of Theatrical Stage Employees and Moving Picture Machine Operators of the United States and Canada (IATSE), Toronto. Local union protests infringements of its rights by New York headquarters. Its chief steward at the CBC charges that the local union has 'no say whatsoever in contract negotiations.' It is charged too that $3 dues are being deducted and sent to New York with the local seeing scarcely a dime.

1959, IATSE, Montreal. US interferency by the IATSE reaches the point of strike-breaking during the CBC Montreal strike. Members of that union in Montreal are ordered to remove their picket lines from the CBC. The orders come from a Canadian source – Hugh Sedgewick of Hamilton, IATSE chief representative in Canada – but he said he got them from New York.

1959-60, Plumbers, Montreal. International headquarters strikes at local 144's autonomy once again. It lifts the local's power to hold meetings and conduct business for a period of almost a year.

1960, Bridge, Structural and Iron Workers, Vancouver. International headquarters dismisses the local union's elected officers and cancels its right to conduct its own business.

1960, United Auto Workers. Paul Siren, a UAW organizer in Canada, on the staff of that union practically since its inception in the 1930s, makes so bold as to support for office a candidate for the Canadian vice-presidency running in opposition to George Burt, the candidate supported by the Reuther administration. Not long after, Siren is peremptorily dismissed.

1962, International Union of Electrical Workers. At a convention of Canadian IUEW locals held in Toronto, international president James B. Carey ousts the Canadian IUEW president C. Hutchens and puts the eleven Canadian staff members under his personal control. One delegate protested 'we live in Canada, a democracy!' Another said, 'You can sell that stuff in the US [but] you can't sell it here.' But Carey got away with it.

The list of violations above is far from complete. Nor would a complete and updated list tell the tale; for what must be taken into account also are those further violations initiated by international headquarters in the United States but carried through within Canada by Canadian districts, central councils, provincial federations, and the Canadian Labour Congress.

These violations are but the surface expression of the deeper wrong, as with accidents and crimes. A constant conformism to avert such reprisals – that is the greatest violation of all. Canadian members fear loss of conditions, contracts, certificates, loss of pensions and other accumulated union benefits; they fear disruption and raids from the United States, if they do what they have to do to free themselves. That does not mean they cannot do it; and sometimes not to do it may be worse than to do it. But generally caution and careful preparation are needed, and preferably co-ordination and multiple action.

The number of overt violations of Canadian rights is diminished, not just by fear-induced conformity, but also by non-conformity. For the fight for Canadian rights goes on constantly, with some gains and some losses, some benefits and some sacrifices; every so often US headquarters forces a general flare-up. The result is an equilibrium between Canadian freedom and US domination. But this is not the placid harmony depicted by Claude Jodoin and E.A. Forsey. It is rather the equilibrium of struggle, the battle for Canadian unionism fought but not yet won.

FOREIGN POLICY AND POLITICAL ACTION

Since the Cold War began, there has been an identity of foreign policy between the Canadian Labour Congress (and its antecedent centres) and the AFL-CIO. More recently that identity has diminished, but in broad lines it still persists. Has US domination of Canada's unions played a part in producing this identity? Dr Forsey of the Canadian Labour Congress has said 'No.' He says that the identity is due rather to a coincidence of attitude between the free trade union movements of the United States and Canada. But what coincidence produced the coincidence? And how free is Canada's free trade union movement? What about the eleven years (1947-1962) of reprisals against Canadian union members who challenged the chief tenets of State Department policy? Of course, Jodoin and Forsey are 'free' – free to agree with Washington. But those who disagree are not so free.

Consider now political action. The kind of problem encountered is illustrated by what happened at the 1959 International Convention of the Brotherhood of Railroad and Steamship Clerks. A Canadian local submitted a resolution asking that the constitution be amended to enable locals in Canada to participate in party politics. Speaking in support of that proposal, a BRSC delegate from Winnipeg (Baatable) said that the present constitutional ban on political action should not be 'applicable to Canadian lodges and members.' This the international president, George Harrison, flatly opposed. So did the resolutions committee, and the reason it gave was typically US imperialist. It said the amendment 'would be a violation of [US] state and federal laws.'

It is certain that policies of this kind have slowed down labour political pro-gress in Canada. It is certain that they have played their part in producing the situation which prevailed on the eve of the 1962 federal election, where scarcely a sixth of total union membership in Canada had affiliated with the New Democratic party, although that party had been initiated by the Cana-dian Labour Congress with a membership of over a million; and even where union affiliation had taken place, as in the United Steel Workers of American and the United Auto Workers, opposition of international officers to such a course was bound to bulwark those elements in the Canadian membership who for one reason or another did not want to support the New Democratic party. This was the trade union organizational reality underlying the parlia-mentary electoral reality, and this reality continued to operate in the 1963 federal election, when the number of successful New Democratic party can-didates declined. Here we have an inkling, at least, of what international unionism means to labour's political progress in Canada.

What has the CLC leadership been doing about it? In 1962, the Canadian Labour Congress vice-president, William Dodge, went to the United States to ask those international unions whose constitutions contained bans on political action to free Canadian organizations from these bans. That was a noble mis-sion, but one he could not press to victory because he linked to it a lie, and that lie was contained in his suggestion that these bans represented the last survival of Canadian labour subordination to the United States. But how could that be true when he was there in a foreign country asking foreigners to do for Canadians what Canadians should be able to do for themselves? The out-come was that some international unions lifted the bans, while others did not; and even in the case of those that did, that was not necessarily the final solu-tion, for there are bans which persist in life long after they have been dropped from constitution. Where there is power, where there is control over pay-cheques, a wink and a nod may suffice.[4]

CANADIAN UNIONISM AND PROGRESSIVE UNIONISM

So far we have dealt with international unionism and its relationship to Cana-dian unions. But there is a superior starting point: Canadian unionism – the total trade union movement of Canada. Beyond that, it is the fight to free that movement from servitude to the United States, the fight for a sovereign Canadian movement. An advanced expression of that fight is the completely Canadian union. Examples are the unions of the Confederation of National Trade Unions (CNTU), the Canadian Brotherhood of Railway, Transport and General Workers (CBRT), the National Union of Public Employees (now in-corporated in Canadian Union of Public Employees), the United Fisherman and Allied Workers Union (UFAWU), the Canadian Textile Council's directly chartered locals in the CLC, and CNTU independent locals, such as the Vancouver Outside Workers. In addition, bodies like the Mine-Mill Canada and the UE Canadian Council, though connected with the US, fulfil, at least in some decisive respects, the function of Canadian unions.

The percentage of Canadian-union membership to the total union membership is a decisive index of Canadian labour progress. Its range of variation through the last half-century is shown by the following statistics: in 1911, it stood at 10.8 per cent – a low connected with a decade of hatchet work by international unions on Canadian unions after the 1902 split in the Trades and Labor Congress; in 1935, it stood at 48.8 per cent – nearly half;[5] in 1955, it stood at 29.5 per cent. These figures do not include UE and Mine-Mill. In 1963, the total of members in such unions was 430,137, *including* UE and Mine-Mill, as compared with a total membership of 1,449,181, or 29.6 per cent of the total.

There is Canadian unionism and there is progressive unionism. The two are distinct, but they are also closely connected. The whole history of the movement attests to this. For example, those international unions which provide the greatest degree of autonomy for the Canadian membership tend to be the progressively led international unions. Conversely, those international unions which refuse autonomy tend to be the more reactionary unions. Those unions that are completely Canadian or virtually Canadian – bodies such as the CNTU, the CTC, the UFAWU, the International Union of Mine-Mill and the Smelter Workers, UE, and the CBRT – tend to be more progressive than the average international union. Many of the unions which in 1963 were not in the CLC were Canadian unions, for example those in the CNTU and the CTC; or they were unions fulfilling the functions of Canadian unions, for instance the UE and Mine-Mill; or they were international unions which had fallen out with the AFL-CIO in the US such as the Teamsters.

It might be useful here to summarize the experience of some progressive unions, and take a brief look at one reactionary union.

The UE has been virtually autonomous in Canada ever since it was founded here in the late 1930s. In 1956, this autonomy was given constitutional recognition by the UE international convention. In the late 1950s, the international Longshoremen and Warehousemen's Union took similar action. An example of the most advanced Canadian autonomy within the international unions is that of Mine-Mill. In 1953, its international convention amended the constitution to provide for its existence in Canada as a distinct Canadian entity. Subsequently, Mine-Mill Canada was established, and this was approved by a referendum vote of the Canadian membership. It is noteworthy that all three unions linked these decisions to the struggle for Canadian independence from US imperialism, the common struggle of Canadian and US workers against their common foe, US imperialism.

But more typical is the case of a reactionary international union which took a negative stand to Canadian rights, despite the energetic measures the Canadian membership took to uphold its rights. In the years 1942-52 in Canada, the United Textile Workers of America grew into an organization of 12,000 members grouped in twenty locals in Ontario, Quebec, and the Maritimes. All this work was done by Canadians. The Canadian membership struggled constantly to expand its autonomy. To this end, it set up a Canadian district which held annual conventions, elected Canadian leadership, and had its own treasury and strike fund based on per capita paid direct from the Canadian locals to the Canadian district headquarters. By 1950, a level of autonomy had been attained in the UTWA unsurpassed by any other international union. All this was the work of the Canadian district and its officers. Part of the general pattern then prevailing in the UTWA of Canada were vigorous negotiations, a constant effort to organize the unorganized and improve conditions, hard-fought struggles for trade union rights, and struggles against raiding by the rival Textile Workers Union of America. This pattern of progressivism and Canadian unionism the headquarters of international UTWA resented and feared, and in 1950 it moved to destroy the Canadian district's autonomy. This challenge the Canadian district met by establishing itself as a distinct Canadian organization called the Canadian Textile Council, while it retained its affiliation with the international union. In 1952, when the CTC was locked in battle with the Dominion Textile Company in Quebec in a major strike, international headquarters decided its time had come. It moved in on the Canadian organization and dismissed the entire staff. The CTC response was to sever all connections with the international union, thereby becoming a sovereign Canadian union in the textile industry. The years that followed have brought their toll of company attacks and raids by US unions; but meanwhile, if only on an exceedingly modest scale, the CTC has persisted as an advanced base of progressivism and Canadian unionism in the textile industry.

BIG BUSINESS AND INTERNATIONAL UNIONS

Historically, it is clear that big business has tended to support international unionism where the alternative was a militant Canadian union. There is the evidence of the 1920s and 1930s: the One Big Union versus the international unions; Nova Scotia Coal Miners versus United Mine Workers of America international headquarters. There is the evidence of the 1940s and 1950s; the Canadian Seamans' Union versus the Seafarers' International Union; the Canadian Textile Council versus the United Textile Workers of America and the Textile Workers Union of America; the International Union of Mine, Mill and Smelter Workers versus the United Steelworkers of America. In all these struggles, the companies swung their weight behind the international unions.

Why does big business prefer international unions? One reason is that the companies look to the stand-pat leadership of the average international union to put a curb on the Canadian membership. Consider David Dubinsky, international president of the International Ladies Garment Workers Union: at the 1962 international convention of his union, he charged that peace marchers were, wittingly or otherwise, tools of Moscow. Capitalists in Canada see the point in maintaining connection with a person such as this: they can use reactionary leaders in the United States as a counterweight to the Canadian working class' efforts for peace. Hence at Drummondville, Quebec, in the mid-1950s, the Canadian Celanese Company blocked a CNTU bid at organization, but did not shut the door tight on the United Textile Workers of America.

In a brief submitted to the Royal Commission on Canada's Economic Prospects in 1957, two federal government experts, I. Brecher and S.S. Riesman, stated: 'Headquarters officials sometimes participate directly in Canadian negotiations ... with an observable bias towards moderation and restraint ... To the limited extent that intervention from headquarters has occurred, the influence has characteristically been in a moderating direction. There are good reasons ... The top executive is frequently a well-paid group ... they would quite naturally be expected to have much the same respect for conservatism as can be attributed to any high-income managerial group occupying a position of substantial authority.'

Another reason why big business in Canada may prefer international unions is the physical and organizational distance between the Canadian membership and international headquarters in Chicago, Cleveland, Washington, or New York. This facilitates top-level manoeuvring between management and high-placed union officers behind the backs of the Canadian membership. Here are three examples: In 1946, the president of the Dominion Textile Company, Blair Gordon, wrote a letter to the United Textile Workers of America international headquarters at Washington, in which he asked the Americans to provide a Canadian leadership more to the liking of the company. In 1949, there was a coincidence of activities involving the US State Department, the federal Liberal government, and the executive councils of the American Federation of Labor and Trades and Labor Congress, whose combined result was the expulsion of the Canadian Seamen's Union from the Trades and Labor Congress, the smashing of the strike conducted by the union, and finally the smashing of the union itself. In 1959, the Dominion Bridge Company in British Columbia and the international headquarters of the Bridge, Structural and Iron Workers Union conducted negotiations behind the backs of the union membership then on strike.

It should be remembered, above all, that many of the companies are American and that their parent companies in the United States have already established relations with international unions in the US. Sometimes master agreements are negotiated in the United States and extended, with comparative ease, into Canada.

We have listed above some of the reasons why big business in Canada prefers international unions. The ultimate preference of big business, of course, is no union at all. Hence, when an international union in Canada does get involved in a struggle, big business will not hesitate to fight that union, and in that fight it may turn against the union that very quality which in the first place it found attractive – its international character. This helps explain the recurrent big business cry of 'foreign union.' Two examples in recent years are declarations by N.R. Crump of the CPR and Fox of St Lawrence Paper. Attacks such as these would harness Canadianism to anti-labour purposes. They are attacks in force because they are aimed at a genuine weakness in the labour movement. The way to defeat them is to win the given struggle, whether it be conducted by a Canadian or international union, but beyond that to move as swiftly as possible to a completely Canadian trade union movement.

International unionism is a key link in the system of US domination of Canada. We need only look at the trade union movement and monopoly capital in the United States to see a union movement that has been more class collaborationist, less inclined to fight the foreign and domestic policies of its ruling class, more committed to capitalism than the trade union movement of any other important capitalist country. Monopoly capital in the United States is more powerful than monopoly capital in any other important capitalist country. The result is an abnormally unfavourable balance of forces between capital and labour in the United States as compared with most other developed capitalist countries. This unfavourable balance of forces tends to be transmitted to Canada by the system of international unionism. There is a constant export of labour conservatism to Canada. It has been going on for sixty years. It has played its part in producing in Canada a labour movement of a special kind, one which in some ways is more disunited and more backward than is the labour movement of any other advanced capitalist country: one which correspondingly has failed to grasp the magnificent opportunity presented to it in the 1960s when US imperialism became weaker on a world scale while the movement for Canadian independence became stronger.[6]

The export of labour conservatism manifests itself in various ways, sometimes directly through the international unions themselves, sometimes from the harassing activities of employer and government agencies in the United States. The unions in the United States are under constant pressure from such legislation, as the Taft-Hartley and Landrum-Griffin acts. In terms of practical politics, an international union which did not act to keep its locals in Canada 'clean' would be in the black books of anti-labour circles in the US; and when the US labour leaders are dealing with these anti-labour circles, even when they are trying to fight them, generally it is not the rights of the Canadian membership which stand uppermost; on the contrary, these rights may well be deemed expendable.

Through such chains of connections, international unions become a major link in US economic aggression on Canada. A right-wing clique dominates the US trade union movement, a clique centred in the leadership of the Building Trade unions, the International Ladies' Garment Workers Union, the Brotherhood of Railroad and Steamship Clerks, and several other unions. It is significant that the leaders of these same unions constitute also the hard core of the right-wing in the Canadian Labour Congress. It is also significant that this Canadian clique is most fanatical in its support of US foreign policy, is most vicious in opposing Canadian autonomy and Canadian unionism, is most prone to ride roughshod over the rights of its membership in Canada, is most ready to use the Canadian Labour Congress for its own aims as it used the antecedent centres in the past, and is most ready to threaten the Congress with dismemberment, with the formation of a dual centre when, under pressure from the Canadian membership, the CLC begins to show a bit of opposition to US designs.

In Canada international unionism and class collaborationism through right-wing union leadership form an intermeshed, interacting combination which historically has dominated the trade union movement. This interconnection shows in the arguments used by right-wing labour leaders in Canada to justify international unionism. 'International unions for international business' was the slogan advanced by the executive council of the Canadian Labour Congress in 1960. It said that international unions provided an example of 'good international relations' which had 'paid off.' Just as many companies operating in Canada are American, similar close ties between trade unions members of these countries should be maintained. But what is the so-called international structure of the North American economy, if not a euphemism for US domination of the Canadian economy? And, given that domination, is it not true that the kind of labour movement this country needs is one which is sovereign and not subject to pressure from the base imperialist country?

Not 'international unions for international business' but 'Canadian unions for international business; Canadian unions to combat international business' should be the operative slogan of the Canadian labour movement.[7]

A FIGHT ON TWO FRONTS

It is tragic that during the Cold War years, in the midst of growing US in-roads in Canada, the issue of Canadian unionism was brought more to the fore.

When the matter came up at trade union conventions in the 1950s and early 1960s, often it was for defensive reasons – some new assault by international headquarters, some new chopping of heads, some new barrier to political action, some new challenge to an independent foreign policy for Canada. The issue of Canadian unionism as such has not been recognized enough as a principled question, as a principle, a passion, deeply imbedded in the reality, needs, and aspirations of the workers, one which must find its creative solution. More than ever, the continuation of the rotten system of international unionism in Canada becomes a decisive internal weakness of the organized labour movement, an impediment to its forward progress on the front of conditions, peace, and Canadian independence. Let this be recognized, and it follows that the trade union struggle in Canada cannot be conducted on one front alone but on two fronts. The fight for militancy is inseparable from the fight for Canadian unionism, and vice versa. The fight should be conducted on both fronts, and the danger which constantly assails progressives in Canada – that of intervention from the US – will begin to diminish and their prospects for victory will begin to increase. And, as the fight develops on both fronts, it will become increasingly clear that the system of international unionism in Canada is not just a weak link in the chain of Canadian organized labour, but is also a weak link in the chain of American capitalism and its dominion over Canada; and this because international unionism is one of those links in the system of US domination of Canada which is most within reach of the organized workers in this country, once they decide firmly to be masters in their own house, masters of their own movement.

We say then that, given this truth, this reality, and the basic attitude of the workers, it is tragic that in recent years there have been no serious sustained, massive battles on these issues. There have been skirmishes: for example, the debate at the Canadian Congress of Labour convention of 1955. At that convention, progressives demanded that the Congress take a stand for Canadian unionism in view of Canada's growing domination by the United States. They asked why there should be a situation where the United Mine Workers of America in Canada should not be in the Canadian Congress of Labour simply because its parent body in the United States had decided to withhold per capita tax. 'Why should we consider ourselves as children when it comes to running our own affairs in the trade union movement?' asked Sam Jankins of the BC Marine and Shipyard Workers Union. This was a sensible question to ask of a trade union centre founded in the name of a Canadian movement.

It will be recalled that the Canadian Congress of Labour was established in 1940 as a merger of the All-Canadian Congress of Labour and the CIO unions expelled from the Trades and Labour Congress on US orders. Between the CCL's militant Canadian origins and the right-wing clique which had come to dominate it in Cold War years, however, the gap was great indeed. The administration's response to these all-too-modest proposals of the progressives was negative. There was dark talk about people who followed 'that particular line.' More sophisticated reasons were also advanced, reasons to placate the majority which demanded something better than red-baiting. George Burt, UAW director in Canada, said Canadians were members of international unions 'because of the power we derive from membership in the international unions.' Surely the source of the UAW's strength in Canada is not the US membership at Detroit, but the Canadian membership at Windsor, Oshawa, and St Catharines. Canadian auto workers are the only auto workers in the world who have an international union. Auto workers in France, Britain, Italy, the Soviet Union, the United States itself (for there the UAW fulfils the function of a national union) have national unions, not international unions, and are none the weaker for it.

George Burt referred to premier Hepburn's attack against the internationals in 1937. It is true that Hepburn in the 1930s, like Smallwood in the 1950s, was prepared to pin the US label on the union he was fighting, but his real target was the process of self-organization by Canada's industrial workers then going on in auto, steel, electrical industries, and hard-rock mining. For that matter, if we go back to the founding years of the USWA in the 1930s, it may well be asked whether we would not have been further ahead if we had established merely working co-operation with the CIO while maintaining a completely independent organization in Canada. Certain it is, however, that the auto workers at the time, and the Left which was influential among them, decided otherwise. So Burt was turning on the very people who, rightly or wrongly but, generally speaking, sincerely, had helped bring the CIO into Canada and had helped advance him to leadership. At the 1956 CCL convention, J.K. Bell of the Nova Scotia Marine and Shipyard Workers Union reminded Burt about this, but he also added: 'It might have been all right [in the 1930s] but I think Canadians have since developed and want their own labour movement.'

How then, shall we sum up the place of international unionism in Canadian labour history? In the final decade of the nineteenth century contradictions began to develop between the *substance* Canadian unionism, and the *mode* international unionism, so that the central contradiction began to be posed: *Canadian unionism versus international unionism*. This contradiction developed through the first five decades of the twentieth century. It gave rise to new centres, such as the National Trades and Labour Congress, the One Big Union, the Confederation of National Trade Unions, the All-Canadian Congress of Labour, and the Workers Unity League. It also expressed itself within the Trades and Labor Congress of Canada, the Canadian Congress of Labour, and its successor, the Canadian Labour Congress.

There is much that is positive in labour's history. Many a union battle in Canada, however, has been fought under the banner of the international unions; and there has been constant solidarity between Canadian and US organized workers' movements in Canada and the United States. Yet unions would have been built in Canada, and relations of solidarity would have been established between US and Canadian workers, had there been a sovereign movement in Canada and a sovereign movement in the United States. What is positive in international unionism then is not the *appearance* or the *mode* - international unionism, but the *essence* or the *substance* - Canadian unionism.

International unionism has also meant strike-breaking, jurisdictional chaos imposed on Canada's workers, repeated disruption of Canadian labour unity, and persistence of archaic craft structures as opposed to a scientific plan of industrial unionism.

International unionism has imposed balkanization on Canada's organized workers. It has frustrated development of a system of Canada-wide industrial unions - general unions proper, such as exist in Britain, Australia, France, Italy, the Soviet Union, indeed, in practically every country.

Beyond that, international unionism has meant the reinforcing of the tendency to local isolation in Canada. The constituting of central organs (trade union centres, provincial federations, city central councils) or even the constituting of a central political party such as the New Democratic party could not compensate for this lack of structural identity at the base. The result has been to hold back unification of Canada's workers for economic, legislative, and political action; and to impede the development of the kind of labour movement in Canada which could begin in a serious way to undertake central class objectives such as the shorter work day, total organization of the unorganized, Canadian independence, and peace.

The negative effects of international unionism apply also on the country as a whole. International unionism has been a major link in the system of US domination of Canada, has provided US imperialism with a base in Canada, one worth more to it than outright acquisition of a province or outright ownership of a number of major industries. Again and again, in central crises of the class struggle in Canada - in the conscription crisis of 1917, in the Winnipeg general strike of 1919, in the fight for unity and peace during the 1930s, in the momentous struggles of the Cold War era - the system of international unionism has operated as a major reserve of reaction to defeat the working class. It has converted Canada into a guinea pig for labour imperialism, the labour front of US imperialism; the kind of labour imperialism which, during the Cold War years, the reactionary US labour leaders, the Dubinskys, Meanys, and Harrisons, tried to impose on the peoples of Latin America, Western Europe, Asia, and Africa.

Again, international unionism has served as a vital link in the system of class collaborationism, the system of capital domination of labour from within. Again and again, the right wings in Canada and in the United States combined their forces and provided each other with a reserve of strength to prop up their domination of the unions. The result has been bad, not just for Canada's organized workers, but also for US organized workers.

The conclusion is clear. The winning of a sovereign trade union movement – a sovereign Canadian union for each industry, a sovereign movement for the country as a whole – stands as a central class objective for Canada's organized workers. The prime objective should be, not autonomy within the international union, but a system of sovereign Canadian unions:[8] Where direct action to break links is not possible, the struggle should be conducted for Canadian autonomy within the international union. But that must mean, not just the facade of autonomy, but the content: a Canadian district, a Canadian constitution, a Canadian leadership elected by the Canadian membership, a Canadian treasury, a Canadian strike fund, and the right of the Canadian membership to secession. And even where such autonomy has been established, it should be regarded as but a second best, a transition link to the form which is proper and classical for Canada – the sovereign Canadian union: a body which will be master in its own house, but will also be free to establish such links of solidarity as it sees fit with organized workers in the United States or anywhere else.

This is what can prevail by the will of Canada's workers.

NOTES

1 This threat was heard in 1962-63 in connection with a dispute between the Carpenters (United Brotherhood of Carpenters and Joiners) and the International Woodworkers of America. The Carpenters walked out of the 1962 convention on that issue, and subsequently they suspended payment of per capita to the Congress. At the time, it was said that the Carpenters and some other international unions were considering the organization of a rival centre.

2 In 1958, in fifty-three of seventy international unions, permission was required from headquarters before a local could strike with full support of the union.

3 In 1960, Donald Secord, CBRT secretary-treasurer, cited a similar case. Canadian members in one international who were demanding additional rights were told that if this demand were granted, the next thing would be that Catholics and Protestants would put forward similar requests, not to speak of the people of Alaska.

4 A further indication of the policy pursued by the CLC leadership is Dodge's address to the 1961 international convention of the United Brewery Flour, Cereal, Soft Drink and Distillery Workers of America at Baltimore, Maryland. There he defined 'legislative program, political action ... foreign trade and International affairs' as those areas where there should be autonomy, and he went on to say that 'in administrative, financial and consti-

tutional matters, autonomy is not as important.' *Canadian Labour* (Oct. 1961.)

5   This underlines the significance of the decision by communists and progressives in the late 1930s to dissolve or merge the Canadian unions established in the late 1920s and early 1930s into international unions of the CIO and AFL. That was probably a mistake, though it had its positive side, and was connected with the circumstances of the day. It is a fact, however, that from its inception in 1922 until 1964, the Communist party of Canada, though performing yeoman's work in the fight for Canadian unionism both as a party and through its adherents, has never clearly understood this struggle – and this is one big reason for the setbacks it has suffered.

6   The use of international fraternal organizations by US imperialism in its conquest of Canada is not confined to the labour movement. It involves also various religious bodies and fraternal organizations such as Jehovah's Witnesses, the Zionists, Rotary International, the Shriners. Revealing was this incident at the University of Toronto in 1960 involving a coloured woman student who was denied membership in a fraternity. It turned out that the US headquarters of the fraternity had advised the officers of the Toronto chapter that admission of a coloured person would involve the organization in difficulties with its chapters located in the Southern United States.

7   Further evidence revealing the interconnection between class collaborationism and international unionism is the joint TLC-CCL brief submitted in 1957 to the Royal Commission on Canada's Economic Prospects. In upholding international unions, this brief advances arguments more palatable to management than to labour. It speaks about the 'moderation' of international unions. It considers ten objections to international unions. Of these, eight are employer-type objections, and only two are worker-type objections. It deals with the problem of strikes – that is to say, the right of Canadian members of international unions to strike, not from the standpoint of the Canadians' right to strike, but rather their *right not to strike*. That is an employer-tilted approach; for, as far as the employers are concerned, the freer the workers are *not* to strike, the better they (the employers) like it. But as far as the workers are concerned, the freer they (the workers) are to strike (implicit in which is the right *not* to strike), the better they (the workers) like it.

8   The Communist party of Canada, which should be a leader in this field, has confined itself in practice to the 'Canadian autonomy' slogan. This has been one important factor holding up progress to building a Canadian trade union movement.

THE END

REFERENCES

Chapter 1.

1. H. A. Innis, *The Fur Trade in Canada* (New Haven, 1930), p. 221.
2. Ibid., p. 245.
3. H. A. Innis and A. R. M. Lower, ed., *Select Documents in Canadian Economic History, 1783-1885* (Toronto, 1933), II, p. 271.
4. Ibid., p. 290.
5. Ibid.
6. Ibid., p. 295.
7. Ibid., pp. 295-297.
8. Ibid., p. 296.
9. Ibid., p. 297.
10. Ibid., p. 289.
11. Ibid., p. 104.
12. Ibid., p. 114.
13. Ibid., p. 108.
14. Hon. Andrew Haydon, *Pioneer Sketches in the District of Bathurst* (Toronto, 1925), pp. 100-126.
15. Stanley B. Ryerson, *1837 : The Birth of Canadian Democracy,* (Toronto n.d.), p. 71.
16. *Quebec Gazette,* May 13, 1834.
17. H. A. Innis and A. R. M. Lower, *Select Documents . . .* II, p. 241.
18. R. H. Coats, "The Labour Movement in Canada, 1914", *Canada and Its Provinces* (Toronto, 1913-1917), IX, p. 292.
19. R. H. Coats, in *Canada and Its Provinces,* IX, p. 292.
20. *La Minerve,* January 5, 1832.
21. The Montreal *Herald,* Jan. 28, 1833; the Montreal *Vindicator,* Jan. 29, Feb., Apr. 5, Dec. 3, 1833.
22. *La Minerve,* June 30, 1834; The *Vindicator,* May 30, 1834.
23. *Vindicator,* Feb. 1, 1833.
24. Ibid., Jan. 29, 1833.
25. Ibid., Feb. 1, 1833.
26. Ibid., Feb. 8, 1833.
27. Ibid.
28. Ibid., Apr. 5, 1833.
29. Ibid., Feb. 28, 1834.
30. Ibid., Feb. 25, 1834.
31. Ibid.
32. The Montreal *Gazette,* Mar. 4, 1834.
33. *Vindicator,* Mar. 11, 1834.
34. *Gazette,* Mar. 4, 1834.
35. *Vindicator,* Mar. 14, 1834.
36. Montreal *Daily Advertiser,* July 28, 1834.
37. *Vindicator,* Mar. 14, Apr. 4, 1834.
38. Ibid., Mar. 14, 1834.
39. *La Minerve,* June 30, 1834.
40. *Vindicator,* Mar. 14, 1834.

41. Ibid., May 2, 1834.
42. Ibid., Sept. 23, 1835.
43. R. H. Coats, in *Canada and Its Provinces,* IX, p. 292.
44. *Colonial Advocate,* Mar. 10, 1831.
45. Ibid., Mar. 10, 1831.
46. Ibid., Oct. 17, 1833.
47. Toronto Typographical Society, *Minutes,* 1845 (Toronto: Archives, local 91, International Typographical Union), p. 4.
48. Ibid., pp. 3-5.
49. Ibid.
50. Ibid., p. 8.
51. Ibid.
52. Article by J. M. Conner in *Souvenir Program* (Toronto: Archives, local 91, I.T.U.) See also J. M. Conner, "Trade Unions in Toronto", in J. A. Middleton, *Municipality of Toronto,* II, pp. 555-556.
53. Margaret Mackintosh, *An Outline of Trade Union History in Great Britain, the United States and Canada* (Ottawa, Department of Labour, 1938), p. 9.
54. Ibid.
55. *New Brunswick Courier,* February 16, 1833.
56. *Vindicator,* Mar. 11, 1834.
57. William Z. Foster, *Outline History of the World Trade Union Movement,* (New York, 1956), p. 38.
58. Beatrice and Sidney Webb, *History of Trade Unionism* (London, 1920), p. 733.
59. J. W. Buckley, *Monograph on the Tolpuddle Martyrs* (Unpublished Manuscript, Toronto Public Reference Library).
60. Ibid.
61. Ibid.
62. Ibid.
63. Ibid.
64. *Colonial Advocate,* May 4, 1826.
65. *Vindicator,* Apr. 22 and Dec. 16, 1834.
66. A. D. De Celles, "Lettres de 1835 et de 1836", Royal Society of Canada, *Proceedings* (Ottawa, 1914), Third Series, VII, pp. 169-179; *La Minerve,* Mar. 7, 10, 1836.
67. *Gazette,* Oct. 28, 1834; *Herald,* Oct. 28, 1834; *Daily Advertiser,* Oct. 29, 1834; *Vindicator,* Oct. 30, 1834.
68. Toronto Typographical Society, *Minutes,* 1845, p. 7.
69. *Advocate,* (Toronto) Mar. 18, 1834.
70. Ibid., July 31, 1834.
71. Ibid., Mar. 6, 1834.
72. *Vindicator,* June 14, 1836.
73. J. M. Conner, "Trade Unions in Toronto", pp. 555-556.
74. Stanley B. Ryerson, *French Canada* (Toronto, 1943), p. 40.
75. Robert Christie. *A History of the late province of Lower Canada* (Montreal, 1866), V., pp. 59-66.
76. *Vindicator,* June 30, 1837; *Constitution,* June 27-28, 1837.
77. *Vindicator,* May 16, 1837.

78. *Advocate,* June 29, 1837.
79. *Vindicator,* May 16, 1837.
80. Ibid.
81. Ibid., July 14, 1837.
82. Stanley B. Ryerson, *1837: Birth of Canadian Democracy,* p. 123.
83. *Vindicator,* Sept. 5, 1837.
84. *La Minerve,* Sept. 7, 1837.
85. *Vindicator,* Sept. 12, 1837.
86. *La Minerve,* Oct. 16, 1837.
87. Robert Christie, *A History . . . . . Lower Canada,* V., pp. 59-66.
88. *Vindicator,* May 26, 1837.
89. *Constitution,* Feb. 1, 1837.
90. Charles Lindsey, *The Life and Times of William Lyon Mackenzie* (Toronto, 1862), II, p. 55.
91. Ibid., pp. 52-55.
92. *Advocate,* Nov. 15, 1837.
93. Stanley B. Ryerson, *1837: Birth of Canadian Democracy,* p. 75.
94. Ibid.
95. Aegidius Fauteux, *Patriotes de 1837-1838* (Montréal, 1950), pp. 75-79.
96. Ibid.
97. Rev. John Douglas Borthwick, "Rebellion of 1837-1838", *Diamond Jubilee Publication,* (Montreal, 1898), pp. 91-93.
98. Charles Lindsey, *William Lyon Mackenzie,* II, pp. 373-400.
99. Stanley B. Ryerson, *1837: . . . . . Democracy,* p. 123.
100. Toronto Typographical Society, *Minutes,* Apr. 2, 1845.
101. Ibid.
102. Ibid.
103. Ibid., p. 22.
104. Ibid., July 1845, p. 27.
105. Ibid., May 3, 1845.
106. Ibid., May 5, 1845.
107. Ibid., July 1845.
108. Article by J. M. Conner in *Souvenir Program* (Toronto: Archives local 91, I.T.U.).
109. Ibid.
110. Ibid.
111. Toronto Typographical Society, *Minutes,* 1845, p. 145.
112. Ibid., Feb. 10, 1847.
113. Ibid.
114. Ibid., Jan. 19, 1850, p. 193.
115. Ibid., Feb. 10, 1847.
116. Ibid., Mar. 2, 1850.
117. H. A. Logan, *Trade Unions In Canada,* (Toronto, 1948), p. 31.
118. R. H. Coats, in *Canada and Its Provinces,* IX, p. 293.
119. H. A. Logan, *Trade Unions In Canada,* p. 31.
120. Ibid.
121. Ibid.
122. Ibid.
123. Ibid.

124. H. A. Innis, *Select Documents . . . 1783-1885,* II, p. 801.
125. H. A. Logan, *Trade Unions In Canada,* pp. 30, 31.
126. Ibid., p. 31.
127. Ibid.
128. H. A. Innis, *Select Documents . . . 1783-1885,* II, p. 313.
129. International Typographical Union, local 302, *57th Anniversary Souvenir* (Quebec City).
130. Ibid.
131. René Genois, "Historique de l'Union Typographique Internationale de Québec, local 302", *Le Typo,* (Organe du local 302).
132. Ibid.
133. International Typographical Union, local 302, *57th Anniversary Souvenir.*
134. H. A. Logan, *Trade Unions In Canada,* p. 29.
135. Toronto Trades and Labour Council, *Souvenir,* 1898.
136. H. A. Logan, *Trade Unions In Canada,* p. 29.
137. Ibid., p. 30.
138. Ibid., p. 71.
139. René Genois, "Historique . . . . . local 302", p. 26.
140. Toronto Typographical Society, *Minutes,* Aug. 15, 1872.
141. Ibid., Jan. Feb. 1859.
142. Ibid., Mar. 1859.
143. Ibid., Dec. 13, 1865.
144. Ibid., May 19, 1866.
145. Ibid., Aug. 10, 1867; Oct. 9, 1867; Nov. 13, 1867.
146. Toronto Typographical Society, "Annual Report for year 1866", *Minutes,* 1866.
147. Ibid., Jan. 17, 1860.
148. Ibid., Nov. 13, 1867.
149. William Z. Foster, *History of the Three Internationals* (New York, 1955), p. 120.

Chapter 2.

1. Canada, Royal Commission on Dominion-Provincial Relations, *Report* (Ottawa, 1940), I, p. 21.
2. Ibid., p. 22.
3. George Kleiner, *Capital Accumulation in Canada* (M.A. Thesis, McGill University, 1937), p. 89.
4. H. A. Innis, *Select Documents . . . 1783-1885,* II, p. 624.
5. Ibid., p. 618.
6. Ibid., p. 622.
7. Canada, Royal Commission on Dominion-Provincial Relations, Report I, p. 25.
8. Ibid., p. 38.
9. Ibid., pp. 20, 25, 28, 29.
10. Ibid., p. 48; H. A. Innis, *Select Documents . . . ,* pp. 818, 819.
11. Canada, Royal Commission on Dominion-Provincial Relations, *Report,* 1940, I, pp. 47-48.

12. Toronto Typographical Society, *Minutes* (Archives I.T.U., Local 91, Toronto), Mar. 4, 1871, p. 2; Toronto Trades Assembly, *Minutes* (Library, Canadian Labour Congress, Ottawa), p. 1.
13. Toronto Trades Assembly, *Minutes, p. 1.*
14. Ibid., p. 3.
15. Ibid., June 9, 1871.
16. Ibid., p. 9.
17. Ibid., May 19, 1871, p. 7; Ibid., Aug. 4, 1871, p. 18; Ibid., Oct. 1, 1871; Ibid., Nov. 3, 1871, p. 25; Ibid., Mar. 12, 1872, p. 45.
18. Toronto Trades Assembly, *Minutes*, 1872.
19. Ibid.
20. Ibid., Mar. 21, 1872, p. 45; Ibid., pp. 14 and 62.
21. Ibid., pp. 14, 58, 62, 66, 72.
22. Ibid., Apr. 24, 1872, pp. 46, 52; Ibid., Apr. 19, 1872, pp. 39, 61.
23. Ibid., Mar. 12, 1872,pp. 39, 43; Ibid., May 3, 1872, pp. 55, 72.
24. Ibid., p. 46.
25. Ibid., p. 78.
26. Toronto Typographical Society, *Minutes*, Feb. 17 and 24, 1872.
27. Ibid., Mar. 13, 1872, p. 15.
28. Ibid.
29. *Ontario Workman*, May 9, 1872.
30. *Ontario Workman*, Apr. 18, 1872.
31. Ibid.
32. Ibid.
33. Ibid.
34. Ibid.
35. Karl Marx, *Capital*, I, (Modern Library Edition), p. 259, footnote.
36. *Ontario Workman*, Apr. 25, 1872.
36A. Ibid.
37. Ibid., May 16, 23, 1872.
38. Ibid., Issues of May, 1872.
39. *Ontario Workman*, May 30, 1872.
40. Ibid., May 16, May 23, 1872.
41. Ibid., May 23, 1872.
42. Ibid., May 2, May 9, 1872; Toronto Trades Assembly, *Minutes*, May 17, 1872.
43. *Ontario Workman*, May 9, May 16, May 23, 1872.
44. Ibid., May 23, 1872.
45. Toronto Trades Assembly, *Minutes*, May 3, 1872, p. 57; *Ontario Workman*, May 9, 1872.
46. Toronto Trades Assembly, *Minutes*, May 2, 1872, p. 55, May 3, 1872, p. 57; *Ontario Workman*, May 9, 1872.
47. Canadian Labour Union, *Proceedings*, Sept. 1873 .
48. Ibid.
49. Ibid.
50. Ibid.
51. Ibid.
52. *Ontario Workman*, May, June, 1872.
53. Toronto Trades Assembly, *Minutes*, July 7, 1875.

54.   Toronto Typographical Society, *Minutes,* 1877.
54A. Canadian Labour Union, *Proceedings,* Aug. 1877.
55.   Toronto Trades Assembly, *Minutes,* 1875.
56.   Canadian Labour Union, *Proceedings,* 1873.
57.   Canadian Labour Union, *Proceedings,* Aug. 1874.
58.   Ibid., Aug. 1875.
59.   Ibid., Aug. 1876.
60.   Ibid., Aug. 1877.
61.   Toronto Trades Assembly, *Minutes,* May 21, 1872.
62.   Ibid., Mar. 1875 et seq.
63.   Canadian Labour Union, *Proceedings,* July 21, 1875; Toronto Trades Assembly, *Minutes,* Oct. 20 and Nov. 3, 1875.
64.   Toronto Trades Assembly, *Minutes,* Nov. 3, 1875.
65.   Toronto Trades Assembly, *Minutes,* Nov. 3 and 17, 1875; Mar. 1 and 15, 1876.
66.   Canadian Labour Union, *Proceedings,* Aug. 1875.
67.   Ibid., Aug. 1876.
68.   Ibid., Aug. 1877.
69.   Toronto Trades Assembly, *Minutes,* July 1875.
70.   Canadian Labour Union, *Proceedings,* Aug. 1876. ·
71.   Toronto Trades Assembly, *Minutes,* Oct. and Nov. 1872.
72.   Canadian Labour Union, *Proceedings,* 1873, 1874, 1875.
73.   Ibid., 1873, 1876.
74.   Canadian Labour Union, *Proceedings,* 1878.
75.   Canada, Royal Commission on Dominion-Provincial Relations, *Report,* 1940, I.
76.   Canadian Labour Union, *Proceedings,* Aug. 1874.
77.   Ibid., Aug. 1877.
78.   Ibid.
79.   Canada, Royal Commission on Dominion-Provincial Relations, *Report,* 1940, I.
80.   Toronto Trades Assembly, *Minutes,* Mar. 1, 1872.
81.   *Ontario Workman,* May 16 and May 23, 1872.
82.   Toronto Trades Assembly, *Minutes,* July 5, 1872.
83.   *Ontario Workman,* July 18, 1872.
84.   Ibid.
85.   Ibid., Aug. 1, 1872.
86.   Ibid., Aug. 15, 1872.
87.   Carl Wittke, *A History of Canada,* p. 218.
88.   Canadian Labour Union, *Proceedings,* Sept. 1873.
89.   Ibid.
90.   Ibid., Aug. 1876.
91.   Ibid., Aug. 1877.
92.   Toronto Typographical Society, *Minutes,* Dec. 2, 1876.
93.   Ibid., Nov. 11, 1876.
93A. Toronto Trades Assembly, *Minutes,* Oct. 1874.
93B. Ibid., Feb. 9, 1878.
94.   *Ontario Workman,* Feb. 13, 1873.
95.   Ibid., Mar. 13, 1873.
96.   *Daily Leader,* Sept. 25, 1873.

97. *Daily Globe,* Aug. 5, 1876.
98. *Ontario Workman,* Jan. 2, 1873..
98A. Canadian Labour Union, *Proceedings,* Aug. 1876.
98B. Ibid., Aug. 1877.
99. Canadian Labour Union, *Proceedings,* Aug. 1875.
100. Canadian Labour Union, *Proceedings,* Aug. 1877.
101. Ibid.
102. Toronto Trades Assembly, *Minutes,* Feb. 20, 1878, p. 251.
103. Ibid., June 16, 1875 and Dec. 5, 1877.

Chapter 3.

1. Canada, D.S.B., *Canada Year Book,* 1905, pp. 124 and 128.
2. Canada, Royal Commission on the Relations of Capital and Labour (Ottawa, 1889), *Evidence of Ontario,* p. 73.
3. Ibid., *Evidence of Quebec,* p. 368.
4. Ibid., p. 21.
5. Ibid., pp. 21-148.
6. Ibid., pp. 21, 42.
7. Ibid., pp. 21-148.
8. Ibid., p. 95.
9. Ibid., p. 83; pp. 81-91, 123, 125-126.
10. Ibid., pp. 21-148.
11. Ibid., pp. 87, 88, 123, 288.
12. Ibid., pp. 87, 88, 123, 388, 390.
13. Ibid., p. 70.
14. Ibid., pp. 21-148.
15. Ibid., pp. 400-532.
15A. Ibid.
16. Ibid., pp. 271-279.
17. Ibid.
18. Ibid.
19. Ibid., *Evidence of Ontario.*
20. Ibid.
21. Ibid., *Evidence of New Brunswick.*
22. Trades and Labour Congress of Canada, 1887, Third Annual Convention, *Proceedings,* p. 24.
23. Canadian Labour Congress, 1883, *Proceedings,* p. 22.
24. Canada, Royal Commission on the Relations of Capital and Labour, 1889, *Evidence of Nova Scotia.*
25. Ibid., *Evidence of Quebec.*
26. Ibid.
27. Ibid., *Evidence of Ontario.*
28. Ibid.
29. Ibid., *Evidence of Quebec.*
30. Ibid., *Evidence of Ontario,* p. 650.
31. Toronto Trades and Labour Council, *Minutes,* Nov. 1, 1884.
32. Ibid., p. 14; Canada, Royal Commission on the Relations of Capital and Labour, 1889, *Evidence of Quebec.*
32A. Ibid., *Evidence of Nova Scotia.*

33. Ibid., *Evidence of Quebec.*
34. Ibid., *Evidence of Ontario.*
35. Harold Griffin, *British Columbia: The People's Early Story* (Vancouver, 1958), pp. 47-48.
36. Canada, Royal Commission on the Relations of Capital and Labour, 1889, *Evidence of Ontario,* pp. 332, 334, 242, 120, 78; Toronto Trades and Labour Council, *Minutes,* May 21, June 4, July 2, 1886; Douglas Ross Kennedy, *The Knights of Labour in Canada* (M. A. Thesis, University of Western Ontario), pp. 71-74.
37. Canada, Royal Commission on the Relations of Capital and Labour, 1889, *Evidence of Ontario.*
38. Ibid., *Evidence of Quebec.*
39. Ibid., *Evidence of Ontario.*
40. Ibid., *Evidence of Quebec.*
41. Ibid.
42. Harold Griffin, *British Columbia . . . Story.*
43. Victor O. Chan, *The Canadian Knights of Labour, with special reference to the 1880s* (M. A. Thesis, McGill University, 1949), pp. 18, 26, 143; Douglas Ross Kennedy, *The Knights . . . Canada,* pp. 36, 38, 122.
43A. Ibid., p. 173.
43B. Ibid., p. 183.
44. Ibid.
45. Ibid., pp. 193, 196, 197.
46. Ibid., p. 200.
47. Douglas Ross Kennedy, *The Knights . . . Canada,* pp. 100-116.
48. *Evening Palladium,* Dec. 6, 1886.
49. Trades and Labour Congress of Canada, Second Annual Convention, 1886, *Proceedings.*
50. Toronto Trades and Labour Council, *Minutes,* Aug. 17, 1883.
51. Canadian Labour Congress, 1883, *Proceedings,* pp. 8-9.
51A. Ibid., p. 38.
52. Trades and Labour Congress of Canada, Second Annual Convention, 1886, *Proceedings,* p. 32.
53. Ibid., 1887.
54. Ibid., 1888.
55. Ibid., 1889, pp. 3-6.
56. Ibid., 1889, p. 19.
57. Toronto Trades and Labour Council, *Minutes,* 1881.
58. Canada, Royal Commission on the Relations of Capital and Labour, 1889, *Report,* p. 89.
59. Ibid.
60. Canadian Labour Congress, 1883, *Proceedings,* p. 22.
61. Canada, Royal Commission on the Relations of Capital and Labour, 1889, *Evidence of Ontario.*
62. Ibid., *Evidence of Quebec,* p. 374.
63. Canadian Labour Congress, 1883, *Proceedings,* p. 30.
64. Trades and Labour Congress of Canada, Second Annual Convention, 1886, *Proceedings.*
65. Toronto Trades and Labour Council, *Minutes,* Jan. 19, 1883.

66. *Palladium of Labour,* Mar. 3, 1883.
67. Victor O. Chan, *The Canadian Knights of Labour,* pp. 111, 118, 146.
68. Ibid., p. 153.
69. Trades and Labour Congress of Canada, Third Annual Convention, 1887, *Proceedings,* p. 28.
70. *Palladium of Labour,* 1883.
71. Ibid., Mar. 3, 1883.
72. Canada, Royal Commission on the Relations of Capital and Labour, 1889, *Evidence of Ontario.*
73. Ibid.
74. *Palladium of Labour,* Jan. 13, 1883.
75. Canada, Royal Commission on the Relations of Capital and Labour, 1889, *Evidence of Ontario.*
76. *Palladium of Labour,* Jan. 20, 1883.
77. Ibid., Feb. 10, 1883.

Chapter 4.

1. Canada, DBS, *Canada Year Book,* 1905, pp. 2 and 142.
2. *Labour Advocate,* Sept. 18, 1891.
3. *Industrial Banner,* 1897-1899.
4. *Labour Advocate,* Oct. 2, 1891.
5. Ibid., Sept. 24, 1891.
6. Trades and Labour Congress of Canada, Thirteenth Annual Convention, 1898, *Proceedings,* p. 31.
7. Ibid., 1893, pp. 16-17.
8. Ibid., 1894, pp. 15, 16.
9. Ibid., 1899.
10. Ibid.
11. Ibid., 1893, p. 5.
12. *Labour Advocate,* Sept. 11, 1891.
13. Ibid., Mar. 13, 1891.
14. Ibid.
15. Ibid.
16. Allied Printing Trades Council, *Labour Day Souvenir* (Toronto, 1898).
17. Trades and Labour Congress of Canada, Fourteenth Annual Convention, 1899, *Proceedings,* p. 19.
18. *Labour Advocate,* Feb. 11, 1892.
19. Ibid., Dec. 26, 1890.
20. Ibid., Aug. 28, 1891.
21. Allied Printing Trades Council, *Labour Day Souvenir.*
22. *Labour Advocate,* Mar. 27, 1891.
23. Trades and Labour Congress of Canada, Eighth Annual Convention, 1893, *Proceedings,* p. 16.

Chapter 5.

1. Canada, DBS, *Canada Year Book,* 1922-23, p. 430.
2. George Kleiner, *Capital . . . Canada,* p. 105.

3. Canada,DBS, *Canada Year Book,* 1905 and 1916-17.
4. George Kleiner, *Capital . . . Canada,* p. 88.
5. Jurgen Kuczynski, *A Short History of Labour Conditions, Vol. 1, Part 2; The British Empire 1800 to the Present Day* (London, 1942), p. 74.
6. O. J. Firestone, *Canada's Economic Development, 1867 to 1953* (London, 1958), p. 207.
7. Ibid.
8. George Kleiner, *Capital . . . Canada,* p. 117.
9. Ibid.
10. Canada, DBS, *Canada Year Book,* 1905, 1922-23.
11. Canada, Department of Labour, *Annual Report on Strikes and Lockouts,* 1901-1916, 1956.
12. Ibid.
13. *Voice,* June 17, 28, July 2, 4, 6, 1901.
14. Trades and Labour Congress of Canada, Seventeenth Annual Convention, 1902, *Proceedings,* pp. 46-47.
15. *Voice,* June 20, 28, July 2, 4, 6, 1902; *Industrial Banner,* Feb. 1903.
16. Canada, Royal Commission on Industrial Disputes in the Province of British Columbia, 1903, *Proceedings,* p. 748.
17. Ibid., p. 567.
18. Ibid., p. 75.
19. Canada, Department of Labour, *Annual Report on Strikes and Lockouts,* 1915.
20. Ibid., p. 19.
21. Canada, Royal Commission to Inquire into Industrial disputes in the Cotton Factories of the Province of Quebec, *Report* (Ottawa, 1909, pp. 25-28.
22. Ibid., p. 33.
23. Ibid., p. 25.
24. Ibid., p. 7.
25. Ibid., p. 10.
26. Ibid., p. 9.
27. Ibid., p. 18.
28. Canada, Department of Labour, *Annual Report on Strikes and Lockouts,* 1901-1916.

Chapter 6.

1. Trades and Labour Congress of Canada, Fourteenth Annual Convention, 1899, *Proceedings,* p. 7.
2. *Industrial Banner,* June 1907.
3. Ibid.
4. *Voice,* April 17, 1903.
5. Ibid., Sept. 18, 1908.
6. Trades and Labour Congress of Canada, 28th Annual Convention, 1913, *Proceedings,* p. 121.

7. Canada, Royal Commission on Industrial Disputes in the Province of British Columbia, 1903, *Evidence,* p. 792.
8. Ibid., *Report,* p. 75.
9. Trades and Labour Congress of Canada, 27th Annual Convention, 1912, *Proceedings,* p. 48.
10. Montreal Trades and Labour Council, *Minutes,* 1911, p. 144.
11. Trades and Labour Congress of Canada, 27th Annual Convention, 1914, *Proceedings,* p. 44.
12. *Voice,* June 12, 1908.
13. Trades and Labour Congress of Canada, 21st Annual Convention, 1906, *Proceedings,* p. 44.
14. Ibid., 1909, p. 10.
15. *Voice,* Oct. 2, 1908.
16. Trades and Labour Congress of Canada, 25th Annual Convention, 1910, *Proceedings,* p. 11.
17. Ibid., p. 35.
18. Ibid., 1911.
19. Ibid., 1912.
20. *Voice,* July 1, 1907.
21. Data on the struggle for the Ontario Workmen's Compensation Legislation, 1914, is compiled from Trades and Labour Congress of Canada, 1912, *Proceedings* ; and Ibid., 1914, p. 59 ; *Industrial Banner,* Jan. 20, Feb. 6, Mar. 13, Apr. 28, 1914.
22. Trades and Labour Congress of Canada, Eighteenth Annual Convention, 1903, *Proceedings,* p. 59.
23. Ibid., p. 56.
24. Ibid., 1903, p. 59.
25. *Voice,* Oct. 20, 1902.
26. Ibid., Nov. 18, 1904.
27. Trades and Labour Congress of Canada, Eighteenth Annual Convention, 1903, *Proceedings,* p. 32.
28. Ibid., 1906, p. 84.
29. Ibid., 1906, p. 83.
30. Ibid., 1910, p. 45.
31. *Voice,* Sept. 6, 1901.
32. Ibid., Nov. 27, 1908.
33. Canada, Royal Commission on Industrial Disputes in the Province of British Columbia, 1903, *Proceedings,* pp. 541, 543.
34. Ibid., p. 541.
35. *National Affairs Monthly,* Dec. 1955; Montreal *Gazette,* Dec. 23, 1905.
36. *Le Canada,* Dec. 12, 1905.
37. National Affairs Monthly, loc. cit.
38. G. Okulevich, *Russians in Canada (Russkie V. Kanade)* Toronto, 1952.
39. P. Krawchuk, *In the New Land* (Toronto, 1958).
39A. Montreal Trades and Labour Council, *Minutes,* Nov. 17, 1910, p. 108.
40. *Voice,* Oct. 7, 1910.

41. Trades and Labour Congress of Canada, 23rd Annual Convention, 1908, *Proceedings,* p. 80.
42. Ibid., 1912, p. 28.

Chapter 7.

1. *Golden Jubilee History of the Montreal Trades and Labour Council, 1885-1935,* Montreal Trades and Labour Council, 1935.
2. Trades and Labour Congress of Canada, Seventeenth Annual Convention, 1902, *Proceedings,* p. 73; Ibid., 1903, p. 46.
3. *Industrial Banner,* Oct. 17, 1913.
4. Ibid., May 1, 1914.
5. Ibid., Mar. 1904.
6. Montreal Trades and Labour Council, *Minutes,* Feb. 5, 1914.
7. *Industrial Banner,* Sept. 1910.
8. Source for data on Amalgamated Society of Carpenters' expulsion from TLC: Trades and Labour Congress of Canada, 28th Annual Convention, 1913, *Proceedings,* pp. 29-30.
9. Ibid., 1913, p. 27.
10. Ibid., 1913, p. 157.
11. Ibid., 1913, pp. 6-14.
11A. Ibid., 1903, p. 19.
12. Ibid., 1905, p. 2.
12A. Canada, Royal Commission on Industrial Disputes in the Province of British Columbia, 1903, *Evidence,* p. 352.
13. Source for data in this paragraph: National Trades and Labour Congress of Canada, Conventions of 1906, 1908: *Proceedings.*
14. Ibid., 1908, p. 10.
15. Trades and Labour Congress of Canada, 23rd Annual Convention, 1908, *Proceedings.*
16. Ibid., 1911, p. 14.
17. Ibid., 1911, pp. 38-40.
18. Ibid.
19. Ibid., p. 73.
19A. Source for data in this paragraph: Ibid., 1911, p. 79.
19B. Ibid., 1911.
19C. Ibid., 1903.

Chapter 8.

1. Canada, DBS, *Canada Year Book.*
2. George Kleiner, *Capital . . . Canada,* p. 63.
3. Ibid., pp. 98-99.
4. Ibid., pp. 99-102.
5. Ibid., pp. 103-104.
6. Canada, Royal Commission on the Textile Industry, 1938, *Report.*
7. Canada, Royal Commission on Dominion-Provincial Relations, 1940, *Report,* I, p. 69.

8. Trades and Labour Congress of Canada, Sixteenth Annual Convention, 1901, *Proceedings,* p. 76.
9. Ibid., 1906, p. 56.
9A. W. Z. Foster, *History of the Three Internationals.*
10. Trades and Labour Congress of Canada, 24th Annual Convention, 1909, *Proceedings,* p. 10.
10A. Trades and Labour Congress of Canada, 25th Annual Convention, 1910, *Proceedings,* p. 70.
11. Ibid., 1909, p. 9.
11A. C. Wittke, *History of Canada,* pp. 266-270.
12. *Industrial Banner,* Sept. 1911.
13. *Voice,* June 6, 1913.
14. Trades and Labour Congress of Canada, 26th Annual Convention, 1911, *Proceedings,* p. 74.
15. Ibid., 1912, p. 7.
16. Ibid.
17. Ibid.
18. Source for data on 1913 TLC Convention: Ibid., 1913, p. 156, etc.

Chapter 9.

1. *Industrial Banner,* Aug. 7, 1914.
2. Trades and Labour Congress of Canada, 32nd Annual Convention, 1917, *Proceedings.*
3. Canada, Department of Labour, *Annual Report on Labour Organization,* 1914, pp. 21-24.
4. Trades and Labour Congress of Canada, 29th Annual Convention, 1914, *Proceedings,* p. 129.
5. Ibid., p. 4.
6. Ibid., p. 15.
7. Ibid., 1916, p. 6.
8. Ibid., 1918, p. 31.
8A. Ibid., 1917, p. 82.
9. Ibid., 1914.
9A. Ibid., 1914, p. 111.
10. Ibid., 1917.
11. Canada, House of Commons, *Debates,* Aug. 8, 1917.
12. C. Wittke, *History of Canada* (New York, 1941), Fifth Edition, p. 309.
13. Canada, House of Commons, *Debates,* Apr. 19, 1918.
14. Ibid., Aug. 2, 1917.
15. Trades and Labour Congress of Canada, 31st Annual Convention, 1916, *Proceedings,* p. 106.
16. Canada, Department of Labour, *Labour Organization in Canada,* 1960.
17. Canada, Department of Labour, *Strikes and Lockouts,* 1917, 1918.
18. Ibid., 1916.
19. Trades and Labour Congress of Canada, 32nd Annual Convention, 1917, *Proceedings.*
20. Canada, *Labour Organization in Canada,* 1917, p. 27.

21. Ibid., p. 82.
22. Canada, House of Commons, *Debates,* June 28, 1917.
23. Montreal *Gazette*, July 4, 1917.
24. Ibid., July 16, 1917.
25. Canada, House of Commons, *Debates,* July 21, 1917.
26. *Labour World,* Dec. 9, 1917.
27. Canada, Department of Labour, *Annual Report on Labour Organization in Canada,* 1917.
27A. Ibid.
28. Ibid., 1917 and 1918.
29. Trades and Labour Congress of Canada, 32nd Annual Convention, 1917, *Proceedings,* p. 138.
30. Ibid., p. 135.
31. Ibid., 1917.
32. Ibid.
33. Ibid.
34. Ibid.
35. Ibid.
36. Ibid.
37. Ibid.
38. Ibid.
39. Ibid.
40. Ibid.
41. Ibid.
42. Ibid., 1917.
43. Samuel Gompers, *American Labor and the War* (New York, 1919), pp. 141-158.
44. W. T. R. Preston, *My Generation of Politics and Politicians* (Toronto, 1927), pp. 368-370.
45. Canada, Department of Labour, *Labour Organization in Canada,* 1958, p. 7.
46. Canada, Department of Labour, *Strikes and Lockouts,* 1956.
47. Canada, Department of Labour, *Annual Report on Labour Organization in Canada,* 1918, p. 60.
48. Canada, House of Commons, *Debates,* Apr. 2, 3, 1918.
49. Trades and Labour Congress of Canada, 33rd Annual Convention, 1918, *Proceedings,* p. 103.
50. Ibid.
51. Samuel Gompers, *American Labor and the War,* pp. 141-158.
52. Trades and Labour Congress of Canada, 33rd Annual Convention, 1918, *Proceedings,* p. 116.
52A. Ibid., 1918.
53. Ibid.

Chapter 10.

1. Canada, Department of Labour, *Labour Organizations in Canada,* 1963.
2. Canada, Department of Labour, *Strikes and Lockouts in Canada,* 1963.

3. Stephen B. Leacock, "My Affair with My Landlord", *Laugh With Leacock: An Anthology* (New York, 1934).
4. Canada, House of Commons, *Debates,* Mar. 18, 1919.
5. C. Wittke, *History of Canada,* p. 305.
6. D. C. Masters, *The Winnipeg General Strike* (Toronto, 1950), p. 28.
7. Ibid., p. 4.
8. Ibid.
9. Canada, House of Commons, *Debates,* Mar. 11, 1919.
10. Ibid.
11. Ibid., Apr. 28, 1919.
12. D. C. Masters, *The Winnipeg General Strike.*
13. *B.C. Federationist,* Mar. 14, 1919.
14. Source for data on 1919 Convention of B.C. Federation of Labour: B.C. Federation of Labour, 1919, *Proceedings,* pp. 28-36.
15. Western Canada Labour Conference, 1919, *Proceedings,* pp. 24, 33.
16. Ibid., p. 11.
17. Ibid.
18. Ibid., p. 30.
19. Ibid., pp. 28, 33.
20. D. C. Masters, *The Winnipeg General Strike.*
21. H. A. Robson, Canada, Royal Commission to enquire into and report upon the causes and effects of the General Strike which recently existed in the City of Winnipeg for a period of six weeks, including the methods of calling and carrying on such strike, 1919, *Report,* p. 9.
22. *Western Labour News,* May 23, 1919.
23. Montreal *Gazette,* Aug. 1, 1919.
24. *Western Labour News,* May 17, 1919.
25. H. A. Robson, Royal Commission . . . General Strike . . . 1919, *Report,* p. 5.
26. *Western Labour News,* June 28, 1919.
27. D. C. Masters, *The Winnipeg General Strike,* p. 57.
28. Wilfrid Harris Crook, *The General Strike* (University of North Carolina, 1931), pp. 545-546.
29. D. C. Masters, *The Winnipeg General Strike,* p. 44.
30. W. H. Crook, *The General Strike,* p. 543.
31. *Western Labour News,* May 17, 1919.
32. Montreal *Gazette,* June 17, 1919.
33. *Western Labour News,* May 19, 1919.
34. Ibid.
35. Ibid.
36. H. A. Robson, Royal Commission . . . General Strike . . . 1919, *Report,* p. 545. *Western-Labour News,* May 21, 1919.
37. *Western Labour News,* May 21, 1919.
38. Ibid., May 28, 31, 1919.
39. Ibid., May 22, 1919.
40. Ibid., May 29, 1919.
41. Ibid., May 27, 1919.

42. Canada, House of Commons, *Debates,* May 27, 1919.
42A. Ibid.
43. Ibid.
44. D. C. Masters, *The Winnipeg General Strike,* p. 71.
45. Canada, House of Commons, *Debates,* June 6, 1919.
46. W. H. Crook, *The General Strike,* p. 550.
47. Ibid.
48. Ibid., p. 552.
49. Ibid., p. 550.
50. Ibid., pp. 552-553.
51. W. H. Crook, *The General Strike,* p. 550.
52. *Western Labour News,* June 5, 1919.
53. Canada, Department of Labour, *Labour Organization in Canada,* 1919.
54. W. H. Crook, *The General Strike,* pp. 550-552.
55. *Western Labour News,* June 5, 1919.
56. W. H. Crook, *The General Strike,* p. 550.
57. D. C. Masters, *The Winnipeg General Strike,* p. 60.
58. W. H. Crook, *The General Strike,* p. 550.
59. *Western Labour News,* May 31, 1919.
59A. Ibid.
60. Ibid.
61. *Western Labour News,* May 30, 31, 1919; W. H. Crook, *The General Strike,* p. 550.
62. *Western Labour News,* June 2, 1919.
63. *Western Labour News,* May 31, June 5, 1919; D. C. Masters, *The Winnipeg General Strike,* p. 90.
64. *Western Labour News,* June 2, 5, 1919.
65. Canada, House of Commons, *Debates,* June 6, 1919.
66. W. H. Crook, *The General Strike,* p. 225.
67. *Western Labour News,* June 13, 1919.
68. Ibid.
69. Ibid.
70. W. H. Crook, *The General Strike,* p. 554, 555.
71. *Western Labour News,* June 17, 1919.
72. W. H. Crook, *The General Strike,* p. 555.
73. *Western Labour News,* June 17, 1919.
74. *Labour World,* June 7, 1919: Montreal *Gazette,* June 17, 1919.
75. *Western Labour News,* June 14, 1919.
76. Ibid., June 17, 1919.
77. Ibid., June 13, 1919.
78. Ibid., June 18, 1919.
79. Canada, House of Commons, *Debates,* 1926, Vol. IV, p. 4006.
80. W. H. Crook, *The General Strike,* p. 555.
81. D. C. Masters, *The Winnipeg General Strike,* p. 102.
82. W. H. Crook, *The General Strike,* p. 555.
83. *Western Labour News,* June 23, 1919.
84. Montreal *Gazette,* June 20, 1919; *Western Labour News,* June 23, 1919.
85. *Western Labour News,* June 23, 1919.

86. Ibid., June 18, 1919.
87. Ibid., June 23, 1919.
88. W. H. Crook, *The General Strike,* p. 557.
89. H. A. Robson, Royal Commission . . . Winnipeg Strike, 1919, *Report,* p. 2.
90. *Western Labour News,* June 23, 1919.
91. Ibid., July 2, 1919; W. H. Crook, *The General Strike,* p. 557.
92. *Western Labour News,* June 30, 1919.
93. Ibid., June 19, 21, 30, July 2, 8, 10, 19, 1919.
94. Ibid., July 3, 5, 7, 1919.
95. Ibid., July 3, 1919.
96. Ibid., July 7, 1919.
97. Ibid., July 10, 1919.

Chapter 11.

1. Canada, House of Commons, *Debates,* June 2, 1919.
2. D. C. Masters, *The Winnipeg General Strike,* p. 112.
3. H. A. Robson, Royal Commission . . . General Strike . . . 1919, *Report,* p. 19.
4. Canada, House of Commons, *Debates,* June 2, 1926.
5. Ibid.
6. Ibid.
7. D. C. Masters, *The Winnipeg General Strike,* p. 77.
8. *Western Labour News,* July 3, 1919.
9. W. H. Crook, *The General Strike,* p. 555.
10. Canada, House of Commons, *Debates,* June 2, 1926.
11. *B.C. Federationist,* May 30, 1919.
12. W. H. Crook, *The General Strike,* p. 552.
13. Canada, House of Commons, *Debates,* June 2, 1919.
14. W. H. Crook, *The General Strike,* p. 552.
15. Ibid., p. 550.
16. *Western Labour News,* June 28, 1919.
17. Montreal *Gazette,* June 16, 1919.
18. *Western Labour News,* June 20, 1919; H. A. Robson, Royal Commission . . . General Strike . . . 1919, *Report,* p. 23; D. C. Masters, *The Winnipeg General Strike,* p. 102; Montreal *Gazette,* Aug. 1, 1919.
19. D. C. Masters, *The Winnipeg General Strike,* pp. 101-102.
19A. Canada, House of Commons, *Debates,* June 2, 1926.
20. Canada, House of Commons, *Debates,* June 2, 1926.
21. *Western Labour News,* May 30, 1919.
22. Ibid., May 20, 1919.
23. Ibid., May 18, 1919.
24. Ibid., May 29, 1919.
25. Ibid.
26. Ibid., May 24, 1919.
27. Ibid., June 18, 1919.
28. Ibid., June 9, 1919.

29. Canada, House of Commons, *Debates*, June 2, 1919; *Western Labour News*, June 9, 1919.
30. Montreal *Gazette*, June 18, 1919.
31. *Western Labour News*, June 20, 1919.
32. Canada, House of Commons, *Debates*, June 2, 1919.
33. *Western Labour News*, July 2, 1919.

Chapter 12.

1. Western Canada Labour Conference, 1919, *Proceedings*, p. 27.
2. Ibid., p. 47.
3. *Western Labour News*, July 10, 1919.
4. Trades and Labour Congress of Canada, 34th Annual Convention, 1919, *Proceedings*, p. 172.
5. B.C. Federation of Labour, 1920, *Proceedings*, p. 4.
6. Canada, Department of Labour, *Annual Report on Labour Organization in Canada*, 1919, 1920, p. 23 ff.
7. Ibid.
8. Ibid., 1922.
9. B.C. Federation of Labour, 1920, *Proceedings*, p. 9.
10. Louis-Laurent Hardy, *Brève Histoire du Syndicalisme Ouvrier au Canada* (Montréal, 1958), pp. 71-72.
11. Ibid., p. 73.
12. Canada, Department of Labour, *Annual Report on Labour Organization in Canada*, 1921, p. 25.
13. Montreal Trades and Labour Council, *Minutes*, Sept. 7, 1916; July 19, 1917.
14. Trades and Labour Congress of Canada, 35th Annual Convention, 1920, *Proceedings*, p. 114.
15. Canada, House of Commons, *Debates*, Apr. 6, 1921.
16. Canada, Department of Labour, *Annual Report on Labour Organization in Canada*, 1921, p. 25.
17. Ibid., pp. 26, 27.
18. Ibid., p. 27.
19. Ibid., pp. 26-27.
20. Ibid., 1922, p. 165.
21. Ibid., 1923, p. 160.
22. Ibid., 1922, p. 173.
23. Ibid.
24. Ibid., 1924, p. 163.

Chapter 13.

1. Trades and Labour Congress of Canada, 35th Annual Convention, 1919, *Proceedings*, p. 134.
2. Ibid., p. 191.
3. Ibid., 1921, pp. 165-171.
4. Ibid., 1923, pp. 92-99.
5. Ibid., 1924, p. 101.
6. Ibid., 1925, pp. 142-146.

7. Ibid., 1926, pp. 149-151.
8. Ibid., 1928, pp. 126-128.
9. Ibid., 1927, pp. 102-103.
10. Ibid., 1917, p. 43.
11. Canada, Department of Labour, *Annual Report on Labour Organization in Canada,* 1921, p. 55 ff.
12. Ibid., p. 51.
13. Ibid., 1923, p. 201 ff.
14. Trades and Labour Congress of Canada, 38th Annual Convention, 1923, *Proceedings,* p. 99.

Chapter 14.

1. Trades and Labour Congress of Canada, 35th Annual Convention, *Proceedings,* 1920.
2. Canada, Royal Commission on Industrial Relations, 1919, *Report,* pp. 14, 16-17.
3. Canada, Department of Labour, *Labour Gazette, Supplement,* 1919, p. 19.
4. William Z. Foster, *Misleaders of Labor* (New York, 1927), p. 74.
5. Ibid., p. 75.
6. Trades and Labour Congress of Canada, 42nd Annual Convention, 1927, *Proceedings,* p. 105.
7. Ibid., 1925.
8. Ibid., 1929.
9. W. Z. Foster, *Misleaders of Labor,* p. 10; pp. 58-60; pp. 118-119.
10. Ibid., pp. 83, 245.
11. All-Canadian Congress of Labour, *Canadian Unionist,* Aug. 1929.
12. W. Z. Foster, *Misleaders of Labor,* p. 168.
13. Ibid., p. 130.
14. *Canadian Unionist,* Dec. 1928, p. 111.
15. Ibid., Apr. 1929, p. 181.
16. Ibid., Feb. 1928.
17. Ibid., Jan. 1928, p. 121.
18. Trades and Labour Congress of Canada, 36th Annual Convention, 1921, *Proceedings,* p. 104.
19. *Canadian Unionist,* Dec. 1928, p. 111.
20. Ibid., Nov. 1928, p. 68.
21. Ibid., July 1927.
22. Ibid., 1927.
23. Ibid., Nov. 1928, p. 68.
24. Ibid., June 1927, p. 2.
25. Ibid., Dec. 1929.
26. Canada, Department of Labour, *Annual Report on Labour Organization in Canada,* 1929.
27. *Canadian Unionist,* June 1927.
28. Ibid., Dec. 1928, p. 117.
29. Ibid., May 1929.
30. Ibid., Dec. 1929, p. 86.

31. Trades and Labour Congress of Canada, 33rd Annual Convention, 1918, *Proceedings*, pp. 69, 94; Ibid., 1917, p. 48; *Worker*, Sept. 5, 1923.

32. Canada, Department of Labour, *Annual Report on Labour Organization in Canada*, 1922, p. 169.

33. The *Worker*, Aug. 1, 1923.

34. Canada, House of Commons, *Debates*, May 17, 1921; Canada, Department of Labour, *Annual Report on Labour Organization in Canada*, 1923, p. 191.

35. Canada, Department of Labour, *Labour Organization in Canada*, 1923, p. 187.

36. Ibid.

37. The *Worker*, Aug. 1, 1923.

38. Canada, Department of Labour, *Labour Organization in Canada*, 1923, p. 192.

39. The *Worker*, Mar. 29, 1924 (Quoting Financial Post, Mar. 14, 1924).

39A. Ibid., Sept. 26, 1923.

40. Ibid., Mar. 7, 1923.

41. Ibid., Oct. 3, 1923.

42. Canada, House of Commons, *Debates*, Apr. 21, 1925; *Maritime Labour Herald*, Mar. 7, 1925.

43. The *Worker*, Mar. 21, Apr. 25, 1925.

44. Canada, House of Commons, *Debates*, Apr. 21, 1925.

45. The *Worker*, Aug. 25, 1928.

46. *Canadian Unionist*, Aug. 18, 1928.

47. The *Worker*, Oct. 15, 1928.

48. Ibid.

49. The *Worker*, Sept. 21, 1929.

50. Ibid., Apr. 1928; Ibid., Nov. 2, 1928.

51. Ibid., Apr. 7, 1928.

52. Ibid.

52A. *Toronto Telegram*, Nov. 2, 1928.

53. Trades and Labour Congress of Canada, 32nd Annual Convention, 1927, *Proceedings*, p. 161.

54. Ibid.

55. The *Worker*, Sept. 3, 1927.

56. *Canadian Unionist*, Oct. 1927, p. 86.

57. Canada, Department of Labour, *Annual Report on Labour Organization in Canada*, 1925, p. 140; Ibid., 1926, p. 156.

58. *Canadian Unionist*, 1927.

59. Ibid., Feb. 1928, p. 139.

60. Trades and Labour Congress of Canada, 33rd Annual Convention, 1928, *Proceedings*.

61. Ibid., 1923.

62. Ibid., 1924.

Chapter 15.

1. Trades and Labour Congress of Canada, 45th Annual Convention, 1930, *Proceedings,* p. 146.
2. Canada, Royal Commission on Price Spreads, 1925, *Minutes of Proceedings and Evidence,* I, p. 1354; *Report,* pp. 118, 154.
3. Trades and Labour Congress of Canada, 45th Annual Convention, 1930, *Proceedings,* pp. 146, 147.
4. Ibid., p. 178.
5. Ibid., 1932, p. 149.
6. Ibid., 1931, pp. 137-141.
6A. The *Worker,* Sept. 19, 26, Oct. 3, 1931.
7. Trades and Labour Congress of Canada, 46th Annual Convention, 1931, *Proceedings,* p. 179.
7A. Trades and Labour Congress of Canada, 47th Annual Convention, 1932, *Proceedings.*
8. Sources for data in this paragraph: Ibid., 1931, pp. 198-202.
8A. Ibid., 1933, pp. 188-189.
9. Ibid., 1937, p. 174.
10. Ibid., 1938, p. 52.
10A. Ibid., 1939, p. 48.
10B. Ibid.
10C. Ibid., pp. 147-157.
11. Canada, House of Commons, *Debates,* Apr. 17, 1939.
12. American Federation of Labour, 1938, *Report of the Proceedings,* p. 504.

Chapter 16.

1. Canada, Department of Labour, *Labour Organizations in Canada,* 1963.
1A. Canada, House of Commons, *Debates,* Apr. 29, 1942, May 14, 1941.
2. Ibid., Oct. 9, 1945.
3. Trades and Labour Congress of Canada, 58th Annual Convention, 1943, *Proceedings,* p. 61.
4. Canada, House of Commons, *Debates,* Oct. 9, 1945.
5. Ibid., Aug. 29, 1946.
5A. *U.E. News,* July 19, 1946.
6. Canada, Department of Labour, *Labour Organization in Canada,* 1958, p. 7.
6A. Ibid.
7. Canada, DBS, *Review of Man-Hours and Hourly Earnings,* 1957, pp. 17, 19.
7A. Trades and Labour Congress of Canada, 63rd Annual Convention, 1948, *Proceedings,* pp. 156-157.
7B. Ibid., p. 160.
8. Canada, House of Commons, *Debates,* June 14, 1948.
9. *Canadian Tribune,* June 26, Oct. 11, 1948.
10. *Searchlight,* Sept. 30, 1948; *Canadian Tribune,* Sept. 20, 1948.

11. *Trades and Labour Congress Journal,* XXVIII, No. 3, Mar. 1949, pp. 11-13.
12. Trades and Labour Congress of Canada, 63rd Annual Convention, 1948, *Proceedings,* p. 149.
12A. Ibid.
13. Ibid., pp. 155-208.
13A. Ibid., p. 157.
14. *Trades and Labour Congress Journal,* Mar. 1949, pp. 12-13.
15. Ibid., p. 12.
16. Ibid.

Chapter 17.

1. Montreal *Star,* Apr. 14, 1949; *Canadian Tribune,* Apr. 18, 1949.
2. Canada, House of Commons, *Debates,* Apr. 8, 1949.
3. *Canadian Tribune,* June 6, 1949.
4. Trades and Labour Congress of Canada, 64th Annual Convention, *Proceedings,* 1949.
5. Ibid.
6. Ibid.
7. Ibid.
8. Ibid.
9. Montreal *Gazette,* Aug. 11, 1950.
10. Ibid., Aug. 19, 1950.
11. B. K. Sandwell, "The Recent Rail Strike", *Queen's Quarterly,* vol. 57, 1950.
12. Montreal *Gazette,* Aug. 29, 1950.
13. Ibid.
14. Canada, House of Commons, *Debates,* Aug. 30, 1950.
15. Montreal *Gazette,* Aug. 30, 1950.
16. Ibid.
17. Ibid., Aug. 24, 1950.
18. Trades and Labour Congress of Canada, 65th Annual Convention, 1950, *Proceedings.*
19. Ibid.
20. Ibid.
21. Ibid.
22. Ibid.
23. Trades and Labour Congress of Canada, 65th Annual Convention, 1950, *Proceedings.*
24. Ibid.
25. Ibid.
26. Ibid.
27. Ibid.
28. Ibid.
29. Ibid.
30. Canadian Congress of Labour, Canadian and Catholic Confederation of Labour, Trades and Labour Congress of Canada, the Railway Transportation Brotherhoods Joint Brief to the Federal Government, "Submission on Price Control", *Trades and Labour Congress Journal,* March 1951, *p. 17.*

31. Trades and Labour Congress of Canada, 67th Annual Convention, 1952, *Proceedings.*
32. United Fishermen and Allied Workers Union, Proceedings, 1954 Convention.
33. Ibid.
34. Ibid.
35. Montreal *Gazette,* May 26, 1952; Montreal *Star,* May 26, 1952.
36. Montreal *Star,* May 26, 1952; Montreal *Gazette,* May 28, 1952; Montreal *Gazette,* June 4, 1952.
37. Montreal *Star,* May 28, 1952.
38. Montreal *Gazette,* May 28, 1952.
39. Montreal *Star,* May 26, 1952.
39A. Montreal *Star,* May 26 and 27, 1952; Montreal *Gazette,* May 27, 1952.
40. A.F.L.-C.I.O. Convention, 1957, *Proceedings,* vol. 2, p. 550.
41. Ibid.
42. Ibid.
43. Canadian Congress of Labour Convention, 1947, *Proceedings.*
44. Ibid.
45. Ibid., 1948.
46. Ibid.
47. Ibid., 1950.
48. Ibid., 1948.
49. Canadian Congress of Labour Convention, 1950, *Proceedings.*
50. Ibid.
51. Ibid.
52. Ibid., 1952.
53. Ibid., 1951.
54. Ibid.
55. Ibid., 1952.
56. Trades and Labour Congress of Canada, 64th Annual Convention, 1949, *Proceedings.*
57. Ibid., 1952.
58. Ibid.
59. Ibid.
60. Ibid.
61. Ibid., 1953.
62. Ibid.
63. Ibid.
64. Ibid.
65. Trades and Labour Congress of Canada, 69th Annual Convention, 1954, *Proceedings.*
66. Ibid.
67. Ibid.

Chapter 18.

1. Canada, DBS, *Review of Man-hours and hourly Earnings, 1945-1962.*
2. Ibid.

3. *Labor Facts,* Oct. 1959.
4. Ibid.
5. *Le Travail,* Nov. 6, 1959.
6. *Hamilton Spectator,* May 31, 1956.
7. Computed from Canada, DBS, *The Labour Force,* 1945-1958 : Total non-agricultural paid workers without jobs as percentage of total employed and unemployed non-agricultural workers.
8. Canadian Labour Congress, Second Constitutional Convention, 1958, Officers Reports, p. 66.
9. Canada, Department of Labour, *Strikes and Lockouts in Canada.*
10. Compiled from *Strikes and Lockouts in Canada.*
11. Compiled from *Strikes and Lockouts in Canada.*

Chapter 19.

1. Canada, Department of Labour, *Strikes and Lockouts in Canada.*
2. Ibid.
3. Renaude Lapointe, *L'Histoire Bouleversante de Mgr Charbonneau* (Montréal, 1962), p. 56.
4. Pierre Elliott Trudeau, *La Grève de l'Amiante* (Montréal, 1956), p. 252.
5. Source for data on Asbestos strike is Trudeau, op. cit. and newspaper clippings.

INDEX

NC PRESS LTD

NC Press is the publishing arm of the Canadian Liberation Movement. It is truly a peoples' publishing house, distributing books on the struggle for national independence and socialism in Canada and throughout the world.

The History of Quebec A Patriote's Handbook
by Léandre Bergeron 245 pp. $1.50 paper
The History of Quebec: The French Regime
In Pictures! by Léandre Bergeron & Robert Lavaill
48 pp. $1.00
Why is Canada in Vietnam? by Claire Culhane
Introduced by Wilfred Burchett 125 pp. $1.50
paper
More Poems for People by Milton Acorn 120 pp.
$1.75 paper $4.00 cloth   one hour tape $5.00
                                            cassette $4.00
The Prevention of World War III by Harold
Bronson
217 pp. $2.75 paper
The Trade Union Movement of Canada 1827-1959
by Dr. Charles Lipton
400 pp. $3.95 paper $7.95 cloth
towards a people's art –
the History of Canadian and Québécois painting
by Barry Lord 164 pp. $3.95 paper $8.95 cloth
1837 Revolution in the Canadas – as told by Wm.
Lyon Mackenzie edited by Greg. Keilty
175 pp. $2.00 paper $5.95 cloth
A People's History of Prince Edward Island
by Errol Sharpe 175 pp. $2.00 paper $5.95 cloth
Black Canadians – A Long Line of Fighters
by Headley Tullock 100 pp. $1.50 paper
Canadian Unions for Canadian Workers
by Caroline Perly 120 pp. $1.50
In The Ottawa Valley by Jim Brown
24 pp. $.75

Tanzania Publishing House

NC Press is proud to announce that it is the exclusive Canadian distributor for Tanzanian Publishing House.

Québec!

Les Révoltes d'Acadie
Pierre Godin . . . . 158 pp. $1.50

Le Jeune Latbour
A. Gérin Lajoie . . . . 55 pp. $2.00

Famille Sans Nom
Jules Verne . . . . 275 pp. $3.50

Docteur Bethune
Sydney Gordes et Ted Allan . . . . . 313 pp. $5.50

Nègres Blancs d'Amérique
Pierre Vallières . . . . 440 pp. $3.50

**Classes Sociales et Question au Québec,
    1760-1840**
Gilles Bourque . . . . 352 pp. $3.50

Les Québécois
Jacques Berque (ed.) . . . . 300 pp. $3.00

Québec Occupé
Jean-Marc Picotte et al . . . . 250 pp. $3.00

Québec: Immigration Zéro
Jean-Claude Lenormand . . . . 100 pp. $1.00

China!

Quotations from Mao Tse Tung*

                          312 pp.   .50

Selected Readings from the Works of Mao Tse Tung*

                          504 pp.   1.00

On New Democracy*   71 pp.   .25

Imperialism, the Highest Stage of Capitalism*
    by V.I. Lenin   166 pp.   .50

Selected Works of Mao Tse Tung *

Volume One	348 pp.	2.10
Volume Two	472 pp.	2.60
Volume Three	344 pp.	2.10
Volume Four	460 pp.	2.60

* also available in French
A complete catalogue available on request.

Join CLM !

Independence and Socialism

Canada is a colony. Our trade unions, our natural resources, our culture, our universities and our industry — all are controlled from the U.S. There are those who, seeing the extent of this colonialism, believe the battle to be lost. We do not see it that way. We see people across the country rising up against US imperialism: workers struggling to forge militant, democratic Canadian Unions, farmers fighting US agri-business, students opposing the takeover of the universities by increasing numbers of American professors.

JOIN THE CANADIAN LIBERATION MOVEMENT! Join the fight for independent rank-and-file controlled Canadian unions. Participate actively in the struggle to free Canada from U.S. imperialist control.

The CANADIAN LIBERATION MOVEMENT is devoted to building an independent, socialist Canada. It is up to you and to every progressive and patriotic Canadian to become involved to the extent of your resources and abilities in the saving of our nation and in the building of a new and better Canada.

Box 41, Station 'E', Toronto 4, Ontario (964-1139)
Box 620, Station 'B', Ottawa, Ontario
Box 481, Thunder Bay F, Ontario
Box 6272, Station 'F', Hamilton, Ontario
Box 1595, Guelph, Ontario
Box 784, Waterloo, Ontario
Box 5256, Station 'B', Victoria, B.C.

CANADIAN LIBERATION MOVEMENT

TO: Canadian Liberation Movement

___ Please send me more information about the
Canadian Liberation Movement

___ I want to join CLM

Here is a donation of $_____ to help you with your work

NAME . . . .

ADDRESS . . . .

PHONE . . . .